Social Differentiation and
Social Inequality

Social Inequality Series
Marta Tienda and David B. Grusky, Series Editors

Social Differentiation and Social Inequality: Essays in Honor of John Pock, edited by James N. Baron, David B. Grusky, and Donald J. Treiman

Can Education Be Equalized? The Swedish Case in Comparative Perspective, edited by Robert Erikson and Jan O. Jonsson

Generating Social Stratification: Toward a New Research Agenda, edited by Alan C. Kerckhoff

The New Role of Women: Family Formation in Modern Societies, edited by Hans-Peter Blossfeld

Social Stratification: Class, Race, and Gender in Sociological Perspective, edited by David B. Grusky

Careers and Creativity: Social Forces in the Arts, Harrison C. White

Persistent Inequality: Changing Educational Attainment in Thirteen Countries, edited by Yossi Shavit and Hans-Peter Blossfeld

The Arab Minority in Israel's Economy: Patterns of Ethnic Inequality, Noah Lewin-Epstein and Moshe Semyonov

Equality and Achievement in Education, James S. Coleman

FORTHCOMING

Between Two Worlds: Southeast Asian Refugee Youth in America, Ruben G. Rumbaut and Kenji Ima

Prejudice or Productivity: Ethnicity, Languages, and Discrimination in Labor Markets, M.D.R. Evans

Inequality and Aging, John Henretta and Angela O'Rand

Children, Schools, and Inequality, Doris R. Entwisle and Karl Len Alexander

Social Differentiation and Social Inequality

Essays in Honor of John Pock

EDITED BY

James N. Baron
David B. Grusky
Donald J. Treiman

WestviewPress
A Division of HarperCollins*Publishers*

Social Inequality Series

All rights reserved. Printed in the United States of America. No part of this publication may be reproduced or transmitted in any form or by any means, electronic or mechanical, including photocopy, recording, or any information storage and retrieval system, without permission in writing from the publisher.

Copyright © 1996 by Westview Press, A Division of HarperCollins Publishers, Inc.

Published in 1996 in the United States of America by Westview Press, 5500 Central Avenue, Boulder, Colorado 80301-2877, and in the United Kingdom by Westview Press, 12 Hid's Copse Road, Cumnor Hill, Oxford OX2 9JJ

A CIP catalog record for this book is available from the Library of Congress.
ISBN 0-8133-8883-X

The paper used in this publication meets the requirements of the American National Standard for Permanence of Paper for Printed Library Materials Z39.48-1984.

10   9   8   7   6   5   4   3   2   1

Contents

Preface and Acknowledgments ix

PART ONE
Introduction

1   How Pock Shaped Me, *Paul M. Siegel*   3

PART TWO
The Contours of Social Differentiation

2   The Logic of Employment Systems,
    Neil Fligstein and Haldor Byrkjeflot   11

3   Income Differences Among 31 Ethnic Groups
    in Los Angeles, *Donald J. Treiman and Hye-kyung Lee*   37

4   The Structure of Career Mobility in Microscopic
    Perspective, *Jesper B. Sørensen and David B. Grusky*   83

PART THREE
Demographic Aspects of Social Differentiation

5   Demography and the Evolution of Educational
    Inequality, *Robert D. Mare*   117

6   The Decline of Infant Mortality in China:
    Sichuan, 1949–1988, *William M. Mason, William Lavely,
    Hiromi Ono, and Angelique Chan*   153

PART FOUR
Gender and Social Differentiation

7	Vive la Différence! Continuity and Change in the Gender Wage Gap, 1967–1987, *Martina Morris*	211
8	Gender Inequalities in the Distribution of Responsibility, *Carol A. Heimer*	241
9	Currents and Anchors: Structure and Change in Australian Gender Role Attitudes, 1984–1989, *M.D.R. Evans and Karen Oppenheim Mason*	275
10	The Social Construction of Modern Intelligence: An Exploration of Gender-Differentiated Boundaries, *William Tudor*	303

PART FIVE
Conclusion

11	Social Differentiation and Inequality: Some Reflections on the State of the Field, *James N. Baron, David B. Grusky, and Donald J. Treiman*	345

PART SIX
Appendixes

A	Biographical Sketches of Contributors	369
B	Reed College Students Who Became Professional Sociologists, 1957–1991	377
	About the Book and Editors	383

Preface and Acknowledgments

The essays included in this volume honor a truly gifted teacher and sociologist, John C. Pock. After a brief stint at the University of Illinois, Pock moved in 1955 to Reed College, a highly regarded but very small liberal arts institution (roughly 1,000 students) located in Portland, Oregon. Pock has spent the rest of his career (to date) there. During his forty-year tenure at Reed College, the sociology department usually had only two faculty members. Even so, during this period as many as 104 students graduated with majors in sociology and 69 established professional careers as sociologists. (A listing, which is assuredly incomplete, of Reed students during Pock's tenure who went on to professional careers in sociology is presented in an appendix to this volume.) Many of these sociologists have been extremely successful and influential within the discipline. Reed sociologists have taught or are teaching at the University of California at Berkeley, the University of Chicago, Columbia, Cornell, Duke, Michigan, Northwestern, Stanford, UCLA, Wisconsin, and other leading U.S. academic departments. Others have been employed as researchers in such prominent institutions within and outside the United States as RAND, the National Academy of Sciences, the National Opinion Research Center, the East-West Center, the U.S. Census Bureau and Bureau of Labor Statistics, the Sloan Foundation, and the Australian National University.

In honor of John Pock's fortieth anniversary as a teacher at Reed College, we have organized this volume to pay tribute to his long-term impact on the field of sociology through the students he has trained. Pock's interests are enormously broad and diverse, and therefore it is not a surprise that Reed sociologists have contributed to a wide variety of subfields within sociology. Nonetheless, there has been a substantial concentration among Pock's former students in the study of social differentiation and social inequality, broadly conceived, and we have chosen to organize this volume around that theme.

Despite this thematic emphasis, the chapters in this volume are conspicuously diverse in their subject matter and methods, reflecting the wide variety of scholarship within contemporary sociology that bears on the determinants, correlates, and consequences of social inequality. Reed sociologists may share a common intellectual "family of origin," but it has led them to different intellectual destinations, even within the field of stratification and inequality. Indeed, in organizing this volume and writing our concluding chapter, we discovered that—despite close similarities in our training, shared loyalty to John Pock and this project, and mutual respect for one another—we did not always see eye to eye on substantive issues. Still, we take collective responsibility both for the concluding chapter and for the volume as a whole, and emphasize this by listing ourselves alphabetically.

This absence of consensus about the key issues regarding stratification and inequality and the best methods for pursuing them is characteristic of the field in general. Accordingly, we have opted to write a concluding chapter to this volume, which uses the various papers in this volume produced by Pock's students—as well as the topics *not* represented in their contributions—as a window into the field of stratification and a means of suggesting some promising directions for future theory and research.

We are indebted to many people who assisted and supported us in preparing this volume. Dr. Steven Koblik, president of Reed College, graciously provided support to help defray some of the publication costs. Professor Mark Gould (Reed '67) of Haverford College generously offered to organize a special session of the 1995 American Sociological Association (ASA) annual meeting in Washington, D.C., consisting of papers from this festschrift honoring John Pock.

We obviously owe a great debt to the talented and overcommitted Reed sociologists who contributed chapters to this volume. Unfortunately, there were more thoughtful manuscripts submitted than we could publish, given space limitations. We apologize to those authors whose essays could not be included and express our deep gratitude for their willingness to participate in this celebration of John Pock's contributions to sociology. We are also indebted to various Reed alumni who offered support and assistance on behalf of this project at various stages. Any listing of these individuals is certain to omit some who deserve mention, but we would especially like to thank Francine Cancian, Marin Clarkberg, Galen Cranz, David Elesh, Dean Gerstein, Mark Gould, Kathryn Kost, Gwendolyn Lewis, Harry Makler, Martina Morris, and Gerald Suttles.

We appreciate the support of Professor Marta Tienda, editor of the Westview Press Series on Social Inequality, and Dean Birkenkamp of Westview Press, without whose endorsement and support this project would not have been approved. We gratefully acknowledge the skill and cooperation of Peter Obst in typesetting and Alice Colwell in copyediting. Linda Taoka and Aishya Earls did a masterful job of coordinating the flow of paper among the three of us and between us, the authors, and the production personnel. Mara Corrada of the American Sociological Association provided us with a listing from the ASA data base of Reed College graduates who are or have been ASA members.

This project was begun during Treiman's tenure as a Fellow at the Center for Advanced Study in the Behavioral Sciences, which put us all on the Stanford campus during the academic year 1992–93. The Center has been very supportive of Reed graduates. In all, at least eight Reed sociologists have been Fellows at the Center.

Finally, we acknowledge our abiding affection for John Pock and the enduring intellectual debt we owe him.

James N. Baron
David B. Grusky
Donald J. Treiman

Social Differentiation and
Social Inequality

PART ONE

Introduction

1

How Pock Shaped Me

Paul M. Siegel

> *It is a fact that whether or not the students flock to a teacher is determined in large measure, larger than one would believe possible, by purely external things ...*
> — (Weber 1922)

This collection of quantitative empirical sociology is presented in tribute to and celebration of our teacher, John Pock. I have the honor of trying to explain who he is and, thus, why this book. I would like to make this an equally quantitative empirical analysis of John Pock's pedagogy. But one of the things I *didn't* learn from John was what to do with single cases (in this instance, a singular case). I did learn to avoid or mistrust conclusions that depended upon the single example or counterexample and not to confuse experience with empirical analysis. So perforce, I have chosen and intend the more personal, introspective task. Those of John's students represented by contributions to this volume, the larger number who produced Reed theses under John's tutelage, the 104 who have graduated from Reed as sociology majors since 1957, and the even larger number of persons who were students in a course or two of John's (some of whom went on to professional careers as sociologists), all bear marks of his thought and teaching. The marks are not all the same, and their bearers may not recognize them for what they are. Doubtless, not all of them are effects John intended. It seems important to me to speak to John about these marks—to number them in thanks. I don't know how John the teacher changed over forty years of his career at Reed or how his students' experience of him varied. So this must remain a personal account of how Pock influenced me.

Some years back, the American Sociological Association recognized John for his distinguished contribution to sociology in America. The citation read in part:

> Professor Pock's teaching effectiveness derives from the stimulating and challenging didactic regimen he has developed over the years. This program is based on fundamental principles of social organization, structured in such a way that a perceptive and diligent student can come to understand these principles both as objects of study and as subjective experiences. The Awards Committee considers this citation an appropriate tribute to a man who has devoted his professional life to introducing young minds to the challenge and excitement of sociology as a discipline. (ASA 1982)

Some set of "fundamental principles of social organization" is the object of study in many undergraduate sociology programs (though not all, not even in the dream time). John's was a very good set. He presented sociology as if it were a coherent field of inquiry. In later years John was outraged at the suggestion that the Reed department's offerings should consist *exclusively* of focused, semester courses (watered-down versions of "upper-division" courses) so independent of each other that a student could start sociology anywhere.[1] He taught as if sociology warranted an introductory course covering the field and as if there were a viewpoint and sensitivity to be gained in such an introduction that was essential to further work in the field. There have been periods in the twentieth century when that was not a bizarre idea, though for much of the era the profession seems incoherent, as if it were in the hands of the Vandals.

In the late 1950s, the introductory course was, in fact, an introduction to sociology and anthropology, and it was taught by John, the other member of the sociology faculty (Howard Jolly), and the entire anthropology department (David French). Not too many years earlier what had been a sociology/anthropology department had split. John was adamant that there was no such thing as sociology/anthropology. Some students, majors, and graduates of that era were not as clear as he about whether that meant there were two different things or only one thing. I tended to overlook the epistemological differences between the departments at Reed, which were probably downplayed compared to the gulf between the modal professional sociological empiricist and the modal professional anthropologist. I'm not sure where this fits with my own tension between knowing from experience and understanding through formalization.

Creating the impression that sociology was a unified field may have been easier to do in a tiny department in a small liberal arts college than in a diverse department within a large research university, but illusion or no, it had an enduring effect. I left Reed with a sense of intellectual responsibility for the entire spectrum of sociology—I was supposed to be able to read and argue any of it—and it all had to fit together, somehow. It took a long time before I stopped feeling guilty for not reading the journals from cover to cover.

The Distinguished Contribution to Teaching citation also alludes to the fact that a large proportion of Reed sociology graduates went on to graduate school. Two-thirds of the 104 Reed sociology graduates from 1956 to 1995 are known to have received a graduate degree![2] An even larger number must have attended graduate school. In October 1992 the membership of the American Sociological Association included 56 persons who indicated Reed as their baccalaureate institution[3] The National Science Foundation doctorate data[4] show that between 1966 and 1993; 63 persons who received a Ph.D. in sociology reported Reed as their baccalaureate institution. While Reed used to boast that high proportions of its graduates across many fields sought and won higher degrees, it may have been an effect of the qualities undergraduates brought to the place as much as the effect of Reed's collection of outstanding teachers. But the magnitude of the contribution that those 63 doctors of philosophy in sociology represent must not be diminished by mere quibbling about causality. They are an important measure of John's contribution to sociology. It is a bequest few can match.

John sent me off to graduate school tagged a theorist. I suppose that was a distinction he made among his students (some of them weren't theorists); I didn't think it a compliment. "Theorists" somehow escaped the discipline of the merely empirical. In any case, I went to the University of Chicago, surely not a locus of theory. Still, I spent much of my career trying to make a coherent human ecology. While it never worked as a theory, and it never led to a research program, it did articulate a vast range of structures from urban social organization to systems in which people play minor roles. And it gave me an excuse to read way outside sociology. I like to think there were a few students lured into sociology by the apparent cohesion of my introduction to human ecology.

The common elements of students' subjective experience of the fundamental principles of social organization doubtless owed much to our common vulnerability, naiveté, and intellectual innocence, along with our diligence and perceptiveness. Before I'd signed up for the introductory course, I'd been warned about the final (or was it midterm?) exam: The "true/false and why" questions (for each question you were supposed to answer whether it was true or false and write a paragraph explaining and defending your answer) were regarded as particularly penetrating and difficult by my informant. I remember thinking that being asked to justify one's answer was a great acknowledgment of one's ability to think. I also remember thinking there were no right answers, just good arguments, and that was OK. I still remember one of those questions I got wrong—in the country of the blind the one-eyed man is king—though I can't recall what my answer was. And I recall being disabused of the notion that we students and nascent sociologists were at liberty to create any world we could verbally defend.

My *experience* of the fundamental principles of social organization also owed much to Reed College and its insistence that its faculty, students, and administrators constituted a community. I'm sure this is not universal among John's students, but I spent a lot of fruitful time discovering that sociology was a real field by seeing that some dynamics of the Reed community exemplified principles of social organization. I wrote impassioned student newspaper editorials on the basis of these examples. I think John took them as evidence I had learned something.

I think John tried to use the Reed community as a pedagogic tool, and not always with success. Sometimes his intended uses ran up against contrary social consequences. Early in his teaching career (not long after his graduate student days), John used to give parties in his home for all the students taking sociology. The number of students was so large, and John and Helen's living room so small, that he was forced to give several parties, with different students invited to each, in order to accommodate them all. When John discovered that students were imputing motives and evaluations to the guest lists, he abandoned the effort to include everyone, with no little disappointment, I think, and a caustic evaluation of the covetousness of students.

I attribute to John my sense that formal organizations, like those in which I have spent most of my life, are social machines that can be fathomed. Under his influence, the adolescent view of society and large-scale organizations as malicious and arbitrary epiphenomena gave way to an appreciation of the order of social structures of sentiment and rationality and of the limits of trying to comprehend them as merely rational. When I thought about it, I attributed John's organizational perspective to his service in the armed forces and his having grown up in Chicago, which *was* organized, in contrast to the anarchy of Los Angeles, where I grew up. It occurs to me now that John's organizational smarts offered students an exciting demonstration of the possibility of converting knowledge-from-experience into empirically defensible understanding. I gather that "population" or "demography" came to play a large part in John's thinking and teaching. I don't remember its presence when I was at Reed, so either it came later or I slept through it.

John held out empirical research as the *sine qua non* of competent sociology. He firmly believed that students should *do* responsible research. Part of the way he made sociology an exciting undertaking for me was by transforming my concerns into empirically researchable questions.

Perhaps more important, he nurtured the sense that one must recast issues into arguments in which facts matter, do it in a way that makes clear *which* facts matter, and then get the facts. Along the way, the concerns and issues came more and more to be anchored in sociology, and less and less to arise out of unmediated experience and social concerns. But, of course, that's what's supposed to happen to undergraduates. As an adult empiricist, I thought it crucial to frame the pursuit of empirical evidence in the theoretical and rhetorical terms to which the evidence was supposed to speak. I worried my students unmercifully as much about their reasoning as their technical proficiency. I attribute to John whatever I have been able to convey of the art of framing research questions in the context of arguments. The techniques and methods I learned elsewhere, but the intent and the quiet passion were fostered by John.

When I first knew him, John was a bundle of energy: not a frenzy of activity, and certainly not a bundle of the kind of energy that animates crystals or wood nymphs, but rather the energy of a dynamo. He was short, tanned, trim, and crew-cut. He still is, though stockier and grayer. He was intellectually tough and demanded the same of students. He seemed to feel betrayed because not all his faculty colleagues made such demands. I think that many of his students share the notion that tough-mindedness is a fundamental mark of academic and professional excellence. I think we share it with John. It was part of his successful pedagogy.

There was a period when middle-class youth at small liberal arts colleges hungered for the kind of tough-minded certainty about the social world that John's sociology seemed to offer. It was as sexy as Marxism, and easier to do. And it seemed to license a certain alluring disdain for more particularistic approaches to understanding social experience. I'm not sure this facet of tough-mindedness retains its appeal in the context of today's changed, if not correct, sensibilities. It was, I think, a major feature of the charisma of John's cynicism.

I have had former students thank me for some lesson they thought they learned in a class I dimly remember teaching (more often than not at 8:00 in the morning). I've been pleased that students later found something laudable to associate with my matinal torture and overlooked their distortions of substance or attribution for the insinuation I might have done something worthy. I hope John will do the same, though I can't ignore the recollection of A.J.P. Taylor's review of a festschrift for him in which he found some of his students still didn't get it right.

Notes

1. I heard this in conversation with John in the late 1980s.

2. Based on Reed College Alumni Office records. Of course not all of these degrees were in sociology.

3. Thirty-two had graduated in sociology after 1955. Twenty-two were not on the Alumni Office's list of sociology graduates. These data cannot support very precise inferences.

4. Of course, these data are only available without individual identification. One must presume that some would *not* appear on a list of Reed *sociology* graduates. National Science Foundation, Doctorate Records File, Survey of Earned Doctorates, 1966–1993. (Available, if not published, on the WWW via the NSF's CASPAR Database System. Start from http://www.nsf.gov/.)

References

American Sociological Association (ASA). 1982. *Footnotes* 10:1.

Weber, Max. 1922. "Wissenschaft als Beruf." in *Gesammelte Aufsätze zur Wissenschaftslehre.* Tübingen: J.C.B. Mohr.

PART TWO

The Contours of Social Differentiation

2

The Logic of Employment Systems

Neil Fligstein and Haldor Byrkjeflot

It has now been about 20 years since sociologists have begun to take the problem of the structure of work seriously in empirical research on stratification. The "new structuralism" has tried to embed the employment relation in larger units of analysis, such as organizations, sectors, classes, labor market segments, and even nation-states (for some examples, see Baron and Bielby 1980; Baron 1984; Hodson 1986; Wright 1979; Hodson, Kaufman, and Fligstein 1981; Doeringer and Piore 1971; Edwards 1979; Lincoln and Kalleberg 1990). Recent theoretical work (Hodson 1986; Kalleberg 1988; Fligstein and Fernandez 1988) has tried to view the production of labor relations as the interaction between groups of laborers and employers with varying amounts of resources.

This latter approach has the positive effect of introducing dynamics into the formation of labor markets. But it stops short of specifying how resources and bargaining positions become established in the first place, that is, what the institutions are that shape and are shaped by the contours of group interactions. Baron (1984) has reviewed the literature on organizations and stratification, but almost none of the works he cites try to use a more institutional approach to the problem of stratification.

If the system of employment relations is thought of as a large-scale institutional project, then one can begin to ask a different set of questions. How do such systems come into existence in the first place? What are their internal logics? Is it possible to tell if they are in some form of fundamental crisis that might bring about a reorganization of employment relations? How do states intervene in employment relations at each phase of their transformation? What is the impact of the increased internationalization of the economy on employment systems?

Our approach begins with considering what type of institution employment relations comprise. The basic case we wish to make is that employment systems are cultural and social constructions that reflect a societal tendency of important actors toward enforcing certain forms of careers and social organization. In capitalist societies this tendency emerges from the interactions of organized actors in three sectors of society: the state, the educational system, and the industrial field. Our central argument is that at the origins of industrialization these actors reach a political compromise on how to structure their relations. This compromise then becomes a set of cultural practices and understandings that functions as a template or worldview that helps actors make sense of their worlds and operates as a tool for the construction of action and career expectations. It also influences the construction of subsequent interaction across industries. This cultural construction is an identity that allows disparate groups of actors to come together to form social units such as unions, industries, firms, and professions. These are not identities in a social psychological sense (although they can be) but rather sets of meanings that actors can share and use to define situations, interests, and action (Swidler 1986; White 1992).

We identify three employment systems that have emerged historically in advanced capitalist industrial countries: vocationalism, professionalism, and managerialism. Vocationalism refers to a conception of work and career that emphasizes occupational communities, focuses on industrial unions, and relies on vocational training (either formal or on the job) for new personnel. The typical career is marked by a commitment to one industry. Professionalism is a conception of work that references a professional peer group, uses associations to maintain collegiality, and relies on universities for the training of personnel. Careers are centered on professions, not firms or industries, and once in a system of professions an individual tends to stay for life.[1] Managerialism reflects a commitment to a given work organization, is characterized by company unions, and relies on general schooling as a filter for admittance to the organization and on firm-specific job training over the life cycle. The typical career is with one corporation.

In the sections that follow, we first consider the problem of creating institutions like employment systems generally. This necessitates specifying elements of a theory of institutionalization that emphasize the role of states, firms, and other organized groups. We then detail the unique types of dynamics from which real employment systems emerge, which allows us to answer the questions posed above about the emergence, logics, and transformation of employment systems. Finally, we sketch how this view helps us make sense of the dominant systems of employment relations that have emerged in Western Europe, the United States, and Japan.

There are a number of interesting implications of the view we propose here. First, one can use this approach to attempt to identify and examine crucial historical moments in employment systems. Second, one can begin to understand how the existence of employment systems results from the mutual support of multiple sectors (or what can be called organizational fields) and that this tends to limit the possibilities for transformation of employment systems across sectors. So, for instance, the discussions in the United States about reforming the educational system to promote vocationalism is going on without regard to existing employment relations in large firms, which promote managerialism or professionalism. Such reforms are likely to have little effect because a shift to a vocational educational system ignores the operation of labor markets that are structured by managerialism and professionalism. Third, one can also see how, once in place, conflict in employment relations will be dynamic but limited by larger arrangements. Fourth, the unique systems of employment relations that have evolved across modern capitalist societies are deeply rooted in the unique development of each society and the mutual interaction of sectors. This creates a kind of path dependence that means that institutions are not easily borrowed or transplanted except under the most dire circumstances. This helps explain why sexism, racism, credentialism, and other forms of discriminatory labor market practices, once in place, are so difficult to dislodge.

Institutionalization as a General Social Process

What is new about the "new institutional theory" in organizational theory is that action in organizations takes place in what are called organizational fields (DiMaggio 1988; Powell and DiMaggio 1991). An organizational field is defined as the group of organizations that take one another into account in their behavior (Fligstein 1990). Organizational fields come into existence when actors in different organizational spheres recognize their interdependence and find a way collectively to frame action vis-à-vis one another. The purpose of organizational fields is to promote stability for the organizations that populate the field by finding a political compromise that will allow interaction to proceed.

One can conceive of this attempt to create a stable world as an institutional project. This requires solving three problems. First, actors must find a political solution that allows some groups of organizations to create stable outcomes for their members. Second, in order to find such an arrangement, they need to create a cultural conception of control (Fligstein 1990) that produces a local order in their field. These cultural frames define shared meanings about how to act and how to interpret the actions of others. They are also oriented to enforcing a certain view of the world and the pecking order of the organizational field. Finally, the dominant groups in the organizational field need the means to fend off challengers to their order. This can be done directly, through threats, or by using the law, usually with either the tacit or explicit approval of the state (Fligstein and McAdam 1993; Campbell, Hollingsworth, and Lindberg 1991).

Modern states claim to make rules for interaction in their territories. Hence, by definition states become the final arbiters of organizational fields within a certain geographic terrain. But states are the sites of contestation between opposing forces in organizational fields. Thus the way in which a state intervenes and on whose side is a matter of the configuration of political forces when the governance structure comes into existence.[2]

Solving the problem of finding a stable social outcome is not simple or predestined. Indeed, institutionalization projects can end up in disaster as frequently as they do in success. New organizational fields are most likely to emerge in proximity to old organizational fields. Models of action will often be borrowed from the nearby fields.

One of the critical problems is finding a stable set of understandings in the organizational field. The most powerful actors in an organizational field have the upper hand in setting the rules for others. This is because they have the resources to enforce such an order. Often even powerful groups are unable to enforce a social order by themselves. In this situation strategic actors must find a way to build a political coalition that brings along a substantial number of important organizational actors.

Once an organizational field comes into existence, it may be remarkably stable. A given social order is reinforced by the participants in that order. Those who benefit the most have a huge stake in maintaining business as usual. Those who are being victimized by the field constantly try to contest what is occurring. Once institutionalized, conceptions of control are powerful devices to keep an organizational field stable.

This suggests that the sources of change in existing organizational fields are likely to come from outside the field. Because the dominant organizational actors within a field continue to reinforce a given order, they are unlikely to be the source of a new order. It is very difficult for them to perceive when their strategies are failing to get them through turbulent times, so their basic approach in a crisis is to press forward with current conceptions of control.

So, for example, in the United States the dominant conception of the employment relation is that workers should be mobile factors of production and can be laid off whenever economic downturn occurs. Workers should treat the downturn as "their" problem and they should thus move to where the jobs are. This contrasts with the view in Western Europe that firms should not lay workers off and that cutting hours is preferable. Further, the state is the employer of last resort, and state-sponsored projects are highly regarded. These very different views have resulted in quite different actions in the economic crisis of the early 1990s.

Employment Systems as Institutional Projects

This abstract discussion proves quite useful to a consideration of the problem of the creation of employment systems across societies. We define employment systems as the rules governing relations between groups of workers and employers that concern the general logics of how groups define careers and how they organize to maintain these conceptions. These general logics inform more concrete sets of rules that help explain the organization of labor markets, the mobility of labor and managers, and the ways in which employers and workers organize. We do not mean just the set of practices traditionally conceived to be part of a system of industrial relations, that is, unions and professional and employer associations. We contend that it is necessary to include institutions and organizations linked to the education of workers, professionals, and managers and the skill-formation functions within the firm, since these institutions are essential in defining the logic and range of developmental possibilities within any employment system.[3]

In this section we begin with an abstract discussion of the relevant groups that make up the organizational field of employment systems in industrial societies. Then we examine how these groups might align themselves in an ideal-typical set of situations to produce the dominance of one of three conceptions of control: managerialism, vocationalism, and professionalism. We want to view these outcomes as the result of the different strengths among the competing groups.

In capitalist economies the means of production is held primarily in private hands. As part of these property rights, the owners and managers of capital claim the right to control employment relations. Employers and their representative groups focus mainly on getting states to guarantee their rights to control employment systems. In most Marxist theories it is assumed that the state will come down on the side of the owners of capital (Miliband 1969).

We want to problematize this relation and argue that one can presume that if the most powerful forces in society are owners and managers of capital, then they can organize the field of employment relations and realize their institutional project. But to do so generally in society, they must have the state and either the professions or worker representatives as active partners in the process.

The power of workers and professionals has two sources: skill and status differences and the ability to control labor and skills supply. They build associations and unions in order to gain power. We think that a potentially large number of groups could form around these various tactics. But in practice there are two major conceptions that groups use to control employment relations: those that we associate with blue-collar and those that we associate with white-collar work. Larson (1977) has argued that there are no major differences in the strategies of these groups. Both focus on controlling occupational skills or labor supply as their primary source of power.

Abbott (1988) argues in his "regional" theory of division of labor, however, that there is a difference. White-collar workers focus on professionalization as their major tactic of control. Professional projects try to use the abstract expertise of a group as grounds for self-governance of that group. The new literature on professions also notes that they employ universities in their struggle for governance, focus their control projects on the state, and constantly try to invade other groups' professional territory. Professions, then, may use different organizational tactics and seek allies among educators, states, and other professions in order to promote their interests. A question increasingly discussed in the professionalization literature is the possibility of another type of alliance: between professions and managers. In a number of societies, the management function itself has become increasingly professionalized. The management function may either be conceived of as a generalist position attached to organizations as wholes or it may be defined as a specialized activity attached to the type of activity performed in the organization. It is likely that a high degree of professionalization or functional generalization of the management function will lead to a preference for professionals as allies in the struggle with workers, whereas managers who identify with specialized functions in the firm, such as production, will prefer other types of alliances (Abbott 1988, 1989; Armstrong 1984; Burrage 1990; Byrkjeflot 1993; Fligstein 1990).

The constitution of rules regarding employment relations turns on the organizational and entrepreneurial capacities of these various parties, the general political and economic environment, and the particular historical period in which employment systems come into existence. We think it is possible to abstract away from historical particularism to identify several ideal-typical outcomes of this kind of struggle for the creation of employment systems.

Earlier we asserted that three ideal-typical institutional sets of arrangements appeared to dominate the existing types of employment systems: managerialism, vocationalism, and professionalism. Table 2.1 summarizes our characterization of these employment systems. We think these types closely reflect the relative power of the five potentially orga-

TABLE 2.1 The Logic of Employment Systems

Attribute	Vocationalism	Professionalism	Managerialism
Affiliative unit	Industrial trade union	Professional association	Firm (or company union)
Training	"On-the-job"	Postgraduate education	Universities
Intragenerational mobility (career)	Intraoccupational	Intraoccupational	Intrafirm

nized groups in society. If firms have the upper hand, they will tend toward institutionalizing managerialism as the model of employment relations. Here, managers will control who enters the firms, and they will use internal labor markets as devices to create primary and secondary labor markets. Firms and societies dominated by managerialism will tend to have company unions, use status credentials as the primary filter for admittance into the organization, and engage in firm-specific training over the life cycle to create careers for valued employees. The typical career is with one corporation. This model is similar to what Burawoy (1985) calls hegemonic despotism, Edwards's (1979) bureaucratic control, and how Williamson (1975, 1985) views the employment relation.

Challenges to firm control over labor markets can come from many sources. We argue that strong worker organization produces vocationalism. These groups focus on producing occupational career tracks. We call this conception of control vocationalism because it relies on vocational training, either on the job or in certified programs where the training is done both at work and in classrooms. The distinction between management and workers is not as strong in such systems, since the management function is less professionalized and since lower management often is recruited from worker ranks. The people doing the hiring of new workers and lower supervisors are influenced by a worker perspective because they have the same vocational training as those they recruit. The typical career is marked by a commitment to one occupation or a field of occupations within an industry.

White-collar workers will be inclined toward professionalism, whereby privilege is exerted because of expert knowledge (Stinchcombe 1959). Professionalism is a conception of work that references a professional expert peer group, uses associations to maintain collegiality, and relies on universities for training personnel. There are at least two variants of professionalism, however, depending on the extent to which professions rely on the state or on private associations. In state professionalism the state takes a direct role in the construction of a professional system, whereas private associations have the initiative in associational professionalism. Careers in both these variants are centered on expertise or fields of knowledge and are therefore not firm- or industry-specific.

The challenge when speaking about employment systems is to bring the education system into the analysis. Here we agree with Abbott when he says that "the 12 years spent in school by most citizens ... clearly provide the implicit model for later industrial relations. ... Education is the main girder supporting modern staffing structures" (Abbott 1989:287–8). We argue that the extent to which a society develops vocationalist, managerial, or professional systems will depend on the structure of the whole system from kindergarten to graduate studies.

Marxist scholars (Bowles and Gintis 1976) have tended to see the educational system as a source of reproduction and legitimation of capitalist inequalities. While we agree that schools function to reproduce employment systems once they are formed, they can have pivotal effects in two sorts of ways. First, at critical moments where the possibility exists for employment systems to emerge, actors in the educational system allied with managers, professionals, workers, or the state can weigh in to institutionalize some system of employment relations. This is particularly important for groups trying to establish themselves as professionals. Universities serve as bases of power to legitimate the claims of these groups to control certification.

Second, once in place, educational elites can affect the supply of different types of groups. In this way there can be feedback into employment systems that could tend to reproduce or undermine them. The massive production of lawyers in the United States in the 1970s and 1980s has altered many features of the employment relation, including the propensity of workers to use the court system to exert control. Another example is the attempt of medical schools to control the labor supply of physicians in the United States, thereby increasing the relative incomes and autonomy of physicians (Starr 1982).

To the degree that educators form a distinct group within societies, they will be divided along lines reflecting the relative size and power of their potential client populations. Primary and secondary schools will compete with community colleges and universities for funding and influence. The conception of control embedded in vocationalism will tend to be supported by secondary schools and community colleges, while professionalism will tend to garner support from the universities. In a society such as that in the United States, where the university system underwent huge expansion in the postwar era, one would expect a surge in the number of professions and their ability to gain certification.

Variations and Transformations in Employment Systems

These ideal-typical accounts can be usefully modified in three ways in order to make them more useful for analysis. First, it is important to consider how mixes of these pure types might produce stable institutional outcomes. It is also important to consider how one might use the analysis of institutional change that was described in the last section to specify the conditions under which one might identify the trajectory of a given set of institutions governing employment relations. In other words, how can we tell if a system is coming into existence, is stable and perhaps spreading, or is open to transformation? Finally, it is helpful to suggest how one might use this perspective to ask and answer questions about historical systems of employment relations.

Mixed types of employment relations could come into existence in a number of ways. For one, since different sectors of the economy have emerged at different historical moments, one system of employment relations might dominate certain sectors of the economy and another might dominate others. Thus the dominance of one system of employment relations depends on the relative power of organized groups at the moment of the founding of the industry.

There is another way in which the industrial structure of a country can affect the mix of employment systems. It may be that firms located in large-scale industries or the so-called core (Averitt 1968; Beck, Horan, and Tolbert 1978; Hodson, Kaufman, and Fligstein 1981) may tend to be dominated by managerialism, while firms in the periphery might have a mixed mode of employment relations, combining vocationalism (e.g., U.S. construction sector) or professionalism (e.g., business services) with managerialism. This is because some smaller firms that employ skilled labor have fewer abilities to resist workers' attempts at organization, particularly professionals.

Finally, political compromises between organized groups might produce mixed outcomes that incorporate features of several of the systems. One can easily imagine an alliance between managerialism and professionalism (Brint 1994): Managers would claim to control their firms but would grant professionals independent status in certain expert occupations and rely on expert advice for the structuring of their organizations. Societal variations in the trend toward externalization of professional business services in modern economies might symbolize the degree to which professionals have been able to reach a compromise with their employers.[4] Similarly, one could imagine a situation where managerialism and vocationalism coexisted. In certain large firms, managers and workers might negotiate internal labor markets such that workers control work rules and seniority and managers and professionals control the organization of work (such as the U.S. automobile industry).

The Dynamics of Systems of Employment Relations

The purpose of this section is to consider where employment systems come from and how they become institutionalized. Employment systems reflect the construction of interests produced by the structural positions of groups. But to some degree they are also political and social constructions that reflect reactions to other groups and the experiences of similarly placed groups in other countries and other times. This suggests that the initial timing and conditions of employment relations have important effects for the formation of institutions around the employment relations in a given society. At crucial points in time, power constellations in society and differentiated patterns in education have crystallized into institutions that have continued to shape employment systems even after those initial conditions have changed.

Every society is composed of a huge number of organizational fields connected in a great many ways. A given field may be both dependent on some and at the same time dominant over others. States connect directly and indirectly to every existing organizational field. Thus organizations and various organized groups often find themselves as participants in a multitude of fields.

The large-scale institutional project described here—that is, the making of a society-wide employment system—requires interaction among participants in a broad variety of fields. One could argue that at the early stages of rapid capitalist development a large number of organizational fields (those organized around large-scale product markets) faced the problem of developing stable employment relations. The process by which these relations emerged should be the focus of sustained study. One would need to identify key organizations and actors and how they tried to resolve their problems in the context of their organizational fields. One would want to be sensitive to how those solutions proved more general and spread to other fields. Finally, our perspective suggests that states had to be involved in the ratification, if not the creation, of stable employment relations. Thus the constitution of the policy domain of employment relations needs to be a constant area of focus.

Using the language developed earlier, we might ask, How do the various organized forces come together to establish a stable employment system at the level of organizational fields? We would expect that this problem would be most acute for rapidly growing sectors of the economy where there were not previously well known employment relations.

Initial conditions are important in several ways. Some states developed interventionist strategies into their economies at an early historical junction, whereas others were less developed and remained regulatory (Dobbin 1994). States provided social insurance schemes, and the character of state regulation of labor relations could create important advantages for workers and professions in their different bargaining positions vis-à-vis employers (Burawoy 1985:126). The relative power of workers and firms depended on the importance of skill level in the production system and the supply of skilled labor.

It is useful to describe the extreme cases. Where states were not interventionist, where skilled labor was not undersupplied, and where employers were large and had resources, one would expect managerialism. Where states were interventionist, where labor and professionals had skills in short supply relative to the demand of the production system, and where firms were not particularly large, one would expect vocationalism. Where states were interventionist and workers and firms less organized or in a stalemate, state professionalism would dominate. Finally, where states were not interventionist and workers and firms less organized, there would be associational professionalism.

If we understand employment systems as conceptions of control certified by the state and institutionalized at crucial junctures in history, it would also be relevant to find out what industries were dominant at that time. One would expect that the most rapidly growing industries were the site for experiments in institutions surrounding the employment relation (Stinchcombe 1965). Once these took hold and were ratified or legalized by the state, they would spread to organizational fields where similar conditions held sway. Once a system of employment relations was institutionalized more generally, one would expect that it would greatly shape the possibilities for new systems of employment to come into existence. The emergence or rapid growth of an industrial or technical educational system would be influenced by the set of employment relations in the most important industries at the time. The system would be producing individuals who would take up positions in the new industries and in the policy domain of employment relations. Then too, as new industrial fields opened up, the first place that managers and workers would look for models of employment relations would be nearby industries.

New systems of employment relations are likely to have two sources. As already mentioned, new industries would emerge with different balances of power among important groups. More interesting is the case where employment relations would be transformed in existing industries. We believe changes in employment relations in existing industries would depend on the failure of conceptions of employment relations in supporting economic growth (economic crisis) or the failure of the education system to produce motivated and adequately skilled workers (motivation crisis).

The balance of power within employment relations would have to be perceived to be creating negative conditions for dominant groups in order to convince these groups to shift their tactics. In a general economic downturn (like the Great Depression of the 1930s), one would expect systems of employment relations to come under pressure from all of the groups involved. If the largest firms began to go bankrupt or if the skills supply situation changed dramatically, then existing systems would be threatened. In another scenario, crises generated by states (wars and political upheaval) could easily undermine employment systems (Baron, Dobbin, and Jennings 1986). States could intervene either directly to alter the functioning of labor markets or indirectly through the passage of what appeared to be unrelated legislation. Finally, invasion of the major industries of a given society by other firms utilizing different employment relations could force reorganization of remaining firms' employment relations.

Insights into Comparative Employment Systems

This is not the place to undertake a substantial comparison of the voluminous historical and sociological histories of the employment relations in the industrialized societies. It is useful, however, to try and bring this theoretical apparatus to bear on what we know about the employment systems and institutional history of the United States, Germany, Japan, and France.

Since the approach here is ideal-typical, we want to view the tendencies of these societies as they currently appear to be configured. Some of what we have to say is speculative precisely because the research to investigate many of the points we have made has not been done. From our perspective, Germany most clearly conforms to the vocational model, France seems to best fit the state professional model, Japan fits the managerialist model, and the United States appears to reflect a compromise between the managerial and professional models. It is probably the case that in each society there are examples of industries organized according to each of the models. But since states are arguably the units that legitimate employment systems, it is plausible to begin with the hypothesis that a single system might emerge. An ambitious research agenda would ask whether or not societies could be characterized in this way and, if so, how the system was modified across sectors over time.

Germany: Vocationalism

The story of the deal struck in the 1870s between Otto von Bismarck and the state, on the one hand, and heavy industry, on the other, is well known. Germany was a late industrializer that developed cartels and a high degree of integration in the economy by the involvement of states and banks. Germany was particularly strong in producer goods and export industries, and the explicit aim was to catch up to Britain and other more advanced industrialized countries and develop strong military power. However, the employment system that developed was most strongly influenced by the strength of German workers' associations. We argue that this relative strength led to key concessions granted by the state and firms in their search for rapid industrial development and led to the eventual accession of a vocationalist system.

What is particularly interesting is the way the state developed an advanced system of welfare provision early on and how the education system was structured to create differentiated skills (Muller, Ringer, and Simon 1987). The welfare system facilitated the emergence of unions by granting them independence from their employers. The functionally differentiated technical education system made it difficult for potential professional groups and managers to appropriate workers' skills (Caplan 1990).

This combination gave unions the impetus to organize across firms and within industries. The state intervened in labor relations but in the long run was unable to stop the union buildup and the growth of the Social Democratic Party. The state was more successful in establishing a distinction between white and blue-collar workers. The social insurance law granted white-collar workers and civil servants privileges, and this made an alliance between these groups and workers more unlikely. There were, however, no legal restrictions that kept discontented white-collar workers from unionizing, and strong labor unions were established among engineers as well as other white-collar groups in the twentieth century. Craft workers, however, appear to have been successful in matching skills supply with demand. Because of its emphasis on producer goods, the German economy was very skill-intensive, and this tended to favor the organization of workers.

United States: Managerial Professionalism

The U.S. case shows very clearly a mix of employment systems. It also shows a diversified education system and a system of social insurance provision less directed by the state than in most other industrialized countries. Working-class organization in the United States has been weak, and the link between workers and professionals, which could theoretically lead to vocationalist employment relations, did not emerge. It is for this reason that we say that managerialist employment relations predominated early in the century and that they were increasingly joined by professionalist ones. The rise of professionalist employment relations appears to be in newer sectors of the economy and therefore did not supplant the managerialist system. In the core of the U.S. economy, there appears to have been some compromise between managerialist and vocationalist models beginning in the 1930s.

In the late nineteenth century, a strong labor movement seemed to be developing in the United States. But in a series of labor struggles established unions such as the Knights of Labor were systematically defeated and destroyed by the employers' associations. The federal and state governments either did nothing or were openly hostile toward union organizing efforts (Voss 1993). By 1920 managerialist tendencies in U.S. employment relations came into strong play. It is no surprise that Taylorism and Fordism dominated the structuring of the employment system.

The U.S. labor movement continued to resist this development, however, and the Wagner Act (1937) legalized unions. After bloody struggles in a number of core industries, unions and firms agreed to a mix of managerialism and vocationalism in those industries. The employment system that developed in the automobile, steel, and other core industries reflected the relatively greater organized power of workers in those industries. In peripheral industries managerialism dominated.

The real expansion of professionals in the United States came after World War II. We speculate that this expansion was fueled by the great increase in the size of the college-educated population. Through the GI Bill millions of returning veterans enrolled in universities and their advanced training produced a market for professionals in the postwar era. A large number of professionalization projects were also undertaken. Documenting the number and success of groups that attempted to professionalize would be a significant research effort.

By and large the owners and managers of firms have not resisted the professionalization of various classes of their employees. Large and medium-sized businesses alike have sought out the expertise of these professionals, whether they are consultants, specialists, engineers, or academic groups. The role of the state in this process has been relatively reactive. The certification of professionals has been left to professional associations. The educational elites located in universities have promoted this process precisely because it has strengthened their claim over scarce societal resources.

France: State Professionalism

France displays a third variant of industrial development. There, a diversified consumer industry evolved early on, without developing the high level of bank involvement, concentration, and emphasis on producer goods that characterize late developers. Lash and Urry have argued that this was because France was really quite industrially advanced. In the same way as did Britain, France experienced the "penalty of taking the lead" (Veblen 1939). The state was, however, much more interventionist and modern than in Britain. The French government had a long history of intervention in employment relations and the education system; the state thus promoted the agenda of state professionalist employment relations.

The key feature that led to state domination of the employment system was the inability of employer or worker organization to dominate industrial relations. So in different historical periods the battle between workers and employers often turned violent and potentially revolutionary. The organizational apparatuses that could be brought to bear on this conflict were found in the state and among the professions attached to it. Credentials became the coin of the realm, and the development of elite educational institutions worked to create an elite that viewed its role as the direction of society through the government, not through the private economy. The present employment system, then, is the result of state intervention in the economy and the gradual penetration of the economy by "cadres" and professionals with state credentials.

Boltanski's study (1987) of the making of this group, the emergence of which he traces to the economic crisis in the 1930s, might be interpreted as an analysis of the institutionalization of a state professionalist conception of control in the French economy. Exactly how this conception of control is institutionalized as an employment system, however, is difficult to detect from Boltanski's work. In order to understand this we need more information about how the state certified the relationship between white-collar and blue-collar groups in French society and what kind of institutionalized division of labor emerged among the major groups (Boltanski 1987; Lash and Urry 1987).

Japan: Managerialism

Burawoy characterizes Japan as a society "in which the state offers little or no social insurance and abstains from the regulation of factory apparatuses" (Burawoy 1985:144). As we see it, the purest example of managerialism exists in that society. Japan is also, along with Germany, the classic case of a late developing nation displaying the "advantages of backwardness" (Veblen 1939). Industrialization came to Japan later than to the other three countries. The Japanese emphasised production of producer goods and export, as did the Germans, but the Japanese task structure, the degree of internationalization, and the organizational models in these industries were different. In general, Japanese labor was not well organized, but Japanese firms were. The Japanese state led industrialization before World War II, but the economy remained in the private hands of a small number of families, who were given wide latitude in their handling of labor relations.

After World War II, labor laws and antitrust laws similar to those in the United States were established in Japan in a top-down approach. There was an intensified period of class struggle before the Korean War, but this ended in the early 1950s. The result of these struggles was the creation of enterprise unions, a much less interventionist state in labor affairs than the United States, and the establishment of a new type of business group (the Keiretsu). The major victory for workers was the permanent employment system—the main compromise in the Japanese system that makes it a less than pure case of managerialism.

This last aspect is particularly relevant here. It is important to note that the high degree of job security granted Japanese workers that were part of this system was limited to the core firms in Japanese industry. In recessions core firms would force their peripheral suppliers and customers to accept extra workers. This would continue down the chain until the smallest firms would be forced to lay off their workers (Lincoln and Kalleberg 1990). This combined a hegemonic system in the core with a despotic system with insecure jobs in the peripheral industries. As Whitehill pointed out, however, "life-time employment, whether actually experienced or not, remains an ideal norm to which all companies, large and small, aspire" (Whitehill 1990:131).

Rohlen has argued that the Japanese school system represents a particularly strong legitimation of the prevailing organizational structures and that the uniformity at the lower levels combined with an intensely status-stratified system at higher levels creates dedicated and docile workers (Rohlen 1983). The reason for the intense competition among students at the lower levels is that they need to be accepted at a high-status university in order to be granted entry into the permanent employment system. It is because of this strong expectation of lifetime employment within a single company among the highest educated that Japanese firms continue to develop extensive in-house educational programs. Once the university graduates are part of this system, however, they have to accept the notion of a broad career. Job rotation, usually every three to five years, is an expected part of every manager's career advancement.

Japanese managers are neither pure generalists, as are American managers, nor narrowly specialized in one occupation, as are the Germans; rather, they are multi-specialists. The major distinction in the core firms in

Japan is between top executives and employees. The line separating blue-collar workers from white-collar workers is much more blurred in Japan than in any of the other countries examined here (Koike and Inoki 1990; Kuwahara 1989; Whitehill 1990).

Research Agendas

We think that our approach has two important implications. It suggests that systems of employment relations have a unique social origin that can be studied only historically. But we have also provided a causal analysis that specifies the conditions under which one outcome or another is likely. The cases illustrate how historical processes in each society that reflected the path into industrialization had profound effects on the system of employment that emerged. Where firms were strong, more managerialist systems emerged (i.e., Japan); where workers were strong, more vocationalist systems emerged (i.e., Germany). Where the sides were forced to compromise, mixtures of systems came into being (i.e., France, the United States). Once general arrangements emerged in the societies, educational systems came to buttress them.

It is useful to consider some of the implications of the perspective developed here for existing and future research. Most of the research on the "new structuralism" has been ahistorical and focused exclusively on the U.S. case. There have been exceptions (for instance, Baron, Dobbin, and Jennings 1986; Edwards 1979), but they have not altered the terms of the discussion. The thrust of the theoretical perspective put forward here is that the time is ripe for opening the field of stratification and organizations to more historical, more comparative, and more political and institutional approaches.

Our approach encourages scholars to take up the issues of the formation, crisis, and transformation of employment systems; we have offered a set of conceptual distinctions about the important features of employment systems. We have also provided rudimentary hypotheses about how pure cases might turn out. Taken together, these arguments can inform more sustained analyses of employment systems and begin to show how systems reflect compromises and whether current assaults on them are likely to yield change.

One of the most pressing research projects this suggests is a consideration of the historical accuracy of our general view about the types of employment systems in advanced industrial countries. Are there single systems of employment relations in modern industrial societies? Do our ideal types capture the most important distinctions among systems of employment relations? If societies contain multiple systems, is that explained by sectoral differences (i.e., core/periphery effects), path dependence (i.e., the moment of emergence), or compromises within sectors—or perhaps combinations of all three? It may be possible to synthesize what is known from disparate literatures (labor history, the history and study of professions, managerial history) to fill in some of the gaps, but it is certainly the case that much remains to be done.

It is useful to study systems of employment relations beyond their originating moments in industrialization. A set of severe external crises (two world wars, the depression of the 1930s) and huge institutional reorganizations have resulted. We have generally only stumbled onto these effects serendipitously. But it is important to study these events and their aftermaths more closely to see how the terms of employment were altered as a consequence. So, for instance, World War II did not appear to change the employment system in Germany, but it may have in Japan.

The framework we have developed can be applied to examine how the current organization of employment relations accounts for patterns of stratification we currently observe. It is useful to develop a case. The research on gender stratification in organizations in the United States has generally demonstrated that women are highly segregated within jobs in firms (Bielby and Baron 1984) and that as women move into male-oriented occupations a process of resegregation occurs (Reskin and Roos 1990). The search for causes of this have focused almost exclusively on employer or male worker choices. The empirical problem is that a theoretical argument that justifies this focus must rely on self-conscious sexist attitudes of employers and workers, the proof of which has so far eluded researchers.

Our argument suggests an alternative view. If the gender division of labor is inscribed in the evolution of the employment system, then even as women attain higher credentials, they meet with resistance from entrenched institutional arrangements. If we are correct in thinking that the United States has a mixed managerial-professional system, then one would expect that in occupations governed by managerialism "older" sex segregation practices would emerge as occupations changed their sex composition. Thus one would expect resegregation to occur. In occupations governed by professionalism or in new or emerging industries, there might be changes toward a less extreme division of labor. There is some evidence to support this prediction (Wright and Jacobs 1994; Jacobs 1989, 1992).

These changes will be held back by the standard institutional arrangements that new organizations will borrow from existing ones. It may be that the most effective tactics to changing these patterns will require collective action or the production of laws (Dobbin et al. 1993; Sutton et al. 1994). The rise of the women's movement, the increases in the number of women professionals and managers, and the emergence of equal employment opportunity (EEO) laws could have altered the institutional arrangements in some occupations and industries. These are testable hypotheses. We think similar styles of arguments can be made with regard to racism and credentialism.

It would also be possible to study the evolution of employment systems within or across industries as they emerge. One would argue that employment practices in a given newly emerging industry would owe greatly to existing practices from "nearby" industries. A succession of practices would reflect the ongoing political struggle to define these practices and the relative resources of various groups of workers and managers. So, for example, in new industries such as the computer industry and the biotechnology industry, one would expect professional models of employment relations to dominate early in the process. The initial power would be with engineers and other professionals. This could lock in, but one could also see that as technologies settled down power might shift back to managers, who would try to impose more orderly labor markets. One interesting feature of high-technology industries is that technology does change, and that makes it difficult for managers to control the situation, implying that professionalism might dominate.

We earlier argued that existing employment systems, once in place, would prove to be stable. We argued that such systems would prove to serve the interests of important groups and would usually only be transformed when they were in severe crisis. One source of crisis that might affect stable employment systems in advanced capitalist countries is the internationalization of the world's economy.

The nature and trajectory of the Japanese and German employment systems are a matter of some academic and political attention. The critical question is whether these distinctive systems of employment relations can weather the increase in international competition. Our argument is that these current institutional arrangements provide managers in these societies with ways to react to short-term economic crises. So while the lifetime employment system in Japan is under duress, its survival depends on firms' being able to shift workers across organizations. How long and how far this can go will determine if the conditions for institutional transformation exist. Similarly, the economic crisis in Germany has started to force employers to rethink their employment systems. Shortening the work week would be a solution that reflects the strategy of adjustment that characterizes the existing system of employment relations. But if these adjustments fail, then the wholesale transformation of the system is possible. The employment system in the United States appears to be, for the time being, the most stable. The managerial-professional model allows firms to shed workers in downturns and contract to keep workers they favor and need.

Finally, it is important to link more closely the development of educational institutions in a society to the system of employment relations. Once systems of education have expanded, they can have unintended effects on employment relations. We have argued that the professionalization projects of the postwar era in the United States have been fueled to a large degree by the expansion of higher education and its supporters in state and federal governments. It would be useful to explore this process through the institutions involved and seek out evidence to solidify this type of argument.

Conclusions

The theoretical arguments we have proposed have drawn their inspiration from three literatures: the "new" institutionalism in organizational theory, the "old" institutional economics, and Marxism. The argument about the "new" institutionalism was made most explicit. It is useful briefly to link our project to these other traditions.

There were two strands of the "old" institutional economics. The first focused on how noneconomic institutions shaped economic action (Veblen 1940; Commons 1934). This literature took for granted that political processes were at the core of the construction of institutions. A later version of this tradition informed analyses of labor markets (Kerr 1954; Dunlop 1957; Doeringer and Piore 1971). Here, the view was that groups would try to exercise control over atomistic labor market processes by constructing labor market segments, characterized by bargaining arrangements that would invoke credentials, constrain labor supply, and try to raise wages. Their basic insight was that labor markets could be negotiated, and this would affect a large number of outcomes. Our institutional analysis begins with a bargaining view of the players involved in the formation of employment systems.

Marxism, of course, has a great deal to say about the employment system (Edwards 1979; Burawoy 1985; Braverman 1974). The basic insight is that capitalists and workers face off over issues of control in the labor force and that capitalists generally have the upper hand. We concur with this argument as well. If one limits oneself to just the advanced industrial societies, managerialism and to a lesser degree professionalism dominate employment relations. The number of societies where vocationalism is the core model is small, and Germany is the purest case. We think this comes about because capitalists tend to be much better organized, have more resources, and can frequently call on states to intervene in their favor.

The Logic of Employment Systems

But we think that Marxism and the "old" institutional economics share several problems that are somewhat resolved by the "new" institutionalism. States should be treated as both exogenous and part of the process by which employment relations are negotiated. States do not only intervene on the side of capitalists (as in Marxism) or merely provide protection for privileged groups of workers (as in institutional economics). They must be seen as partners to bargains. Further, workers are sometimes able to organize alternative institutions within the framework of capitalism. Therefore, the class struggle approach needs to be problematized to allow for more possible outcomes, such as professionalism, vocationalism, and the various political compromises we have discussed.

Third, neither theory has a theory of institutions. This means they cannot make sense of how institutions become stable. Once institutions are in place, they are difficult to dislodge for two reasons: They are templates for action, and they organize existing interests and reward certain groups who then have a great deal at stake in defending them. The process of institutionalization suggests why systems of employment relations can last for long periods of time. Both institutional economics and Marxism focus narrowly on the relation between workers and capitalists. Our perspective broadens that relation and embeds it in larger societal arrangements, including states, educational systems, existing models of employment relations, and the previous history of those arrangements.

A final difference of opinion follows from our institutionalist framework as well. From our perspective, changes in employment relations are not likely to be endogenous to the bargaining process, as Marxism and institutional economics suggest, but exogenous. To change an employment system will require a crisis in the existing system, one usually caused by exogenous shocks. If a given bargain is held in place by a given distribution of resources, new bargains will require those distributions to change. This will most frequently occur during major events and their aftermath, such as wars and depressions, or the force of international competition.

We think that a political-institutional approach to studying employment systems gives scholars a great deal of leverage in understanding what has happened, what is possible, and what strategies make the most sense given current institutional arrangements. We also think it explains why employment systems are so resistant to change. The purpose of this theorizing is to suggest that projects couched in these more historical, political, and institutional terms are likely to prove fruitful in showing more clearly how stratification and organizational processes are intertwined.

Notes

This work was presented at the annual meeting of the American Sociological Association in Los Angeles, August 1994. We would like to thank Jim Baron, Frank Dobbin, and David Grusky for comments on an earlier draft.

1. As we shall see later, it is useful to distinguish between state professionalism and associational professionalism.

2. Here we define "governance structure" as a state-sanctioned institutional setup legitimizing certain conceptions of control and delegitimizing others.

3. We use the term "skill formation" to describe the mix of (1) formal schooling, (2) certified training on the job with or without external involvement, and (3) on-the-job training. The mixture of these three types is an important cultural as well as economic factor, with direct implications for employment systems.

4. The independence of professionals in the market for business services does not necessarily mean that these groups have established a particularly powerful position vis-à-vis managers. It might be exactly because they are so firmly under management control and do not represent any challenge that they are allowed to produce their services in the market.

References

Abbott, Andrew D. 1988. *The System of Professions: An Essay on the Division of Expert Labor.* Chicago: University of Chicago Press.

———. 1989. "The New Occupational Structure—What Are the Questions?" *Work and Occupations* 16:273–91.

Armstrong, P. 1984. "Competition Between the Organizational Professions and the Evolution of Management Control Strategies." In Kenneth Thompson (ed.), *Work, Employment and Unemployment.* Philadelphia: Open University Press and Milton Keynes.

Averitt, Robert T. 1968. *The Dual Economy: The Dynamics of American Industry Structure.* New York: Norton.

Baron, James N. 1984. "Organizational Perspectives on Stratification." *Annual Review of Sociology* 10:37–69.

Baron, James N., and William T. Bielby. 1980. "Bringing the Firms Back in." *American Sociological Review* 45:737–66.

Baron, James N., Frank R. Dobbin, and P. Devereaux Jennings. 1986. "War and Peace: The Evolution of Modern Personnel–Administration in U.S. Industry." *American Journal of Sociology* 92:350–83.

Beck, E.M., Patrick M. Horan, and Charles M. Tolbert II. 1978. "Stratification in a Dual Economy: A Sectoral Model of Earnings Determination." *American Sociological Review* 43:704–20.

Bielby, William T., and James N. Baron. 1984. "A Woman's Place Is with Other Women: Sex Segregation Within Firms." In Barbara F. Reskin (ed.), *Sex Segregation in the Workplace: Trends, Explanations, and Remedies.* Washington, DC: National Academy Press.

Boltanski, Luc. 1987. *The Making of a Class: Cadres in French Society.* Cambridge: Cambridge University Press.
Bowles, Samuel, and Herbert Gintis. 1976. *Schooling in Capitalist America: Educational Reform and the Contradictions of Economic Life.* New York: Basic Books.
Braverman, Harry. 1974. *Labor and Monopoly Capitalism: The Degradation of Work in the Twentieth Century.* New York: Monthly Review Press.
Brint, Steven G. 1994. *In an Age of Experts: The Changing Role of Experts in Politics and Public Life.* Princeton, NJ: Princeton University Press.
Burawoy, Michael. 1985. *The Politics of Production: Factory Regimes Under Capitalism and Socialism.* London: Verso.
Burrage, Michael. 1990. "Beyond a Sub-set: The Professional Aspirations of Manual Workers in France, the United States and Britain." In Michael Burrage and Rolf Torstendahl (eds.), *Professions in Theory and History: Rethinking the Study of the Professions.* London: Sage.
Byrkjeflot, Haldor. 1993. "Engineering and Management in Germany and the USA: The Origins of Diversity in Organizational Forms." Dissertation prospectus, Department of Sociology, University of California—Berkeley.
Campbell, John L., J. Rogers Hollingsworth, and Leon N. Lindberg. 1991. *Governance of the American Economy.* Cambridge: Cambridge University Press.
Caplan, J. 1990. "Professions as a Vocation: The German Civil Service." In Geoffrey Cocks and Konrad H. Jarausch (eds.), *German Professions, 1800–1950.* London: Sage.
Commons, John R. 1934. *Institutional Economics: Its Place in Political Economy.* New York: Macmillan.
DiMaggio, Paul J. 1988. "Interest and Agency in Institutional Theory." In Lynne Zucker (ed.), *Institutional Patterns and Organizations: Culture and Environment.* Cambridge, MA: Ballinger Press.
Dobbin, Frank. 1994. *Forging Industrial Policy: The United States, Britain, and France in the Railway Age.* New York: Cambridge University Press.
Dobbin, Frank., John R. Sutton, John W. Meyer, and W. Richard Scott. 1993. "Equal Opportunity Law and the Construction of Internal Labor Markets." *American Journal of Sociology* 99:396–427.
Doeringer, Peter B, and Michael J. Piore. 1971. *Internal Labor Markets and Manpower Analysis.* Lexington, MA: D.C. Heath.
Dunlop, John. 1957. "The Task of Contemporary Wage Theory." In George W. Taylor (ed.), *New Concepts in Wage Determination.* New York: McGraw-Hill.
Edwards, R. 1979. *Contested Terrain: The Transformation of the Work Place in the Twentieth Century.* New York: Basic Books.
Fligstein, Neil. 1990. *The Transformation of Corporate Control.* Cambridge: Harvard University Press.
Fligstein, Neil, and Roberto M. Fernandez. 1988. "Worker Power, Firm Power, and the Structure of Labor Markets." *Sociological Quarterly* 29:5–28.
Fligstein, Neil, and Doug McAdam. 1993. "A Political-cultural Approach to the Problem of Strategic Action." Manuscript, Department of Sociology, University of California–Berkeley.
Hodson, Randy. 1986. "Modeling the Effects of Industrial Structure on Wages and Benefits." *Work and Occupations* 13:488–510.

Hodson, Randy, and Robert L. Kaufman. 1982. "Economic Dualism: A Critical Review." *American Sociological Review* 47:728–39.

Kaufman, Robert L., Randy Hodson, and Neil D. Fligstein. 1981. "Defrocking Dualism: A New Approach to Industrial Sectors." *Social Science Research* 10:1–31.

Jacobs, Jerry A. 1989. *Revolving Doors: Sex Segregation and Women's Careers.* Stanford, CA: Stanford University Press.

———. 1992. "Women's Entry into Management: Trends in Earnings, Authority, and Values Among Salaried Managers." *Administrative Science Quarterly* 37:282–301.

Kalleberg, Arne L. 1988. "Comparative Perspectives on Work Structures and Inequality." *Annual Review of Sociology* 14:203–25.

Kalleberg, Arne L., and James R. Lincoln. 1988. "The Structure of Earnings Inequality in the United States and Japan." *American Journal of Sociology* 94:S121–53.

Kerr, C. 1954, "The Balkanization of Labor Markets." In E. Wright Bakke (ed.), *Labor Mobility and Economic Opportunity: Essays by E. Wright Bakke (and Others).* Cambridge: MIT Press.

Koike, Kazuo, and Takenori Inoki (eds.). 1990. *Skill Formation in Japan and Southeast Asia.* Tokyo: Tokyo University Press.

Kuwahara, Y. 1989. *Managerial Staffing in Large Japanese Companies.* Honolulu: Industrial Relations Center, University of Hawaii.

Lash, Scott, and John Urry. 1987. *The End of Organized Capitalism.* Madison: University of Wisconsin Press.

Larson, Magali S. 1977. *The Rise of Professionalism: A Sociological Analysis.* Berkeley: University of California Press.

Lincoln, James R., and Arne L. Kalleberg. 1990. *Culture, Control, and Commitment: A Study of Work Organization and Work Attitudes in the United States and Japan.* Cambridge: Cambridge University Press.

Miliband, Ralph. 1969. *The State in Capitalist Society.* New York: Basic Books.

Müller, Detlef K., Fritz Ringer, and Brian Simon (eds.). 1987. *The Rise of the Modern Educational System: Structural Change and Social Reproduction, 1870–1920.* Cambridge: Cambridge University Press.

Powell, Walter W., and Paul J. DiMaggio (eds.). 1991. *The New Institutionalism in Organizational Analysis.* Chicago: University of Chicago Press.

Reskin, Barbara F., and Patricia A. Roos. 1990. *Job Queues, Gender Queues: Explaining Women's Inroads into Male Occupations.* Philadelphia: Temple University Press.

Rohlen, Thomas P. 1983. *Japan's High Schools.* Berkeley: University of California Press.

Starr, Paul. 1982. *The Social Transformation of American Medicine.* New York: Basic Books.

Stinchcombe, Arthur L. 1959. "Bureaucratic and Craft Administration of Production." *Administrative Science Quarterly* 4:168–87.

———. 1965. "Social Structure and Organizations." In James G. March (ed.), *Handbook of Organizations.* Chicago: Rand McNally.

Sutton, John R., Frank Dobbin, John W. Meyer, and W. Richard Scott. 1994. "The Legalization of the Workplace." *American Journal of Sociology* 99:944–71.
Swidler, Ann. 1986. "Culture in Action: Symbols and Strategies." *American Sociological Review* 51:273–86.
Veblen, Thorstein. 1904. *The Theory of Business Enterprise.* New York: Charles Scribner's Sons.
———. 1939. *Imperial Germany and the Industrial Revolution.* New York: Viking.
Voss, Kim. 1993. *The Making of American Exceptionalism: The Knights of Labor and Class Formation in the Nineteenth Century.* Ithaca, N.Y.: Cornell University Press.
White, Harrison. 1992. *Identity and Control: A Structural Theory of Social Action.* Princeton, NJ: Princeton University Press.
Whitehill, Arthur M. 1990. *Japanese Management: Tradition and Transition.* London: Routledge, Kegan Paul.
Williamson, Oliver E. 1975. *Markets and Hierarchies, Analysis and Antitrust Implications: A Study in the Economics of Internal Organization.* New York: Free Press.
———. 1985. *The Economic Institutions of Capitalism: Firms, Markets, Relational Contracting.* New York: Free Press.
Wright, Erik Olin. 1979. *Class Structure and Income Determination.* New York: Academic Press.
Wright, Rosemary, and Jerry A. Jacobs. 1994. "Male Flight from Computer Work: A New Look at Occupational Resegregation and Ghettoization." *American Sociological Review* 59:511–36.

3

Income Differences Among 31 Ethnic Groups in Los Angeles

Donald J. Treiman and Hye-kyung Lee

The Los Angeles metropolitan area, with a current population of more than 15 million—about the size of the Netherlands—is sometimes called the "capital of the Pacific Rim" or, more derisively, the "capital of the Third World." Boosters are fond of pointing out that if the metropolitan area were a separate country, it would have the eleventh largest economy in the world (Security Pacific Bank 1988:8). But what is truly distinctive about Los Angeles is what is captured in the second epithet—the fact that over the past quarter century it has become the major destination of immigrants in the world. Since 1970, when most of the population was of European origin[1] ("Anglo," in the local parlance), nearly 3 million international immigrants, most from Latin America and Asia, have settled in the area.[2] By 1990, 27.3 percent of the population were foreign-born. Just under half the population (48.6 percent) was of European origin and nearly one-third (32.4 percent) was of Latin American origin; 9.3 percent were of Asian origin, 7.1 percent were of African origin, and 1.8 percent were of Middle Eastern origin.[3] In Los Angeles County, the core of the metropolitan area, the shift to a non-European origin population was even more pronounced: The corresponding percentages were 39.3, 37.4, 10.8, 9.4, and 2.4; and one-third (32.7 percent) of the population was foreign-born. Finally, 151 different languages were spoken in the five-county metropolitan area and 132 in Los Angeles County.[4]

The shift in the population of Los Angeles from a mainly native-born to a substantially immigrant population has been occurring at a time when the economy of the area, in common with much of the remainder of the country, has been undergoing very substantial restructuring away from heavy manufacturing and toward low-paying, low-skill jobs in light manufacturing, for example, furniture and garment manufacture (Schimek 1989). In addition, Los Angeles (along with New York, London, and Tokyo) has become a "capital of capital" (Soja 1987), which has resulted in an increase both in high-end jobs in banking, finance, and professional services and low-end jobs in hotels, restaurants, and other service industries.

The combination of massive and (as we shall see) very diverse immigration together with substantial shifts in the economy of the area gives rise to an obvious question: How have new immigrants been incorporated into the economy of Los Angeles? Have they followed the traditional immigrant route of concentration in low-level jobs, or have they found a greater variety of opportunities? With the shift from an "Anglo"-dominated to a truly multiethnic population, has there been a corresponding shift to true "equality of opportunity," the ability of persons of all ethnic origins to secure jobs and income commensurate with their individual qualifications, their "human capital"?

In this chapter we consider these questions. We begin with a socioeconomic profile of the 31 largest ethnic groups in the metropolitan area. As we will see, there is enormous diversity, especially in incomes—the ratio of the mean incomes of the richest and poorest groups is about five to one, and the sources of income differ substantially across groups. We then consider to what extent ethnic-group differences in income can be attributed to ethnic group differences in human-capital. As it turns out, human capital differences are part of but by no means the whole story. We consider why this is so by analyzing whether ethnic groups differ in the kinds of jobs they hold net of human capital differences. It turns out that they do. We then show that when ethnic group differences in both human capital and job characteristics are taken into account, ethnic group differences in income are largely, although not entirely, explained. We conclude with a discussion of how ethnic differences in income arise and some conjectures about what explains the differences that remain net of human capital assets and occupational characteristics.

Data

The data used in this analysis are from the 5 percent Public Use Microdata Sample (PUMS) from the 1990 U.S. Census of Population (U.S. Bureau of the Census 1993). From the California Microdata File, we extracted all persons residing in the five counties constituting the Los Angeles metropolitan area (Los Angeles, Orange, Riverside, San Bernardino, and Ventura Counties). Although these counties cover a vast region of Southern California, from the Pacific Ocean to the Arizona border, over 90 percent of their combined population live within 60 miles of the Los Angeles city hall, and on a variety of measures the region clearly constitutes a single metropolis and a single labor market (Security Pacific Bank 1979, 1988). The area had a population of something over 14 million in 1990, and the 5 percent sample consists of 705,938 persons.

In the present analysis we restrict the sample to males age 20–64 who were not in school at the time of the data collection, had worked at any time in 1989, and had nonzero incomes in 1989. We excluded those without income and, for the regression analyses, the 374 men who reported negative incomes. These restrictions reduce the sample to 162,982 and, for the regression analysis, to 162,608. We focus on men because in this population there are complex interactions among ethnicity, gender, and socioeconomic attributes. Separate analyses of men and women would therefore be warranted, which would have nearly doubled the length of this essay. We leave such an analysis for another time. We restrict the sample to men age 20–64 in order to avoid the usual biases associated with age at entry into the labor force (those destined for high-paying jobs are likely still to be in school until around age 20) and continuing employment after the conventional retirement age (which tends to be restricted to those either at the very high or the very low end of the occupational status distribution).

For the analysis, we have divided the sample into 31 ethnic categories: eight Asian origin groups, nine Latin American origin groups, six European origin groups, three Middle Eastern origin groups, three African origin groups, American Indians, and an "other" category. As Table 3.1 shows, there is great internal variability within the aggregated categories. Hence, much that is interesting about the immigrant and ethnic groups of Los Angeles is lost when comparisons are restricted to gross categories such as "Asians," "Hispanics," or "whites." We will have more to say about this later.

Since our interest was in producing a detailed account of differences in the way various groups are incorporated into the economy of Los Angeles, we tried to create the most detailed classification that could sustain the analysis. To do this, we distinguished every identifiable non-European-origin group with at least 20,000 persons in the population of the metropolitan area (and hence at least 1,000 persons in the 5 percent PUMS sample), and every European-origin group with at least 20,000 *foreign-born* persons in the population. The specification of a 1,000-person minimum in the sample seemed a workable criterion since it would produce at least a few hundred respondents from each ethnic group, even from subsets of the population such as the employed males age 20–64 uti-

TABLE 3.1 Selected Socioeconomic Characteristics of 31 Ethnic Groups, Los Angeles Metropolitan Area, 1990 (Male Labor Force Age 20–64))

Ethnic Group	Mean Income in 1989	Percent Upper Non-manual[a]	Mean Years of School	Percent Speaking Non-English Language at Home	Percent Foreign Born	Percent Immigrated 1980 or Later	Percent Immigrated 1987 or Later	Mean Years of Labor Force Experience	Percent of Total Male Labor Force	N
Total	36,058	27.5	12.5	37.7	33.3	15.5	4.1	19.8	100.0	162,982
Asian origin										
Asian Indian	43,396	51.4	15.5	85.5	97.6	46.8	10.0	18.1	.6	920
Cambodian	23,107	15.6	10.5	97.0	99.3	61.5	2.2	19.0	.1	135
Chinese	36,665	43.1	14.1	88.3	87.0	42.5	8.9	20.3	2.0	3,179
Filipino	27,571	26.7	14.3	87.7	88.1	45.4	10.9	19.6	1.9	3,040
Japanese	45,998	44.9	14.5	41.4	32.1	16.2	7.9	20.9	1.3	2,151
Korean	37,206	32.2	14.2	96.5	97.7	53.3	12.3	21.0	1.2	1,935
Vietnamese	25,872	21.5	12.7	98.4	98.9	52.5	6.6	18.0	.8	1,341
Other Asian	29,549	26.6	13.5	71.4	69.2	34.4	6.9	18.7	.7	1,065
Total	34,906	35.1	14.1	81.6	80.8	41.4	9.3	19.8	8.4	13,766
Latin American origin										
Cuban	31,797	23.6	12.1	87.8	85.6	14.1	1.3	22.9	.4	681
Guatemalan	14,307	4.9	8.3	97.8	98.3	69.1	22.5	18.5	.8	1,296
Mexican	19,891	8.0	9.2	82.9	67.3	31.1	9.0	19.1	24.5	39,978

Nicaraguan	19,114	14.7	11.6	95.2	93.4	59.9	18.0	18.0	.2	272
Puerto Rican	28,521	18.9	12.2	68.6	4.6[b]	10.3[c]	4.1	18.8	.4	681
Salvadoran	14,214	5.7	8.2	96.9	98.7	67.9	12.4	18.7	1.3	2,192
South American	27,596	21.9	12.6	90.9	90.2	34.7	8.1	19.8	.6	999
Other Central American	20,690	11.6	10.3	94.5	92.5	51.7	15.6	18.6	.2	346
Other Hispanic	22,700	14.2	10.4	77.5	71.6	39.7	9.9	19.3	1.6	2,538
Total	20,079	8.9	9.4	83.8	69.9	34.0	9.5	19.1	30.1	48,983
European origin										
English	49,220	42.1	14.3	2.6	7.1	2.4	.7	22.0	7.7	12,539
German	45,077	35.7	13.9	5.1	3.3	.4	.2	19.9	12.2	19,925
Italian	45,440	34.7	13.8	9.8	6.2	1.1	.2	19.4	3.3	5,301
Polish	51,455	45.1	14.6	10.3	10.6	4.3	.9	19.7	1.6	2,585
Russian	69,458	56.5	15.5	10.0	7.6	2.2	.7	21.4	1.6	2,608
Other European	43,815	35.1	13.8	8.1	7.6	2.2	.6	20.0	27.0	43,980
Total	45,979	37.1	14.0	6.8	6.5	1.8	.5	20.2	53.3	86,938
Middle Eastern origin										
Armenian	41,390	32.9	13.1	76.5	74.2	28.7	8.6	21.7	.6	1,009
Iranian	43,066	47.4	15.5	90.6	97.5	38.2	7.1	17.3	.5	870
Other ME., North African	44,532	39.3	14.0	70.5	76.2	32.6	7.4	19.0	.7	1,210
Total	43,093	39.5	14.1	78.1	81.5	32.9	7.7	19.4	1.9	3,089

(continued)

41

TABLE 3.1 (continued)

Ethnic Group	Mean Income in 1989	Percent Upper Non-manual[a]	Mean Years of School	Percent Speaking Non-English Language at Home	Percent Foreign Born	Percent Immigrated 1980 or Later	Percent Immigrated 1987 or Later	Mean Years of Labor Force Experience	Percent of Total Male Labor Force	N
African origin										
U.S. blacks	27,561	20.0	13.0	4.1	0.0	.1[d]	.0	19.4	5.2	8,509
West Indian	26,166	21.5	12.7	14.9	80.7	24.1	7.0	20.5	.1	228
Foreign born blacks (exc. W.I.)	28,092	27.3	13.9	47.9	100.0	42.8	7.1	17.1	.2	311
Total	27,544	20.3	13.0	5.9	5.5	2.2	.4	19.3	5.6	9,048
American Indian	28,672	20.2	12.8	14.3	3.7	1.9	.6	19.3	.5	803
Other	28,483	19.7	11.8	46.8	34.4	16.9	1.7	19.0	.2	355

[a] Percent in administrative or professional occupations, as defined in the 1990 U.S. Census Classification of Industries and Occupations (U.S. Bureau of the Census 1992).

[b] These could be persons who immigrated to Puerto Rico from other countries and later came to Los Angeles. Or they could have erroneously thought of Puerto Rico as a foreign country.

[c] This number clearly is in error since it is larger than the number of "foreign-born" Puerto Ricans. Perhaps some respondents gave the year they immigrated from Puerto Rico to the mainland.

[d] There should be no positive responses to the year of immigration to the United States since this category includes only those born here.

lized here. The decision to separately identify European-origin groups only when they included at least 1,000 foreign-born persons reflected our special interest in immigrant groups but also kept the number of groups from increasing substantially.

Defining ethnic groups in the U.S. census is not an easy matter, since the census utilizes a hodgepodge of lumpy and overlapping indicators. (An example of the lumpiness: "white" is one race, but each of the Asian origin groups shown in Table 3.1 is treated as a separate "race"; an example of the overlap: those of "Hispanic origin" may be of any race.) After exploring a number of options, we settled upon a classification based on a combination of the "Hispanic origin," "race," "ancestry 1," and "place of birth" questions. We first distinguished those of Hispanic origin from others and then used the Hispanic-origin question and the ancestry question to make further distinctions among Latin American origin groups; we included those of Iberian origin—Spanish and Portuguese—in the "other European origin" category. For the remainder (the non-Hispanic origin population) we then distinguished those of Asian, African, and American Indian origin on the basis of race. For Asians, the race variable was sufficient to distinguish each group, except that we moved "other Hispanics" who claimed an Asian race into the appropriate Asian category. This mainly applies to Filipinos, who sometimes claim to be "other Hispanics." For those of African origin, we distinguished those with West Indian origins on the basis of ancestry and non-West Indian foreign-born blacks on the basis of place of birth. From the remainder we distinguished those of Middle Eastern origin (Armenians, Iranians, and others) on the basis of ancestry. From the remainder we then distinguished those of European origin on the basis of race ("white") and used the ancestry variable to make further distinctions. The small percentage of the population that did not meet any of these criteria was included in a residual category, "other."[5]

Descriptive Information

Table 3.1 provides pertinent social and economic information about each of the 31 ethnic groups. Note first the absolute and relative size of each of the categories. The right-hand column gives the number of persons in each ethnic group included in the sample. The groups range in size from 135 Cambodians, who constitute about one-tenth of 1 percent of the sample (as we can see from the next column to the left), to 43,980 of "other European origin"—non-Hispanic whites who do not identify their main ancestry as English, German, Italian, Polish, or Russian—who constitute just over a quarter of the sample. Just over half of the employed men in the Los Angeles metropolitan area are of European origin, nearly one-third are of Latin American origin, 8 percent are of Asian origin, 6 percent are of African origin, and the remainder are of Middle Eastern, American Indian, or "other" origin. Multiplying the number of cases in the sample by 20 gives an approximate estimate of the size of each group in the population. Thus there were about 2,700 (= 135*20) Cambodian men age 20–64 in the metropolitan labor force in 1990, and so on.

Income differences among ethnic groups are very substantial, even when the aggregate groups normally analyzed are considered. Those of European origin average about $46,000 per year, and those of Middle Eastern origin do nearly as well, averaging about $43,000 per year. Then come Asians (averaging about $35,000), blacks (averaging about $28,000), and finally those of Latin American origin, who average about $20,000. But these gross distinctions mask important variation between specific groups within the aggregate categories. While the incomes of all European origin groups are relatively high, those of Russian origin (who are mainly Jews—see Rosenthal 1975) do much better than all of the remaining groups, earning nearly 60 percent more per year than those of "other European origin." Similarly, Japanese earn about twice as much as do Cambodians, and Cubans earn more than twice as much as do those from Guatemala and El Salvador.

Income differences among ethnic groups are substantially but not completely mirrored in differences in education and occupational status. In general, those of Asian, European, and Middle Eastern origin have relatively high socioeconomic status: Members of these groups average about two years of college and more than one-third are professionals or managers. Blacks average a year less education, and only about 20 percent are in professional or managerial jobs. Those of Latin American origin average less than nine years of schooling, and less than 10 percent have professional or managerial jobs. However, just as with income, there are important ethnic-group differences in both education and the likelihood of holding a professional or managerial job within the aggregate categories. For example, on average, Asian Indians have five years more schooling than do Cambodians (15.5 compared to 10.5), and those from South America have over four years more schooling than those from El Salvador (12.6 compared to 8.2). Similarly, more than half of the Indians but only 16 percent of the Vietnamese have professional or managerial jobs, and the same is true of more than 20 percent of the Cubans and less than 5 percent of the Guatemalans.

The same story of aggregate differences but of important variations between specific groups within each aggregate category can be seen by inspection of the columns indicating the percentage foreign-born and the percentage speaking a language other than English at home. In general, large fractions of those from Asian, Latin American, and Middle Eastern origins and small fractions of the remaining groups are foreign-born and speak a non-English language at home. But among the Asians, the Japanese stand out as a largely native-born group—the low level of recent immigration from Japan reflecting its position as a wealthy nation. And among Latin Americans, those of Mexican origin and "other Hispanic origin" (who appear to be mainly Mexican origin) stand out as distinctively more likely to be native-born than the remainder.[6]

Table 3.2 shows the sources of total income for each ethnic group. In all ethnic groups most men have wage and salary earnings. But there are important variations among the groups with respect to the percentage with income from self-employment and the percentage with income from interest and rents. With respect to self-employment income, the Koreans are distinctive, as is well known (Light and Bonacich 1988): More than one-third are self-employed, followed by the three groups of Middle Eastern origin and Russians, which have self-employment rates ranging from 25 to 30 percent. At the other extreme, less than 10 percent of Filipinos, most of those of Latin American origin, and blacks (except West Indians) have self-employment income. As these figures indicate, the within-aggregate-group differences are striking: Koreans versus Filipinos; South Americans and Cubans versus Mexicans and Central Americans; and Russians versus the remaining European-origin groups.

Similarly striking contrasts emerge with respect to the percentage who have income from interest or rents: around half of those of Chinese, Japanese, and Russian origin; more than one-third of Asian Indians and the remaining European-origin groups; and less than 10 percent of those of Mexican or Central American origins. Among those with income from interest or rents, the largest returns are for Asian Indians, Koreans, all of the Middle Eastern-origin groups, foreign-born (non-West Indian) blacks, and all of the European-origin groups, but especially those of Russian origin.

What Tables 3.1 and 3.2 convey is the complexity of the story. The ethnic groups considered here have distinctive patterns of migration to Los Angeles and of incorporation in the local economy. Clearly, these histories must be taken into account in order to explain group differences in average income. But we would have one sort of story if income differences between ethnic groups are simply a matter of group differences in human capital and a different sort of story if substantial differences remain after human-capital attributes are taken into account. In the former case the focus would be on the factors accounting for differentially selective migration, while in the latter case it would be necessary to consider variations in the way different ethnic groups fare in Los Angeles.

TABLE 3.2 Components of 1989 Income for 31 Ethnic Groups in Los Angeles (Male Labor Force Age 20–64)

Ethnic group	Percent with				Mean Income of Those with Income			
	Wage and Salary Earnings	Self-employment Income	Interest, Rental Income	Income from Other Sources	Wage and Salary Earnings	Self-employment Income	Interest, Rental Income	Income from Other Sources
Total	91.6	13.9	26.6	7.1	33,090	28,004	4,986	7,312
Asian origin								
Asian Indian	90.9	18.7	39.3	2.8	38,949	31,416	5,076	4,673
Cambodian	88.9	13.3	21.5	8.9	20,153	30,650	2,234	7,049
Chinese	89.6	18.2	47.8	4.8	33,111	24,058	4,888	5,741
Filipino	96.2	7.1	22.9	5.7	26,370	18,436	2,386	5,896
Japanese	90.5	15.7	47.9	6.1	43,534	27,356	3,693	8,927
Korean	71.9	36.3	22.3	2.4	32,919	32,984	6,538	3,421
Vietnamese	92.8	11.7	21.3	7.2	24,738	18,270	1,924	5,194
Other Asian	92.0	12.1	20.8	4.2	27,573	26,929	3,329	5,224
Total	89.3	16.8	33.2	5.0	32,117	27,090	4,131	6,105
Latin American origin								
Cuban	86.0	17.6	22.2	5.7	30,585	25,566	3,063	5,139
Guatemalan	95.1	6.5	2.7	3.2	13,815	15,786	1,755	3,277
Mexican	95.3	6.6	7.6	5.2	19,105	18,366	3,375	4,027
Nicaraguan	95.2	5.1	7.7	4.8	18,731	21,708	997	1,762
Puerto Rican	95.4	6.8	16.0	9.3	26,947	29,430	2,202	4,980
Salvadoran	95.0	6.4	3.4	3.0	13,874	13,983	1,723	2,384
South American	86.9	18.7	14.8	4.4	25,387	25,352	3,720	5,468

Other Central American	91.3	10.7	9.8	2.6	19,932	21,164	887	5,203
Other Hispanic	94.4	9.2	11.5	5.1	21,137	21,264	4,654	4,828
Total	94.9	7.2	7.9	5.1	19,210	19,126	3,359	4,072
European origin								
English	89.9	17.6	43.8	9.2	45,062	30,678	5,417	9,872
German	91.0	16.4	39.0	8.3	41,415	28,855	4,945	8,785
Italian	89.5	18.3	34.4	6.9	41,892	31,449	4,991	7,281
Polish	90.6	18.3	44.5	6.5	47,203	30,746	5,698	8,280
Russian	85.0	27.6	53.6	7.7	62,009	39,731	9,777	6,447
Other European	90.3	17.0	34.3	8.4	40,277	29,655	5,030	8,394
Total	90.2	17.4	37.6	8.3	42,148	30,261	5,299	8,607
Middle Eastern origin								
Armenian	78.4	30.2	28.5	5.5	38,130	29,044	8,106	7,432
Iranian	82.5	25.9	30.8	3.1	39,148	32,873	6,527	7,908
Other M.E., North African	82.7	25.1	30.6	3.6	39,994	35,114	7,651	7,828
Total	81.3	27.0	30.0	4.1	39,165	32,289	7,467	7,672
African origin								
U.S. blacks	95.0	8.3	11.9	9.9	25,895	23,267	3,112	6,893
West Indian	91.2	11.4	11.8	5.3	25,029	25,444	1,848	4,037
Foreign-born blacks (exc. W.I.)	93.6	9.0	13.5	7.4	26,205	26,076	5,939	5,711
Total	94.8	8.4	12.0	9.7	25,885	23,446	3,191	6,794
American Indian	93.4	10.7	18.7	9.1	27,281	18,597	3,099	6,830
Other	92.7	10.7	13.2	5.4	27,017	25,318	3,196	5,818

Analytic Strategy

To decide between these alternatives, we develop a model of income attainment that allows us to estimate the effect of ethnic group membership net of the human-capital assets of individuals and, of course, the effect of personal characteristics net of ethnic-group membership. We do this by estimating two equations. We first estimate an equation of the form

$$\widehat{\ln(Y)} = a + \sum b_i X_i \qquad (1)$$

where Y is the total income received in 1979 and the X_i are personal characteristics thought to affect income. We then estimate an equation of the form

$$\widehat{\ln(Y)} = a + \sum b_i X_i + \sum c_j G_j \qquad (2)$$

where Y and the X_i are human capital attributes and the G_i are dummy variables for the ethnic groups, scored one for individuals who are members of the group and zero otherwise. We will have more to say in the next section about the interpretation of these two equations (and of corresponding equations that include job characteristics as additional independent variables). But first we need to define the variables included in them.

Dependent Variable

Income. $\ln(Y)$ = the natural log of total income in 1989 from all sources. The total income variable was created by the Census Bureau as the sum of income reported from each of eight sources: wage and salary earnings; earnings from nonfarm self employment; earnings from farm self-employment; income from interest, dividends, and rents; income from social security; income from public assistance; retirement income; and income from other sources. Total income from all sources is analyzed rather than wage and salary earnings because other sources of income, particularly income from self-employment, vary substantially among ethnic groups, as we have seen. Moreover, it is the total income differences, not merely earnings differences, that are consequential. In our preliminary analysis we estimated the income equations using both the metric and log form of income and investigated various heteroskedasticity measures. Because the log form produces a better fit to the data (the R^2s are higher) and because the distributions of the variables are much better behaved, we report the analysis based on the log form of the income variable. To facilitate handling the logged income variable, we omitted the 374 men who reported negative incomes. Thus the analysis is restricted to men with positive incomes in 1989. There are two additional advantages to the log form. First, individual income tends to be distributed log-normally so the log of income is distributed normally, a convenient property. Second, and more important, when the dependent variable is in (natural) log form, the coefficients associated with the independent variables can be interpreted as indicating approximately the proportional increase in the dependent variable for a one-unit increase in the independent variable.[7]

The remaining variables fall into three groups: measures of human capital attributes, characteristics of the jobs held by respondents, and a set of dummy variables distinguishing the 31 ethnic groups.

Human Capital Attributes

Education. E = years of school completed, which is a standard summary measure of educational attainment. It is well established that amount of schooling is the single strongest determinant of occupational status (e.g., Treiman and Ganzeboom 1990:117). We also include the square of education, to permit the possibility that the value of each additional year of education increases as the level of education increases (Treiman and Terrell 1975). If it does, the coefficient associated with the squared term will be positive.

Education completed in the United States. U is a dummy variable indicating whether the respondent's education was completed in the U.S. ($U = 1$) or abroad ($U = 0$). Since the census includes no direct indicator of where education was completed, we estimated this variable by assuming that the men in our sample began school at age six and completed their education without interruption. This provided the year in which they completed their education. If this year was later than the midpoint of the period of immigration to the United States, they were assumed to have completed their education in the United States (as were those who immigrated prior to 1965 or were native-born).[8] The reason for including this variable was our suspicion that education completed abroad is not as valuable as education completed in the United States because of the greater relevance of American education to the United States labor market as well as the presence of specific vocational guidance that is a standard part of the curriculum in the United States To test the claim that returns to education completed in the United States are greater than returns to education completed abroad, we included the interaction terms EU and E^2U.

Labor force experience. Income is known to increase substantially with labor force experience, but in a curvilinear fashion—at first rapidly but then more slowly (Treiman and Roos 1983). We thus include both a main term and a squared term for labor force experience, with the expectation that the coefficients of the squared term will be negative. Since the census includes no direct measure of years of labor force experience, we approximate total labor force experience in the conventional way, as T = age − education − 6.[9]

English language competence. $L_2 \ldots L_5$ is a set of dummy variables indicating the degree of English-language competence. The hypothesis is, of course, that English-language competence has a positive net effect on income. The omitted category consists of those who are monolingual in English. Members of the remaining categories all speak a language other than English at home. L_1 is scored one for those who, by the report of whoever completed the census form (themselves or another member of their household), speak English "very well" and zero otherwise. L_2 is scored one for those who speak English "well" and zero otherwise. L_3 is scored one for those who speak English "not well" and zero otherwise. L_4 is scored one for those who do not speak English at all and zero otherwise.

Recent immigration. R is a dummy variable scored one for those who immigrated to the United States between 1988 and 1990 and zero otherwise. The assumption is that very recent immigrants will not yet have learned the ropes nor acquired the contacts necessary to be economically successful. The disadvantaged position of very recent immigrants is reflected in the folk terms applied by many immigrant groups to newcomers: *greenhorns, fobs* (for "fresh off the boat"), and so on.

Job Characteristics

While some analysts (e.g., Grusky and Baron, in personal communication) regard income as an attribute of jobs like any other—for example, the nature of the employment relationship (employer, employee, etc.), the status of the occupation that defines the job, and so on—others (e.g., Duncan 1961; Ganzeboom, de Graaf, and Treiman 1992) regard jobs as intervening between education and income. In this formulation, which we prefer, human-capital assets qualify individuals for jobs with certain attributes; the kind of jobs people do plus their performance on the job plus other attributes together determine their income. Since there is a good deal of variance in the incomes of individuals who do nominally identical jobs—we need look no further than our own university departments to be convinced of this—it seems sensible to us to treat job attributes as one, but only one, of the sets of factors that affect the income of individuals. To assess the effect of job attributes as intervening between human-capital and income, we estimate a second set of equations corresponding to equation 1 and equation 2 but that include both human-capital factors and job attributes as independent variables. The job attributes we analyze are the following.

Employment status. ($C_1 \ldots C_3$). Immigrants (and members of different ethnic groups) may be incorporated into the labor force in a variety of ways, with important consequences for their income. Most will be employed as wage or salary workers (the reference category), but some will have sufficient capital to establish enterprises, and still others will work without regular pay in family enterprises. Those who establish incorporated businesses—and therefore are listed by the census as employees of their own businesses (C_1)—should have the highest incomes, since they are in a position to take profits. By contrast, it is unclear whether self-employment in an unincorporated business (C_2) is an advantage or disadvantage relative to a wage or salary. What surely is true is that small businesses often entail extremely long hours of labor, so that the return to hour spent working is likely to be smaller for the self-employed than for wage or salary workers. Finally, those who work without regular pay in family enterprises (C_3) are likely to have low personal incomes. In most cases they will be the spouse or the grown children of the owner of the enterprise and thus will partake of whatever income from the business accrues to the family.

Time spent working. H = the natural logarithm of the usual hours worked per week in 1989. W = the natural logarithm of the number of weeks worked in 1989. Together, these variables take account of the possibility that ethnic differences in hours worked per year partly account for ethnic differences in annual income. Since the dependent variable is not earnings but rather income, the coefficients are not quite measures of effects on earnings but are close.[10]

Occupation. Because we are interested in the way different ethnic groups are incorporated into the economic life of Los Angeles, it is more useful to represent occupational position by a set of dummy variables for occupational categories than to utilize a global summary measure. We have distinguished the 13 occupational categories shown in Table 3.3 plus the reference category, managers and administrators. The 13 categories shown in the table are ordered in terms of their mean income.

Ethnic Group Membership

$G_1 \ldots G_{31}$ is a set of dummy variables representing the 31 ethnic groups described in the "Data" section above. Each variable is scored one for individuals who are members of the ethnic group and zero otherwise.

Results

Table 3.3 shows the coefficients associated with four models predicting (ln) income. Model 1 includes only the human-capital variables listed; model 2 includes in addition the 30 dummy variables for ethnic groups.

TABLE 3.3 Coefficients of Models of Determinants of (ln) Total Income for 31 Ethnic Groups in Los Angeles (Male Labor Force 20–64)

	Model 1 (human capital)	Model 2 (human capital plus ethnic dummies)	Model 3 (human capital plus job features)	Model 4 (human capital, job features, and ethnic dummies)
R^2	.330	.343	.551	.556
Standard Error of Estimate	.800	.793	.656	.652
BIC	−64,977	−67,803	−129,846	−131,306
Intercept	8.649	8.781	4.224	4.370
E: Years of schooling	.0036	.0042	.0104	.0100
E^2: Squared years of schooling	.00339	.00304	.00190	.00177
U: Completed education in U.S.	−.301	−.272	−.010	−.002
EU: Years of school by U.S. completion	.0318	.0248	−.0016	−.0055
E^2U: Squared years of school by U.S. completion	.000159	.000400	.000977	.001100
X: Years of labor force experience	.0658	.0651	.0468	.0468
X^2: Squared labor force experience	−.000965	−.000971	−.000601	−.000613
L_1: Speaks English "very well"[a]	−.102	−.013	−.076	−.010
L_2: Speaks English "well"	−.164	−.072	−.126	−.058
L_3: Speaks English "not well"	−.360	−.268	−.264	−.197
L_4: Speaks English "not at all"	−.515	−.417	−.360	−.290
R: Immigrated 1987–1990	−.352	−.357	−.176	−.181
C_1: Self-employed (unincorporated)[b]			−.061	−.077
C_2: Employee of own corporation			.308	.293

52

C_3: Help out in family business	−.802	−.816
H: ln(hours usually worked per week)	.529	.519
W: ln(weeks worked per year in 1989)	.796	.792
O_1: Professionals[c]	−.069	−.066
O_2: Sales personnel (high)	−.061	−.065
O_3: Technicians	−.135	−.127
O_4: Clerical workers	−.364	−.337
O_5: Skilled manual workers	−.213	−.203
O_6: Transportation operators	−.291	−.266
O_7: Sales clerks	−.428	−.424
O_8: Protective service workers	−.237	−.209
O_9: Machine operators	−.345	−.322
O_{10}: Other service workers	−.565	−.538
O_{11}: Laborers	−.410	−.387
O_{12}: Farming, forestry, fishing workers	−.503	−.489
O_{13}: Private household service workers	−.888	−.860

[a] The reference category is those who speak only English at home.
[b] The reference category is wage and salary workers.
[c] The reference category is managers and administrators. Occupational groups are arrayed in the order of their mean observed income with no controls.

Models 3 and 4 parallel models 1 and 2 except that they also include variables for the job characteristics.

Human Capital

Consider model 1 first. There is little that is surprising here. By and large, the variables behave as expected. Net of education, labor force experience, and recency of immigration, those who speak a non-English language at home but who speak English "very well" experience a 10 percent reduction in income relative to native English speakers. As English-language competence declines, the income gap relative to native speakers increases, so that the cost of not speaking English at all is to reduce average incomes by more than one-third net of other factors. Precisely, those who do not speak English at all have expected incomes about 60 percent ($.598 = e^{-.515}$) as large as those of native speakers. Similarly, recent immigrants earn about 30 percent less ($.703 = e^{-.352}$) than do longer-term immigrants or the native-born with similar education, labor force experience, and English-language skill.

The coefficients associated with years of school completed, where education was completed, and labor force experience cannot be interpreted directly from Table 3.3 because of the presence of squared terms and interaction terms. To facilitate interpretation, we graph the effects of years of education completed in the United States and abroad (in Figure 3.1) and labor force experience (in Figure 3.2). These graphs are estimated by evaluating equation 1 at the mean of the remaining variables to produce an equation in two unknowns, which can then be graphed. For example, Figure 3.1 is derived from

$$\widehat{\ln(Y)} = .0036(E) + .00339(E^2) - .301(U) + .0318(EU) + .000159(E^2U)$$
$$+ a + \sum b_i \bar{X}_i$$

$$\widehat{\ln(Y)} = .0036(E) + .00339(E^2) - .301(U) + .0318(EU) + .000159(E^2U)$$
$$+ 9.476,$$

(3)

where $\sum b_i \bar{X}_i$ is the product of the coefficients associated with and means of all the variables in the model except those involving education.[11] For those who completed their education in the United States, $U = 1$, and therefore the equation simplifies to

$$\widehat{\ln(Y)} = (.0036 + .0318)E + (.00339 + .000159)E^2 + (-.301 + 9.476)$$
$$= .0354(E) + .00355(E^2) + 9.175 \qquad (4)$$

FIGURE 3.1 Expected Income by Years of School Completed, Net of Other Human Capital Attributes, Los Angeles Metropolitan Area, 1990 (Male Labor Force Age 20–64)

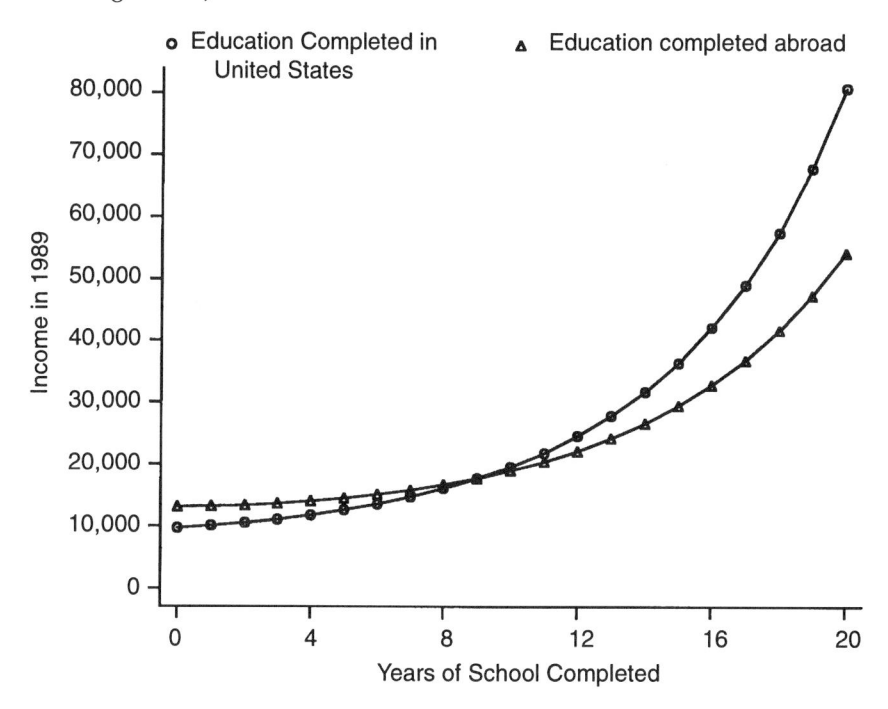

FIGURE 3.2 Expected Income by Years of Labor Force Experience, Net of Other Human Capital Attributes, Los Angeles Metropolitan Area (Area Male Labor Force Age 20–64)

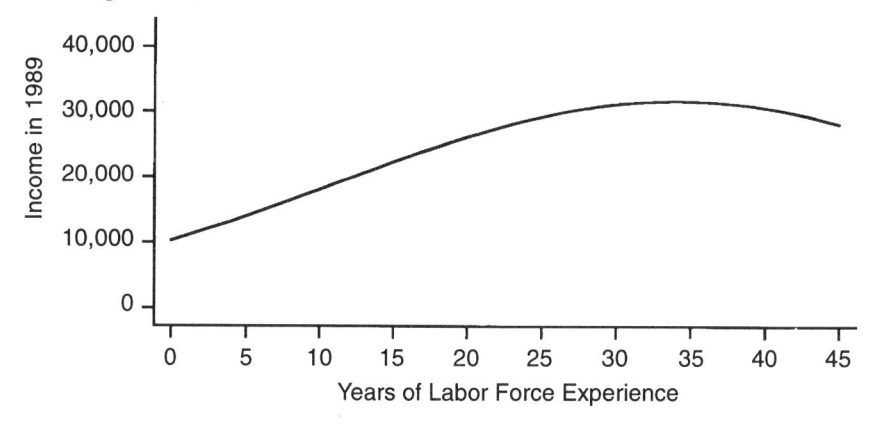

and for those who completed their education abroad $U = 0$ and therefore the equation simplifies to

$$\widehat{\ln(Y)} = .0036(E) + .00339(E^2) + 9.476 . \tag{5}$$

Equations 4 and 5 are graphed in Figure 3.1. Figure 3.2 is created in a similar way.

Figure 3.1 reveals that, as expected, income increases with education and returns to higher levels of education are greater than returns to lower levels of education. Also, as expected, returns to education completed in the United States are greater than returns to education completed abroad, although this result reverses at very low levels of schooling. Among those with less than nine years of schooling, men whose education was completed abroad do a bit better, on average, than equally poorly educated men who completed their education in the United States. In the U.S., where secondary education is both free and required, it is likely that those who get less than nine years of schooling are seriously dysfunctional in a variety of ways. By contrast, for those who completed their education abroad, particularly those from Latin America, many men obtain very little schooling through no fault of their own. Thus even immigrants very poorly educated by American standards may be *positively* selected with respect to skill, motivation, discipline, and intelligence, whereas poorly educated Americans may be *negatively* selected with respect to the same traits.

As expected, income increases with labor force experience, but at a decreasing rate, and begins to decline at 34 years of experience.[12] As has been observed elsewhere (e.g., Treiman, McKeever, and Fodor 1996), the effect of labor force experience on income is small relative to the effect of education.

So far we have a conventional analysis of the effect of human-capital on income attainment. The central focus of this chapter, however, is on whether there are ethnic-group differences in returns to human-capital. To assess these, we estimated model 2. Model 2 is identical to model 1 except that it includes in addition to the variables in model 1 a set of 30 dummy variables for ethnic-group membership, $G_1 \ldots G_{22}, G_{24} \ldots G_{31}$ (G_{23}, "other European origin," is the omitted category). The inclusion of dummy variables for the ethnic groups permits the decomposition of group differences in income into a portion associated with group differences with respect to the variables shown in Table 3.3 and a portion associated with other factors. The results of this decomposition are shown in Table 3.4.

TABLE 3.4 Decomposition of Ethnic Group Differences in Mean Income

		Ratio of Adjusted Group Mean to Overall Mean	
Ethnic Group	Ratio of Observed Group Mean to Overall Mean	Model 2: Controlling for Human Capital	Model 4: Controlling for Human Capital and Job Characteristics
Asian origin			
Asian Indian	1.20	1.01	.99
Cambodian	.64	.82	.95
Chinese	1.02	.95	.94
Filipino	.76	.82	.87
Japanese	1.28	1.23	1.14
Korean	1.03	1.01	.98
Vietnamese	.72	.89	.94
Other Asian	.82	.90	.92
Total	.97	.96[a]	.96
Latin American origin			
Cuban	.88	1.04	1.01
Guatemalan	.40	.78	.82
Mexican	.55	.91	.93
Nicaraguan	.53	.81	.83
Puerto Rican	.79	.95	1.00
Salvadoran	.39	.77	.81
South American	.77	.91	.93
Other Central American	.57	.86	.90
Other Hispanic	.63	.83	.88
Total	.56	.89	.92
European origin			
English	1.37	1.10	1.08
German	1.25	1.12	1.07
Italian	1.26	1.16	1.11
Polish	1.43	1.13	1.08

(continued)

TABLE 3.4 (continued)

	Ratio of Observed Group Mean to Overall Mean	Ratio of Adjusted Group Mean to Overall Mean	
Ethnic Group		Model 2: Controlling for Human Capital	Model 4: Controlling for Human Capital and Job Characteristics
Russian	1.93	1.25	1.19
Other European	1.22	1.08	1.06
Total	1.28	1.10	1.07
Middle Eastern origin			
Armenian	1.15	1.08	1.03
Iranian	1.19	1.06	1.00
Other M.E., N. African	1.24	1.13	1.07
Total	1.20	1.09	1.04
African origin			
U.S. blacks	.76	.74	.85
West Indian	.73	.84	.89
Foreign-born blacks (exc. W.I.)	.78	.81	.87
Total	.76	.75	.85
American Indian	.80	.81	.87
Other	.79	.89	.91

[a] The averages for major ethnic groups are derived by taking the antilog of the weighted average of the adjusted coefficients for the component ethnic categories.

Before discussing Table 3.4, however, we note that the coefficients for the individual level variables shown for model 2 in Table 3.3 are on the whole very similar to the corresponding coefficients for model 1. The only important differences are the stronger effects of English-language competence in model 1. Moreover, the variance explained by model 2 is hardly greater than that explained by model 1, an increment of .013.[13] Taken together, these results suggest that ethnic-group differences in average income are largely due to ethnic differences with respect to the variables in Table 3.3. Still, this is not the whole story, as we shall see.

Table 3.4 shows a decomposition of ethnic differences in mean income into two components: a portion due to group differences in the factors measured in Table 3.3 and a portion due to group differences in other factors. Column 1 shows the ratio of the actual mean income of each group to the overall mean; this is just a transformation of the values in the left-hand column of Table 3.1. Columns 2 and 3 express the ratio of each group's *expected* mean to the overall mean, controlling for the variables in Table 3.3. The coefficients in column 2 are just transformations of the coefficients associated with the dummy variables for ethnic group membership in model 2, where the transformation involved first converting the coefficients to deviations from the grand mean rather than deviations from the omitted category[14] and then taking antilogs. Column 3 shows the corresponding coefficients derived from model 4.

Consider first the figures in column 1. As we have already noted in discussing Table 3.1, there are very large differences between groups in average income. Column 1 expresses these in ratio to the overall mean and shows a range of about 40 percent of the overall mean for Guatemalans and Salvadorans to 193 percent of the overall mean for those of Russian origin. All the black and Hispanic groups have ratios of less than unity and all of the European-origin and Middle Eastern groups have ratios of greater than unity, while the Asian-origin groups are less consistent.

The more interesting figures, however, are those in column 2, which show the ratio of each group's average income to the overall mean income *net of the variables in model 2.* These coefficients can be interpreted as indicating the effect of ethnic-group membership on income among individuals who are indistinguishable with respect to the human-capital attributes assessed in Table 3.3. Of course, what the effect of ethnic-group membership means is unclear. Logically, the coefficients associated with ethnic-group membership are surrogates for whatever variables not included in the equation are correlated with ethnic-group membership and correlated with income. Still, inspection of the pattern of coefficients in column 2 provides some clues.

It is evident that ethnic-group differences in human-capital—in years of schooling, English-language competence, labor force experience, and recency of immigration to the United States—account for a substantial fraction, but by no means all, of the observed group differences in average income. One way to see this is to compare various measures of variability across ethnic groups with respect to observed incomes and expected incomes net of human-capital factors. Consider the two series involving ratios. Both the range across the ratios and the weighted standard deviation of the ratios (weighted by the relative population size) are reduced by two-thirds when human-capital factors are controlled and the unweighted standard deviation of the ratios is reduced by nearly 60 percent. In this sense we can say that ethnic-group differences in human capital—primarily the level of education but also English-language competence, length of labor force experience, and recency of immigration—account for about two-thirds of group variability in income.

But what about the remaining third? How can we account for ethnic differences in average income that do not simply reflect ethnic differences in human-capital assets? Why do those of European and Middle Eastern origin, Japanese, and Cubans do better than would be expected on the basis of their human capital; Asian Indians and Koreans about as expected; and the remaining groups less well than expected?

We have already suggested that the various ethnic groups of Los Angeles are incorporated into the economy in very different ways, depending upon the particular circumstances of their arrival. Los Angeles is, after all, a city of immigrants—if not from other countries then from other parts of the United States. That group differences in returns to human capital are large—which is what is implied by the coefficients in column 2—suggests that Los Angeles is a *multi*ethnic rather than a *non*ethnic society. Far from being the individualistic place it sometimes is portrayed to be, where success depends only upon one's skill and drive and luck, Los Angeles is a place where ethnicity matters, where one's life chances depend upon the kind of niche one's group has found in the economic life of the city. These niches, in turn, are the product of the historical circumstances that produced particular kinds of immigrant flows at particular historical periods.

While the number of ethnic groups analyzed here precludes a full accounting of the circumstances of each group, we can get some handle on the processes involved by considering the extent and pattern of ethnic differences in income remaining when account is taken not only of group differences in human capital but also of group differences in job characteristics.

Human Capital and Job Characteristics

The coefficients in column 3 of Table 3.4 are similar to those in column 2 but are derived from the ethnic-group coefficients from model 4. Before assessing the remaining effect of ethnic-group membership, we need to consider how human-capital factors and job characteristics jointly affect income. That is, we need first to compare the coefficients for the human-capital variables in the two right-hand columns of Table 3.3 with the corresponding coefficients in the two left-hand columns and, second, to consider the role of job characteristics as determinants of income net of human-capital differences.

Not surprisingly, the coefficients associated with the human-capital variables continue to behave as expected, albeit they are somewhat smaller than the corresponding coefficients for models 1 and 2. This is exactly as we would expect: The characteristics of the jobs people do are partly dependent upon their human capital, and job characteristics intervene between human capital and income. The reduced effect of the human capital variables is easy to see in the case of English-language competence and recency of immigration. Introducing job characteristics reduces the expected income gap between those who cannot speak English at all and those who speak English only from 40 percent ($.598 = e^{-.515}$) when ethnicity is not controlled, or 34 percent ($.659 = e^{-.417}$) when ethnicity is controlled, to 30 percent ($.698 = e^{-.360}$) and 25 percent ($.748 = e^{-.290}$), respectively. Similarly, controlling for job characteristics reduces the cost of very recent immigration by about half. The effects of education and work experience are similarly reduced, although the effects cannot be so readily seen without graphing the relationships (as in Figures 3.1 and 3.2). We do not show these graphs here because of limitations of space.

Now consider the effect of job characteristics on income, controlling for human-capital factors. As anticipated, those who are employees of their own corporations—an indicator of owning a corporation large enough or profitable enough to warrant incorporation—do well. Their incomes average about one-third more than those of otherwise similar wage and salary workers. In contrast, those helping in family businesses without pay have very low independent incomes—less than half of those of wage and salary workers—although presumably they benefit from the collective profits of the enterprise.

Weeks worked in 1989 and hours per week usually worked in 1989 are expressed in log form. For such variables, the associated regression coefficients are interpreted as indicating the percentage change in the dependent variable for a 1 *percent* change in the independent variable; such coefficients are known in the economics literature as elasticity coefficients. Hours and weeks worked are converted to log form because we would expect increases in earnings to be proportional to increases in hours spent working. Interestingly, weeks worked per year is more important than hours worked per week (the elasticities are, respectively, .80 and .53), perhaps because a large fraction of the labor force is paid on a salaried rather than an hourly wage basis and differences in the normal work week (e.g., 35 or 37.5 or 40 hours) are not reflected in pay differentials.

Finally, occupational groups differ substantially in their mean income, net of human capital differences and differences in the other job characteristics. Relative to their education, English-language competence, and so on, managers, professionals, and high status sales personnel have the highest incomes, followed by technicians; then by skilled manual workers, protective service workers, and transportation operators; then by clerical workers and machine operators; then by sales clerks and laborers; then by other service workers and agricultural workers; and finally by private household service workers.

Together, human-capital attributes and job characteristics account for more than half of the variance in (ln) incomes, far more than human capital alone. Controlling for ethnic-group membership has little effect on the remaining variables except for English-language competence: Just as for model 2, controlling for ethnic-group membership in model 4 reduces the importance of English-language competence as a determinant of income. Moreover, the addition of dummy variables for ethnic-group membership increases the explained variance by only one half a percentage point, which suggests that few ethnic-group differences in income remain once account is taken of qualifications (the human-capital attributes) and the types of jobs people hold.

To assess remaining ethnic-group differences in income, net of both human-capital factors and job characteristics, we can inspect the coefficients in the right-hand column of Table 3.4. It is evident that controlling for job characteristics as well as human capital reduces the ethnic differences in income still further. All but one of the residual ratios is reduced relative to the corresponding coefficients in column 2 (only the Chinese coefficient remains essentially unchanged). Comparing the same measures of variability in the ethnic group coefficients as before, we find that both the range across the ratios and the weighted standard deviation of the ratios is reduced by about three-quarters and the unweighted standard deviation of the ratios by more than 70 percent. Thus most of the variability in incomes across ethnic groups in Los Angeles can be explained by ethnic-group differences in human capital and in the kinds of jobs men hold.

In particular, the large difference in the average incomes of Asians and Hispanics observed in column 1 is almost entirely accounted for by differences between these groups with respect to the variables shown in Table 3.3, particularly the human-capital variables: The ratio of average incomes is reduced from 1.73 to 1.08 when only human capital is controlled (column 2) and to 1.04 when job characteristics are also controlled (column 3). This result puts a rather different light on journalistic accounts of the unusual success of Asian immigrants, which tend to emphasize cultural values. The considerable success of recent Asian immigrants, especially in comparison to other groups such as immigrants from Latin America, is the consequence of selective migration—the average Asian immigrant arrives with at least some college education and—judging from the figures in Table 3.2 and Appendix Table 3A.3—

with considerable financial capital as well. By contrast, the average Latin American immigrant arrives with little education and little capital. It is no great surprise, then, that the Asians do better in the struggle for socioeconomic success.

Remaining Ethnic-Group Differences in Income

The differences between ethnic groups that remain after controlling for human capital and job characteristics, although quite small, are very systematic. Net of their human capital and the sort of work they do, men of European origin have about a 7 percent income advantage relative to the average earner, those of Middle Eastern origin have a 4 percent net advantage, those of Asian origin a 4 percent disadvantage, those of Latin American origin an 8 percent disadvantage, and those of African origin a 15 percent disadvantage. All of the European-origin and Middle Eastern groups except Iranians have above average net incomes, with Iranians exactly average, while all of the Asian, Latin American, and black groups have below average net incomes, with the exception of Puerto Ricans and Cubans, who are just about average, and Japanese, who have the second highest net incomes of all, exceeded only by those of Russian origin.

Seldom are results so clear-cut. Yet the explanation for these remaining differences is far from clear. While the nearly perfect division of "whites" and "non-whites" into groups with, respectively, higher and lower incomes than expected from their human capital and job characteristics invites an inference of some sort of "discrimination," it is not evident what the mechanisms of discrimination might be. This is particularly true because when occupational status (TSEI)[15] is predicted from human-capital attributes plus ethnic-group membership—in an analysis not shown here because of space limitations—the coefficients associated with the ethnic dummies are very highly correlated with the coefficients reported in the right-hand column of Table 3.4 ($r = .80$). This tells us that groups that have higher than expected *occupational status* returns to their human capital also tend to a considerable degree to have higher than expected *income* returns to their human capital *and job characteristics*. So whatever mechanisms of status differentiation of ethnic groups are operative appear to be quite general, creating a distinctive advantage or disadvantage with respect to both occupational and income attainment. Moreover, with one exception, the differences in the coefficients for particular ethnic groups within aggregated origin groups are large relative to the differences among the aggregated groups, as is evident from inspection of the right-hand column of Table 3.4. This again suggests that we need to turn to the particular history and circumstances of each ethnic group and not to settle for generalizations about "whites," "Asians," "Hispanics," and "blacks."

Blacks. The exception is for those of African origin, who have an aggregate coefficient of .85 and disaggregated coefficients that are not much different. The .85 coefficient tells us that blacks earn only about 85 percent of what would be expected given their human capital and job characteristics. Moreover, black incomes are only about 75 percent as large as would be expected from their human-capital characteristics alone (column 2 of Table 3.4), which differ little from those of European origin: Virtually all are competent at English and were born in the United States, and blacks get only about one year less schooling on average than do those of Asian, European, and Middle Eastern origin. Yet black incomes are far lower. That the ratio of actual to expected incomes is substantially lower when only human-capital characteristics are considered than when job characteristics are controlled as well implies that blacks are far less able than average to convert their human capital into desirable jobs—an inference that is clearly supported by the evidence in Appendix Table 3A.2. Finally, both West Indian and other foreign-born blacks suffer the same fate as those born in the United States, which again undercuts claims about a culture of dependency (Sowell 1978:41–8) as a major explanation of the income gap. Rather, an inference of continuing and substantial discrimination against blacks seems difficult to avoid. But, again, it is important to pin down the exact mechanisms involved.

One obvious distinction between blacks and other groups is the much greater residential segregation than is true of any other group, which holds for Los Angeles even more than elsewhere (Massey and Denton 1989, 1993). Given the lack of capital within the black community (Oliver and Shapiro 1995:86, 94), which precludes the establishment of black enterprises, residential segregation puts blacks at a severe disadvantage when it comes to competing for jobs (Wilson 1987). In short, blacks are disadvantaged at every turn.

Russians. At the other extreme are those of Russian origin, who earn about 25 percent more than would be expected from their human-capital and about 19 percent more than would be expected from their human-capital plus the kinds of jobs they hold. These are mainly Jews whose parents and grandparents immigrated to the United States around the turn of the century (Rosenthal 1975). But the Jews were the "Asians of yesterday," to turn the phrase around. That is, in the context of late nineteenth and early twentieth century immigration, the Jews arrived with a substantial competitive advantage over their fellow immigrants: literacy and urban origins. Although for the most part they had little material capital, they had great human capital. In consequence, they were enormously successful, and they were able to pass their advantages on to their children and grandchildren, who, as these data show, are very well educated and disproportionately likely to work at professional and administrative jobs, own businesses, and control considerable wealth. Since we have taken account of group differences in education, occupational status, and self-employment propensities, it is probable that the substantial wealth of those of Russian origin is implicated in their unusually high income net of these factors (cf. Chiswick 1983). But, again, the limitations of our data preclude further analysis here.

Japanese. The other group with strikingly high incomes net of human capital and job characteristics is the Japanese-origin population. This group is distinctive in another way as well: It is the only non-European-origin group with substantially higher income than would be expected on the basis of its human capital and job characteristics. From a socioeconomic point of view, those of Japanese origin are similar to those of European origin. Actually, there are two quite distinctive Japanese communities in Los Angeles: those from families that arrived in the late nineteenth or early twentieth century, who are thus fourth- or fifth-generation Americans, and the foreign-born, who are to a large extent not immigrants at all but temporary sojourners, sent by their enterprises to work in America for a few years (among the foreign-born, 25 percent arrived in the United States in 1987 or later and 32 percent were managers, both more than for any other ethnic group). Japan is distinctive among Asian countries in that—not surprisingly for a wealthy country—there is very little current immigration. In consequence, most people of Japanese origin in Los Angeles were born in the United States. Native-born men of Japanese origin are very similar to those of European origin: 82 percent speak only English at home, and they have similar levels of education and work at similar jobs. Foreign-born Japanese are actually quite similar to the native-born except that they are more likely to be managers than to be professionals (whereas the native-born are more likely to be professionals) and tend to have higher incomes, averaging $50,730 (in contrast to $43,938 for the native-born), which is exceeded only by those of Polish and Russian origin.

Mexicans and Central Americans. Like the Japanese population, the Mexican population can be divided into the native-born (about one-third) and immigrants (about two-thirds). These two populations are sharply differentiated. The foreign-born population is similar to those from Guatemala and El Salvador. They are even less well educated, averaging 7.8 years of school; substantial fractions are very recent immigrants—46 percent since 1980 and 13 percent since 1987; more than half have substantial difficulty with English—34 percent speak English "not well" and 18 percent do not speak English at all; only a very small fraction hold professional or managerial jobs—4.7 percent; and they are disproportionately likely to work at service jobs (14.5 percent), semi- or unskilled laboring jobs (39.5 percent), or agricultural jobs, mainly as gardeners (9.3

percent). Not surprising, their average income is also very low, $16,252, commensurate with those from Guatemala and El Salvador—most of whom also arrived very recently with little education and limited English.

The native-born population of Mexican origin is much better educated, averaging 12.0 years of schooling, and is correspondingly more likely to work at managerial or professional jobs (14.4 percent) and less likely to work at service jobs (6.3 percent), semi- or unskilled manual jobs (28.4 percent), or agricultural jobs (2.8 percent). However, the superior education and occupational status of the native-born does not translate into any greater likelihood of self employment. Neither group has much income from self-employment nor is likely to own their own incorporated businesses. Finally, in contrast to the Japanese, a majority of even native-born men of Mexican origin are not monolingual English speakers: 55 percent speak Spanish at home.

In short, despite sharp differences between the foreign- and native-born, the Mexican origin population as a whole still is what it has been historically—a largely working-class population—which means that when newcomers arrive their information networks tend to be restricted to knowledge of working-class jobs. Moreover, even though there is a very large ethnic enclave in East Los Angeles and a number of other sizable areas of Latino settlement, there has never been a commensurate development of ethnic enterprise. As Appendix Table 3A.4 shows, those of Mexican origin are very unlikely to own businesses, and the businesses they do own tend to be very small. Thus there is little opportunity to find work in an enterprise owned by a co-ethnic. Most men of Mexican origin work for non-Hispanics and thus gain none of the advantages of employment in ethnic enterprises (Portes and Bach 1985: ch. 6 and 7).

Filipinos. Among Asians, Filipinos are a distinctive group. While on average they are as well educated as Chinese, Japanese, and Koreans, they are much less likely to become managers, professionals, or high-level sales workers than are members of the other three groups (see Table 3.1 and Appendix Table 3A.2) and also are far less likely to engage in entrepreneurial activity, as indicated by the dearth of self-employment activity or income (see Table 3.2 and Appendix Tables 3A.3 and 3A.4). The reasons for this are not entirely clear but may be related both to circumstances in the Philippines and to the historical character of Filipino immigration to the United States. Some have suggested that industrial development was deliberately suppressed by American colonial authorities in order to secure a market for American goods and that commerce was left to the Chinese in order to ensure a labor supply for hacienda agriculture (Shalom 1986; Anderson 1988). Perhaps as a result, there is no "Little Manila" comparable to Little Tokyo, Koreatown, Little Saigon,

Chinatown, or Monterey Park (a large and very wealthy Chinese community just east of downtown Los Angeles), and an attempt to develop a commercial center in an area of relatively dense Filipino concentration near Koreatown failed (Espiritu 1992). Thus the kinds of occupational opportunities that develop in ethnic enclaves may not be available to Filipinos. Second, Filipinos initially came to the United States—mainly to Hawaii and California—as agricultural laborers, much like Mexican immigrants (Allen 1977:195–6). So, even when immigration broadened after 1965 (Liu, Ong, and Rosenstein 1991), there was no established commercial community to provide jobs. Finally, a seeming advantage—generalized English-language competence because English is the language of instruction in the Philippines (Min 1986:55)—actually may have disadvantaged Filipinos by putting them into direct competition with the native-born for jobs, especially professional jobs. The result is that, uniquely among Asians, Filipinos have substantially lower incomes than would be expected from their human capital and the kind of work they do.

Koreans. Koreans are distinctive in a different way. Compared to other groups with comparable education, they are unusually deficient in English. For example, among Chinese and foreign-born Japanese, fewer than one-quarter speak English "not well" or "not at all," whereas this is true of 34 percent of Koreans (see Appendix Table 3A.1). As a consequence, many men who worked at professional jobs in Korea become entrepreneurs in the United States, often opening small businesses in inner-city neighborhoods (Light and Bonacich 1988). The well-known conflict between Koreans and blacks arises directly from the presence of Korean petty merchants in black neighborhoods (Light and Bonacich 1988:211–7). But Koreans also are able to operate businesses in the large and thriving enclave known locally as Koreatown, where most of their activity is conducted in Korean. Indeed, in 1980 about 40 percent of Koreans in Los Angeles County were employed by other Koreans, which resulted in a total of 62 percent either self-employed, helping in family enterprises, or employed in the Korean enclave (Light and Bonacich 1988:3). The distinctive mode of incorporation of Koreans into the economy is reflected in Appendix Table 3A.3, which shows that 40 percent of Koreans, more than any other group, are self-employed. Additional analysis, not shown for lack of space, indicates that net of the human capital variables in Table 3.3, Koreans were more than twice as likely than average to own their own incorporated businesses—a rate higher than all other groups except for those of Russian or Middle Eastern origin. Since these odds are net of English-language competence, they suggest that once a particular mode of incorporation—in this case entrepreneurship—becomes established, it is exploited in preference to alternative possibilities. This probably reflects the acquisition of social capital, in Coleman's (1988) sense—specifically the collective knowledge in the ethnic community about how to establish a business and the lack of corresponding knowledge about how to obtain and retain jobs outside the ethnic community.

Middle Easterners. Finally, those of Middle Eastern origin—Armenians, Iranians, and men from elsewhere in the Middle East or North Africa—are quite similar to men of European origin except for their unusual propensity to own their own businesses. As Appendix Table 3A.3 shows, along with Koreans and those of Russian origin, men of Middle Eastern origin are far more likely to be self-employed than are members of other groups. Iranians who fled Iran after the fall of the shah and Armenians who also fled Iran or the civil war in Lebanon[16] apparently were able to bring substantial amounts of capital with them, enabling them to establish businesses in the United States. But Iranians are also disproportionately likely to be self-employed professionals, which reflects the fact that many came to the United States as students (Bozorgmehr and Sabagh 1988).

Common patterns. The general point that emerges from this review of the circumstances of specific ethnic groups is that group resources matter. It is not simply that some immigrants arrive with substantial education and/or substantial funds to invest but that some groups are composed of a high proportion of such people and others of a very low proportion. When a substantial fraction of the ethnic community is well endowed with skills and funds, it is likely that a vibrant ethnic community will develop, which will provide jobs and opportunities for its less fortunate members, enabling them to do better than would be expected from their individual attributes. And of course the opposite is true when the ethnic community is poorly endowed with such assets, particularly financial assets.

Conclusions

As we have seen, Los Angeles is enormously diverse, the new home to people from dozens—indeed hundreds—of places, both elsewhere in the United States and abroad. Despite fires, floods, earthquakes, and riots, and a shaky economy to boot, people keep flooding in, following their families or compatriots or pioneering a migration stream. For them, Los Angeles is the land of opportunity—a destination that, whatever its troubles, is preferable to the place from which they have come. They come hoping for success, for good jobs that pay well—or at least for a better life than the one they left behind. Presumably, most find such a life, or else the migration stream would dry up; people would return home or move on.

But of course some do much better than others, just as we would expect: There is no society in which some individuals do not achieve more than others. More to the point, some groups do better than others. Why is this so? What we have shown here is that to a very considerable degree group differences in income simply reflect group differences in the factors that affect income. While the ethnic groups of the Los Angeles area vary widely in their average incomes, they also vary widely in their education, their ability to speak English, and the likelihood that they are very recent immigrants. Group differences in these human-capital endowments account for about two-thirds of the group differences in average incomes. This fraction goes up to about three-fourths when account is also taken of group differences in the ability to convert human capital into desirable jobs.

But what about the remaining fraction? If ethnicity didn't matter, there would be no remaining fraction. Ethnic differences in income net of human capital differences and differences in job characteristics, although generally small, are highly systematic. They appear to reflect two general processes. The first is some sort of systematic distinction between "whites" and "non-whites": Whites do a little better than would be expected on the basis of their human capital and job characteristics, and non-whites do a little less well. Second, those groups that have been unable to generate substantial ethnic enterprise because they arrived without financial capital and were incorporated into the local economy in working-class roles—Filipinos, Central Americans, and blacks—have fared particularly badly.

Still, there are many exceptions to these generalizations, which reflect the distinctive histories of each group sketched in the previous section. While the search for generalizations is an admirable sociological goal, sometimes the richness of the story is in the specifics. The rich diversity of Los Angeles, one of the world's most fascinating cities, is a case in point.

Notes

An earlier version of this essay, based on 1980 census data, was prepared while the first author was an ASA/NSF/Census research fellow at the U.S. Bureau of the Census in 1987–1988. That version was presented at the annual meeting of the Population Association of America, April 1988; a meeting of the Research Committee on Social Stratification and Social Mobility, International Sociological Association, Haifa, Israel, April 1988; and Reed College, November 1988. We thank Jim Baron, David Grusky, and Nelson Lim for helpful comments on earlier drafts and David McFarland for special advice to the senior author.

1. In 1970, 13.8 percent of the population were of "Hispanic heritage" and 8.3 percent were black; those of Asian origin were not numerous enough to be

counted as a separate category. Also, 9.8 percent were foreign-born. Computations are from U.S. Bureau of the Census 1973.

2. This is the net immigration figure. The 1990 population of the area includes about 2.8 million people who immigrated to the United States since 1970.

3. The remaining .8 percent were of American Indian or "other" origin.

4. We counted each language spoken by at least one person in the 5 percent sample.

5. Anyone wishing to examine the SPSS code used to make these distinctions should contact the first author via e-mail: treiman@dudley.sscnet.ucla.edu.

6. Puerto Ricans born in Puerto Rico are, of course, counted as native-born in the Census classification.

7. To see this, consider the equation $\ln(Y) = a + b(X)$. Now consider two individuals who differ by one unit with respect to X. Their expected values with respect to $\ln(Y)$ can be expressed by $\ln(Y_1) = a + b(X_1)$ and $\ln(Y_2) = a + b(X_2)$

So, subtracting, $\ln(Y_1) - \ln(Y_2) = (a - a) + b(X_1 - X_2) = b$.

But we know from the properties of logs that $\ln(Y_1) - \ln(Y_2) = \ln(Y_1/Y_2)$.

So we have $\ln(Y_1/Y_2) = b$.

Then, taking the antilog of both sides, we have $Y_1/Y_2 = e^b$.

Now let's look at the relationship of b to $e^b = Y_1/Y_2$ for various values of b.

b	e^b	b	e^b
.01	1.01	−.01	.99
.05	1.05	−.05	.95
.10	1.11	−.10	.90
.15	1.16	−.15	.86
.20	1.22	−.20	.82
.30	1.35	−.30	.74
.40	1.49	−.40	.67

So we see that for b less than about .2, b is a good approximation to the expected proportional increase in Y for a one unit increase in X. For larger values of b, b underestimates the proportional increase in Y.

8. While the assumption that all pre-1965 immigrants completed their education in the United States is surely not strictly correct, whatever error is introduced is unlikely to be very consequential since those who both left school and immigrated prior to 1965 had a minimum of 25 years of U.S. labor force experience by 1990 and therefore the impact of where they completed their education is likely to be trivial.

9. This estimate closely approximates actual labor force experience for men (Treiman and Roos 1983:620–1, n.9).

10. Lee (1987:147), in an analysis of the determinants of income among Koreans and Filipinos in Los Angeles, gets nearly identical results using a measure of earnings (the sum of wage and salary earnings, earnings from nonfarm self-employment, and earnings from farm self-employment) and a measure of total income from all sources.

11. Actually, this is not precisely correct. We substituted the square of the mean number of years of labor force experience so that the constant would correctly reflect the expected value for a man with average labor force experience. Note that the mean of the squared term is not identical to the square of the mean. Also, by taking the means (= the proportions) for the dummy variables, we have in some sense represented the "typical" English-language competence and recency of arrival in the United States.

12. It can be shown that for an equation of the form $\hat{Y} = a + b(X) + c(X^2)$ where $\hat{Y}$ = expected (ln) income and X = years of labor force experience, the maximum (ln) income, m, is given by $m = a - b^2/4c$, and the number of years at which the maximum is reached, F, is given by $F = -b/2c$. In the present case, we have $\hat{Y} = 9.24 + .0658(X) - .000965(X^2)$, which implies that $F = 34.1$ and $m = 10.36$, which in turn implies that the maximum expected income is $31,571 (= $e^{10.36}$).

13. The increment in R^2 is statistically significant beyond the .01 level; because of the extremely large sample size, virtually any coefficient will be statistically significant. We also report the Bayesian information coefficient (BIC), introduced by Raftery (1995). BIC is a measure of whether a model is true, given the data. The more negative the BIC, the more likely the model is true. For an OLS regression model, k, $BIC_k = n \left[\ln(1 - R_k^2)\right] + p_k \left[\ln(n)\right]$, where p_k = the number of independent variables and n = the number of cases in the sample. In the present case the more negative BIC implies that model 2 is more likely to be true than model 1.

14. To express coefficients as deviations from the grand mean, we compute

$$a_{ij} = b_{ij} - \sum_j p_{ij} b_{ij},$$

where a_{ij} = the transformed coefficient for the jth category of predictor i, b_{ij} = the corresponding dummy variable regression coefficient, and p_{ij} = the proportion of cases in the jth category of predictor i (Andrews et al. 1973:46).

15. We use a version of the well-known Socioeconomic Index of Occupations originally developed by Duncan (1961) and updated for the 1990 census categories by Hauser and Warren (1996). The Hauser-Warren version (TSEI) is a weighted average of the percentage of incumbents of each occupation with at least some college in 1990 and the percentage earning at least $14.30 per hour in 1989; see Hauser and Warren 1996 for details.

16. The foreign-born of Armenian ancestry are from a wide variety of places but mainly from the former Soviet Union, Iran, and Lebanon. For corresponding 1980 data, see Der-Martirosian, Sabagh, and Bozorgmehr 1993.

References

Allen, James P. 1977. "Recent Immigration from the Philippines and Filipino Communities in the United States." *Geographical Review* 67:195–208.

Anderson, Benedict. 1988. "Cacique Democracy in the Philippines: Origins and Dreams." *New Left Review* 169 (May–June):3–33.

Andrews, Frank M.; James N. Morgan; John A. Sonquist; and Laura Klem. 1973. *Multiple Classification Analysis: A Report on a Computer Program for Multiple*

Regression Using Categorical Predictors. Second edition. Ann Arbor: University of Michigan, Institute for Social Research.

Bozorgmehr, Mehdi, and Georges Sabagh. 1988. "High Status Immigrants: A Statistical Profile of Iranians in the United States." *Iranian Studies* 21:5–36.

Chiswick, Barry R. 1983. "The Earnings and Human Capital of American Jews." *Journal of Human Resources* 18:313–36.

Coleman, James S. 1988. "Social Capital in the Creation of Human Capital." *American Journal of Sociology* 94 (Supplement):S95–S120.

Der-Martirosian, Claudia; Georges Sabagh; and Mehdi Bozorgmehr. 1993. "Subethnicity: Armenians in Los Angeles." Pp. 243–58 in Ivan Light and Parminder Bhachu (eds.), *Immigration and Entrepreneurship: Culture, Capital, and Ethnic Networks.* New Brunswick, NJ: Transaction Publishers.

Duncan, Otis Dudley. 1961. "A Socioeconomic Index for All Occupations." Pp. 109–38 in Albert J. Reiss Jr. (ed.), *Occupations and Social Status.* New York: Free Press.

Espiritu, Augusto F. 1992. "The Rise and Fall of the Filipino Town Campaign in Los Angeles: A Study in Filipino American Leadership." Master's thesis, Department of Asian American Studies, UCLA.

Ganzeboom, Harry B. G.; Paul de Graaf; and Donald J. Treiman. 1992. "An International Scale of Occupational Status." *Social Science Research* 21:1–56.

Hauser, Robert M., and John Robert Warren. 1996. "A Socioeconomic Index for Occupations in the 1990 Census." Working Paper 96–01. Madison: Center for Demography and Ecology, University of Wisconsin-Madison.

Lee, Hye-kyung. 1987. "Socioeconomic Attainment of Recent Korean and Filipino Immigrant Men and Women in the Los Angeles Metropolitan Area, 1980." Ph.D. dissertation, Department of Sociology, UCLA.

Light, Ivan, and Edna Bonacich. 1988. *Immigrant Entrepreneurs: Koreans in Los Angeles, 1965–82.* Berkeley: University of California Press.

Liu, John M.; Paul M. Ong; and Carolyn Rosenstein. 1991. "Dual Chain Migration: Post-1965 Filipino Immigration to the United States." *International Migration Review* 25:487–513.

Massey, Douglas, and Nancy A. Denton. 1989. "Hypersegregation in U.S. Metropolitan Areas: Black and Hispanic Segregation Along Five Dimensions." *Demography* 26:373–91.

———. 1993. *American Apartheid: Segregation and the Making of the Underclass.* Cambridge: Harvard University Press.

Min, Pyong Gap. 1986. "Filipino and Korean Immigrants in Small Business: A Comparative Analysis." *Amerasia Journal* 13:53–72.

Oliver, Melvin L., and Thomas M. Shapiro. 1995. *Black Wealth, White Wealth: A New Perspective on Racial Inequality.* New York: Routledge.

Portes, Alejandro, and Robert L. Bach. 1985. *Latin Journey: Cuban and Mexican Immigrants in the United States.* Berkeley: University of California Press.

Raftery, A. E. 1995. "Bayesian Model Selection in Social Research." In *Sociological Methodology 1995.* Washington, DC: American Sociological Association.

Rosenthal, Erich. 1975. "The Equivalence of United States Census Data for Persons of Russian Stock or Descent with American Jews: An Evaluation." *Demography* 12:275–90.

Schimek, Paul. 1989. "Earnings Polarization and the Proliferation of Low-Wage Work." Pp. 27–51 in Paul Ong, et al., *The Widening Divide: Income Inequality and Poverty in Los Angeles*. Los Angeles: UCLA Graduate School of Architecture and Urban Planning.

Security Pacific Bank. 1979. *The Sixty Mile Circle*. Los Angeles: Security Pacific Bank.

———. 1988. *Portrait for Progress—Entering the 21st Century: The Economy of Los Angeles County and the Sixty-mile Circle Region*. Los Angeles: Security Pacific Bank.

Shalom, Stephen R. 1986. *The United States and the Philippines: A Study of Neocolonialism*. Quezon City: New Day Publishers.

Soja, Edward D. 1987. "Economic Restructuring and the Internationalization of the Los Angeles Region." Pp. 178–98 in Michael P. Smith and Joe R. Feagin (eds.), *The Capitalist City: Global Restructuring and Community Politics*. New York: Basil Blackwell.

Sowell, Thomas. 1978. "Three Black Histories." Pp. 7–64 in Thomas Sowell (ed.), *Essays and Data on American Ethnic Groups*. Washington, DC: Urban Institute.

Treiman, Donald J., and Harry B. G. Ganzeboom. 1990. "Cross-national Comparative Status Attainment Research." *Research in Social Stratification and Mobility* 9:105–27.

Treiman, Donald J.; Matthew McKeever; and Eva Fodor. 1996. "Racial Differences in Occupational Status and Income in South Africa, 1980 and 1991." *Demography* 33, 1 (February).

Treiman, Donald J., and Patricia A. Roos. 1983. "Sex and Earnings in Industrial Society: A Nine-nation Comparison." *American Journal of Sociology* 89:613–50.

Treiman, Donald J., and Kermit Terrell. 1975. "Sex and the Process of Status Attainment: A Comparison of Working Women and Men." *American Sociological Review* 40:174–201.

U.S. Bureau of the Census. 1973. *U.S. Census of Population 1970*. Volume 1: *Characteristics of the Population*. Part 6: *California*. Section 1. Washington, DC: U.S. Government Printing Office.

———. 1991a. *1987 Economic Censuses. Survey of Minority-Owned Business Enterprises. Asian Americans, American Indians, and Other Minorities*. Washington, DC: U.S. Government Printing Office.

———. 1991b. *1987 Economic Censuses. Survey of Minority-Owned Business Enterprises. Hispanic*. Washington, DC: U.S. Government Printing Office.

———. 1991c. *1987 Economic Censuses. Survey of Minority-Owned Business Enterprises. Summary*. Washington, DC: U.S. Government Printing Office.

———. 1992. *Census of Population and Housing, 1990. Alphabetical Index of Industries and Occupations*. Washington, DC: U.S. Government Printing Office.

———. 1993. *Census of Population and Housing, 1990. United States—Public-Use Microdata Sample: 5-percent Sample* [machine-readable data file]. Ann Arbor, MI: Interuniversity Consortium for Political and Social Research [distributor] (ICPSR 9952, second release, August).

Wilson, William J. 1987. *The Truly Disadvantaged: The Inner City, the Underclass, and Public Policy*. Chicago: University of Chicago Press.

Appendix to Chapter 3

TABLE 3A.1 Percentage Distribution of English Language Competence, 31 Ethnic Groups, Los Angeles Metropolitan Area, 1990 (Male Labor Force Age 20–64)

	\multicolumn{5}{c}{*Percentage Distribution of English-Language Competence*}
Ethnic Group	*Speak Only English at Home*	*Very Well*	*Well*	*Not Well*	*Not at All*
Total	62.3	15.6	9.7	8.7	3.7
Asian origin					
Asian Indian	14.5	66.1	16.7	2.5	.2
Cambodian	3.0	24.4	37.0	33.3	2.2
Chinese	11.7	32.4	34.4	18.2	3.3
Filipino	12.3	62.0	23.4	2.1	.2
Japanese	58.7	16.4	15.7	8.6	.7
Korean	3.5	24.8	37.8	30.8	3.0
Vietnamese	1.6	24.4	51.3	21.3	1.4
Other Asian	28.6	37.8	25.6	7.6	.5
Total	18.5	37.2	29.3	13.5	1.5
Latin American origin					
Cuban	12.2	46.3	22.9	14.9	3.7
Guatemalan	2.2	17.5	27.2	36.0	17.2
Mexican	17.1	27.7	19.4	23.8	12.0
Nicaraguan	4.8	30.9	28.3	23.5	12.5
Puerto Rican	31.4	48.6	12.4	5.9	1.8
Salvadoran	3.1	19.8	28.1	32.9	16.1
South American	9.1	39.5	30.7	17.4	3.3
Other Central American	5.5	36.3	25.0	22.7	10.5
Other Hispanic	22.5	29.8	19.8	19.0	9.0
Total	16.2	28.1	20.3	23.7	11.8
European origin					
English	97.4	2.0	.3	.2	.0
German	94.9	4.2	.6	.3	.0

(continued)

TABLE 3A.1 (continued)

| | Percentage Distribution of English-Language Competence ||||||
| | Speak Only English at Home | Speak a Foreign Language at Home and Speak English ||||
Ethnic Group		Very Well	Well	Not Well	Not at All
Italian	90.2	7.2	2.2	.4	.0
Polish	89.7	7.0	2.4	.7	.1
Russian	90.0	6.8	2.5	.7	.0
Other European	91.9	6.0	1.4	.5	.1
Total	93.2	5.2	1.2	.4	.0
Middle Eastern origin					
Armenian	23.5	38.1	25.8	10.9	1.8
Iranian	9.5	59.0	26.0	5.1	.5
Other M.E. and N. African	29.6	48.3	18.0	3.9	.2
Total	21.9	48.0	22.8	6.5	.8
African origin					
U.S. blacks	95.9	3.2	.5	.4	.0
West Indian	85.0	11.5	3.1	.4	.0
Foreign-born blacks (except W.I.)	52.3	39.0	6.8	1.9	.0
Total	94.1	4.6	.8	.5	.0
American Indian	85.6	11.6	2.0	.8	.0
Other	53.2	23.7	11.0	9.0	3.1

TABLE 3A.2 Percentage Distribution Across Occupation Groups, 31 Ethnic Groups, Los Angeles Metropolitan Area, 1990 (Male Labor Force Age 20–64)

Ethnic Group	Managers	Professionals	High Sales	Technicians	Clerical	Skilled Manual	Trans. Ops.	Sales Clerks	Protective Service	Machine Ops.	Other Ser.	Laborers	Agricultural Workers	Private Household Service
Total	14.7	12.8	8.1	3.5	7.1	19.8	5.9	3.0	2.3	8.0	6.5	5.5	2.6	.1
Asian origin														
Asian Indian	21.4	30.0	9.6	5.4	8.0	6.6	2.2	8.0	1.0	3.7	2.1	1.6	.3	0
Cambodian	6.7	8.9	7.4	5.9	11.9	20.7	.7	5.9	.7	18.5	10.4	2.2	0	0
Chinese	20.8	22.3	11.4	5.4	6.6	9.4	1.5	3.2	.3	4.5	12.3	1.6	.4	.2
Filipino	14.1	12.6	4.6	8.6	18.7	12.7	3.1	2.9	3.0	7.2	8.2	3.5	.8	.2
Japanese	23.5	21.4	9.9	5.8	8.1	11.0	1.4	2.6	1.2	2.4	5.3	2.3	5.0	.0
Korean	19.9	12.4	19.4	2.8	4.8	16.4	1.1	9.2	.6	5.4	5.2	1.9	.9	.2
Vietnamese	6.8	14.7	5.1	12.3	7.8	18.6	2.6	3.3	.4	17.4	6.5	3.1	1.5	0
Other Asian	16.2	10.3	7.5	4.7	11.4	19.6	4.5	4.0	2.0	6.9	7.3	3.7	1.8	.1
Total	17.8	17.3	9.7	6.4	9.9	13.0	2.2	4.3	1.3	6.4	7.6	2.5	1.5	.1
Latin American origin														
Cuban	12.6	11.0	11.2	3.8	8.7	19.2	7.8	3.8	1.6	7.5	8.2	3.5	1.0	0
Guatemalan	3.2	1.6	2.3	.8	5.2	25.4	8.5	2.9	1.3	20.4	15.7	9.8	2.4	.5
Mexican	5.1	3.0	3.0	1.5	5.8	23.4	7.9	2.1	1.4	17.2	11.7	10.8	7.2	.1

Nicaraguan	8.1	6.6	7.7	1.5	8.1	21.7	8.1	3.3	2.6	15.4	8.5	6.3	2.2	0
Puerto Rican	9.4	9.6	5.0	4.7	11.7	20.4	9.0	2.9	3.2	8.5	7.2	6.5	1.8	.1
Salvadoran	3.9	1.9	2.6	1.3	5.4	25.2	8.4	3.8	.9	18.3	14.8	10.0	3.4	.1
South American	12.1	9.8	8.0	3.3	8.1	20.8	6.5	4.7	.9	10.6	9.1	4.6	1.3	.1
Other Central American	7.5	4.0	5.2	1.7	6.1	27.2	7.8	3.5	1.7	11.3	10.1	11.3	1.7	.9
Other Hispanic	8.0	6.2	4.7	2.7	7.4	23.2	7.4	2.8	1.9	12.6	11.3	8.5	3.3	.2
Total	5.5	3.4	3.4	1.6	6.0	23.4	7.9	2.3	1.4	16.6	11.8	10.3	6.3	.1
European origin														
English	22.3	19.8	10.3	4.5	6.7	16.6	4.3	2.7	2.8	3.5	2.6	2.7	.9	.0
German	19.3	16.5	10.4	4.0	6.6	21.1	5.4	2.8	2.9	3.9	2.8	3.4	1.0	.0
Italian	19.8	14.9	12.9	3.5	7.4	19.0	4.1	3.5	2.9	3.6	4.3	3.5	.6	.0
Polish	20.9	24.2	11.7	4.1	6.1	15.0	3.1	3.4	2.1	3.6	2.6	2.4	.7	.1
Russian	25.4	31.1	16.0	3.3	4.6	7.8	1.9	3.8	1.2	1.6	1.9	1.1	.3	0
Other European	18.7	16.4	10.3	4.0	6.7	20.3	5.6	3.2	2.7	3.9	3.6	3.5	1.1	.0
Total	19.7	17.5	10.7	4.0	6.6	19.4	5.1	3.1	2.7	3.8	3.2	3.3	1.0	.0

(*continued*)

TABLE 3A.2 (continued)

Ethnic Group	Managers	Professionals	High Sales	Technicians	Clerical	Skilled Manual	Trans. Ops.	Sales Clerks	Protective Service	Machine Ops.	Other Ser.	Laborers	Agricultural Workers	Private Household Service
Middle Eastern origin														
Armenian	17.7	15.2	12.3	2.9	5.1	23.6	5.2	5.5	.8	5.6	2.4	2.9	1.0	0
Iranian	22.2	25.2	19.4	3.3	4.4	10.2	2.4	6.4	.1	1.3	2.8	2.3	0	0
Other M.E. and N. African	22.6	16.8	15.6	3.6	4.2	14.4	4.1	6.1	1.7	3.2	3.7	3.3	.5	.1
Total	20.9	18.6	15.6	3.3	4.5	16.2	4.0	6.0	1.0	3.5	3.0	2.9	.5	.0
African origin														
U.S. blacks	10.3	9.7	5.0	3.3	14.5	15.4	9.5	2.7	6.2	6.0	9.5	6.7	1.1	.1
West Indian	11.4	10.1	3.5	4.4	12.7	21.9	7.9	5.3	4.8	3.5	8.8	4.4	.9	.4
Foreign-born blacks (exc. W.I.)	12.2	15.1	6.8	3.5	10.9	13.5	9.3	4.2	4.5	5.1	9.0	4.5	1.0	.3
Total	10.4	9.9	5.0	3.3	14.4	15.5	9.4	2.8	6.1	5.9	9.5	6.6	1.1	.1
American Indian	11.1	9.1	5.1	3.2	6.8	27.4	8.1	2.0	4.2	6.6	6.8	7.8	1.6	0
Other	11.0	8.7	4.8	3.7	8.2	21.7	9.3	4.2	2.8	9.6	7.3	7.0	1.7	0

TABLE 3A.3 Selected Characteristics of Jobs Held, 31 Ethnic Groups, Los Angeles Metropolitan Area, 1990 (Male Labor Force Age 20–64)

	Percentage Distribution of Employment Status				Mean	
Ethnic Group	Employee	Self Employed	Own Corporation	Helping in Family Business	Hours Worked per Week	Weeks Worked per Year
Total	86.5	9.8	3.6	.1	43.1	46.4
Asian origin						
Asian Indian	83.4	10.8	5.5	.3	44.2	47.2
Cambodian	87.4	11.9	.7	.0	41.2	43.5
Chinese	79.8	12.0	7.9	.3	43.1	46.6
Filipino	93.9	4.5	1.6	.0	41.7	46.7
Japanese	83.3	10.8	5.8	.1	44.4	48.6
Korean	58.9	31.0	9.2	.9	46.6	45.9
Vietnamese	89.9	8.0	2.0	.1	40.6	46.2
Other Asian	87.7	8.5	3.6	.2	42.7	46.3
Total	82.4	12.1	5.2	.4	43.2	46.8
Latin American origin						
Cuban	81.1	15.3	3.4	.3	42.8	46.7
Guatemalan	93.3	5.0	1.6	.1	40.9	43.5
Mexican	93.3	5.2	1.4	.1	41.5	44.9
Nicaraguan	91.9	4.8	2.6	.7	41.0	44.8
Puerto Rican	93.1	5.0	1.8	.1	42.8	45.5
Salvadoran	93.5	5.3	1.1	.1	40.9	44.2

(*continued*)

TABLE 3A.3 (continued)

	Percentage Distribution of Employment Status				Mean	
Ethnic Group	Employee	Self Employed	Own Corporation	Helping in Family Business	Hours Worked per Week	Weeks Worked per Year
South American	81.5	15.0	3.5	.0	42.7	45.6
Other Central American	89.6	8.7	1.7	.0	41.0	44.9
Other Hispanic	91.1	6.1	2.7	.0	41.9	44.4
Total	92.7	5.6	1.5	.1	41.6	44.8
European origin						
English	83.5	11.6	4.7	.1	43.9	47.5
German	85.0	10.9	4.1	.1	44.0	47.7
Italian	82.2	12.8	4.9	.1	43.9	47.7
Polish	81.6	11.3	7.0	.1	44.4	47.8
Russian	69.8	18.5	11.6	.1	45.1	47.8
Other European	84.0	11.6	4.3	.1	44.0	47.3
Total	83.5	11.7	4.6	.1	44.0	47.5
Middle Eastern origin						
Armenian	66.3	24.9	8.6	.2	44.3	46.5
Iranian	67.8	19.8	12.4	.0	45.5	47.2
Other M.E. and N. African	71.5	19.8	8.6	.2	44.5	46.8
Total	68.8	21.4	9.7	.1	44.7	46.8
African origin						
U.S. blacks	93.1	5.6	1.3	.1	41.4	44.6
West Indian	88.2	10.1	1.8	.0	42.1	45.9

Foreign-born blacks (exc. W.I.)	90.4	6.8	2.6	.3	42.3	46.0
Total	92.9	5.7	1.3	.1	41.4	44.7
American Indian	90.5	7.5	1.9	.1	43.4	44.9
Other	88.2	8.2	3.7	.0	43.6	46.2

TABLE 3A.4 Statistics on Business Ownership for Selected Ethnic Groups, Los Angeles County, 1987

			Firms with Paid Employees		
Ethnic Group	Firms per Capita[a]	Mean Sales and Receipts ($ thousands)	Percent of All Firms	Mean Number of Employees	Mean Sales and Receipts ($ thousands)
Asian					
Asian Indian	.17	149	26	4.0	407
Chinese	.11	122	27	4.8	334
Filipino	.05	44	13	2.4	210
Japanese	.12	84	19	4.1	314
Korean	.21	145	32	4.4	346
Vietnamese	.12	61	22	4.6	180
Hispanic					
Cuban	.08	91	23	4.8	302
Mexican	.03	59	18	3.5	218
Puerto Rican	.05	86	20	3.0	346
Black	.05	54	15	3.1	251

[a] Denominator estimated from the 1990 census file as the number of adults (persons age 20 and older) not enrolled in school, multiplied by 20.

Source: U.S. Bureau of the Census 1991a: table 7; 1991b: table 7; 1991c: table 4. Since we could not readily locate the figures for blacks, we estimated them by subtracting the figures for Hispanics and Asians from the total figures reported in 1991c.

4

The Structure of Career Mobility in Microscopic Perspective

Jesper B. Sørensen and David B. Grusky

Although more attention has been lavished on mobility tables than perhaps any other type of sociological data, only rarely have sociologists sought to map the underlying contours of mobility between actual *occupations*, where these are understood as functionally defined positions in the division of labor (cf. Rytina 1992; Evans and Laumann 1978). The prevailing practice has been to examine patterns of mobility between "classes" or "strata" formed by aggregating detailed jobs or occupations in terms of their measured (or presumed) work conditions, market position, consumption practices, mobility chances, or socioeconomic standing. While there is surely no consensus on any single class schema, the shared and unchallenged assumption has been that some sort of aggregation into supraoccupational categories is appropriate. The latter assumption has limited empirical inquiry into such fundamental matters as (1) the extent of social closure at the detailed occupational level, (2) the size and location of interoccupational cleavages, disjunctures, and discontinuities in mobility chances, and (3) the macrolevel sources and causes of occupational persistence and mobility. This chapter provides new insights into these issues by presenting a disaggregate occupational classification and calibrating it against one of the standard data sets in the field.

The tabular and event history approaches to mobility analysis differ in many respects, but they evidently share the foregoing preference for extreme aggregation. In some cases, event history analysts use language suggestive of a suboccupational level of analysis, but such language is easily misunderstood. It should be borne in mind that many, if not most, event history analysts resort to modeling job shifts between categories that are defined in terms of occupational status, thus implying that the de facto level of analysis is in fact supraoccupational. The typical researcher will of course distinguish between upward and downward "job shifts" (e.g., Sørensen and Tuma 1981); however, jobs nonetheless disappear from the analysis because researchers rely upon occupational status in ascertaining the directionality of moves, thereby introducing an implicit aggregation of not just jobs but occupations as well.[1] In similar fashion, conventional analyses of "grade mobility" may confound patterns of exchange between and within occupations, since a great many diverse occupations are typically classified into the same grade (e.g., DiPrete 1989).

We would therefore suggest that the principal difference between event history and tabular traditions is not so much the level of analysis at which they operate but rather the particular types of occupational aggregation that are privileged. Whereas the tabular tradition operates within a (not always Marxian) class analytic approach, the event history literature shares with the older path analytic tradition (e.g., Blau and Duncan 1967) a taste for socioeconomic aggregations of occupations. It is ironic that occupations themselves are missing from these analyses despite the great respect that mobility scholars pay to the conventional view that occupations are the "backbone" of the modern stratification system (Parkin 1971:18; also, Blau and Duncan 1967:6–7; Featherman and Hauser 1977:4). We shall attempt here to analyze mobility data in ways that take this conventional view more seriously.

The popularity of aggregate categories can be attributed to such pragmatic considerations as (1) the relatively small samples available for mobility research and the consequent sparseness of disaggregate tables, (2) the convenience of introducing new models and methods with aggregate cross-classifications, and (3) the forces of sociological tradition and convention. The aggregate categories that mobility researchers routinely apply are thus regarded as analytically convenient rather than true collectivities of the realist variety (Holton and Turner 1989; cf. Goldthorpe and Marshall 1992; Wright 1985). Indeed, if a realist model of inequality is to be preferred, there is much to be said for ratcheting the level of analysis down to the detailed occupation itself. We have argued elsewhere that occupational categories are the fundamental units of modern labor markets and the main bases of social closure, collective action, and identity formation (see Grusky and Sørensen 1995). In documenting this claim, we would begin by noting that workers frequently invoke and deploy detailed occupational categories (e.g., doctor, plumber), whereas the aggregate languages of class and status are spoken almost exclusively in academic institutions. The labor market is likewise rife with associations (e.g., unions, professional associations) that act on behalf of *detailed* occupational groupings. By contrast, there are no supraoccupational organizations that represent aggregate classes (see Murphy 1988), nor are there formally institutionalized barriers to mobility that are truly aggregate in scope. This line of reasoning suggests that the life chances of workers are governed by their occupations more so than their aggregate classes (see Grusky and Sørensen 1995 for further details).

The mobility analyses presented here explore the implications of adopting disaggregate models that correspond to such lay representations of inequality. We proceed by first speculating on the contours of persistence and exchange that our disaggregated analyses will likely reveal. After outlining these hypotheses and possible criticisms of them, we introduce our detailed occupational classification and the data on which it is based. We conclude by discussing our mobility models and the implications of these models for contemporary theories of mobility.

Disaggregation and Persistence

It is instructive to begin our discussion of occupational persistence by rehearsing the received wisdom on such matters. In conventional analyses of career mobility, the densities of class persistence invariably take on a U-shape, with the most extreme rigidities appearing at the top and bottom of the class structure (Featherman and Hauser 1978; Stier and Grusky 1990). This pattern is revealed, for example, in the three-dimensional graph of Figure 4.1, where we have displayed the underlying densities of career mobility reported by Featherman and Hauser (1978). As shown here, the densities of upper nonmanual and farming persistence are quite strong, whereas the densities in the interior of the occupational structure are relatively weak. The results presented in Figure 4.1 are based on the standard levels model introduced by Hauser (1978), but it should be emphasized that the contours of persistence are similar under nearly all competing specifications of the mobility regime (cf. MacDonald 1981).

Although the U-shape of Figure 4.1 has been represented as one of the fundamental features of modern mobility, it may ultimately prove to be an artifact of the highly aggregate classification schemes that sociologists conventionally adopt. As we suggested earlier, one might expect to find considerable heterogeneity in the underlying contours of persistence, since closure and exclusion are secured at the level of occupations rather than classes. The manual sector, for instance, may well be poorly formed in the aggregate, yet it comprises many occupations that have successfully deployed such exclusionary tactics as unionization, closed hiring, and credentialing. At the same time, some professional occupations have failed to achieve fully their exclusionary objectives (e.g., nurses), while others have neither pursued nor articulated such objectives in any sustained fashion (e.g., artists). The aggregate statistics of standard mobility

FIGURE 4.1 Densities of Mobility and Persistence Under Featherman-Hauser Levels Model

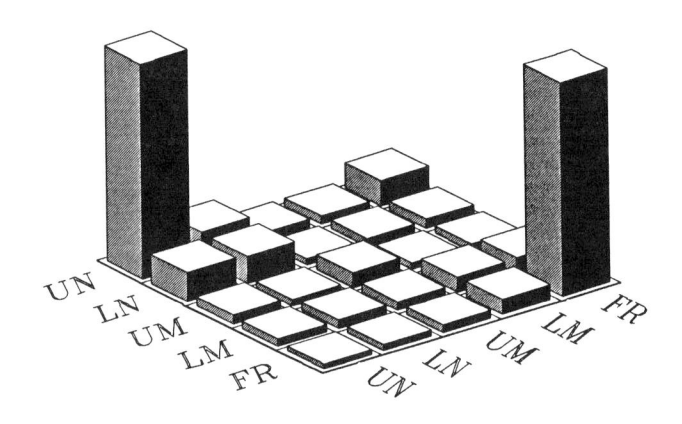

Note: The occupational categories are labeled as follows: UN = upper nonmanual; LN = lower nonmanual; UM = upper manual; LM = lower manual; FR = farm. The left-hand labels index occupational origins, and the right-hand labels index occupational destinations.

Source: Featherman and Hauser 1978: table 4.13

analysis thus conceal the disparate forms and types of closure that prevail within any given class. While manual workers are no doubt more likely than professionals to favor unionism over credentialism, this tendency holds only imperfectly and conceals considerable interoccupational variability in the success with which these exclusionary strategies have been pursued in each class.

The further difficulty with aggregate analyses is that they necessarily confound occupational persistence with intraclass mobility. If the densities of persistence are typically stronger than those of mobility, one would then expect closure to be greatest within aggregate classes that are so homogeneous (e.g., farming) as to encompass little in the way of implied mobility. By contrast, the persistence parameters for heterogeneous classes (e.g., craft labor) will likely be muted, since they disproportionately reflect the weak tendencies for intraclass mobility among the many disparate occupations that constitute such classes (e.g., bakers, carpenters, mechanics). This suggests that our well-known contour maps of mobility may be quite sensitive to the level of aggregation that has been assumed. Moreover, if the above argument is carried to its logical conclusion, it further implies that the densities of class persistence can be raised or lowered at will simply by defining a class category more or less narrowly.

The corollary to this claim is that conventional aggregate analyses may underestimate the extent of social closure in the mobility regime. To be sure, the *observed* mobility rate will perforce increase with disaggregation, since the proportion of the sample falling on the main diagonal will always shrink when class categories are more sharply defined. The effects of disaggregation on patterns of association are rather less obvious; that is, once the marginal effects in a mobility table are parsed out, the operative question is whether the shrinkage on the main diagonal (caused by disaggregation) is more or less severe than the corresponding shrinkage of the margins themselves. While there is good reason to suspect that intracategory heterogeneity will mute the densities of persistence, this hypothesis has not, to date, been convincingly tested.

The analyses reported by Stier and Grusky (1990) are nonetheless suggestive on this matter. In characterizing their results, they emphasize that many middle-class occupations are surprisingly closed, and that the overall clustering on the main diagonal is perhaps more extreme than prior analysts had appreciated (see Stier and Grusky 1990:746). At the same time, the Stier-Grusky analyses can scarcely be characterized as disaggregate, since they rest on an 18-category classification that necessarily combines disparate occupations into heterogeneous categories.

The analyses of Rytina (1992) are of course *extremely* disaggregate by comparison (i.e., 308 categories). While Rytina (1992:1) concludes that true occupational inheritance is a "comparatively rare phenomenon," we believe that his classification is so disaggregate that the resulting definition of inheritance is *too* narrow and exclusive (see Hauser and Logan 1992 for related problems). We ought not assume that all disaggregation, no matter how extreme, is sociologically desirable; indeed, we would anticipate diminishing returns to disaggregation, since the benefits of distinguishing truly disparate occupations (e.g., baker and carpenter) will at some point be offset by the costs of subdividing occupations that belong to the same generic "mobility family" (e.g., carpenters and apprentice carpenters). The moral to our story, then, is that one should prefer occupational classifications that represent a sociologically informed middle ground. Although such classifications are not now available, they can be readily constructed from standard occupational data (see the section on Constructing a Disaggregate Mobility Table).

Disaggregation and Exchange

The received wisdom on off-diagonal exchange may also require revision when conventional mobility tables are disaggregated. In analyses of standard 5 × 5 tables, the manual-nonmanual cleavage proves to be especially large, while the upper and lower sectors of the manual class are marked by a further, albeit smaller, divide (see Featherman and Hauser 1978; see also Grusky and Fukumoto 1989; Fukumoto and Grusky 1993). The former result appears as a plateau comprising the northwest quadrant of the Featherman-Hauser design matrix, while the latter appears as a low-lying formation in the southeast quadrant of this same matrix (see Figure 4.1). When Featherman and Hauser (1978:195-8) analyzed an elaborated 12-category classification, they found additional rifts and fissures, yet all were less substantial than the foregoing major divides (see also Snipp 1985).

It is unclear whether further disaggregation will be equally benign. If it is, then much of the interoccupational variability in mobility chances should be located *between* aggregate classes rather than *within* them. There are, of course, any number of alternative outcomes that would require more fundamental revisions in our understanding of mobility regimes. For example, the disaggregate results might suggest (1) a gradational mobility regime in which intraclass heterogeneity is so substantial as to eliminate the manual-nonmanual cleavage as well as all other class divides or (2) a fractured mobility regime in which the principal disjunctures and divides occur within conventional classes rather than between them. In examining these possibilities, we shall carry out exploratory analyses of the sort introduced by Goodman (1981b), yet we shall do so with highly disaggregate data and hence ratchet down the level at which primitive (i.e., untested) classificatory decisions are made (see also Breiger 1981; Jacobs and Breiger 1988).

We hope this approach will provide new insights of an explanatory as well as descriptive sort. In a now classic article, Hout (1984) has argued that off-diagonal exchange is explained not merely by the vertical standing of occupations (as indexed by their socioeconomic status) but also by their relative autonomy and an additional "farming effect" that captures the fundamental disjuncture between farm and nonfarm mobility chances (also, Hout 1988, 1989; Hout and Jackson 1986). The resulting model has rightly become a standard in the field. However, further debate on the sources of exchange should not be closed off altogether, since the posited dimensions have not yet been exhaustively tested against various plausible alternatives. We therefore approach the issue of explanation de novo by fitting association models that identify the underlying dimensions of exchange without imposing any explicit constraints on the data (see Goodman 1987; Smith and Garnier 1987). These multidimensional models are estimable only because disaggregation affords us the requisite degrees of freedom to tease out highly correlated dimensions.

Constructing a Disaggregate Mobility Table

If one wishes to work at the disaggregate level, the data requirements are substantial and can only be met by pooling across multiple sources. We proceed, then, by drawing data from both the 1962 and 1973 Occupational Changes in a Generation (OCG) Surveys (Blau and Duncan 1967; Featherman and Hauser 1978). Although our analyses will not allow for known intersurvey trends in the parameters of mobility (Hout 1984; Featherman and Hauser 1978), the observed changes are surely not strong enough to lead us too far astray. At the same time, we hope that trend analyses will ultimately be carried out at the disaggregate level, since doing so would yield important evidence on the sources of stasis and change. The parameter estimates from our own (more limited) models must of course be interpreted as averaging over the small changes that have been observed in the American mobility regime in recent decades.

The OCG data pertain, unfortunately, to men alone. We further restricted the analyses to respondents who were members of the experienced civilian labor force and were 25 to 64 years old at the time of the surveys. After imposing these restrictions and applying the OCG weights, we constructed a conventional mobility table in which the rows and columns refer to origins and destinations respectively. That is, the rows of our mobility table index the "first occupations" of the OCG respondents, while the columns index the corresponding "current occupations" (see Featherman and Hauser 1978). When the missing responses on these variables are eliminated, the pooled sample size is reduced to 40,127 and the mean cell count for the final mobility table becomes 8.2.[2]

In constructing this table, we had no alternative but to devise a new occupational classification, since the currently available ones are either too detailed (e.g., three-digit census classifications), not detailed enough (e.g., standard class categories), or not readily applied to American occupational data (e.g., two-digit International Standard Classification of Occupations).[3] There are, of course, *some* middle-range classifications available for American data, yet they invariably rest on such extraneous criteria as socioeconomic status, life chances, or mobility prospects. For example, Rytina (1992) has combined census occupations into socioeconomic categories, while Breiger (1981) has aggregated occupations on the basis of mobility chances, and Blau and Duncan (1967) have popularized a 17-category classification based, at least partly, on industrial distinctions (see also Jacobs and Breiger 1988; Stier and Grusky 1990). We would readily concede that aggregations of this sort are useful; however, the resulting categories cannot properly be regarded as occupations, since they rest on criteria other than functional similarities in the social division of labor.

We take a more narrowly occupational approach here. Although we have thus proceeded by aggregating census occupations in terms of their functional tasks, the resulting classification also indirectly captures work conditions and market situations (Lockwood 1958). In constructing this classification, we were guided principally by the work descriptions provided in the *Dictionary of Occupational Titles* (1949, 1965, 1977), but we further attended to the aggregations embedded in other classification systems (e.g., the International Standard Classification of Occupations).[4] The results of our efforts are listed in the Appendix. As reported there, we have mapped each of the three-digit 1960 census codes into one (and only one) of 70 middle-range occupational titles. We then distributed these titles into seven strata and sorted them in order of descending socioeconomic status.

Models of Mobility

We analyze our 70 × 70 classification with log-multiplicative association models (Goodman 1979, 1981a, 1981b, 1981c, 1987; Smith and Garnier 1987). The distinctive feature of such models is that they freely scale origin and destination categories without conditioning on any a priori scorings or orderings of the data. In its most general form, the log-multiplicative model can be represented as follows:

$$F_{ij} = \alpha \, \beta_i \, \gamma_j \exp\left(\sum_{m=1}^{M} \Phi_m \mu_{im} \nu_{jm} \right) \qquad (1)$$

where i indexes origins (with $i = 1, \ldots, I$), j indexes destinations (with $j = 1, \ldots, J$), F_{ij} refers to the expected value in the ijth cell, α is the grand mean, β_i is the marginal effect for the ith row, γ_j is the marginal effect for the jth column, Φ_m is the intrinsic association pertaining to the mth dimension, μ_{im} is the scale value for the ith row and mth dimension, and ν_{jm} is the scale value for the jth column and mth dimension.

The foregoing model estimates M association parameters and M sets of row and column scores. While mobility scholars have conventionally estimated one-dimensional association models (e.g., Grusky and Hauser 1984), our disaggregate table is large enough to fit additional dimensions and thereby formally test the three-variable model proposed by Hout (1984). We shall also test for asymmetries of the sort that Blau and Duncan (1967) postulated (also, MacDonald 1981); that is, given the one-to-one correspondence between our row and column categories, we can plausibly impose the further constraint that $\mu_{im} = \nu_{jm}$ (for $i = j$). This equality constraint generates a set of "homogeneous" multidimensional association models (see Goodman 1979).

We have identified the model of equation 1 by forcing the row and column scores to sum to zero, by fixing the sum of their squares at zero, and by constraining the multiple dimensions of association to be orthogonal to one another.[5] These constraints can be represented as follows:

$$\sum_{i=1}^{I} \mu_{im} = 0, \quad \sum_{j=1}^{J} v_{jm} = 0 \tag{2}$$

$$\sum_{i=1}^{I} \mu_{im}^2 = 1, \quad \sum_{j=1}^{J} v_{jm}^2 = 1 \tag{3}$$

$$\sum_{i=1}^{I} \mu_{im} \mu_{im'} = 0, \quad \sum_{j=1}^{J} v_{jm} v_{jm'} = 0 \tag{4}$$

where $m \neq m'$, and the remaining notation is defined as above. If only one dimension is estimated (i.e., $M = 1$), then Φ_m reduces to Φ and the orthogonality constraints of equation 4 are no longer relevant.

We are perhaps obliged to defend our model against the recent claim (see Stier and Grusky 1990) that analyses of career mobility are best carried out with categorical specifications. The latter argument is not wholly inconsistent with our present modeling strategy; in fact, association models are no longer antithetical to categorical interpretations of mobility, since the introduction of multiple dimensions allows for complex disjunctures that could previously be captured only by fitting categorical terms. The well-known competition between categorical and gradational models of mobility has therefore effectively ended. In the past, mobility scholars selected categorical or gradational models on the basis of conceptual preferences or predispositions (see Erikson and Goldthorpe 1992), whereas now such matters can be addressed empirically by examining the number and type of dimensions underlying the mobility regime.

Selecting a Model

We begin our formal analyses by asking whether standard aggregations conceal much intrastratum heterogeneity in mobility chances. As shown in Table 4.1, over 57 percent of the total disaggregate association is generated within our seven strata, while the remaining 43 percent is generated between these strata. In interpreting this result, some scholars might emphasize that most of the origin-by-destination association is concealed by aggregation, whereas others might be impressed by the amount of association (i.e., 43 percent) that a mere 36 degrees of freedom can explain. We incline toward the former view; indeed, given that mobility scholars have spent the last half century analyzing the minority component of association, it is perhaps high time to begin analyzing the large residue that has so far been ignored (but see Rytina 1992). The intellectual payoff to disaggregation is, at the very least, likely to be greater than that secured by carrying out yet another reanalysis of aggregate mobility.

We have thus applied a series of log-multiplicative association models to our full 70 × 70 mobility table. The fit statistics presented in Table 4.2 indicate that our most complex model (see line D2) accounts for 88.7 percent of the total association and correctly allocates over 92.2 percent of all respondents. This result suggests that association models can be readily elaborated to account for disaggregate mobility. Although the impressive fit statistics of Table 4.2 are attributable in part to the (standard) device of blocking the main diagonal, it is nonetheless striking that our association models fit substantially better than the baseline model of quasi-independence (see line A2). If a standard chi-square decomposition is carried out, we find that our simplest association model (see line B1) accounts for 49.1 percent of the total off-diagonal association [(16,188−8,243)/16,188 = .491], while our most complex model accounts for as much as 66.4 percent of this association [(16,188−5,440)/16,188 = .664).

The fit statistics reported in Table 4.2 do not unambiguously identify a single preferred model. If we were to rely solely on a BIC criterion (Raftery 1986), we would opt for the homogeneous variant of the three-dimensional model (see line D1). At the same time, the test statistics

TABLE 4.1 Decomposition of the Total Association in Disaggregate Mobility Table into Components Within and Between Major Strata

Models	L^2	df	L^2_h/L^2_t
1. Total association $\{O\}\{D\}$	48,098	4,761	100.0
2. Between strata $\{O_s\}\{D_s\}$	20,644	36	42.9
3. Within strata	27,454	4,725	57.1

Note: O = occupational origin; D = occupational destination; O_s = stratum origin; D_s = stratum destination

Career Mobility in Microscopic Perspective

TABLE 4.2 Log-Linear and Log-Multiplicative Association Models Applied to Disaggregate Mobility Table

Models	L^2	df	L_h^2/L_t^2	Δ	L^2/df	BIC
A. Baseline models						
1. Independence	48,098	4,761	100.0	30.8	10.10	−2,378
2. Quasi-Independence	16,188	4,691	33.7	18.2	3.45	−33,546
3. Quasi-Symmetry	2,593	2,346	5.4	5.1	1.11	−22,279
B. One-dimensional models						
1. Homogeneous	8,243	4,622	17.1	10.9	1.78	−40,759
2. Heterogeneous	7,980	4,554	16.6	10.6	1.75	−40,302
C. Two-dimensional models						
1. Homogeneous	7,151	4,554	14.9	9.6	1.57	−41,130
2. Heterogeneous	6,596	4,419	13.7	9.1	1.49	−40,255
D. Three-dimensional models						
1. Homogeneous	6,198	4,487	12.9	8.7	1.38	−41,374
2. Heterogeneous	5,440	4,286	11.3	7.8	1.27	−40,000

Note: The association models reported here were all fitted with the main diagonal blanked out.

imply that the row and column scores differ significantly from one another, and the L^2/df ratio likewise suggests that our heterogeneous three-dimensional solution is to be preferred relative to all alternatives (save quasi-symmetry). While Hout (1984) is correct, then, in insisting on a three-dimensional model, it is unclear whether the heterogeneous or homogeneous version of this model should be selected here. In the present context, we see little harm in opting for the more complex specification, and we shall accordingly carry out most of our analyses with the model of line D2. By doing so, we allow our readers, rather than BIC, to decide whether the (clearly significant) departures from quasi-symmetry are of sociological interest.

The Structure of Occupational Persistence

We first deploy this model to explore the contours of persistence. As emphasized in our introductory comments, we are principally interested in whether conventional analyses have been unduly misleading, and we therefore contrast our preferred estimates with those secured when the data are aggregated into the seven strata defined in the Appendix. The resulting 7×7 table returns an L^2 statistic of 265 when the main diagonal is blocked and a one-dimensional homogeneous association model is applied. In the analyses that follow, we rely on this simple model exclusively, if only because it has become one of the standards in the field. It is nonetheless reassuring that the contours of immobility are largely the same under most other conventional specifications (e.g., levels models).

The first column of Table 4.3 presents the total densities of immobility under this standard model, while the second column provides the corresponding densities under our preferred model of line D2 (Table 4.2). These densities are calculated as follows:

$$D_{ij} = \ln [\exp (\sum_{m=1}^{M} \Phi_m \mu_{im} \nu_{jm}) \delta_i]$$

$$= \ln [F_{ij} / (\alpha \beta_i \gamma_j)] \tag{5}$$

where δ_i refers to the immobility parameter for the ith class, and the remaining parameters are defined as before (see equation 1). In our 7×7 classification, the definition of D_{ij} simplifies because M equals one and μ_i equals ν_j (for $i = j$), but the formula of equation 5 otherwise applies equally to the aggregate and disaggregate cases (see Featherman and Hauser 1978:150-61 for analogously defined mobility ratios). The aggregate values of D_{ij} (see column 1) can thus be safely contrasted with the disaggregate values (see column 2) calculated by averaging across the detailed occupations that make up each stratum. Although we subsequently examine the densities of immobility for all 70 occupations, our comparative interests are best served by first examining the central tendency within each stratum. We have likewise reported the within-stratum variances of D_{ij} (see column 3).

In each of the seven strata, the entries in column 2 are larger than their counterparts in column 1 (see Table 4.3), thereby implying that the densities of persistence are attenuated when occupations are aggregated. This "aggregation bias" is quite substantial; that is, the average difference between corresponding entries in columns 1 and 2 is 2.22, which means that the underlying densities of occupational persistence are 9.24 times greater than those of stratum persistence [$\exp(2.22) = 9.24$]. The most dramatic evidence of aggregation bias can be found within strata comprising occupations that have frequently deployed such exclusionary tactics as credentialing, unionization, and closed hiring. For example, the value of

Career Mobility in Microscopic Perspective

TABLE 4.3 The Structure of Persistence for Aggregate and Disaggregate Mobility Tables

Stratum	Stratum Densities	Detailed Occ. Densities Mean	Variance
1. Professional	2.72	6.17	3.53
2. Manager	1.07	4.20	8.48
3. Clerical	0.98	2.84	4.10
4. Sales	1.01	2.12	2.00
5. Craft and operative	0.90	3.81	2.06
6. Service	1.26	3.57	2.64
7. Farm	3.22	4.01	0.75

Note: The densities reported here are in additive form. The stratum densities are taken from a one-dimensional homogeneous association model, and the detailed occupation densities are taken from a three-dimensional hetrogeneous association model (model D2, Table 4.2). For purposes of presentation, the variances have been multiplied by a factor of 100.

D_{ij} increases for professionals by a factor of 31.5 [exp(6.17–2.72) = 31.5], while it increases for managers and craft workers by factors of 22.9 and 18.4 respectively [exp(4.20–1.07) = 22.9; exp(3.81–0.90) = 18.4]. In all such cases, aggregate models misspecify the contours of persistence, since closure is secured through associations or unions that operate at the (detailed) occupational level.

We have graphed the full set of densities in Figure 4.2. As revealed here, the U-shaped curve that appears in aggregate analyses is now more difficult to discern, and not simply because there are pockets of extreme immobility in the skilled manual sector. We find further evidence of such hyper-rigidity in routine nonmanual sectors of the occupational structure (e.g., clerical, sales, service) that have conventionally been regarded as mere "staging posts" for workers engaged in upward mobility projects (see Goldthorpe 1980). Moreover, while the farming sector has long been characterized as the principal region of extreme closure, we now find that the densities of immobility for many professional and managerial occupations rival the corresponding densities for farming. The overall picture that emerges, then, suggests that (1) there is far more immobility than has heretofore been appreciated, (2) the middle regions of the occupational structure can no longer be characterized as zones of great fluidity, and (3)

96

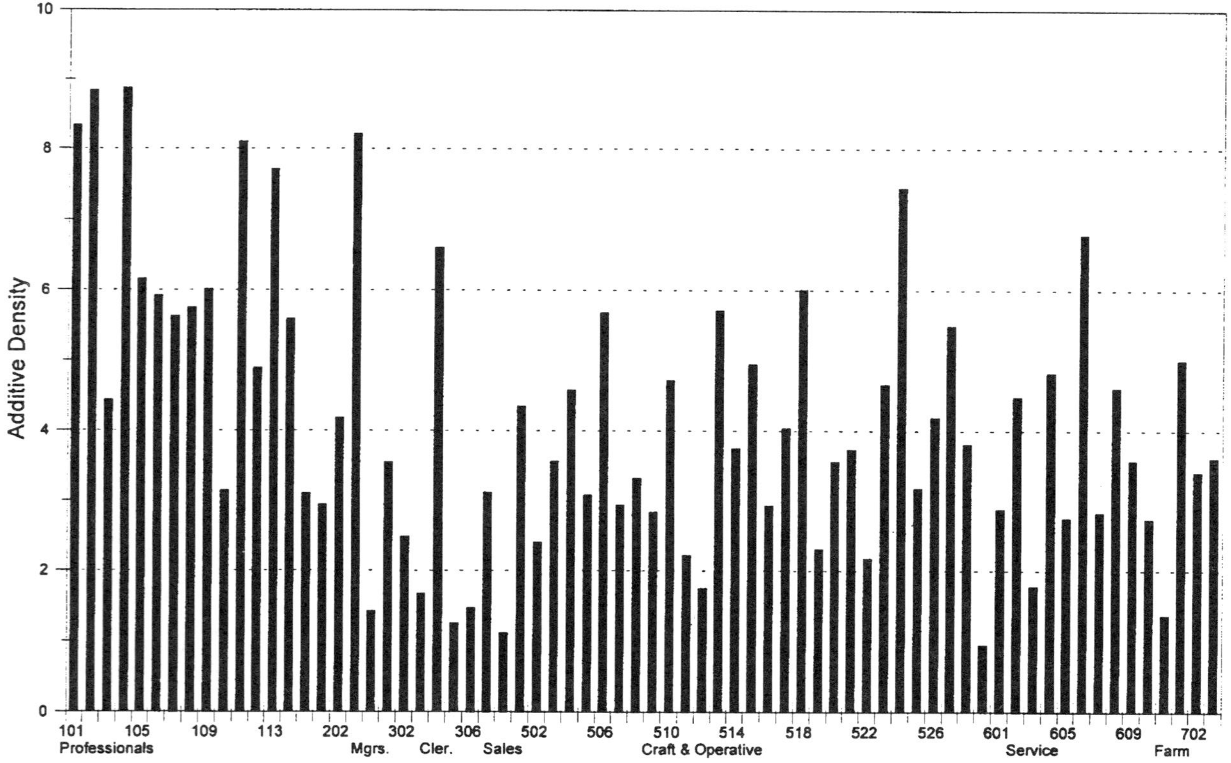

FIGURE 4.2 Total Densities on Main Diagonal Under Three-Dimensional Heterogenous Association Model

pockets of hyper-rigidity appear in virtually all sectors of the class structure.

This variability in the densities of persistence may well be explicable in sociological terms. We can distinguish in this regard between artifactual, descriptive, and structural explanations of the relative strength of D_{ij}. Although a great many accounts stressing artifactual sources are currently on offer (e.g., Rytina 1992), the most straightforward one rests on our prior observation that heterogeneous categories are characterized by relatively weak exchanges among the constituent occupations. As Sorokin (1927/1959:439) noted long ago, "the closer the affinity between occupations, the more intensive among them is mutual interchange of their members; and, *vice versa*, the greater the difference between occupations, the less is the number of individuals who shift from one group to another." This line of reasoning suggests that the D_{ij} can be raised or lowered at will simply by defining an occupational category more or less narrowly. The extreme immobility of farmers, for instance, might therefore be interpreted as reflecting the relative homogeneity of the farming stratum rather than the effects of spatial isolation, landownership, or other intrinsic features of the occupation. The results of Figure 4.2 lend some credence to such a story, since the gap between farm and nonfarm immobility indeed closes when nonfarm occupations are disaggregated into categories as homogeneous as those pertaining to farming. By the same logic, one might further conclude that the remaining variability in D_{ij} is equally artifactual, with the driving force in all cases being intercategory differences in the extent to which occupations are homogeneous groupings.

We suspect that the holding power of occupations would nonetheless vary even if these artifactual effects could be wholly purged. While there is a long tradition of constructing (nonartifactual) theories of persistence, the SAT model (Hout 1984, 1988, 1989) stands out as one of the few attempts to formalize such theories (see also Erikson and Goldthorpe 1992; Evans and Laumann 1978).[6] We have applied this model to our highly disaggregate data by regressing the densities of persistence (i.e., D_{ij}) on detailed measures of status, autonomy, and specialized training.[7] As we earlier noted, the SAT model is best characterized as an inspired hypothesis, since the posited dimensions have not yet been exhaustively tested against various plausible alternatives.[8] For purposes of comparison, we have thus regressed D_{ij} on standard measures of substantive complexity (with respect to data, people, and things), all of which have again been operationalized at the detailed occupational level.[9] The rationale underlying this DPT Model is seemingly straightforward; namely, insofar as complex occupations require substantial occupation-specific investments in training, the incentives for extraoccupational mobility are correspondingly reduced (see Stier and Grusky 1990). Under the above formulation, the DPT model might well be advanced as a serious account of persistence, yet our principal intention here is merely to calibrate the SAT model against a quite arbitrarily chosen alternative. The results of Table 4.4 indicate that (1) much of the interoccupational variability in persistence remains unexplained under either model, (2) the coefficient of variation for the SAT model is slightly smaller than that for our alternative DPT model, and (3) none of the SAT variables remains significant (at $\alpha = .05$) when our two models are overlaid on one another (see column 3, Table 4.4). These results bear out our earlier suggestion that scholars of mobility may have settled prematurely on an SAT formulation.

The models of Table 4.4 might be characterized as descriptive in orientation, since they rest on generic features of occupations (e.g., socioeconomic status) rather than those that directly generate social closure and exclusion. We think that sociologists might usefully develop models that

TABLE 4.4 Regression of Total Occupational Persistence on External Variables

	Model		
Variables	SAT	DPT	Hybrid
STAT	0.013	–	0.011
	(0.161)		(0.128)
AUTON	0.056*	–	0.052
	(0.225)		(0.208)
TRAIN	0.388	–	0.461
	(0.301)		(0.358)
COM1	–	0.022	−0.277
		(0.024)	(−.300)
COM2	–	0.634*	0.439*
		(0.595)	(0.412)
COM3	–	0.243*	0.071
		(0.289)	(0.084)
Constant	1.816*	9.646*	3.718
R^2	0.226	0.242	0.321

Note: The coefficients in parentheses are standardized. STAT = Duncan socioeconomic index; AUTON = autonomy; TRAIN = specialized training; COM1 = substantive complexity pertaining to data; COM2 = substantive complexity pertaining to people; COM3 = substantive complexity pertaining to things. All significant coefficients (at $\alpha = 0.05$) are asterisked.

are more nearly "structural" in form (e.g., Duncan 1975). That is, just as modern models of fertility rest on the proximate physiological sources of reproduction (see Menken 1987), so too one might model immobility in terms of the proximate occupational sources of reproduction. We do not wish to suggest that the descriptive effects of generic variables are altogether uninteresting; however, insofar as such effects reflect exclusionary mechanisms and processes that operate at the (detailed) occupational level, one is well advised to condition on a structural model in which these proximate sources of immobility are explicitly specified. The results of Figure 4.2 suggest, for example, that holding power is strengthened (1) when occupational incumbents are spatially isolated from competing occupational opportunities (e.g., fishermen, forestry workers), (2) when exclusionary tactics such as credentialing and unionization are successfully deployed (e.g., accountants, printers), (3) when workers share all-encompassing lifestyles of the sort classically characterized as "vocations" (e.g., locomotive operators, cabinetmakers), (4) when workplaces are occupationally homogeneous and thereby limit contact with alternative employment possibilities (e.g., professors), and (5) when occupational incumbents own physical capital in the form of a farm, business, or professional practice (e.g., farmers, funeral directors, health professionals). While we do not attempt to construct a formal structural model here, the preceding list of variables is, in our view, a useful starting point for such an exercise (see also Evans and Laumann 1978; Spilerman 1977).

The Structure of Occupational Exchange

The estimates from our association models also speak to the implications of aggregation for interoccupational exchange. The principal question at hand is whether aggregate classes "emerge" from our disaggregate data and hence provide empirical justification for conventional analyses of mobility (see Breiger 1981 for related analyses; see also Jacobs and Breiger 1988). If patterns of exchange have indeed been adequately represented in prior analyses, we should find that classes are internally homogeneous and that the major cleavages in mobility chances are located between classes rather than within them. In addressing this matter, we can safely summarize the data by graphing the scale values from our homogeneous model (line D1, Table 4.2), since we have found that the more complex heterogeneous specification does not, at least in this context, provide additional information of much consequence. The resulting three-dimensional graph is presented in Figure 4.3.[11]

The data points of Figure 4.3 suggest a tripartite division into (1) a professional-managerial "new class" (e.g., Ehrenreich and Ehrenreich 1979; Gouldner 1979), (2) an agricultural class of farmers, farm laborers, and

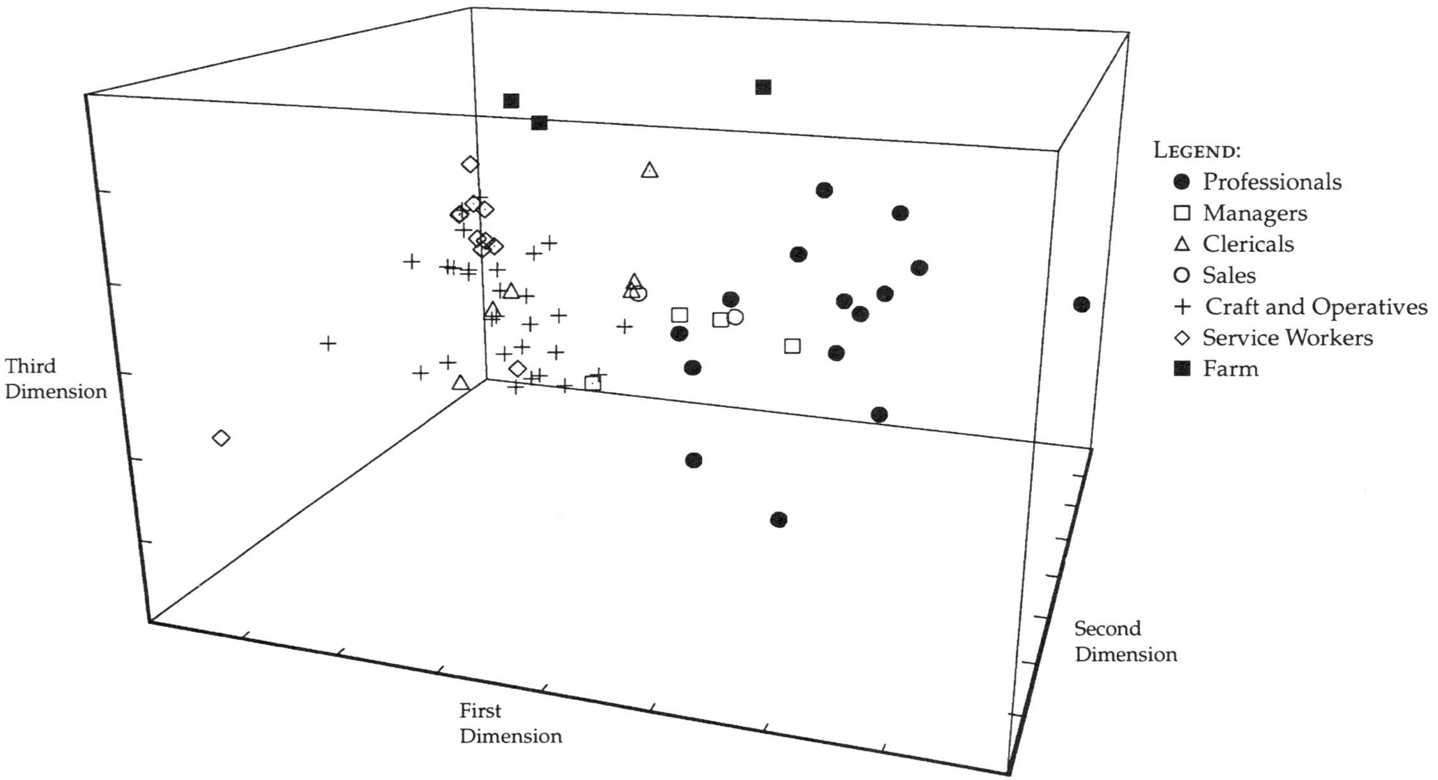

FIGURE 4.3 Scale Values for Three-Dimensional Homogeneous Association Model

farm managers, and (3) a working class of craft, service, and clerical labor. The detailed occupations falling within the latter class appear as a jumble of overlapping data points; indeed, if the detailed occupations within this class were aggregated inductively, one would be forced to define new clusterings that differ from the conventional ones of craft, service, and clerical labor. This is not to suggest that an alternative aggregation emerges here with any clarity. As Figure 4.3 reveals, these intermediary occupations are tightly clustered without any obvious cleavages or dividing lines, thus bearing out the long-standing claim that industrialism "obliterates all distinctions of labor" (Marx 1894/1964:480). Moreover, some clerical occupations are located in the very center of the working class, while others have evidently resisted proletarianization of the sort that Braverman (1974) describes. This result is surely inconsistent with the standard practice of aggregating clerical labor into a single category.

If conventional aggregations cannot be sustained in the middle of the occupational structure, there is nonetheless evidence of a distinct professional-managerial class at the very top of this structure. Although this class is clearly set off from the manual sector, its constituent occupations are also highly dispersed in space, so much so that the resulting "class" spreads out across nearly half the entire figure. This intraclass heterogeneity is *not* reducible to the conventional distinction between salaried and self-employed professionals that Hope (1972:173–9) has emphasized. In examining the right-hand sector of Figure 4.3, we find that some of the occupations indeed involve high rates of self-employment (e.g., accountants), while others are largely staffed by salaried employees (e.g., workers in religion). The principal conclusion that emerges, then, is that standard aggregate categories conceal considerable heterogeneity that is not readily interpretable in conventional ways. In carrying out a de novo aggregation, we would no doubt settle on a conventional farm category, but otherwise our inductive categories would not closely correspond to conventional ones.

The typology of Table 4.5 codifies the various ways in which aggregate classes may or may not be empirically defensible (cf. Jacobs and Breiger 1988). The farming class, for example, approximates the ideal of complete structuration, since it is both internally homogeneous and spatially isolated from all other classes. The working class of craft, service, and clerical labor is more poorly formed; to be sure, its constituent occupations are tightly clustered into dense networks of exchange, but they are also centrally located and accordingly participate in large counterbalancing streams of extraclass flows. By contrast, the professional-managerial class is isolated from the center of the mobility regime, yet it is simultaneously dispersed over much space and is, in this respect, poorly formed. The

TABLE 4.5 Types of Aggregate Class Structuration

Type	Interclass Distances	Intraclass Homogeneity
Complete structuration	High	High
Partial structuration: Type A	Low	High
Partial structuration: Type B	High	Low
Poor structuration	Low	Low

latter two classes provide our clearest examples of type A and type B structuration.

The foregoing results are usefully recast in terms of expected densities. In Figure 4.4, we have projected these densities on a vertical axis, with the height of the bars given by

$$D_{ij}^* = \exp\left(\sum_{m=1}^{M} \Phi_m \mu_{im} \nu_{jm} \right), \qquad (6)$$

where μ_{im} and ν_{jm} are now drawn from our preferred heterogeneous specification in which asymmetries are freely estimated (see line D2, Table 4.2). The resulting graph bears out the interpretations elaborated above. In the far background of Figure 4.4, we find that the densities of farming persistence are consistently strong, thus implying that the farming class is indeed as well formed as mobility analysts implicitly assume. The densities of professional-managerial persistence are more variable, while those of working-class persistence are comparatively weak and are marked by only occasional high-exchange affinities. There is, then, much heterogeneity within each of these classes; however, when one ignores such heterogeneity by averaging across intraclass densities, Figure 4.4 provides little more than a recapitulation of conventional results. That is, the aggregate densities of class persistence in Figure 4.4 are not unlike those of Figure 4.1, with the characteristic U-shape emerging in both cases. In interpreting this result, we should recall that Figure 4.4 represents not the total densities of persistence and exchange but rather those that remain after all residual immobility, as captured by δ_i, has first been purged (see equation 6). We can therefore conclude that the U-shaped diagonal of aggregate tables reflects the structure of short-distance mobility rather than true immobility at the level of detailed occupations. In aggregate analyses of mobility, the densities of working-class persistence are muted, since they are confounded with low-frequency exchange off the microdiagonal.

If the intraclass heterogeneity of Figure 4.4 merely reflects corresponding heterogeneity in the variables that govern mobility, then our results might well be consistent with conventional explanatory accounts. We have examined this possibility in Table 4.6 by correlating the scale values from our heterogeneous specification (line D2, Table 4.2) with the explanatory variables favored by Hout (1984). As we earlier noted, Hout (1984) has argued that off-diagonal exchange is explained not merely by the vertical standing of occupations but also by their relative autonomy and an additional "farming effect" that captures the disjuncture between farm and nonfarm mobility chances.[12] For purposes of comparison, we have contrasted this conventional account with our own DPT specification, where the latter rests on the three measures of substantive complexity that we earlier introduced. The resulting correlation matrix suggests that (1) the first dimension of mobility is, as expected, principally socioeconomic in its underlying structure, (2) the second and third dimensions cannot be adequately explained by the variables of either model, and (3) these residual dimensions are nonetheless most strongly correlated with the variables indexing farming (i.e., FARM) and the substantive complexity of jobs (i.e., COM3).[13] This set of results hardly constitutes a rousing performance by what has become the premier explanatory model in the field.[14] Indeed, the effects of farming are relatively weak, while those of autonomy are exceedingly so. In emphasizing the above problems, we do not mean to suggest that the DPT model is itself plausible but only that it is no less so than the SAT convention.

Conclusions

The preceding analyses have been inspired by closure theory as elaborated by Parkin (1979), Collins (1979), and others (e.g., Manza 1992; Murphy 1988). In modeling patterns of mobility, we have thus emphasized the various ways in which social closure is secured, with the most important of these being the well-known institutional devices of private property and credentialism. As Parkin notes, the institution of private property "prevents general access to the means of production," while that of credentialism "controls and monitors entry to key positions in the division of labor" (Parkin 1979:48). Although closure theory provides a (relatively) new language for understanding how class boundaries are defended, the actual class mappings posited by closure theorists have so far proven to be standard aggregate fare. For example, Parkin (1979:58) proposes a two-class solution for modern capitalism, with the exclusion-

FIGURE 4.4 Densities of Mobility and Persistence for Three-Dimensional Heterogeneous Association Model

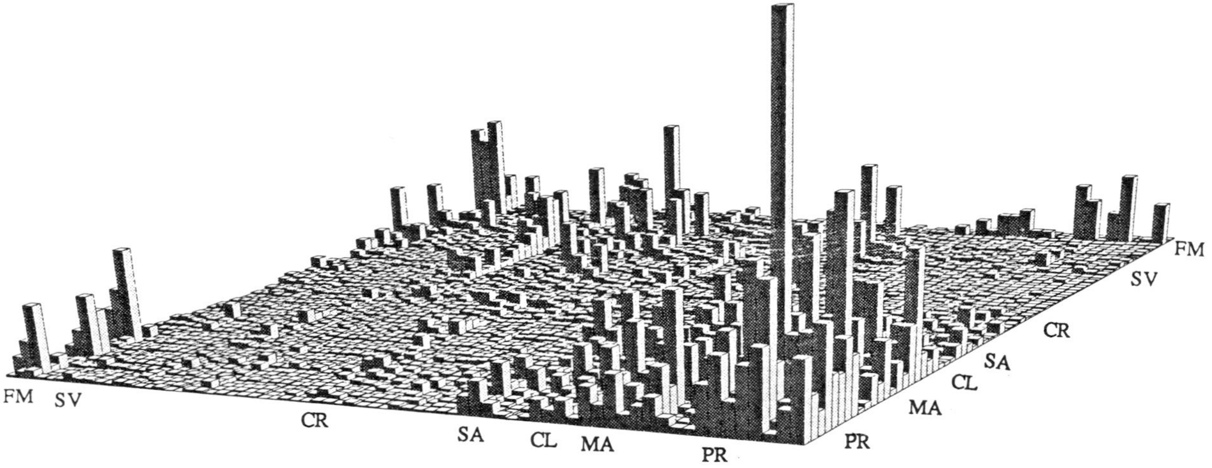

Note: The occupational categories are labeled as follows: PR = professionals; MA = managers; CL = clericals; SA = sales; CR = craft and operatives; SV = service workers; FM = farm. The left-hand labels index occupational origins, and the right-hand labels index occupational destinations. For purposes of presentation, the 96 cells with densities greater than 11 were rescaled by the formula: $10 + (D^{*}_{ij} - 10)^{2/3}$.

TABLE 4.6 Correlations Between Scale Values and External Variables for Three-Dimensional Heterogeneous Association Model

	\multicolumn{6}{c}{External Variables}
Scale Values	STAT	AUTON	FARM	COM1	COM2	COM3
μ_{i1}	0.828	0.131	0.094	0.773	0.655	0.514
μ_{i2}	0.347	−0.268	−0.474	0.093	0.037	0.156
μ_{i3}	0.152	−0.094	−0.051	0.195	−0.072	−0.479
v_{j1}	0.841	0.011	0.126	0.757	0.705	0.503
v_{j2}	0.220	−0.198	−0.373	0.128	−0.166	0.090
v_{j3}	0.116	−0.076	−0.239	−0.036	−0.104	−0.446

Note: μ_{i1} = first dimension row scores; μ_{i2} = second dimension row scores; μ_{i3} = third dimension row scores v_{j1} = first dimension column scores; v_{j2} = second dimension column scores; v_{j3} = third dimension column scores; STAT = Duncan socioeconomic index; AUTON = autonomy; FARM = farming dummy variable; COM1 = substantive complexity pertaining to data; COM2 = substantive complexity pertaining to people; COM3 = substantive complexity pertaining to things.

ary class comprising those who control productive capital and professional services, and the subordinate class comprising all those who are excluded from these positions of control (also, Giddens 1973:107–12; Weber 1922/1968).

The question that emerges here is whether an aggregate formulation is a necessary feature of closure theory or merely a superfluous adjunct. We favor the latter interpretation. If closure theory could somehow be reinvented without the coloration of class analytic convention, its authors would likely emphasize that the fundamental institutions of closure (i.e., professional associations, craft unions) represent the interests of *occupational* incumbents and thus impose barriers to *occupational* entry. As Murphy (1988:174) concedes, the closure rules of advanced capitalism are "not defined broadly, [but] are usually imposed by an association representing the credential-holders themselves." We appreciate that many occupations are relatively unformed; however, where explicit rules of closure *have* been successfully established, one typically finds them implemented at the level of occupations rather than classes. The longstanding attempt to identify a single "exclusionary bourgeoisie" (Parkin 1979) is therefore doubly problematic. That is, such conceptual efforts not only misrepresent the analytic level at which exclusionary barriers are drawn, but they also ignore the many pockets of exclusionary closure that are found within craft, service, and other subordinate occupations.

This disaggregate version of closure theory is clearly inconsistent with the standard practice of carrying out class analyses of social mobility. The results from these conventional analyses have been variously interpreted, but it is becoming increasingly fashionable to characterize modern exchange as so fluid, permeable, and inchoate that "exclusionary institutions do not seem to be designed first and foremost to solve the problem of class reproduction" (Parkin 1979:62; see also Kingston 1994). The latter conclusion is potentially misleading, since it rests on data that conceal exclusionary practices operating at the occupational level. There are at least two ways in which occupation-specific credentials protect incumbents from the hazards of the marketplace: they provide long-term "tenure" by guaranteeing the competence of credential-holders for the duration of their careers, and they require such lengthy training (e.g., advanced schooling) that only workers at the beginning of their careers will seek to undertake the necessary investment (Sørensen 1983; Sørensen and Kalleberg 1981). The principal barriers to inflow and outflow are thereby occupational in nature, and our estimate of persistence will be correspondingly muted insofar as mobility scholars continue to pitch their analyses at the level of aggregate classes.

This argument is supported by our results. When conventional mobility tables are disaggregated, we find that the "holding power" of many detailed occupations is quite strong, whereas that of aggregate classes is comparatively weak. If, then, the amount of intragenerational closure revealed in conventional research falls short of what reproduction theorists promised us (e.g., Bourdieu and Passeron 1977), this is not because bourgeois forms of closure are necessarily unreliable but rather because researchers have misspecified the analytic level at which closure is secured. We have also found that conventional aggregate classes conceal considerable heterogeneity in patterns of persistence and exchange. As revealed in Figure 4.2, pockets of hyper-rigidity appear in virtually all sectors of the occupational structure, thus belying the standard view that social closure is most prominent at the socioeconomic extremes. The sociological convention on interoccupational exchange is likewise misleading, since the principal cleavages and disjunctures in mobility chances are located within major classes rather than between them (see especially Figure 4.3). This set of results suggests that contour mappings of career mobility are quite sensitive to the level of aggregation that is adopted.

Although our analyses have been largely descriptive in orientation, we have also estimated a series of supplementary explanatory models, all of which yielded results of a largely negative sort. When our data are disaggregated to the occupational level, we find that conventional generic variables cannot provide a powerful account of occupational holding power, nor can they adequately explain the residual (nonsocioeconomic) dimensions underlying interoccupational exchange. We would therefore advocate for structural models that explain mobility and persistence in terms of more proximate occupational characteristics (e.g., Duncan 1975). These models can now be realistically pursued because disaggregation affords us the requisite degrees of freedom to measure and distinguish occupational effects that are strongly intercorrelated.

Notes

Direct all correspondence to Jesper B. Sørensen, Department of Sociology, University of Notre Dame, Notre Dame, Indiana, 46556. This research was carried out with support from the Presidential Young Investigator Program of the National Science Foundation (NSF SES-8858467) and the Stanford Center for the Study of Families, Children, and Youth. The data were kindly provided by the National Opinion Research Center and the University of Wisconsin Data and Program Library Service. We have presented earlier drafts of this essay to the American Sociological Association (Los Angeles, California), the Stanford Center for the Study of Families, Children, and Youth (Stanford, California), and the Working Group on the Problems of the Low-Income Population (Madison, Wisconsin). We are most grateful for the comments of James Baron, Diane Burton, Robert Hauser, Robert Mare, Robert Szafran, Szonja Szelényi, Donald Treiman, and Kimberly Weeden. The opinions expressed herein are nonetheless those of the authors alone.

1. To be sure, the residual category of "lateral shifts" is also conventionally analyzed, and here suboccupational forms of mobility perforce reappear. This residual category is nonetheless an amalgam of various levels of analysis, since it encompasses both job shifts occurring within the same occupation and those occurring between occupations that share the same status score.

2. The total number of sampling zeroes in our 70 × 70 table is 2,229.

3. While we were preparing this chapter, Kalmijn (1994) published a 70-category classification that bears some similarity to our own. This classification merges three-digit occupations that are "roughly similar with respect to industry and type of work" but at the same time distinguishes titles that are "similar in type of work and different in earnings or education" (Kalmijn 1994:429–30).

4. We were obviously obliged to accept the primitive classification decisions embedded in three-digit census codes. If we had instead recoded the original individual-level data, we would no doubt have produced a rather different classification.

5. We have also identified the marginal effects by constraining them to sum to zero.

6. The SAT model was originally devised for intergenerational mobility tables. Although some mobility scholars (e.g., Stier and Grusky 1990) have applied the

same model to intragenerational data, such extensions are not necessarily consistent with the intentions of Hout (1984).

7. These measures were operationalized with General Social Survey data (1974–1990) in accord with the protocol described by Hout (1984:1389–90).

8. The dependent variable in our specification is total persistence, whereas Hout (1984) sought to explain the residue of persistence that remained after purging all clustering arising by virtue of interoccupational distances.

9. These measures are drawn from the full set of 15 General Social Surveys covering the years between 1974 and 1990. The variables COM1, COM2, and COM3 are scored on an interval scale ranging from low to high complexity (see Cain and Treiman 1981).

10. We have constructed this list by carefully examining the results of Figure 4.2. If one wished to test formally the model implied by our listing, it would therefore be appropriate to rely on other data.

11. The axes for each dimension in Figure 4.3 have been scaled by the global association parameter (Φ_m) pertaining to that dimension.

12. We have again operationalized these variables in accord with the protocol that Hout (1984:1389–90) specifies.

13. In interpreting Table 4.6, we should bear in mind that the scale values have been orthogonalized (see equation 4), whereas the explanatory variables of interest are no doubt correlated with one another.

14. The SAT model may well provide a better account of intergenerational exchange. We shall test this fallback claim in a subsequent paper.

References

Blau, Peter M., and Otis D. Duncan. 1967. *The American Occupational Structure.* New York: Wiley.

Bourdieu, Pierre, and Jean-Claude Passeron. 1977. *Reproduction.* Beverly Hills, CA: Sage.

Braverman, Harry. 1974. *Labor and Monopoly Capital: The Degradation of Work in the Twentieth Century.* New York: Monthly Review Press.

Breiger, Ronald L. 1981. "The Social Class Structure of Occupational Mobility." *American Journal of Sociology* 87:578–611.

Cain, Pamela S., and Donald J. Treiman. 1981. "The Dictionary of Occupational Titles as a Source of Occupational Data." *American Sociological Review* 46:253–78.

Collins, Randall. 1979. *The Credential Society: An Historical Sociology of Education and Stratification.* New York: Academic.

Dictionary of Occupational Titles. 2nd Edition. 1949. Washington, DC: U.S. Government Printing Office.

Dictionary of Occupational Titles. 3rd Edition. 1965. Washington, DC: U.S. Government Printing Office.

Dictionary of Occupational Titles. 4th Edition. 1977. Washington, DC: U.S. Government Printing Office.

DiPrete, Thomas A. 1989. *The Bureaucratic Labor Market.* New York: Plenum Press.

Duncan, Otis D. 1975. *Introduction to Structural Equation Models*. New York: Academic Press.

Ehrenreich, Barbara, and John Ehrenreich. 1979. "The Professional-Managerial Class." Pp. 5–45 in Pat Walker (ed.), *Between Labor and Capital*. Boston: South End Press.

Erikson, Robert, and John H. Goldthorpe. 1992. *The Constant Flux: A Study of Class Mobility in Industrial Societies*. Oxford: Clarendon Press.

Evans, Mariah D., and Edward O. Laumann. 1978. "Professional Commitment: Myth or Reality?" Pp. 3–40 in Donald J. Treiman and Robert V. Robinson (eds.), *Research in Social Stratification and Mobility*. Greenwich, CT: JAI Press.

Featherman, David L., and Robert M. Hauser. 1977. "Commonalities in Social Stratification and Assumptions About Status Mobility in the United States." Pp. 3–50 in Robert M. Hauser and David L. Featherman (eds.), *The Process of Stratification: Trends and Analyses*. New York: Academic Press.

———. 1978. *Opportunity and Change*. New York: Academic Press.

Fukumoto, Ivan K., and David B. Grusky. 1993. "Social Mobility and Class Structure in Early-Industrial France." Pp. 40–67 in Andrew Miles and David Vincent (eds.), *Building European Society: Occupational Change and Social Mobility in Europe, 1840–1940*. Manchester: Manchester University Press.

Giddens, Anthony. 1973. *The Class Structure of the Advanced Societies*. New York: Harper and Row.

Goldthorpe, John H. 1980. *Social Mobility and Class Structure in Modern Britain*. Oxford: Clarendon Press.

Goldthorpe, John H., and Gordon Marshall. 1992. "The Promising Future of Class Analysis: A Response to Recent Critiques." *Sociology* 26:381–400.

Goodman, Leo A. 1979. "Multiplicative Models for the Analysis of Occupational Mobility Tables and Other Kinds of Cross-Classification Tables." *American Journal of Sociology* 84:804–19.

———. 1981a. "Association Models and Canonical Correlation in the Analysis of Cross-Classifications Having Ordered Categories." *Journal of the American Statistical Association* 76:320–34.

———. 1981b. "Criteria for Determining Whether Certain Categories in a Cross-Classification Table Should Be Combined, with Special Reference to Occupational Categories in an Occupational Mobility Table." *American Journal of Sociology* 87:612–50.

———. 1981c. "Three Elementary Views of Log Linear Models for the Analysis of Cross-Classifications Having Ordered Categories." Pp. 193–239 in Samuel Leinhardt (ed.), *Sociological Methodology, 1981*. San Francisco: Jossey-Bass.

———. 1987. "New Methods for Analyzing the Intrinsic Character of Qualitative Variables Using Cross-Classified Data." *American Journal of Sociology* 93:529–83.

Gouldner, Alvin. 1979. *The Future of Intellectuals and the Rise of the New Class*. New York: Seabury.

Grusky, David B., and Ivan K. Fukumoto. 1989. "A Sociological Approach to Historical Social Mobility." *Journal of Social History* 23:221–32.

Grusky, David B., and Robert M. Hauser. 1984. "Comparative Social Mobility Revisited: Models of Convergence and Divergence in 16 Countries." *American Sociological Review* 49:19–38.

Grusky, David B., and Jesper B. Sørensen. 1995. "Are Class Models Salvageable?" Working paper, Department of Sociology, Stanford University.

Hauser, Robert M. 1978. "A Structural Model of the Mobility Table." *Social Forces* 56:919–53.

Hauser, Robert M., and John A. Logan. 1992. "How Not to Measure Intergenerational Occupational Persistence." *American Journal of Sociology* 97:1689–711.

Holton, Robert J., and Bryan S. Turner. 1989. *Max Weber on Economy and Society*. London: Routledge and Kegan Paul.

Hope, Keith. 1972. "Quantifying Constraints on Social Mobility: The Latent Hierarchies of a Contingency Table." Pp. 121–90 in Keith Hope (ed.), *The Analysis of Social Mobility: Methods and Approaches*. Oxford: Clarendon Press.

Hout, Michael. 1984. "Status, Autonomy, and Training in Occupational Mobility." *American Journal of Sociology* 89:1379–409.

———. 1988. "More Universalism, Less Structural Mobility: The American Occupational Structure in the 1980s." *American Journal of Sociology* 93:1358–1400.

———. 1989. *Following in Father's Footsteps*. Cambridge: Harvard University Press.

Hout, Michael, and John A. Jackson. 1986. "Dimensions of Occupational Mobility in the Republic of Ireland." *European Sociological Review* 2:114–37.

Jacobs, Jerry A., and Ronald L. Breiger. 1988. "Careers, Industries, and Occupations." Pp. 43–63 in George Farkas and Paula England (eds.), *Industries, Firms, and Jobs*. New York: Plenum Press.

Kalmijn, Matthijs. 1994. "Assortative Mating by Cultural and Economic Occupational Status." *American Journal of Sociology* 100:422–52.

Kingston, Paul W. 1994. "Are There Classes in the United States?" Pp. 3–41 in Robert Althauser and Michael Wallace (eds.), *Research in Social Stratification and Mobility*, Volume 13. Greenwich, CT: JAI Press.

Lockwood, David. 1958. *The Blackcoated Worker*. London: George Allen and Unwin.

MacDonald, K. I. 1981. "On the Formulation of a Structural Model of the Mobility Table." *Social Forces* 60:557–71.

Manza, Jeff. 1992. "Classes, Status Groups, and Social Closure: A Critique of Neo-Weberian Social Theory." Pp. 275–302 in Ben Agger (ed.), *Current Perspectives in Social Theory*. Greenwich, CT: JAI Press.

Marx, Karl. (1894) 1964. *Selected Works*, Volume 1. Moscow: Progress Publishers.

Menken, Jane. 1987. "Proximate Determinants of Fertility and Mortality: A Review of Recent Findings." *Sociological Forum* 2:697–717.

Murphy, Raymond. 1988. *Social Closure: The Theory of Monopolization and Exclusion*. Oxford: Clarendon Press.

Parkin, Frank. 1971. *Class Inequality and Political Order: Social Stratification in Capitalist and Communist Societies*. New York: Praeger Press.

———. 1979. *Marxism and Class Theory: A Bourgeois Critique*. New York: Columbia University Press.

Raftery, Adrian. 1986. "Choosing Models for Cross-Classifications." *American Sociological Review* 51:145–6.

Rytina, Steven L. 1992. "Return to Normality: Simple Structure for the Mobility Table and the Symmetric Scaling of Intergenerational Continuity." Working paper, Department of Sociology, McGill University.
Smith, Herbert L., and Maurice A. Garnier. 1987. "Scaling via Models for the Analysis of Association: Social Background and Educational Careers in France." Pp. 205–45 in Clifford C. Clogg (ed.), *Sociological Methodology, 1987.* San Francisco: Jossey-Bass.
Snipp, C. Matthew. 1985. "Occupational Mobility and Social Class: Insights from Men's Career Mobility." *American Sociological Review* 50:475–93.
Sørensen, Aage B. 1983. "Processes of Allocation to Open and Closed Positions in Social Structure." *Zeitschrift für Soziologie* 12:203–24.
Sørensen, Aage B., and Arne L. Kalleberg. 1981. "An Outline of a Theory of the Matching of Persons to Jobs." Pp. 49–74 in Ivar Berg (ed.), *Sociological Perspectives on Labor Markets.* New York: Academic Press.
Sørensen, Aage B., and Nancy B. Tuma. 1981. "Labor Market Structures and Job Mobility." Pp. 67–94 in R. Robinson (ed.), *Research in Social Stratification and Mobility,* Volume 1. Greenwich, CT.: JAI Press.
Sorokin, Pitirim A. (1927) 1959. *Social and Cultural Mobility.* Glencoe, IL: Free Press.
Spilerman, Seymour. 1977. "Careers, Labor Market Structure, and Socioeconomic Achievement." *American Journal of Sociology* 83:551–93.
Stier, Haya, and David B. Grusky. 1990. "An Overlapping Persistence Model of Career Mobility." *American Sociological Review* 55:736–56.
Weber, Max. (1968) 1922. *Economy and Society.* New York: Bedminster Press.
Wright, Erik O. 1985. *Classes.* London: Verso Press.

Appendix to Chapter 4

TABLE 4A.1 Mapping of Detailed Occupational Classification into 1960 Census Occupational Codes

Code	Title	1960 Census Classification
A. Professionals		
101	Jurists	105
102	Health professionals	162, 071, 194, 160, 152, 153, 022
103	Architects and engineers	013, 082, 083, 080, 085, 081, 090, 091, 084, 093, 092
104	Professors and instructors	031, 032, 034, 035, 040, 041, 042, 043, 045, 050, 051, 052, 053, 054, 060, 030
105	Authors, journalists, and related writers	020, 075, 163
106	Scientists	021, 140, 145, 134, 131, 130, 174, 135, 172, 173, 175

(continued)

TABLE 4A.1 (continued)

Code	Title	1960 Census Classification
107	Accountants	000
108	Elementary and secondary school teachers	183, 182, 184
109	Aircraft and ship officers	012, 265
110	Nonmedical technicians	181, 074, 190, 192, 191
111	Funeral directors and embalmers	104
112	Creative Artists	014, 072, 120, 070, 010, 101
113	Workers in religion	023, 170
114	Health semiprofessionals	185, 303, 073, 150, 151, 842, 840, 193
115	Professional, technical, and related workers, n.e.c.	102, 420, 161, 195, 015, 180, 103, 154, 164, 111, 171, 165
B. Managers		
201	Buyers	250, 285, 251
202	Government officials	280, 270, 260
203	Managers and proprietors, lodging and building	262, 821
204	Managers, officials, and proprietors, n.e.c.	254, 290, 253, 275
C. Clerical		
301	Office support staff	345, 360, 342, 325, 341, 302, 320
302	Bookkeepers, cashiers, and related workers	310, 312, 305, 354, 333, 313
303	Postal and mail distribution clerks	340, 323, 315, 324, 351
304	Telephone and telegraph operators	353, 352
305	Stock and shipping clerks	350, 343
306	Clerical workers, n.e.c.	314, 370, 321
D. Sales		
401	Agents and brokers	301, 385, 393, 395, 380, 381
402	Salesman and shop assistants	394, 382, 383

(continued)

TABLE 4A.1   (continued)

Code	Title	1960 Census Classification
E. Craft and operative		
501	Printers and related workers	414, 512, 423, 424, 503, 404, 695, 615
502	Foremen	430
503	Electrical and electronics workers	474, 421, 453, 604
504	Locomotive operators	454, 460, 690, 640, 713
505	Stationary engine operators	701, 520, 712
506	Jewelers, opticians, and precious metal workers	451, 494
507	Blacksmiths, toolmakers, and machinetool operators	402, 431, 492, 530, 502, 452, 653, 614
508	Machinists and millwrights	465, 491, 605
509	Plumbers, welders, and related metal workers	510, 721, 525, 403, 523, 612
510	Food product workers	490, 675
511	Inspectors and checkers	450, 643, 654, 671
512	Mechanics	472, 475, 471, 470, 473, 480, 601, 610, 692, 963
513	Cabinetmakers	410
514	Heavy machinery operators	415, 425
515	Bakers	401
516	Bricklayers, carpenters, and related construction workers	405, 413, 514, 411, 960, 505, 630, 434, 501, 602, 603, 613
517	Metal processors	513, 435, 670, 672
518	Tailors and related workers	524, 651, 432, 680, 705, 535, 515
519	Assemblers	631
520	Painters	495, 694
521	Miners and related workers	685, 634
522	Truck drivers	715, 971, 972
523	Textile workers	710, 461, 720, 673, 652
524	Fishermen	962
525	Longshoremen and freight handlers	965, 973, 841

(continued)

TABLE 4A.1 (continued)

Code	Title	1960 Census Classification
526	Sawyers and lumber inspectors	704, 444
527	Forestry workers	970
528	Craftsmen and kindred workers, n.e.c.	521, 493, 504, 545, 620, 621
529	Operatives and kindred workers, n.e.c.	693, 775, 642, 985, 703, 635
F. Service		
601	Transport conductors	252, 645
602	Protective service workers	850, 853, 852, 854
603	Newsboys and deliverymen	390, 650
604	Housekeeping workers	832, 802, 804, 801, 823
605	Mass transportation operators	714, 641, 691
606	Hairdressers	814, 843
607	Food service workers	825, 835, 875, 815, 830
608	Launderers and dry-cleaners	674, 803
609	Gardeners	964
610	Janitors and cleaners	834, 824
611	Service workers, n.e.c.	304, 632, 851, 890, 810, 812, 813, 831, 874, 820, 860
G. Farm		
701	Farm managers and foremen	222, 901
702	Farmers	200, 903
703	Farm laborers	902, 905
H. Other		
999	Members of armed forces	555
0	Occupation not reported	990, 991, 993, 995, 999

PART THREE

Demographic Aspects of Social Differentiation

5

Demography and the Evolution of Educational Inequality

Robert D. Mare

An often controversial feature of human societies is that not all groups reproduce at the same rate. Differences in fertility rates across social strata arouse concern because they portend changes in patterns of dominance, inequality, or average well-being. For example, a recent, widely publicized book on inequality in the United States expresses apprehension about the presumed "dysgenic" effects of the relatively high rates of fertility among persons with low education and intelligence (Herrnstein and Murray 1994). That fertility rates for low-ability and low-education women are relatively high, the authors argue, is likely to diminish the country's average intellectual ability and to polarize a small "cognitive elite" and a growing number of persons who have limited intellectual and economic capacity. Ironically, others have looked at the same demographic phenomena and drawn diametrically opposite conclusions. For example, in his classic statement about the connections between demography and social stratification, Sibley (1942) warned of the dire effects of reduced immigration and lowered fertility differentials. A large, steady influx of persons with low socioeconomic origins, he believed, is essential to maintain high rates of upward social mobility and to offset the class conflict that occurs in a demographically static society. In this chapter I appraise some of these concerns by examining the effects of variation in demographic rates on trends in the distribution of formal schooling. More specifically, I examine the combined effects of differential fertility, differential mortality, and intergenerational educational mobility on the distribution of educational attainment in the United States for women during the past half century.

Although this essay is stimulated by contemporary public discussion of social inequality, it is motivated by conceptual and technical issues in the analysis of social stratification as well. To understand how a social hierarchy, such as the distribution of formal schooling, is maintained or modified over time, one must examine the process by which a socioeconomically differentiated population reproduces itself. The dominant approach to such problems in the literature on social stratification and mobility has been to focus on the intergenerational transmission of socioeconomic status. The paradigm of intergenerational mobility research, pioneered by Duncan and Hodge (1963) and Blau and Duncan (1967) and sustained by three decades of subsequent work, has been well suited to describing the associations between the socioeconomic positions of parents and offspring and to elucidating the mechanisms that underpin these associations. Yet although these studies show superficially how socioeconomic distributions in one generation give rise to distributions in a subsequent generation, they do not reveal how intergenerational mobility is implicated in changing those distributions from one period to the next. Indeed, Duncan (1966) showed that the measurements of family background used in typical surveys of stratification do not represent any specific cohort or period and thus standard social mobility tables are not the appropriate transition matrices required for transforming a population over time. Unfortunately, Duncan's argument has, for the most part, not served as a challenge to solve this problem. Rather, most researchers have simply lived with this limitation of their models.[1]

As a result of this limitation, stratification research has been ill equipped to handle such aggregate, dynamic questions as: How is the socioeconomic (for example, occupational or educational) distribution for persons or families in one period transformed into the distribution at a later period? How does intergenerational and intragenerational mobility contribute to that transformation? What do status transmission, differentials in levels and timing of fertility, and exogenous change in socioeconomic opportunity contribute to the transformation of socioeconomic hierarchies? How have demographic constraints on opportunity structures affected stratification processes? How have these effects changed over time? These central questions of stratification research require different models from those that are in widespread use and a change in orientation away from exclusive focus on microlevel statistical relationships.

To address these sorts of questions requires that one acknowledge that social mobility occurs within a demographic milieu and that the evolution and transformation of social hierarchies is the joint outcome of demographic metabolism, intergenerational transmission, and opportunity structure. It is important to distinguish between the intergenerational *transmission* of socioeconomic status—that is, the individual- or family-level processes by which parents affect the life chances of their offspring—and the *reproduction* of socioeconomic hierarchies—that is, the population-level processes by which distributions of social statuses and positions persist or evolve. An account of how a socioeconomically diverse population is transformed requires that one take account of not only social mobility but also age structure, differential fertility, assortative mating, family structure, differential mortality, and immigration.[2]

In this essay I employ a simple model for the reproduction of educational hierarchies that takes differential fertility, age structure, differential mortality, and social mobility into account. This is but the first stage in a larger research agenda, which attempts to take fuller account of the interdependence of the intergenerational transmission of inequality and the demographic milieu within which it occurs. The balance of this chapter is as follows. First, I link the present effort to past literature that has presented models and analyses of social mobility, fertility, and socioeconomic reproduction. Second, I present the specific empirical questions that guide this investigation. Third, I review trends in educational attainment and education differences in fertility during the past five decades. This provides the historical and demographic context for this research. Fourth, I describe the analytic approach I take including a projection model that takes account of population heterogeneity in both age and socioeconomic standing and the data sources used in the analysis. Fifth, I present the empirical results. Finally, after summarizing the conclusions of the analysis, I present an agenda for further work on the reproduction of socioeconomic hierarchies.

Links to Previous Literature

Although most sociological research has neglected the interplay between demographic processes and the levels and distributions of socioeconomic traits, several sociologists and demographers have examined the relationship between fertility and intergenerational mobility.[3] Matras (1961, 1967) presented a projection model for a one-sex population differentiated by both age and occupation. Preston (1974) analyzed the implications of differential fertility for differences in occupation distributions and occupational mobility opportunities for black and white men. Preston's approach is an important point of departure for the analyses reported here. Johnson (1980) sketched a two-sex population model of assortative mating, differential fertility, and the intergenerational transmission of religious affiliation. Lam (1986) examined the effects of differential fertility and intergenerational mobility on the time path of income inequality in Brazil. Preston and Campbell (1993) developed a two-sex model for the intergenerational transmission of intelligence (IQ). They showed that, under broad conditions, fixed rates of fertility and assortative mating by level of IQ lead to a stable distribution of IQ rather than, as intuition might suggest, to a distribution that is increasingly concentrated at the level of IQ where fertility is highest.

The present investigation is similar in spirit to these prior studies but also differs in several important respects. First, it focuses on formal educational attainment rather than IQ, occupation, or income. The distribution of formal schooling is clearly of interest for the reasons suggested above. It may, moreover, be especially well suited to an investigation of the effects of differential fertility on distributional outcomes relative to occupation or income. Whereas educational attainment is heavily affected by the resources and preferences of individuals and their families, occupational and income attainment are more strongly constrained by opportunity structures. The arguments I investigate and the models I use assume that social mobility and fertility are separable at the aggregate level. They do not allow for the possibility that patterns of fertility may interact with the structure of available socioeconomic outcomes to force changes in patterns of social mobility (Preston 1974). The latter type of effect occurs when socioeconomic distributions are determined by a relatively fixed distribution of socioeconomic opportunities that are, in turn, established by the demand for labor of various types. It is widely believed that occupational and income mobility are largely determined by demand rather than the supply of individuals with varying characteristics (e.g., Baron 1994). In the twentieth-century United States, however, it is likely that educational opportunities have not been seriously constrained by a relatively fixed number of educational "slots." Insofar as personal and family resources and preferences have been the principal forces behind educational change, it is sensible to analyze the combined effects of differential fertility and mobility on educational outcomes.

Second, the present study examines the effects of differentials in demographic rates in somewhat more detail than most prior studies. Unlike the previous studies that have examined the effects of fertility differentials, the present study considers the separate effects of both the *level* and the *timing* of fertility. To accomplish this, I follow Matras and develop a projection model that incorporates the effects of the age pattern of fertility. In addition, I investigate the effects of differential mortality as well as fertility.

Finally, the emphasis in this analysis is on the effects of the observed historical sequence of fertility rates on educational growth from 1950 to 1990 rather than on the theoretical issue of deriving the equilibrium distributions of socioeconomic outcomes. Whereas these equilibria are useful for illustrating the long-run implications of a given regime of vital rates, they are less well suited to providing an assessment of the quantitative historical importance of demographic rates for changes in socioeconomic distributions.

Research Questions and Conjectures

Within the framework described thus far, I investigate the following questions:

1. Fertility levels during the past several decades have usually varied inversely with the educational attainment of women. This does suggest that more poorly educated women reproduce themselves at a higher rate than women with higher levels of schooling and that ceteris paribus fertility differentials may have reduced average levels of educational attainment below what they would have been in the absence of such differentials. As shown below, however, the strength of these differentials has varied over time, suggesting that the effect might not be uniformly strong. It therefore remains an empirical issue whether the differential fertility of persons of diverse socioeconomic origins affected the trend in average educational attainment and the inequality of schooling during the past 50 years, how large this effect is, and how the current educational distribution would be different if all groups had had the same level of fertility from 1940 to 1990.

2. Insofar as fertility does affect the level and distribution of schooling, are there separate effects of variation in both the *level* and the *timing* of fertility among socioeconomic groups? Given that more highly educated women bear their children, on average, at a later age, that pattern, too, should reduce average educational attainment in the population. (That is, absent historical patterns of fertility timing, education would have been higher.) But it remains an open question how large this effect has been. As discussed more fully below, differentials in the timing of fertility have varied over the past half century. The timing of fertility, moreover, has a secondary effect on population growth compared to fertility levels (for example, Keyfitz 1968), suggesting that timing effects may be smaller than those of the level of fertility.

3. Whatever the historical effect of differential fertility, what are the implications of the large recent patterns of differential fertility? How would the trend in the distribution of schooling have been different if recent fertility differentials had been in effect throughout the past several decades?

4. Does differential mortality have an important effect on the level and distribution of schooling? Mortality differentials should favor higher attainment because women who have more poorly educated children are

less likely to survive to their childbearing years and to survive to adulthood generally. Because mortality rates are low for all groups during this period, however, this effect may not be large.

5. The degree to which fertility affects socioeconomic distributions is conditional on the openness of socioeconomic groups. That is, differential fertility has a stronger effect when socioeconomic groups are more closed to intergenerational mobility and a weaker effect when mobility is greater. How big is this interaction between differential fertility and the rate of intergenerational mobility? If mobility chances were to change, would the effects of demographic rates become more or less important than they are now?

Trends in Educational Attainment, 1940–1990

During the past 50 years in the United States, average educational attainment has grown tremendously. As shown in Table 5.1 and Figure 5.1, which report the educational attainment of women in each decade, formal attainment grew primarily through a decline in the proportion of persons who fail to complete high school and a corresponding growth in those who complete at least some postsecondary schooling. From 1940 to 1990 for 20 to 49-year-old women, average years of school completed increased by about 3.5 years, the percentage who completed more than high school almost quadrupled, and the percentage who failed to complete high school was cut by about four-fifths. Despite substantial educational growth, women who have completed exactly 12 years of schooling remain the modal educational group in 1990.

Table 5.1 also reports Theil's (1972) entropy measure (H) for the distribution of educational attainment in each period. H measures the degree of dispersion of a discrete distribution, in this case the five categories of educational attainment used in Figure 5.1. For a five-category distribution, H varies from zero (all persons are in the same category) to approximately 1.6 (a uniform distribution).[4] By this measure, the inequality of the education distribution for 20 to 49-year-old women increased between 1940 and 1960 and decreased thereafter. This reflects the change in concentration of the education distribution from the lowest levels of attainment, to a greater degree of uniformity across all categories, and finally to the highest levels of attainment. This curvilinear pattern of change in H holds for all ages, but inequality tends to peak in earlier decades for the youngest women and in later decades for the oldest. This is not surprising inasmuch as the growth of schooling occurs primarily as a process of cohort replacement.

Although these trends are well known (see, for example, Mare 1995), one should keep them in mind in considering the impact of trends in fer-

TABLE 5.1 Trends in Women's Educational Attainment in the United States, 1940–1990

Age		1940	1950	1960	1970	1980	1990
20–24	Avg. Yrs. Completed	10.28	10.87	11.44	12.28	12.58	12.83
	H (entropy)	0.607	0.617	0.606	0.598	0.579	0.590
	% < 12 yrs.	51.93	43.16	34.81	21.01	16.38	14.50
	% > 12 yrs.	12.48	16.54	21.31	34.45	40.65	47.03
25–29	Avg. Yrs. Completed	9.96	10.73	11.26	12.08	12.91	13.08
	H (entropy)	0.615	0.619	0.623	0.617	0.611	0.600
	% < 12 yrs.	58.69	45.23	38.46	26.49	15.31	12.99
	% > 12 yrs.	13.23	15.03	18.92	27.74	43.33	45.34
30–34	Avg. Yrs. Completed	9.70	10.38	11.04	11.70	12.79	13.15
	H (entropy)	0.610	0.624	0.628	0.618	0.617	0.600
	% < 12 yrs.	63.22	51.44	42.06	31.53	16.75	12.29
	% > 12 yrs.	14.39	14.35	17.77	22.95	41.17	46.83
35–39	Avg. Yrs. Completed	9.28	9.99	10.85	11.44	12.41	13.21
	H (entropy)	0.577	0.621	0.623	0.622	0.623	0.596
	% < 12 yrs.	68.84	58.31	43.44	35.35	21.45	11.40
	% > 12 yrs.	13.08	14.43	16.39	20.53	34.45	48.02
40–44	Avg. Yrs. Completed	8.99	9.75	10.48	11.23	12.03	13.05
	H (entropy)	0.546	0.614	0.630	0.630	0.626	0.601
	% < 12 yrs.	72.02	62.29	50.22	39.31	26.35	12.88
	% > 12 yrs.	11.46	15.60	15.43	19.34	28.79	44.71
45–49	Avg. Yrs. Completed	8.35	9.32	10.04	11.00	11.80	12.66
	H (entropy)	0.462	0.579	0.626	0.627	0.628	0.617
	% < 12 yrs.	79.49	67.70	57.83	41.87	29.77	17.97
	% > 12 yrs.	8.54	13.86	15.14	17.56	25.69	38.11
20–49	Avg. Yrs. Completed	9.52	10.23	10.85	11.67	12.51	13.02
	H (entropy)	0.591	0.626	0.632	0.628	0.620	0.605
	% < 12 yrs.	64.33	53.78	44.48	31.84	19.77	13.42
	% > 12 yrs.	12.34	15.01	17.44	24.46	37.17	45.38

Source: 1940–1980 U.S. censuses and March 1990 current population survey.

FIGURE 5.1 Trends in the Distribution of Schooling, 1940–1990 Women Aged 20–49

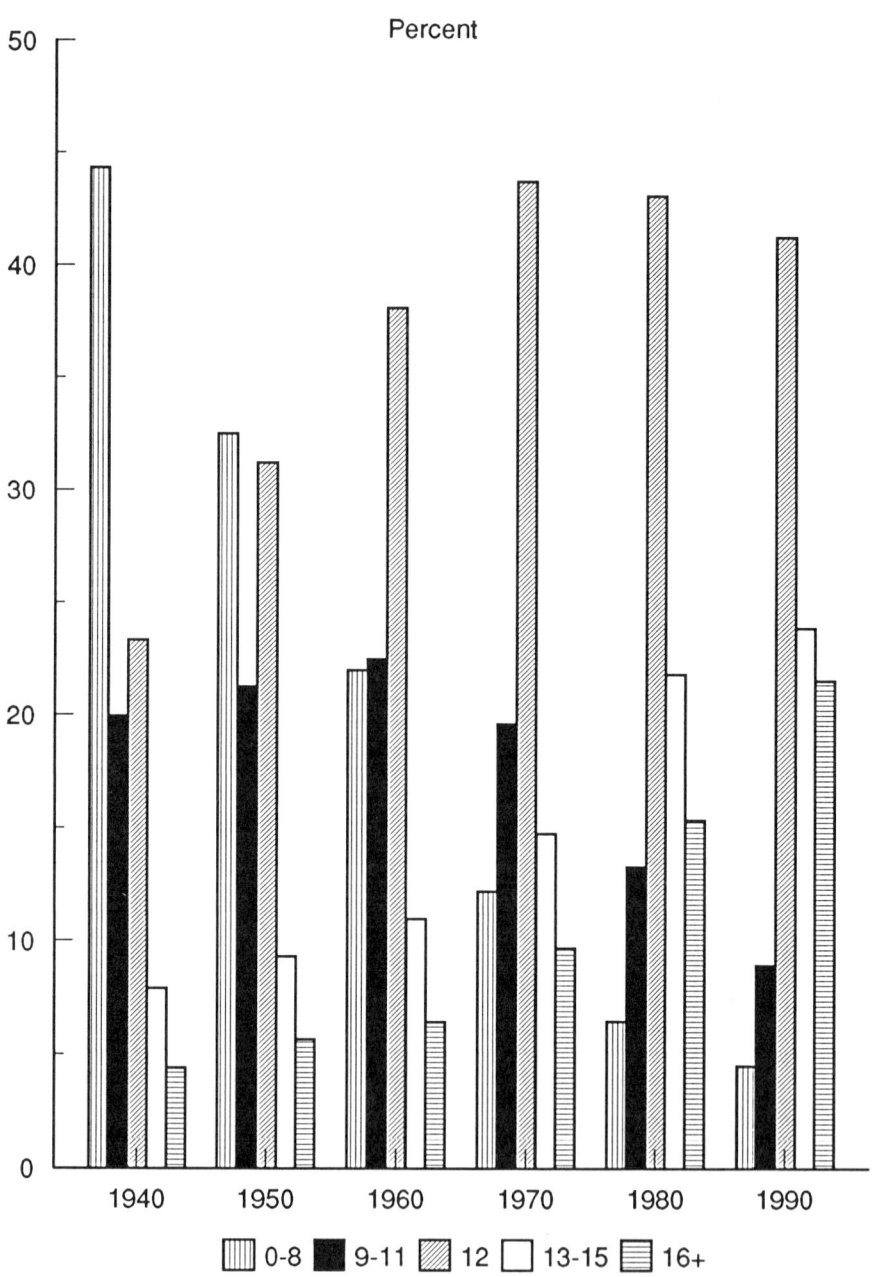

Source: 1940–1980 U.S. census and March current population survey.

tility and mortality on the evolution of educational distributions. Whatever the harmful impact of fertility differentials on average educational attainment, it has not been enough to offset the large surge in attainment during the past 50 years. The size of the estimated effects of demographic rates should, moreover, be appraised in light of the scale of the total observed change in educational attainment over this period.

Trends in Fertility

Both levels and socioeconomic differences in fertility in the United States have fluctuated considerably over the past 50 years. Table 5.2 summarizes the trends in age-specific fertility from 1945 to 1990.[5] (The sources for these fertility estimates are discussed below.) Over this period, women at each level of education experience a common trend in fertility, which rises sharply from immediately after World War II to 1960, which constitutes the peak of the baby boom, and falls precipitously thereafter (e.g., Rindfuss and Sweet 1977). Within most periods women with more schooling tend to bear children at a lower rate than their more poorly educated counterparts, but there are important exceptions to this trend. In 1970 and 1980, women with a high school degree but no further schooling exhibit the highest fertility rates. Strikingly, it is in the most recent year shown in the table that the negative correlation between mother's schooling and fertility is the largest. These large recent differentials are one source of the concern raised in some recent commentary about the implications of differential fertility (Herrnstein and Murray 1994; 348–51).

Education groups vary in the timing as well as the level of their childbearing. For the most part, women with relatively small amounts of schooling tend to bear their children earlier than women who leave school later. Here again, however, 1970 and 1980 are exceptions inasmuch as women who are high school graduates tend to have the lowest mean age of childbearing. Table 5.2 also shows that more highly educated women tend to compress their childbearing into a narrower time interval. In every year the least-educated women have a standard deviation of age at childbearing that is about one and a half years greater than women with a college degree. This pattern reflects that women who leave school later have a shorter period during which they are exposed to the risk of childbearing without the competing activity of school attendance.

The fertility trends shown in Table 5.2 do indicate that women with lower amounts of schooling have higher levels of fertility, earlier fertility, and more broadly spaced fertility than more highly educated women. Taken together, these patterns suggest that the more poorly educated part of the population is growing more rapidly than the better educated part. That there are exceptions to the general pattern of fertility differentials,

TABLE 5.2 Trends in Fertility, 1945–1990

Age	Education	1945	1950	1960	1970	1980	1990
		Age-specific Female Fertility Rates					
	0–8	40.0	64.3	71.5	9.3	14.4	24.6
	9–11	31.3	58.7	85.6	28.8	23.5	28.9
15–19	12	10.6	19.5	30.5	61.4	39.8	42.9
	1–15	5.8	7.9	12.0	26.1	13.3	17.6
	16+	2.7	1.9	3.7	0.0	0.0	0.0
	0–8	71.3	96.1	105.9	70.6	49.2	100.3
	9–11	62.7	95.0	123.7	108.1	85.5	117.6
20–24	12	52.4	83.2	119.9	99.2	70.8	76.4
	13–15	45.3	75.6	104.5	55.1	31.8	33.2
	16+	25.0	34.2	54.1	50.4	24.4	7.4
	0–8	62.0	73.5	90.0	48.6	32.8	75.7
	9–11	55.8	67.2	85.0	58.7	44.9	63.9
25–29	12	58.0	74.3	93.2	70.1	56.8	56.3
	13–15	62.6	85.0	99.8	77.0	57.3	65.9
	16+	57.2	79.6	95.8	83.1	57.5	38.4
	0–8	47.3	50.1	56.8	30.0	18.7	45.9
	9–11	41.8	42.0	49.7	30.0	19.7	30.0
30–34	12	44.1	48.6	55.1	33.3	24.7	30.3
	13–15	47.4	56.5	58.6	37.5	29.8	41.5
	16+	47.6	54.2	63.9	46.3	46.9	41.9
	0–8	28.7	27.8	30.9	16.9	9.4	24.4
	9–11	23.1	23.0	24.9	14.1	7.7	11.9
35–39	12	23.8	24.9	26.2	14.4	7.7	10.1
	13–15	26.3	26.4	26.1	14.2	8.9	14.9
	16+	25.8	30.6	28.3	16.4	14.8	20.2
	0–8	11.9	10.0	12.0	5.8	2.7	6.3
	9–11	8.8	6.6	8.1	3.7	2.0	2.3
40–44	12	7.4	7.4	7.7	4.0	1.6	1.7
	13–15	8.5	9.1	8.9	3.9	1.6	2.6
	16+	7.1	6.4	8.5	3.6	2.3	3.8

(continued)

TABLE 5.2 *(continued)*

Age	Education	1945	1950	1960	1970	1980	1990
		Gross Reproduction Rate					
	0–8	1.31	1.61	1.84	0.91	0.64	1.39
	9–11	1.12	1.46	1.88	1.22	0.92	1.27
15–44	12	0.98	1.29	1.66	1.41	1.01	1.09
	13–15	0.98	1.30	1.55	1.07	0.71	0.88
	16+	0.83	1.03	1.27	1.00	0.73	0.56
		Mean Age of Fertility Schedule					
	0–8	27.3	26.1	26.2	27.3	26.2	26.9
	9–11	27.3	25.7	25.2	25.5	25.0	25.2
15–44	12 –	28.5	27.5	26.7	24.9	24.9	25.0
	13–15	29.2	28.4	27.6	26.8	27.3	27.8
	16+	30.2	29.8	29.2	28.5	29.5	31.4
		Standard Deviation of Age of Fertility Schedule					
	0–8	6.92	6.71	6.69	5.95	5.94	5.96
	9–11	6.70	6.44	6.36	5.60	5.25	5.24
15–44	12	6.10	6.03	5.90	5.91	5.52	5.69
	13–15	5.91	5.74	5.65	5.77	5.37	5.69
	16+	5.51	5.28	5.38	4.84	4.67	4.68

Source: See text (pp.130–1).

however, makes it hard to know how important educational fertility differentials have been for educational growth during the past five decades.

A Projection Model for Demographic and Educational Change

To examine the effects of fertility, mortality, and mobility regimes on trends in educational distributions, I develop a projection model for a population differentiated by socioeconomic categories (in this case, educational attainment). This is a one-sex model and, in the present analysis, is applied only to women. Data on fertility rates for educational attainment groups are much more readily available and of higher quality for women than for men. Despite some differences in educational trends between the sexes, the general pattern of educational growth and distribution during the twentieth century has been similar for men and women.[6] As discussed in the conclusion, it is desirable to elaborate the analysis to incorporate both sexes simultaneously, but this is the subject of future work. Rates of fertility, mortality, and mobility are variables in the projection model. Thus, my strategy is to predict the trend in the distribution of schooling given an initial education distribution and alternative assumptions about demographic rates.

A model for intergenerational educational mobility can be developed through an analogy to well-established models for interregional mobility and population growth. The general discrete-time multiregional projection matrix for a single sex is discussed in detail by Feeney (1970), LeBras (1971), and Rogers (1975). (Broader classes of related models are described by Land and Rogers 1982 and Schoen 1988. The model for educational mobility I use is a special case of the general model. Suppose that a population is divided into A five-year age groups and R groups, which are regions in the context of geographic mobility or socioeconomic categories in the context of social mobility. Let P_t denote an $RA \times 1$ vector of population totals at time t, with typical entry P_{rat}, which is the population in the rth education group and the ath age group in the tth year ($r = 1, \ldots, R$; $a = 0-4, 5-9, \ldots, 45-49$; $t = 0, 5, \ldots, T$). The age-education-specific populations five years later are linked to the totals at time t by a multigroup projection matrix, that is,

$$M_t P_t = P_{t+5}. \tag{1}$$

M is an $RA \times RA$ matrix of transition probabilities with the following structure:

$$M_t = \begin{bmatrix} 0 & 0 & B_{10t} & B_{15t} & B_{20t} & B_{25t} & B_{30t} & B_{35t} & B_{40t} & B_{45t} \\ S_{0t} & 0 & 0 & 0 & 0 & 0 & 0 & 0 & 0 & 0 \\ 0 & S_{5t} & 0 & 0 & 0 & 0 & 0 & 0 & 0 & 0 \\ 0 & 0 & S_{10t} & 0 & 0 & 0 & 0 & 0 & 0 & 0 \\ 0 & 0 & 0 & S_{15t} & 0 & 0 & 0 & 0 & 0 & 0 \\ 0 & 0 & 0 & 0 & S_{20t} & 0 & 0 & 0 & 0 & 0 \\ 0 & 0 & 0 & 0 & 0 & S_{25t} & 0 & 0 & 0 & 0 \\ 0 & 0 & 0 & 0 & 0 & 0 & S_{30t} & 0 & 0 & 0 \\ 0 & 0 & 0 & 0 & 0 & 0 & 0 & S_{35t} & 0 & 0 \\ 0 & 0 & 0 & 0 & 0 & 0 & 0 & 0 & S_{40t} & 0 \end{bmatrix} \tag{2}$$

where the S_{0t}, S_{5t}, ... , S_{40t} are $R \times R$ submatrices of five-year age-specific survival and mobility probabilities and the B_{10t}, B_{15t}, ... , B_{45t} are $R \times R$ submatrices of 5-year age-specific birth and mobility probabilities, adjusted for maternal and childhood mortality. The typical element of submatrix S_{at}, S_{ijat}, is the probability that a woman aged a to $a + 5$ in group i at time t is living five years later in group j ($i = 1, ... , R$; $j = 1, ... , R$). The S_{ijat} reflect the joint processes of region-specific adult mortality and intragenerational mobility. The typical element of submatrix B_{at}, B_{ijat}, is the probability that a woman aged a to $a + 5$ in group i has a child who survives and is living five years later in group j. The B_{ijat} reflect the joint processes of region-specific fertility, adult mortality, child mortality, and intergenerational mobility.

When the multigroup projection model is applied to educational mobility, it is possible to simplify M_t. Inasmuch as one cannot "migrate" from a higher to a lower level of educational attainment (that is, all intragenerational educational mobility is upward), $S_{ijat} = 0$ whenever $i > j$. Thus, all of the S_{at} are upper triangular submatrices. Such a simplification does not apply to the B_{at} because both upward and downward intergenerational educational mobility is possible. One can further simplify the S_{at} if one assumes that all educational attainment is completed by a given age, say c. In this case the S_{at} are diagonal submatrices whenever $a > c$.

In practice I further simplify M_t because of data limitations and my intention to focus the analysis on intergenerational rather than intragenerational mobility. In particular, I assume that ultimate educational attainment is determined at birth; that is, that there is no intragenerational educational mobility.[7] This detracts somewhat from the realism of the model, but it is of no important consequence for the analysis of the effects of demographic rates and intergenerational mobility on education distributions. Furthermore, I focus on the educational distributions of women of childbearing age rather than all adults, although this restriction could easily be relaxed. Finally, I assume that fertility rates for women below age 15 or above age 45 are zero. Given these simplifications, the S_{at} are all diagonal submatrices in which the S_{ijat} equal the age-education-specific five-year survival rates if $i = j$ and equal zero if $i \neq j$. Specifically, when $i = j$, $S_{ijat} = {}_5L_{i,a+5,t} / {}_5L_{iat}$, where ${}_5L_{iat}$ is the life table population between ages a and $a + 5$ for education group i in year t.

A typical element of the B_{at} submatrices, B_{ijat}, incorporates information on the fertility of women aged a to $a + 5$, the survival of women during that age interval, the mortality of children during the first five years of life, and the probabilities that mothers in education group i have daughters who attain education group j. That is,

$$B_{ijat} = {}_5L_{i0t} (F_{iat} + S_{iat} F_{i, a + 5, t}) M_{ijt}, \qquad (3)$$

where ${}_5L_{i0t}$ denotes the life table population between ages zero and five for the offspring of mothers in education group i in year t, F_{iat} denotes the rate of female births to women aged a to $a + 5$ in education group i in year t, S_{iat} denotes the age-education specific 5-year survival rate for women aged a to $a + 5$ in education group i in year t, and M_{ijt} denotes the proportion of mothers in year t in education group i whose daughters attain education group j.[8]

The basic ingredients of the projection model are the age-education-specific female fertility rates (F_{iat}) and survival rates (S_{iat}) and the educational mobility rates (M_{ijt}). By making alternative assumptions about how these quantities vary across education groups and over time, I explore the effects of demographic and mobility regimes on education distributions. Given the model; an assumed pattern of fertility, mortality, and mobility rates; and an initial population distribution, one can derive the subsequent sequence of population distributions. To simulate the impact of fertility patterns on recent educational distributions, it is necessary to use an initial distribution that is sufficiently far in the past that subsequent fertility rates completely determine the current distribution. For example, women aged 20 to 49 years in 1990 were born between 1940 and 1970. Thus to assess the effects of past fertility on this group of women, one must use an initial distribution for 1940 or earlier. For the simulations reported here, I use the age-education distribution of women aged 20 to 49 years in 1940 as the initial distribution. Using the 1950 population, a parallel set of projections yields very similar results to those reported here.

Data

Fertility

Data for estimating the projection model are taken from a variety of published and unpublished sources. For the age-education-specific fertility rates for the years 1945, 1950, 1955, 1960, and 1965, I use Rindfuss and Sweet's estimates derived by the "own children in the household" method from the 1960 and 1970 public use microdata samples of the census (Rindfuss 1976; Rindfuss and Sweet 1977).[9] A weakness of these estimates is that they have not been adjusted for maternal and child mortality, for children away from parents, and for undercount. Whereas the effect of not adjusting for child mortality and children who have left their parents' homes is to undercount the rate at which children are born to less-educated women, the effect of not adjusting for maternal mortality is likely to overestimate this rate. The effect of not adjusting for undercount on fertility differentials is unclear. On balance the net effects of these problems on estimated fertility differences are likely to be small. By this method the numerators of age-specific fertility rates for women aged a at a time t years prior to the census are the numbers of children present in the household who are t years of age at the census. The denominators are the numbers of women of a given education level at the census date who were aged a when the children were born t years before. One advantage of such measures is that the rates for women aged 15 to 19 are based on the reports (and thus the educational statuses) of women who are older than 15 to 19 and who thus have completed their schooling. Compared to contemporaneous fertility measures, the own-children estimates for 15 to 19-year-olds are more consistent with the assumption in the projection model of no intragenerational educational mobility

For 1970, 1975, 1980, 1985, and 1990, I use published vital statistics data on the annual numbers of births to women by educational attainment (National Center for Health Statistics 1975, 1978, 1984, 1988, 1993). To form age-education-specific fertility rates I use population denominators from published tables from the 1975, 1985, and 1990 current population surveys (U.S. Bureau of the Census 1976, 1987, 1992) and the 1970 and 1980 decennial censuses (U.S. Bureau of the Census 1973, 1984). The denominators have been adjusted for changes in the number of states for which information about educational attainment is obtained on the birth certificate. Unlike the fertility estimates based on own children in the household, the vital statistics data do not depend on the adequacy of coverage of children residing with their mothers. These data do, however, have the shortcoming that they are classified by the educational attainment of mothers at the time they give birth rather than by their ultimate educational attainment.[10]

Mortality

Mortality data for this study come from two sources. For adult women, I use the age-education-specific death probabilities from the 1960 Matched Records Study as reported by Kitagawa and Hauser (1973: table 2.8). For infants, I use infant mortality rates computed from the 1964–1966 National Sample Surveys of Natality and Mortality (National Center for Health Statistics 1970) and reported by Kitagawa and Hauser (1973: table 2.9). Mortality estimates specific to education groups are not available prior to 1960. Although estimates are available for the 1980s (Preston and Elo 1994; Elo and Preston 1995), I have elected to rely exclusively on the data for the early 1960s. They capture mortality experience during the middle of the 1940–1990 period and thus represent the conditions experienced by young adults and middle-aged persons in 1990. Using the 1960 and 1964–1966 rates and Model West Regional Model Life Tables, I derive a life table for each educational group (Coale, Demeny, and Vaughn 1983). Figure 5.2, which presents the survival functions for each educational attainment group, is a summary of the life table estimates. These data indicate that persons who have not completed high school experience substantially higher mortality than high school graduates. Among persons who have at least a high school degree, educational mortality differences are small and difficult to distinguish from variation attributable to measurement error.

Educational Mobility

Data on intergenerational mobility are taken from the 1987–1988 National Survey of Families and Households (NSFH) (Sweet, Bumpass, and Call 1988). This survey includes 7,753 women aged 18 and over. To reduce the number of respondents who were still in school at the time of the survey or who were born well before the period to which this analysis applies, I included only women aged 20–69, which reduced the sample to 6,725. In the mobility table used in the analysis, NSFH respondents are the daughters, and their mothers' data are obtained by the respondents' retrospective reports. This arrangement of the data, however, gives disproportionate weight to mothers who had large numbers of children. Thus I weighted each daughter inversely proportional to her reported number of full sisters.[11] I calculated the mobility table for the 5,198 respondents who provided data on their own educational attainment, the education of their mothers, and their number of full sisters.[12]

Educational Attainment Distributions

The data summarized in Table 5.1 and Figure 5.1 on age-specific distributions of schooling for each decade—which are also used to form initial distributions for the projection models—are drawn from published tables from the Decennial Censuses of 1940–1980 and the March 1990 Current Population Survey (U.S. Bureau of the Census 1945, 1953, 1963, 1973, 1984, 1992). Current Population Survey data are used for 1990 because they use a measure of educational attainment that is similar to the one used in the preceding censuses, whereas the 1990 Census measure of attainment is not comparable with previous censuses (Mare 1995). Throughout the analysis, educational attainment is measured in the five categories shown in Table 5.2.

FIGURE 5.2   Estimated Probabilities of Survival [$l(x)$] by Educational Attainment

Survival Probability [l(x)]

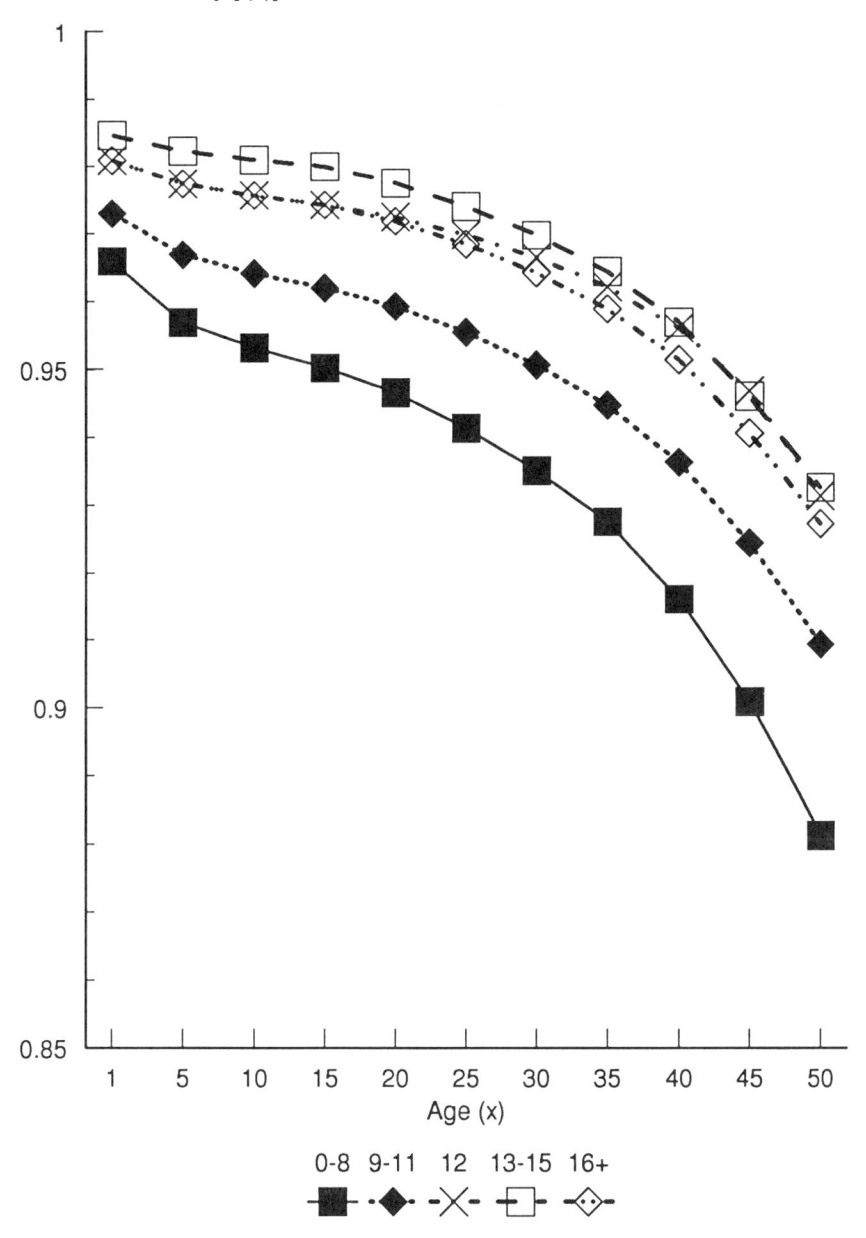

Age (x)

0-8   9-11   12   13-15   16+

Source: See text (pp. 131–2).

Fertility and Mortality Effects Given Observed Mobility Rates

Table 5.3 summarizes the results of a number of simulations that reveal the ways in which differential fertility and mortality may affect the evolution of educational distributions. Each row of the table corresponds to a distinct simulation, and the second through sixth columns indicate the values of the variables that are modified across simulations. "Mobility structure" denotes the assumed pattern of association between mother's and daughter's schooling in the mobility table. The "NSFH" mobility structure denotes the associations observed for women aged 18 and over in the 1987–1988 NSFH data. The other possible values for mobility structure are described below. "Daughter's distribution" denotes the assumed marginal distribution of daughter's schooling in the mobility table. "Mortality," "fertility level," and "fertility timing" denote the assumed vital rates. For these variables, "O" denotes the observed level and pattern of differentials of fertility and mortality, "HSG" indicates that all educational groups have the fertility or mortality of persons with exactly 12 years of schooling (that is, an absence of education differentials), and "1990" indicates that the fertility levels and education differentials for 1990 are in effect throughout the 1940–1990 period. The final four columns of the table present summary statistics for the projected 1990 distribution of educational attainment for 20 to 49-year-old women.

The most important result of this investigation is that the effects of differential fertility and mortality and their interaction with alternative mobility regimes on changes in educational distributions are *very small*. Although one can detect demographic effects that are consistent with common beliefs about the effects of demographic differentials on socioeconomic distributions, these effects are small relative to historical variations in levels of educational attainment.

Fertility Differentials

Simulation 1 in Table 5.3 projects the 1990 schooling distribution under the assumption that the population experiences the observed levels and differentials of fertility and mortality from 1940 to 1990.[13] This simulation yields a projected average number of years of school completed of 12.98. In simulation 2 I assume that in each period from 1940 to 1990 there were no fertility differentials. That is, all women had the same age-specific rates as women with exactly 12 years of schooling. Comparing these two simulations shows that the effects of differential fertility are very small indeed, a difference of only .14 years of schooling over the entire 50-year period. If one focuses on percentages with more or less than 12 years of schooling, one sees similarly small differences. Had there been no fertility differentials, educational attainment would have been higher, but only to a trivial degree.[14]

Level Versus Timing Effects

In conjunction with simulations 1 and 2, simulations 3 and 4 reveal the relative importance of fertility levels and fertility timing in the effect of differential fertility on the 1990 education distribution. When the fertility levels of all education groups are set equal to those of high school graduates but the age pattern of fertility varies across education groups (simulation 3), the projected 1990 distribution is virtually identical to the projected distribution when both the level and the timing of fertility are held constant across education groups (simulation 2). In contrast, when fertility levels vary across education groups but the age pattern of fertility is fixed (simulation 4), the projected distribution is virtually identical to the projected distribution when both the level and the timing of fertility vary across education groups (simulation 1). This shows clearly that the small effect of differential fertility is entirely the result of differences in the *level* of fertility and not differences in the *timing* of fertility.[15]

Recent Fertility Differentials

One reason for the small effects of fertility on the distribution of schooling is that fertility differentials vary in strength and direction between 1940 and 1990 (see Table 5.2). It is therefore of considerable interest to analyze the implications of the fertility differentials in 1990, which are the largest over the five decades considered here. If the 1990 pattern of fertility differentials had been in effect every year from 1940 to 1990, average educational attainment would have been lower (simulation 5). Compared to the distribution implied by observed fertility differentials (simulation 1), average attainment would have been .13 of a year lower. Compared to the distribution implied by no fertility differentials over this period (simulation 2), average attainment would have been .27 of a year lower. We would, after 50 years, have 5.5 percentage points fewer women with some college and 2.2 percentage points more high school dropouts than if there had been no fertility differentials by education. Thus current patterns of differential fertility will have a small negative effect on educational attainment if they persist into the future.

Differential Mortality

The effects of differential mortality on educational distributions are also small. In the absence of mortality differentials from 1940 to 1990 (simulation 6), the average attainment in 1990 would have been .01 years lower than the level implied by observed mortality differentials.

Although the direction of this discrepancy is in keeping with the notion that the superior survival chances of more-educated persons raise average educational attainment, the size of this effect is trivial.

The Effects of Alternative Mobility Regimes

The effects of fertility differentials depend on the degree of intergenerational mobility experienced by a population. When groups are relatively closed to social mobility, the differences in reproductivity across groups result in greater size differences in later years than when groups are relatively open to mobility. It is instructive to examine the size of this interaction between differential fertility and social mobility. In addition it is particularly interesting to know how much stronger the effects of differential fertility would be in a world with lower rates of mobility than those enjoyed by persons in the United States during the past half century. Simulations 7–21 examine the effects of differential fertility and mortality under three alternative mobility regimes: (1) independence of mother's and daughter's educational attainment (perfect mobility) (simulations 7–10), (2) no mobility at all—that is, a regime in which daughters have identical educational attainment to their mothers—(simulations 11–16), and (3) the association between mother's and daughter's schooling that is observed in the NSFH data but a distribution of daughter's schooling that implies no increases in average educational attainment between mothers and daughters (simulations 17–21).

Independence

If mother's and daughter's educational attainments are statistically independent, differential fertility has no effect at all on the distribution of educational attainment (simulations 7–9). This is true by construction because no matter how many children poorly educated women bear and how few highly educated women bear, these children have equal chances of educational success. This represents one extreme on the range of mobility regimes and indicates that the more a population approximates equality of opportunity, the lower the importance of fertility differentials. In contrast, under perfect mobility, the effect of differential mortality on education distributions is not logically required to be nil. Nonetheless, given the size of prevailing mortality differences, the effect is at least as small as under the observed mobility pattern (simulation 10).

No Mobility

To examine the other extreme on the range of mobility—that is, a regime in which daughters achieve exactly the same status as their mothers—it is necessary to modify not only the associations between mother's and daughter's schooling in the observed mobility table but also the marginal distribution of schooling. Much of the intergenerational mobility experienced by the NSFH sample is simply a result of a large secular shift in average levels of schooling between the mothers' and daughters' generations. Thus in a table that represents no mobility it is impossible to retain the same mothers' and daughters' education distributions as are observed in the NSFH data. Instead, I assume a mobility table that is simply the identity matrix, yielding an expected daughter's education distribution that is approximately the same as the 1940 initial distribution. This preserves complete "inheritance" of mother's educational attainment and allows for no "structural mobility" between mothers and daughters. Simulations under this assumption yield, by construction, much lower predicted levels of educational attainment than those based on the observed mobility table (1–6) or on independence of mother's and daughter's schooling subject to the observed marginal distribution of daughter's schooling (7–10). From the standpoint of the present investigation, however, the important issue is how predicted education distributions vary *within* sets of simulations that make a common mobility assumption.

The effects of differential fertility and mortality in the absence of mobility are larger than for the observed mobility regime but still small relative to historical variation in average educational attainment. In the absence of mobility, the observed sequences of fertility and mortality rates imply a 1990 education distribution that averages 9.74 years, 11.1 percent of women with at least some college, and 61.2 percent of women who did not graduate from high school (simulation 11). In the absence of fertility differentials—that is, when all women have the fertility rates of high school graduates in every period—the predicted average 1990 educational attainment is 10.1 years, an increment of .36 of a year, indicating that differential fertility does depress average levels of schooling (simulation 12). The effect of differential fertility is larger in the absence of mobility than for the observed NSFH mobility regime for which the differential fertility effect is only .14 of a year of schooling. As under the observed mobility regime, the depressing effect of differential fertility in the absence of mobility is exclusively the result of differences in level of fertility rather than its timing (simulations 13 and 14). Indeed, when fertility levels are held constant and fertility timing varies across education groups, average attainment is slightly higher than when both level and timing are fixed, suggesting that in the absence of mobility the sequences of differences in timing have a slightly positive effect on educational attainment.

As in the case of the observed mobility table, it is possible to explore the effects of the large 1990 differentials in fertility in the absence of mobility by assuming that the 1990 differentials were in place throughout the 1940–1990 period. Under this assumption the implied 1990 average level of education is 9.49 years, a .25 of a year lower than implied by the observed sequence of fertility rates and .61 of a year lower than implied by the absence of fertility differentials. (Compare simulation 15 to simulations 11 and 12.) These effects are about twice as large as for the NSFH mobility table and illustrate clearly that differential reproductivity has a much bigger effect on relative group size when groups are closed to mobility. These effects, however, remain small relative to the growth in years of schooling between 1940 and 1990.

Observed Mother-Daughter Associations and No Educational Upgrading

An alternative mobility regime, which may better approximate future mobility chances in the United States than any of the regimes considered thus far, is one in which the association between mother's and daughter's schooling is the same as for NSFH respondents but average levels of educational attainment are stable from generation to generation. To approximate this condition, I adjust the marginal distributions of mother's and daughter's schooling in the NSFH mobility table to agree with the 1940 education distribution (simulations 17–21).[16] Under these conditions the pattern of effects under alternative simulations is similar to the ones for the observed mobility table (1–5) and for no mobility (14–18), but the sizes of the effects are closer to those for the observed mobility regime. Average 1990 attainment in the absence of fertility differences (simulation 18) is .2 of a year greater than the level implied by the observed sequence of fertility rates (simulation 17). This compares to the effect of .14 of a year for the observed mobility table and .36 of a year for the model of complete inheritance. Had 1990 fertility patterns been in effect for the entire period under this mobility pattern, average attainment would have been .32 of a year lower than if there had been no fertility differentials. This compares to the effect of .27 of a year for the observed table and .61 of a year for complete inheritance. If relative mobility chances remain unchanged but general educational upgrading is reduced, the impact of differential fertility will continue to be small.

Demographic Rates and Educational Inequality

It is also interesting to examine the effects of alternative fertility regimes on the dispersion as well as the average level of attainment. These effects, which are indicated by the variation in H displayed in the final column of Table 5.3, depend on where a group of women lies on the

TABLE 5.3 Projected Education Distributions Under Alternative Simulations of Fertility, Mortality, and Mobility

Simulation	Mobility Structure	Daughter's Distribution	Mortality	Fertility Level	Fertility Timing	Avg. Yrs.	% > 12	% < 12	H
1.	NSFH	NSFH	O	O	O	12.60	39.6	18.0	0.619
2.	NSFH	NSFH	O	HSG	HSG	12.75	42.2	16.5	0.618
3.	NSFH	NSFH	O	HSG	O	12.75	42.1	16.3	0.616
4.	NSFH	NSFH	O	O	HSG	12.59	39.7	18.1	0.621
5.	NSFH	NSFH	O	1990	1990	12.46	37.3	19.4	0.621
6.	NSFH	NSFH	HSG	O	O	12.58	39.4	18.3	0.621
7.	Indep.	NSFH	O	O	O	12.61	40.2	18.1	0.623
8.	Indep.	NSFH	O	HSG	HSG	12.61	40.2	18.1	0.623
9.	Indep.	NSFH	O	1990	1990	12.61	40.2	18.1	0.623
10.	Indep.	NSFH	HSG	O	O	12.60	40.2	18.3	0.625
11.	No Mobility	1940	O	O	O	9.74	11.1	61.2	0.595
12.	No Mobility	1940	O	HSG	HSG	10.10	13.3	55.7	0.615
13.	No Mobility	1940	O	HSG	O	10.21	14.1	53.7	0.620
14.	No Mobility	1940	O	O	HSG	9.62	10.3	63.1	0.588
15.	No Mobility	1940	O	1990	1990	9.49	9.4	64.6	0.577
16.	No Mobility	1940	HSG	O	O	9.67	10.8	62.2	0.613
17.	NSFH	1940	O	O	O	9.65	12.6	62.4	0.599
18.	NSFH	1940	O	HSG	HSG	9.85	14.1	59.7	0.614
19.	NSFH	1940	O	HSG	O	9.89	14.4	59.1	0.616
20.	NSFH	1940	O	O	HSG	9.61	12.3	63.1	0.596
21.	NSFH	1940	O	1990	1990	9.53	11.7	64.1	0.589

Note: NSFH = women aged 18 and over 1987–1988 National Survey of Families and Households; O = Observed; HSG = high school graduates

TABLE 5.4 Projected Mobility Rates Under Alternative Simulations of Fertility and Mortality

				Upward			Downward		
Simulation	Mortality	Fertility Level	Fertility Timing	1950	1970	1990	1950	1970	1990
1.	O	O	O	43.5	37.1	35.2	18.1	22.5	23.8
2.	O	HSG	HSG	43.1	34.1	32.1	18.3	24.0	26.6
3.	O	HSG	O	42.1	35.3	33.5	19.1	23.9	25.3
4.	O	O	HSG	44.4	36.7	34.1	17.4	22.8	24.8
5.	O	1990	1990	44.3	38.7	36.2	17.6	21.2	23.1

Note: Assumes observed mobility matrix for women aged 18 and over 1987–1988 NSFH; O = Observed; HSG = high schooll graduates

trajectory of educational growth. For the observed mobility regime (simulations 1–6), the variations in the pattern of demographic rates induce only slight changes in the H statistic across simulations.

Under complete inheritance (no mobility), the effects of demographic rates on H are larger and generally in the opposite direction from those for the observed mobility table. Configurations of rates that lower average attainment tend to lower the dispersion of the schooling distribution (compare simulations 18 and 15, for example). The *magnitude* of the changes in H are, like the variations in the mean of the distribution, a reflection of the greater sensitivity of schooling distributions to demographic differentials when mobility is low than when it is high. The direction of the effects, however, is largely a result of the pattern of educational growth. As indicated in Table 5.1, the dispersion of the schooling distribution reaches its maximum during the middle phase of educational growth and then, at high average levels of attainment, shrinks toward its previous size. Thus patterns of fertility or mortality rates that lower average attainment tend to lower the dispersion when an education distribution is similar to the one observed in 1940 (simulations 11–21) and raise the dispersion when a distribution is similar to the one observed in 1990. The effect of differential fertility and mortality on educational inequality, therefore, is heavily dependent on their effects on the mean attainment and on the era in which these effects are observed.

Demographic Rates and Integrational Mobility

Differential fertility is likely to affect not only socioeconomic distributions but also rates of upward and downward mobility. When a large proportion of a population is born to mothers of low socioeconomic standing, there is greater potential for upward mobility than when a small proportion have low socioeconomic origins. Thus differential fertility has an effect on the proportion of persons who are upwardly mobile that is the opposite of its effect on average levels of socioeconomic standing (Preston 1974). Table 5.4 shows how alternative patterns of differential fertility affect expected rates of upward and downward educational mobility for cohorts of women born in 1950, 1970, and 1990. These calculations use the 1940 education distribution as the initial distribution and the observed NSFH educational mobility table.[17] Under all simulations, rates of upward mobility decline and rates of downward mobility increase over cohorts born between 1950 and 1990. This is a natural result of secular educational growth. As more persons reach the top of the distribution, fewer have the potential for upward mobility and more have the potential to move down. Across alternative fertility regimes, mobility rates do vary, but the variations are extremely small. Compared to the mobility rates predicted by the observed sequence of fertility rates (simulation 1), the percentage of women who would be upwardly mobile would be about two points lower in the absence of fertility differentials (simulation 2). If the 1990 fertility pattern were in effect throughout the 1940–1990 period, rates of upward mobility would increase slightly. On balance, the effects of differential fertility on mobility rates are slight.

Conclusions

The analyses reported in this chapter lead to clear answers to the five questions posed at the outset:

1. Differential fertility by educational attainment of mother has retarded the growth of average educational attainment over the past 50 years, but this effect is small. Had there been no fertility differentials between 1940 and 1990, average educational attainment for prime-age women would have been less than one-fifth of a year lower than the actual 1990 attainment level. When one considers that the average educational attainment of women increased by about 3.5 years over this period, this effect is negligible.

2. Whereas the differential *level* of fertility by women's educational attainment depresses average attainment slightly, the differential *timing* of fertility has essentially no effect. This appears to be because education differentials in fertility timing are highly variable. In some periods the expected positive correlation between average age of childbearing and educational attainment is nonexistent.

3. Although 1990 fertility differentials by education are stronger than at any other period since 1945, even these differentials do not have much effect on the distribution of schooling. Had 1990 fertility patterns been in effect for the past 50 years, the average level of educational attainment in the population today would be only slightly lower than it is.

4. Differential mortality raises the average level of educational attainment because less-educated persons die earlier than their more-educated counterparts. This effect, however, is even smaller than the effect of fertility differentials.

5. In a world of perfect mobility (that is, independence of social origins and destinations), differential fertility has no effect on education distributions. The greater the degree of resemblance between mother and daughter on educational attainment (that is, the lower the rate of intergenerational mobility), the greater the effect of differential fertility. In the extreme case in which each daughter has the same educational attainment as her mother, the effects of differential fertility are considerably larger than under the actual regime of intergenerational mobility observed during the past several decades. It is this extreme (and unrealis-

tic) condition that is sometimes mistakenly assumed in discussions of the presumed harmful effect of differential fertility (Preston and Campbell 1993; Lam 1993). Even in this case, however, the impact of differential fertility over a 50-year period is small relative to the overall change in average attainment observed during this period. Moreover, even if we further assume that the large fertility differentials observed in 1990 held for 50 years under this extreme regime of immobility, educational attainment would be only about three-fourths of a year less than the level implied by no differential fertility. This effect is still less than one-fourth of the observed increase in attainment during the past 50 years.

Even under a relatively pessimistic forecast of the prospects for future upward mobility in the United States, it is extremely unlikely that the future will approximate the extreme condition of complete educational immobility. A more realistic scenario is that average attainment levels will converge to a somewhat higher level than they are now, subsequent generations will average similar levels of attainment to those of their parents, and the *association* between parents and offspring will not change much from its historical pattern. This last expectation is in line with the stable patterns of parental effects on offsprings' educational attainment throughout this century (Mare 1981; Hout, Raftery, and Bell 1993). Under these conditions the effects of differential fertility on educational distributions will be very modest.

Research Agenda

The strength of the approach described here is that it enables one to answer aggregate, dynamic questions about the reproduction and evolution of social hierarchies. Such questions cannot be divorced from the demographic mechanisms required to sustain a population, even when, as in the case of the specific illustration presented in this study, demographic effects on socioeconomic distributions are relatively weak. Nonetheless, my analyses are based on a very rudimentary model of socioeconomic reproduction. Obvious extensions of this work are to take account of intercohort changes in social mobility, to use indirect estimation procedures to extend the analysis to periods prior to 1940, and to investigate trends in the distribution of socioeconomic attributes other than educational attainment (such as occupation and income). Of greater importance, however, is the exploration of several key demographic and social complexities that are ignored here.

Two-Sex Versus One-Sex Models

The most serious limitation of the model is that it is confined to one sex. The model does not take account of the ways that marriage markets constrain fertility and how this may vary across persons with varying levels of educational attainment.[18] Taking account of both sexes simultaneously enables one to answer additional questions about how demographic processes influences levels and distributions of socioeconomic characteristics. The degree to which fathers and mothers resemble each other on educational attainment or other socioeconomic attributes affects the degree of inequality experienced by their offspring. When the correlation of spouses' attainments is only moderate, the advantage experienced by a child because of the high attainment of one parent is offset by the lower status of the other parent. When the correlation of spouses' attainments is high, however, the benefit or deficit experienced by a child because of the status of one parent is more often reinforced by the similar status level of the other parent. As the degree of parental resemblance shifts, so may change in the inequality of subsequent generations. The next order of business for the line of investigation proposed here is to develop a two-sex model of fertility and educational mobility. Prototypes for such models already exist (e.g., Preston and Campbell 1993), and the good data available on educational assortative mating (Mare 1991) make these models feasible to estimate.

Changing Household Structure

Once the effects of assortative mating are recognized, it is also necessary to explore the consequences of changing rates of marriage, marital disruption, and nonmarital childbearing, as well as levels of marital homogamy, on socioeconomic distributions in subsequent generations (McLanahan and Sandefur 1994). A large and growing proportion of children raised by single parents may offset or reinforce the effect of the changing covariance of mothers' and fathers' socioeconomic attributes on the intergenerational reproduction of inequality. Thus, in simulating the sequence of socioeconomic distributions, one should take account of the evolving mixture of two-parent and single-parent households in the population.

Parental Age Effects

Whereas the present analysis assumes an invariant mobility matrix across ages of mother, parents' ages when children are born affect children's socioeconomic achievement (Mare and Tzeng 1989; Leng 1990). Children born to older parents fare substantially better than those born to younger parents. As the mean and variance of ages of childbearing have changed over time, this may have contributed to the level and dispersion of socioeconomic outcomes in subsequent generations. Incorporation of parental age effects is a straightforward extension of the projection model.[19]

Three-Generation Effects

Population projection models, as well as most conventional models of social stratification processes, typically assume that the effects of social standing in one generation on the social standing of subsequent generations can be represented fully by social mobility between successive generations. That is, it is assumed that individuals are not affected by their grandparents or great-grandparents once the effects of their parents are taken into account. Yet whether such effects are present is an empirical question that has not been extensively studied. As social mobility data on three generations become available, it will be useful to incorporate multigenerational influences into both individually oriented models of the stratification process and aggregate population models of the sort presented here (Mare and Hauser 1993; Warren and Hauser 1995).

Implications for Racial Inequality

The results in this chapter average over the diverse behaviors of racial and ethnic groups. It is worthwhile to revisit, in light of several decades of social change, Preston's (1974) question of whether differences in socioeconomic achievement between African Americans and whites are partly attributable to racial differences in fertility patterns. Perhaps of greater import is the way that fertility patterns have affected black socioeconomic progress in recent decades. This period has witnessed exceptional growth in the number of blacks who have attained college degrees and even higher educational credentials (for example, Mare 1995). The overwhelming majority of these college graduates have experienced substantial upward intergenerational mobility. These accomplishments benefit not only the persons who achieve them but also, given the intergenerational correlation of educational success, their offspring. On the one hand, therefore, one can hope for an intergenerational "multiplier" effect on black socioeconomic progress. On the other hand, however, patterns of differential fertility may offset this effect. If fertility levels of highly educated African Americans are low, relatively few children are available to benefit from their parents' high level of socioeconomic attainment.[20] Under these conditions most blacks will continue to face the burden of achieving success through the hard route of upward mobility rather than the easier route of maintaining their parents' level of success. One can investigate the degree to which this occurs with the model presented here.[21]

Immigration

In addition to differential fertility and mortality and intergenerational mobility, socioeconomic distributions are also affected by levels and patterns of immigration. Immigration of persons of low socioeconomic origins initially lowers average levels of achievement but is subsequently a source of intra- and intergenerational social mobility (Sibley 1942). A full demographic understanding of the evolution of socioeconomic distributions requires that the model presented in this chapter be elaborated to take account of differences in immigration rates among socioeconomic groups.

Notes

Research for this essay was supported by the National Science Foundation; the University of Wisconsin-Madison; RAND; the Office of the Assistant Secretary for Planning and Evaluation, U.S. Department of Health and Human Services; and the Center for Demography and Ecology of the University of Wisconsin, which is supported by the National Institute of Child Health and Development (NICHD). In preparing this paper, the author benefited from the comments of David B. Grusky, Robert M. Hauser, Samuel H. Preston, Judith A. Seltzer, Donald J. Treiman, Halliman H. Winsborough, and the participants in seminars at UCLA, the University of Pennsylvania, Princeton University, RAND, and the University of Wisconsin.

1. These remarks apply equally to the analysis of social mobility tables and to structural equation models for interval measures of socioeconomic status. The argument also applies equally to approaches to stratification that emphasize psychological, institutional, or economic mechanisms in attempting to account for the intergenerational and intragenerational association of education, occupation, income, or other measures of socioeconomic standing.

2. In fact Blau and Duncan (1967) recognized the role of demographic processes by including detailed analyses of most of these processes in their monograph. Although these analyses were not as influential as the chapters on social mobility and the process of social stratification, they, too, have inspired much subsequent work. Unfortunately, each of these topics has spawned its own, largely independent literature. There has been relatively little effort to synthesize these topics into a common analytic framework.

3. This brief review omits the works in the economics literature that describe behavioral models of social mobility and inequality (for example, Conlisk 1974, Goldberger 1989, and Becker 1992). These models have not been formulated in a way that allows direct investigation of the impact of fertility differentials on socioeconomic distributions, although it may be possible to modify them for this purpose. The review also omits population-genetic models, which do bear close kinship to the models considered here (for example, Cavalli-Sforza and Feldman 1981).

4. H is calculated as $\sum_i p_i \log (1/p_i)$, where p_i denotes the proportion of persons in the ith education category. When the distribution is uniform, $H = 5 \, [.2 \log (1/.2)] \cong 1.6$.

5. The age-specific rates in Table 5.2 indicate the annual number of female children born to 1,000 women of the given age group. The gross reproduction rate

denotes the number of female children born to a hypothetical cohort of women, all of whom survived until the end of their childbearing years, who experienced the age-specific fertility rates of that year. It is estimated as the sum of the age-specific rates for the given year multiplied by 5/1,000. The means and standard deviations of the fertility schedule presented in Table 5.2 are the means and standard deviations respectively of the ages represented in the table weighted by the age-specific fertility rates.

6. Educational inequality has historically been somewhat greater for men than women. That is, disproportionate numbers of men tend to drop out of school very early or who attain the highest possible levels of schooling. These sex differences, however, have declined in recent decades (Mare 1995).

7. In projecting the survival of the population, I also assume that children follow the mortality schedule of their ultimate educational attainment group rather than the mortality schedule of their mother's education group.

8. A further elaboration of this projection matrix would be to allow the mobility rates m_{ijt} to depend on the ages of the mothers. Although the mother's age at the birth of her child affects the child's educational attainment (Mare and Tzeng 1989; Leng 1990), it is beyond the scope of this study to include this refinement of the projection model.

9. I used the 1960 census estimates for 1945 and 1950 and the 1970 census estimates for 1955, 1960, and 1965.

10. The Rindfuss-Sweet estimates and some of the vital statistics estimates assume no fertility below age 15 and above 44. I assume that age-specific fertility rates are zero outside of the 15–44 age interval for all years.

11. In addition I weighted the data by the sampling weights to take account of the disproportionate stratification of the NSFH sample (Sweet, Bumpass, and Call 1988).

12. Women as young as 20 were included to maximize the sample size. As a result, some of the included respondents had not completed their schooling as of the survey data. This may create a small downward bias in respondents' educational attainments. Such respondents, however, are such a small fraction of the sample that this bias can have only a small impact on the analysis.

13. I assume that fertility rates for 1940 are the same as for 1945 because education-specific fertility rates are not available for 1940. This is an unrealistic assumption inasmuch as 1940 was the end of the Great Depression and fertility in 1945 is a result of the mixed effects of World War II and the beginning of the Post-War period. Nonetheless, an alternative analysis in which I use 1950 as the initial distribution and rely only on 1950–1990 fertility rates, yields very similar results to those presented here.

14. The projected education distribution for 1990 in simulation 1 differs slightly from the observed 1990 distribution (see Table 5.1). This discrepancy is the result of several factors, including errors in fertility and mortality rates, immigration, and the fact that the age range of persons included in the mobility matrix is broader than for the observed 1990 distribution. For the purposes of this analysis, however, these discrepancies are unimportant. The effects of demographic rates can be assessed by comparing among alternative simulated distributions, all of which are discrepant from the observed distribution for the same reasons.

15. In simulation 3 the age-specific fertility rates were calculated by multiplying the age specific rate for each education group by the ratio of the gross reproduction rate (GRR) for high school graduates to its own GRR. In simulation 4 fertility rates were calculated by assigning all education groups the age-specific rates of high school graduates and then multiplying the assigned rate for each education group by the ratio of its own GRR to the GRR of high school graduates.

16. Alternative approaches would be to adjust the table to the 1990 education distribution or the distribution for NSFH respondents. These adjustments would yield expected 1990 education distributions more similar to those from simulations 1–10, but would lead to a pattern of differences among simulations that is similar to simulations 17–21.

17. As shown above, under independence, differential fertility has no effect on education distributions and thus has no effect on mobility rates. Under perfect inheritance upward and downward mobility percentages are, by definition, zero irrespective of the pattern of fertility.

18. Of course, it would also be desirable to examine educational trends for the entire population, rather than just the female half of it. This shortcoming, however, can be remedied simply by carrying out a replication of the present analysis on men.

19. Alternatively, one might investigate the closely related issue of the aggregate implications of changing parity (birth order) distributions. At the individual level, however, parental age effects appear to be stronger and more robust than those of birth order (Mare and Tzeng 1989).

20. I am indebted to Samuel Preston for discussions of this point.

21. This effect of differential fertility is separate from and may indeed be compounded by blacks' chances for downward mobility.

References

Baron, James N. 1994. "Reflections on Recent Generations of Mobility Research." Pp. 384–93 in David B. Grusky (ed.), *Social Stratification: Class, Race, and Gender in Sociological Perspective.* Boulder: Westview Press.

Becker, Gary S. 1992. *A Treatise on the Family.* 2nd Edition. Cambridge: Harvard University Press.

Blau, Peter M., and Otis D. Duncan. 1967. *The American Occupational Structure.* New York: Wiley.

Cavalli-Sforza, L. L., and M. W. Feldman. 1981. *Cultural Evolution and Transmission: A Quantitative Approach. Monographs in Population Biology.* Princeton, NJ: Princeton University Press.

Coale, Ansley J., Paul Demeny, and Barbara Vaughn. 1983. *Regional Model Life Tables and Stable Populations.* 2nd Edition. New York: Academic Press.

Conlisk, John. 1974. "Can Equalization of Opportunity Reduce Social Mobility?" *American Economic Review* 64:80–90.

Duncan, Otis Dudley. 1966. "Methodological Issues in the Analysis of Social Mobility." Pp. 51–97 in Neil J. Smelser and Seymour Martin Lipset (eds.), *Social Structure and Mobility in Economic Development.* Chicago: Aldine.

Duncan, Otis Dudley, and Robert W. Hodge. 1963. "Education and Occupational Mobility." *American Journal of Sociology* 68: 629–44.

Elo, Irma T., and Samuel H. Preston. 1995. "Educational Differentials in Mortality: United States, 1979–85." Manuscript, Population Studies Center, University of Pennsylvania.

Feeney, Griffith M. 1970. "Stable Age by Region Distributions." *Demography* 6:341–48.

Goldberger, Arthur S. 1989. "Economic and Mechanical Modes of Intergenerational Transmission." *American Economic Review* 79:504–13.

Herrnstein, Richard J., and Charles Murray. 1994. *The Bell Curve: Intelligence and Class Structure in American Life.* New York: Free Press.

Hout, Michael, Adrian E. Raftery, and Eleanor O. Bell. 1993. "Making the Grade: Educational Stratification in the United States, 1925–1989." Pp. 25–50 In Yossi Shavit and Hans-Peter Blossfeld (eds.), *Persistent Inequality: A Comparative Analysis of Educational Stratification in Thirteen Countries.* Boulder: Westview Press.

Johnson, Robert A. 1980. *Religious Assortative Marriage in the United States.* New York: Academic Press.

Keyfitz, Nathan. 1968. *Introduction to the Mathematics of Population.* Reading, MA: Addison-Wesley.

Kitagawa, Evelyn M., and Philip M. Hauser. 1973. *Differential Mortality in the United States.* Cambridge: Harvard University Press.

Lam, David. 1986. "The Dynamics of Population Growth, Differential Fertility, and Inequality." *American Economic Review* 76:1103–16.

———. 1993. "Comment on Preston and Campbell's 'Differential Fertility and the Distribution of Traits.'" *American Journal of Sociology* 98:1033–9.

Land, Kenneth C., and Andrei Rogers. 1982. *Multidimensional Mathematical Demography.* New York: Academic Press.

LeBras, Henri. 1971. "Équilibre et croissance de populations soumises à des migrations." *Theoretical Population Biology* 2: 100–21.

Leng, Xue. 1990. "The Effects of Parents' Ages on Offspring's Educational Achievement." Master's thesis, Department of Sociology, University of Wisconsin-Madison.

Mare, Robert D. 1981. "Change and Stability in Educational Stratification." *American Sociological Review* 46:72–87.

———. 1991. "Five Decades of Educational Assortative Mating." *American Sociological Review* 56:15–32.

———. 1995. "Changes in Educational Attainment and School Enrollment." In Reynolds Farley (ed.), *State of the Union: America in the 1990s,* Volume 1: *Economic Trends.* New York: Russell Sage Foundation.

Mare, Robert D., and Robert M. Hauser. 1993. "A Survey Module on Families and Social Mobility." Proposal to National Science Foundation.

Mare, Robert D., and Meei-Shenn Tzeng. 1989. "Fathers' Ages and the Social Stratification of Sons." *American Journal of Sociology* 95:108–31.

Matras, Judah. 1961. "Differential Fertility, Intergenerational Occupational Mobility, and Change in Occupational Distribution: Some Elementary Interrelationships." *Population Studies* 15:187–97.

———. 1967. "Social Mobility and Social Structure: Some Insights from the Linear Model." *American Sociological Review* 32:608–14.

McLanahan, Sara, and Gary Sandefur. 1994. *Growing Up with a Single Parent: What Hurts, What Helps.* Cambridge: Harvard University Press.

National Center for Health Statistics. 1970. *The Health of Children—1970.* Washington, DC: U.S. Government Printing Office.

———. 1975. *Vital Statistics of the United States, 1970.* Volume 1, *Natality.* DHEW Pub. No. (HRA) 75–1100. Public Health Service. Washington, DC: U.S. Government Printing Office.

———. 1978. *Vital Statistics of the United States, 1970.* Volume 1, *Natality.* DHEW Pub. No. (PHS) 78–1113. Public Health Service. Washington, DC: U.S. Government Printing Office.

———. 1984. *Vital Statistics of the United States, 1980.* Volume 1, *Natality.* DHHS Pub. No. (PHS) 85–1100. Public Health Service. Washington, DC: U.S. Government Printing Office.

———. 1988. *Vital Statistics of the United States, 1980.* Volume 1, *Natality.* DHHS Pub. No. (PHS) 88–1113. Public Health Service. Washington, DC: U.S. Government Printing Office.

———. 1993. *Monthly Vital Statistics Report* 41, 9(S). Washington, DC: U.S. Government Printing Office.

Preston, Samuel H. 1974. "Differential Fertility, Unwanted Fertility, and Racial Trends in Occupational Achievement." *American Sociological Review* 39:492–506.

Preston, Samuel H., and Cameron Campbell. 1993. "Differential Fertility and the Distribution of Traits: The Case of IQ." *American Journal of Sociology* 98:997–1019.

Preston, Samuel H., and Irma T. Elo. 1994. "Are Educational Differentials in Adult Mortality Increasing in the United States?" Manuscript, Population Studies Center, University of Pennsylvania.

Rindfuss, Ronald R. 1976. "Fertility Rates for Racial and Social Subpopulations with the United States: 1945–1969." CDE Working Paper 76–29. Madison, WI: Center for Demography and Ecology.

Rindfuss, Ronald R., and James A. Sweet. 1977. *Postwar Fertility Trends and Differentials in the United States.* New York: Academic Press.

Rogers, Andrei. 1975. *Introduction to Multiregional Mathematical Demography.* New York: Wiley.

Schoen, Robert. 1988. *Modeling Multigroup Populations.* New York: Plenum Press.

Sibley, Elbridge. 1942. "Some Demographic Clues to Stratification." *American Sociological Review* 7:322–30.

Sweet, James, Larry Bumpass, and Vaughn Call. 1988. "The Design and Content of the National Survey of Families and Households." NSFH Working Paper No. 1. Madison, WI: Center for Demography and Ecology.

Theil, Henri. 1972. *Statistical Decomposition Analysis.* Amsterdam: North-Holland.

U.S. Bureau of the Census. 1945. *Sixteenth Census of the United States: 1940.* Population, Differential Fertility, Women by Number of Children Ever Born. Washington, DC: U.S. Government Printing Office.

———. 1953. *Census of Population: 1950. Special Reports. Women by Number of Children Ever Born.* Washington, D.C.: U.S. Government Printing Office.

———. 1963. *Census of Population: 1960. Volume 1, Characteristics of the Population, Part D, Detailed Population Characteristics, U.S. Summary.* Washington, DC: U.S. Government Printing Office.

———. 1973. *1970 Census of the Population. Volume 1, Characteristics of the Population, Part 1, U.S. Summary.* Washington, DC: U.S. Government Printing Office.

———. 1976. *Educational Attainment in the United States, March 1975.* Current Population Reports Series P-20, No. 295. Washington, DC: U.S. Government Printing Office.

———. 1984. *1980 Census of Population. Volume 1, Characteristics of the Population, Chapter D, Detailed Population Characteristics, Part 1, U.S. Summary.* Washington, DC: U.S. Government Printing Office.

———. 1987. *Educational Attainment in the United States, March 1982 and 1985.* Current Population Reports Series P-20, No. 415. Washington, DC: U.S. Government Printing Office.

———. 1992. *Educational Attainment in the United States, March 1991 and 1990.* Current Population Reports Series P-20, No. 462. Washington, DC: U.S. Government Printing Office.

Warren, John R., and Robert M. Hauser. 1995. "The Process of Stratification in Educational and Occupational Attainments Across Three Generations: New Evidence from the Wisconsin Longitudinal Survey." Manuscript, Department of Sociology, University of Wisconsin-Madison.

6

The Decline of Infant Mortality in China: Sichuan, 1949–1988

*William M. Mason, William Lavely,
Hiromi Ono, and Angelique Chan*

Although the decline of infant mortality in China is one of the great achievements of the post-1949 era, remarkably little is known about its causes. It is widely thought that the decline was driven by the multifaceted social and economic revolution that began with the formation of the People's Republic of China (PRC) in 1949. The first two decades of the PRC were characterized by income redistribution, rising female education, and public health initiatives aimed at eliminating disease vectors and extending basic medical services to the rural population. In the 1970s and 1980s, a family-planning revolution brought marriage and childbearing under bureaucratic control. The dismantling of the collective economy in the 1980s brought rapid growth of income and inequality. Each of these changes could have influenced infant health conditions.

In this chapter we examine the role played by education and other sociodemographic characteristics of individuals and families in the decline of infant mortality. We also use information we have been able to glean from official compendia on changes in the public health infrastructure and the production of food. Lack of appropriate data precludes analysis of the impact of income redistribution in the 1950s and the growth of inequality in the 1980s. We are, however, able to examine the relationship between aggregate income and infant mortality.

The second section of this chapter briefly reviews the literature and discusses the data to be used. As preparation for analysis of the decline of infant mortality, the third section explores cross-sectional and temporal aspects of a single body of data—the Sichuan component of the 1988

National Survey of Fertility and Contraception (NSFC). Using the results of these explorations, in the fourth section we examine possible correlates of the decline of infant mortality, including changes in sociodemographic composition, income, public health activity, and food production.

Background and Data

The growing literature on infant mortality in China has generally not confronted the issue of the mortality decline. From extant empirical research it is impossible to draw quantitative conclusions about the causes of declining infant mortality in one-fifth of the world's population. Instead, analysts working with major surveys conducted in the 1980s, in particular, the 1988 National Survey of Fertility and Contraception and the In-depth Fertility Surveys conducted in several provinces in 1985 and 1987, have shed light on cross-sectional relationships between infant or child mortality and selected social and demographic characteristics of families and individuals (e.g., Choe and Tsuya 1989; Choe, Hao, and Wang 1995; Gu et al. 1991; Ren 1994; Streatfield, Kane and Ruzicka 1991; Tu 1989). There are also studies of specific causes of infant death, birth weight, and other epidemiological issues (e.g., CNCGBDS 1991; Dankert and van Ginneken 1991; Gao 1991; Zhang, Cai, and Lee 1991, 1992; Zhou, Rao, and Zhang 1989). Reports on public health policies and accounts of health conditions in the early years of the People's Republic suggest the effectiveness of vaccination programs and campaigns against disease vectors (e.g., Horn 1969; Lampton 1977; Lucas 1982).

Missing from the body of work cited above are multivariate or bivariate time series analyses of aggregate data; variants thereof that exploit the temporal dimension implicit in the large family-level surveys that elicit birth histories from mothers; and classical demographic decomposition analyses of temporal change (e.g., Kitagawa 1955). To be sure, there are major data availability, suitability and adequacy issues when we attempt to examine the historical record. Nevertheless, this chapter is predicated on the premise that meaningful progress toward a full understanding of the decline of infant mortality in the PRC is a possibility, and the results presented here call on each of the strategies mentioned.[1]

The types of data—availability aside—that might be used to examine the decline of infant mortality in the PRC include aggregate time series; official birth and death registries; censuses or comparable sample surveys fielded at intervals over the period of interest that provide contemporaneous cross-sectional estimates; and large-scale sample surveys with retrospective components (in particular, birth histories and children's mortality histories).

One reason so little is known about the causes of the post-1949 decline of infant mortality is that data of any type for the earlier decades of this period are sparse. The benchmarks are life tables constructed from a national cancer survey of 1973–1975 and the censuses of 1982 and 1990. These put male infant mortality rates (IMRs) in 1973–1975, 1981, and 1990 at 48, 38, and 28, respectively (Banister 1992).[2] However, indirect evidence and intensive post-enumeration surveys suggest that the true IMRs are higher by a considerable margin (Banister 1989; Tu and Liang 1992; Banister 1992).[3] We know of only three infant mortality (IM) time series that span the 1950s and 1960s—when infant mortality is thought to have declined most rapidly. Hill produced the first IM series reaching back to 1950 (Hill 1984). Using several official sources, Banister (1987) constructed improved sex-specific series for the period 1953–1984. However, the only official series is highly abridged for the earlier decades (State Statistical Bureau 1990 in Hayase and Kawamata 1991). None of these series can support the kind of detailed analysis presented here. In particular, they do not lend themselves to consideration of the impact of changing sociodemographic composition of the population.

Owing to the difficulties of obtaining data, probably the only feasible approach to the study of the decline of infant mortality in China for the period of interest is through the use of the two large-scale 1980s sample surveys containing birth and child mortality histories. These surveys have been released in "public use" format to a few selected researchers outside of China.[4] It would be preferable to utilize both bodies of data—not only to increase the sample sizes for the years they have in common but also to extend the length of the infant mortality time series. Unfortunately, that analytic design is not available to us, inasmuch as we have access only to one of the data sets—in our view the best one for our purposes. The present study of infant mortality conditions in Sichuan is based on data from the NSFC, conducted by China's State Family Planning Commission (SFPC) in June 1988 (SFPC 1988). The NSFC, also known as the "2 per 1,000 Survey," is the largest survey of its kind.

In the NSFC all provincial-level units were surveyed (including, for the first time, Tibet). The sampling fraction varied across provinces to reduce sampling errors in relatively sparsely populated, as well as smaller, provinces. The sampling unit of the survey is a political subdivision of the lowest level administrative unit in China: In urban areas this is the "residence small group" (a subunit of the "neighborhood committee"), and in rural areas it is the "village small group" (a subunit of the "administrative village"). There were about 6.7 million such enumeration districts in China, with an average size of about 156 persons. The survey systematically sampled 2 of every 1,000 such enumeration districts (a total of 13,466 districts) and then interviewed every household in each of the selected districts, collecting information on each member of each household. The resulting sample size is approximately 2.1 million persons in the household data set, from which over 500,000 eligible respondents, ever-married women age 15–57, provided pregnancy histories. By contrast, the World Fertility Survey in 40 countries surveyed roughly half that number of women, as did the SFPC's 1982 "1 per 1,000 Survey" in China. Unpublished assessments of the NSFC have concluded that the quality of the data is high (Coale n.d.; Lavely, Mason, and Ono 1991; Zhang and Lu 1991).

We use the birth and mortality histories collected by the NSFC to construct time series of infant mortality for Sichuan. We then assess the salience of various factors measured at the family and child levels (e.g., parental education, child spacing). In addition, we juxtapose time series based on the NSFC with factors available to us only at the aggregate level: income, public health infrastructure, and nutrition.

The use of the birth histories in the NSFC facilitates the testing of "compositional" hypotheses. For example, since maternal education is generally inversely associated with infant mortality in the cross-section, rising levels of female education may help to explain declining infant mortality. Similarly, because infants of very young mothers are generally at greater risk, rising marriage age may have contributed to reduced mortality. These are compositional hypotheses because they are based on the assumption that decline is due to change in population composition rather than change in rates within population strata. Such compositional hypotheses cannot be tested without data that are specific to sociodemographic strata—data of the kind we use here.

If a retrospective survey has analytical advantages, there are also well-known limitations. Birth histories reconstructed from memory are prone to response errors such as event misplacement and omission (Baddeley 1979; Groves 1989; Haaga 1988; Neter and Waksberg 1964; Potter 1977; Som 1973; Sudman and Bradburn 1973). There is also selection bias. Many women who lived in the 1950s did not survive to be interviewed in 1988. The mortality experience of the children of these missing women is likely to have differed from that of the children of surviving women. This is especially true for the children of women who died in a famine or other catastrophe. In 1959–1961 China experienced perhaps the most devastating famine in modern history, which coincided with the radical political movement called the Great Leap Forward (*GLF*), initiated in 1958 (Ashton et al. 1984; Peng 1987). Because the *GLF* and the famine are closely associated in time and are considered to be causally related, we refer to them interchangeably. Births and deaths reported for the famine years may be particularly subject to selective omission because this was a period in which many mothers and entire families perished. In general, there is little we can do about these problems other than to note them and try to understand their influence.

Another kind of selectivity problem arises inevitably from the design of a one-time survey. Any time series of infant mortality constructed from a single cross-sectional survey will suffer from design-induced selectivity that is progressively accentuated the further back in time the respondents are "aged." That is because the greater the distance between the survey date and a child's birth date, the more limited the panel of mothers is to younger ages.[5] In addition, some portion of mothers of births occurring even as little as a decade prior to the survey will have aged out of the sampling frame. Because the risk of infant death varies with maternal age, this will bias mortality estimates for the earlier years. We have attempted to adjust for this bias in the models presented below by including terms for mother's age at the time of a birth. The success of this adjustment depends on the temporal stability of the maternal age at birth effect—partly a matter of assumption.

Owing to the volume of material in our investigations based on the 1988 NSFC, the analysis presented here is limited to Sichuan Province, a mountain-ringed basin in southwest China with a population of 107 million in 1990. In our larger research project, because of the need to restrict the massiveness of the cross-province replications, we use Sichuan data as a "test bed" for exploratory purposes. We have in fact carried out some of the modeling presented here for each province (except Tibet, the data for which are unavailable to us) and at the national level (Mason, Lavely, and Ono 1993). Our analyses of Sichuan are by far the most extensive, and this chapter focuses on that portion concerned with temporal variability.

Were Sichuan an independent country it would be the tenth most populous nation in the world. As a province in the interior, Sichuan lagged the nation economically in the 1980s. In 1986 it ranked 26th out of 29 provinces in income per capita (State Statistical Bureau 1988:55). In earlier decades it was closer to the national median. However, Sichuan has been a leader in fertility control since the inception of the one-child policy in 1979. In short, Sichuan is large and interesting in its own right and thus useful for prototyping analyses to be replicated over provinces.

In turning now to the Sichuan NSFC data, we consider first whether (a) the sample size is large enough to sustain analysis and (b) whether the recall errors and sample and design selectivity inherent in the data so dominate the temporal variation of infant mortality in the Sichuan sample that province-specific analysis is unwarranted.

As Table 6.1 indicates, the Sichuan component of the NSFC sample contains 44,930 births and 3,579 infant deaths—a large sample for some

TABLE 6.1   Births and Infant Deaths by Sex and Residence, Sichuan NSFC

	Births	Deaths	Infant Mortality Rate
Rural male	19,561	1,800	92
Rural female	18,495	1,484	80
Urban	6,874	295	43
Total	44,930	3,579	80

Note: The infant mortality rate is the number of infant deaths per 1,000 births.

Source: National Survey of Fertility and Contraception (NSFC). Counts are based on births for which there are no missing data for a superset of the variables described in this analysis.

purposes—but in this case we wish to study variation in the IMRs over time. Thus Table 6.2 provides the distributions of sample births and deaths by residence (urban vs. rural), sex, and year of birth.[6] Because of the relatively small size of the sample of urban births, we have not attempted to analyze urban infant mortality separately by sex. Furthermore, we consider the urban sample to be too small to support discrete time (interannual) analysis. Thus, with the exception of the initial inspection of the time series, we will use a constrained function of time in our analysis of urban infant mortality in Sichuan.[7] Although Table 6.2 reveals the sex-specific series for rural births and deaths to be sizable even within years, whether the sample sizes will sustain separate analyses by sex also depends on whether the temporal variability has face validity. Figure 6.1 addresses this concern.

The four panels of Figure 6.1 display five Sichuan infant mortality time series for the period 1950–1988, as derived from the raw data contained in Table 6.2. These series are contrasted with Banister's (1987) reconstruction of national infant mortality rates for the period 1950–1984, the only long time series of IMRs for China that we know of. The two data sets are not strictly comparable. The NSFC data refer to Sichuan; Banister's are national. The NSFC data refer to the mortality experience of birth cohorts; Banister's data refer to period mortality.[8]

Still, the two bodies of data reveal patterns that are essentially alike. The Sichuan sample-based series and the national series (Figure 6.1A) begin with high IMRs—between 150 and 200 in the 1950s—rise to a sharp peak during the famine of 1959–1961 and decline rapidly thereafter, leveling off in the 1970s and 1980s. Banister's data peak in 1960, while the NSFC's peak in 1959. We would expect cohort data to lead period data because of the difference in accounting basis, but this probably explains

TABLE 6.2 Counts of Births and Deaths by Year, Sex, and Residence, Sichuan, 1950–1988

	Rural Male		Rural Female		Urban	
Year	Births	Deaths	Births	Deaths	Births	Deaths
1950	61	17	65	11	44	9
1951	66	11	57	12	32	4
1952	127	26	94	18	50	5
1953	157	18	131	22	62	6
1954	186	36	175	25	86	5
1955	204	31	208	27	107	8
1956	232	44	208	42	110	8
1957	280	53	256	27	143	11
1958	297	71	269	49	168	18
1959	182	53	166	50	108	17
1960	130	31	134	32	128	10
1961	164	35	130	28	98	9
1962	338	45	398	58	177	9
1963	681	71	619	68	317	12
1964	635	81	611	71	256	12
1965	651	84	668	63	223	8
1966	798	64	638	59	200	5
1967	625	63	600	48	212	9
1968	815	65	870	58	317	11
1969	814	60	798	59	273	7
1970	863	73	825	46	284	8
1971	975	76	928	67	254	10
1972	966	79	884	56	259	11
1973	945	66	905	60	235	7
1974	997	81	933	61	238	10
1975	874	62	873	61	215	6
1976	656	50	665	31	345	5
1977	524	30	535	29	**242**	7
1978	437	41	416	21	130	6
1979	478	32	438	31	145	4
1980	384	27	365	26	130	5
1981	481	39	469	21	202	9
1982	578	35	512	25	250	5
1983	394	17	385	20	191	6
1984	390	25	328	16	174	4
1985	483	33	444	19	178	5

(continued)

TABLE 6.2 *(continued)*

	Rural Male		Rural Female		Urban	
Year	Births	Deaths	Births	Deaths	Births	Deaths
1986	739	27	692	35	215	3
1987	714	36	605	21	213	7
1988	240	12	198	11	105	1

Note: For 1977, there are no urban births in the data as made available to the authors. We have not found the reason. The embolded frequencies are interpolated and are used only in Figure 6.1.

Source: National Survey of Fertility and Contraception (NSFC). Counts are based on births for which there are no missing data in a superset of the variables described in this analysis.

only part of the discordance. Famine effects began earlier, and lasted longer, in Sichuan than in the rest of China (Peng 1987).

The various recall, selection, and design effects mentioned above have undoubtedly taken their toll on the sample. For these reasons, we make no claims about the absolute levels of the Sichuan IMRs. That they are in remarkable accord with Banister's national series even for the peak famine years (see especially panels A and B) may be misleading. Sichuan was one of two provinces most devastated by the famine (the other being Anhui), and its famine mortality peak should be higher than that of the nation. Nevertheless, the general concordance of the Sichuan pooled rural-urban series with the national series (Figure 6.1A); the generally higher rural, and lower urban, infant mortality (Figure 6.1B); and the usually comparable sex-specific rural infant mortality (Figures 6.1C–D) all taken together suggest considerable face and construct validity for the Sichuan data and support the focus in this chapter on trends over time.[9]

Exploratory Analysis Based on the NSFC

A major consequence of the use of a single survey such as the 1988 NSFC is that on a priori grounds it cannot by itself provide an estimated time series of infant mortality with optimal statistical properties. Although the reasons for this were elaborated above, we restate them here in different terms more clearly linked to data analysis: (1) The cross-sectional sample of women age 15–57 in 1988 is in no way constrained to mirror the infant-mortality-relevant composition of mothers in each prior year back to the starting point of the series. (2) The needed compositional information is unavailable (if it were, we would not need to resort to the

FIGURE 6.1A Sichuan-NSFC IMR (1950–1988) Compared with Banister's IMR (1950–1984) for China

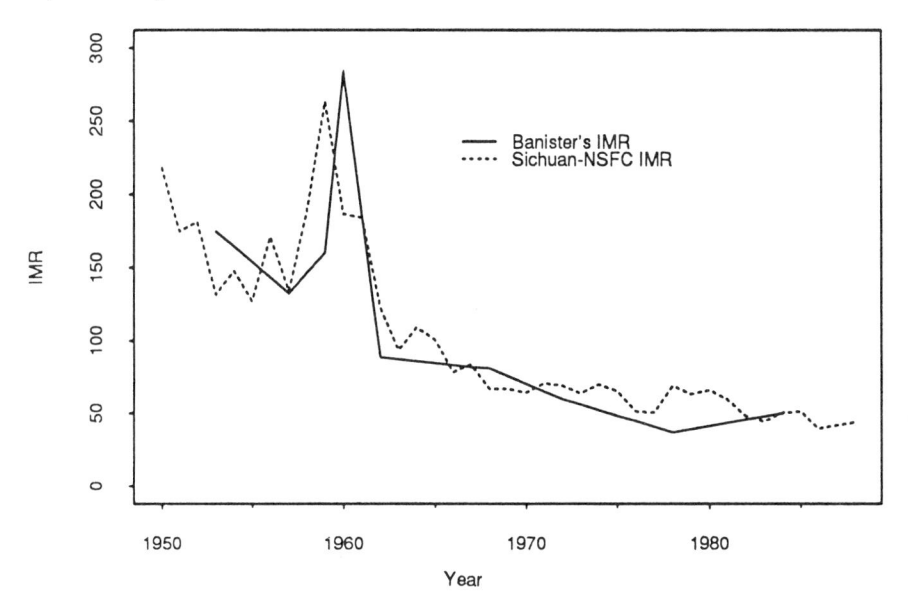

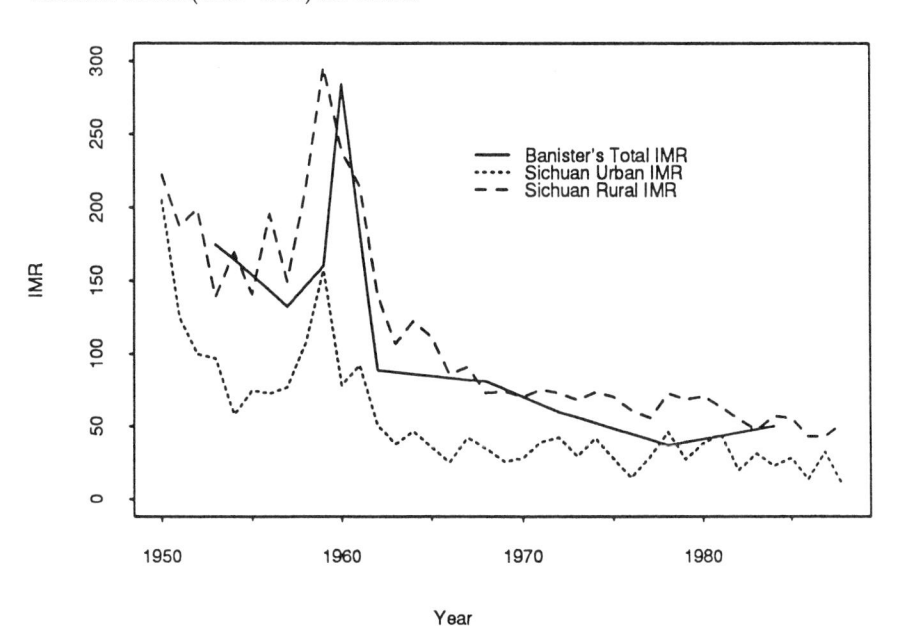

FIGURE 6.1B Sichuan-NSFC Urban and Rural IMR (1950–1988) Compared with Banister's IMR (1950–1984) for China

FIGURE 6.1C Sichuan-NSFC Rural Male IMR (1950–1988) Compared with Banister's Male IMR (1950–1984) for China

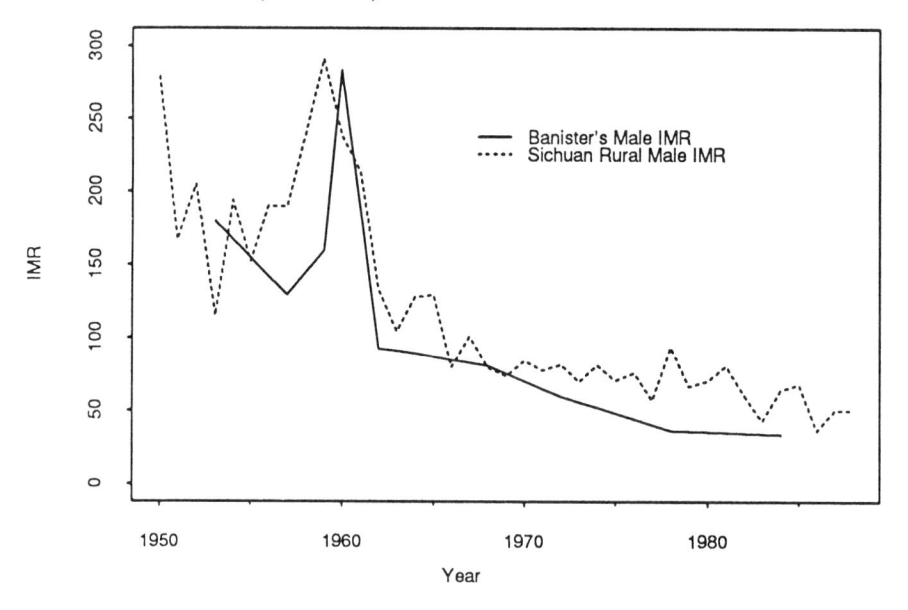

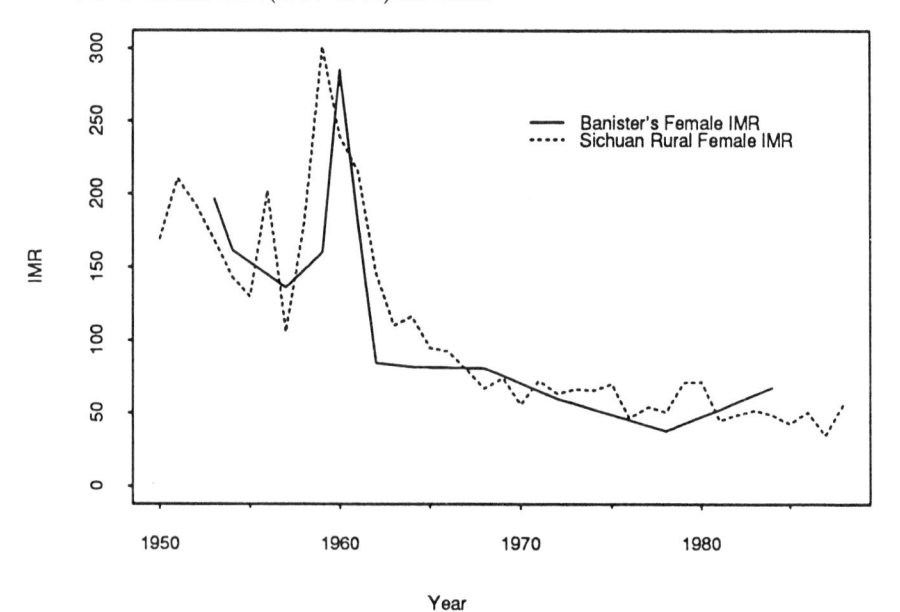

FIGURE 6.1D Sichuan-NSFC Rural Female IMR (1950–1988) Compared with Banister's Female IMR (1950–1984) for China

use of a single survey). (3) The relationship between infant mortality and mortality-relevant composition may actually change over time, though this can be partially assessed even with a single cross-section of mothers. (4) Underreporting and event displacement can not be overcome at the microlevel. About this last problem there is little we can do except to rely on the comparisons offered in Figure 6.1, which clearly indicate that under-reporting and event displacement do *not* overwhelm the general features of temporal variability in infant mortality. With regard to problems 1–3, the generalized linear statistical model provides a helpful framework. Using it, we can discern not only which of the basic markers of family and individual placement within society affect infant mortality, and how and to what extent, but also how these effects have changed over time. In addition the framework provides the foundation for an assessment of the *impact* of changing composition in the markers of family and individual placement on the decline of infant mortality in China.

A Descriptive Modeling Framework

The year-specific Sichuan infant mortality rates in Figure 6.1A are infant deaths per 1,000—equivalently, proportions dying within 12 months multiplied by 1,000. Using births in the NSFC Sichuan sample, these proportions are simply appropriately transformed sample logits from a fitted equation based on the form

$$\omega_{it} = \beta_0 + \sum_{t=1}^{t=T} \beta_t P_{it}, \tag{1}$$

where ω_{it} denotes the (unobserved) logit of infant death for the ith infant in the sample who happens to have been born in the tth year ($i = 1, \ldots, N; t = 1, \ldots, T$), and the P_{it} are dummy variables

$$P_{it} = \begin{cases} 1 & \text{if the } i\text{th child is born in the } t\text{th year;} \\ 0 & \text{if this child is born in a different year.} \end{cases}$$

To identify the β_t we impose the linear restriction $\beta_T = 0$, so that the remaining $T - 1$ year coefficients become contrasts between years t and T.

With the formulation of equation 1, the infant mortality rate in the tth year is

$$\left(\frac{e^{\beta_0 + \beta_t}}{1 + e^{\beta_0 + \beta_t}} \right) 1{,}000 \,.$$

Rates so derived are subject to change if covariates are introduced into the equation. In particular, for the set of covariates $\{X_k\}$, $k = 1, \ldots, K$, if the infant mortality regression becomes

$$\omega_{it} = \beta_0 + \sum_{t=1}^{t=T} \beta_t P_{it} + \sum_{k=1}^{k=K} \gamma_k X_{ik} \qquad (2)$$

the period contrasts are unlikely to equal those of equation 1 because the covariates will not be orthogonal to year. It is obvious that the choice of covariates matters in this context, but why introduce them in the first place? Because without them, we simply have a set of marginal period contrasts and IMRs based on a single cross-section of mothers in 1988, and these marginal contrasts are not warranted to provide statistically unbiased or consistent or in any sense "good" estimates of the IMR time series, despite their apparent plausibility established in Figure 6.1. Although, as noted above, the introduction of covariates cannot solve all problems, failure to control for mortality-salient factors that may be associated with period differences would mean that we have no basis for assessing either the interannual contrasts or the IMRs derived from them. Controlling to the extent possible for the mortality-salient factors means, for example, that the period contrasts hold maternal education constant, and we can also determine whether maternal education and period interact, that is, whether the effect of maternal education varies over time. This provides valuable information about the interannual variability in IMRs.[10]

The specification of equation 2 is also valuable for the estimation of IMRs, as distinguished from period contrasts. To obtain "fitted" year-specific IMRs from equation 2, it is necessary to choose values for the covariates. That is, the fitted year-specific IMRs will depend on the "composition" of the covariates. This is a standardization problem; as in all standardizations, the standardizing distribution(s) must be chosen by the analyst, and there is no "right" answer. These design implications stemming from the use of the NSFC birth and death histories set the agenda for the balance of this section, in which we define the list of covariates for inclusion in equation 2, extend the analytic formulation to survival models, report on interactions, and ultimately use the notion of "composition" to assess the impact of temporally changing sociodemographic and other characteristics on the decline of infant mortality in Sichuan.

Covariates of Infant Mortality

Although its questionnaire is remarkably comprehensive, the NSFC was not designed as a survey of factors pertaining to infant and child health. It contains no behavioral measures relating to prenatal care, birthing conditions, child-specific access to medical care, sanitation practices, power relationships within the family, or living arrangements at the time of birth. Furthermore, some exceedingly interesting information that was collected was apparently never coded and included on the data tapes. For these reasons, the dimensions we have considered as covariates of infant mortality in our explorations are restricted to (1) maternal age at birth; (2) maternal and paternal education; (3) maternal and paternal occupation; (4) parity, birth spacing and multiple birth status; and (5) sibset composition. Initial exploration showed that maternal and paternal education were highly collinear and that maternal education is the more salient predictor of infant mortality. Conversely, we found that paternal occupation dominated maternal occupation. The discussion below is limited accordingly. The list of covariate dimensions utilized here, though far from complete relative to the state of the art, contains seemingly highly relevant—and indeed crucial—demographic factors and markers of familial position, especially given the absence of a major social science research tradition in China focused on infant and child mortality and health.[11] We next discuss these basic socioeconomic and demographic dimensions that on a priori grounds should be related to the risk of infant death in China.

Parental residence. Conditions vary so dramatically between urban and rural settings in China that familial residence cannot be ignored. Some recent research, to maintain consistency with the official summary tables published from the 1990 census, utilizes the tripartite categorization of city, town, and county. That classification scheme effectively subdivides the urban category. Our exploratory analysis of an even more highly detailed categorization of residence suggested that the rural-urban dichotomy used here would suffice. Because of the markedly different life prospects for children born in urban and rural settings, in the microanalyses presented here we estimate separate logistic regressions for infant mortality by residence. A limitation of the data that we are unable to redress is that residence is family-specific at the time of the interview in 1988, not birth-specific. Furthermore, the survey was explicitly not limited to the locally-registered population, and there was considerable migration before 1988. Since most migration between the rural and urban sectors is rural-to-urban (with some variation, as, for example, during the Cultural Revolution), it is likely that the differences between the rural and urban logistic regressions that we shall observe are in fact underestimates.

Maternal education. It is widely observed that the higher the mother's education, the better her infant's chance of survival. There are many reasons for this, such as the educated mother's superior knowledge of sanitation, her status in the household, and her effectiveness in dealing with health systems (Caldwell 1979; Caldwell and Caldwell 1985). Education is measured in five categories combining literacy status and school experience, with the lowest category illiterate and the highest upper-middle-school education and above.

Paternal occupation. We expect a father's social and economic status to influence an infant's chances of survival. Our grouping of the NSFC's occupational codes into the categories of peasant, worker, cadre, and other is a hybrid intended to reflect the main social and economic division of Chinese society into those employed by the state (mainly urban workers) and those outside the state sector (mainly rural peasants).[12] Many "peasants" are in fact engaged in commercial or industrial activities, including services. "Workers" refers to those who are employed by the state in manual occupations and who enjoy the entitlements that pertain to this status. "Cadres" are government officials and administrators in state organizations and enterprises.[13]

Maternal age at birth. We expect a ∪-shaped function in which births at youngest and oldest ages are at greatest risk, a widely observed pattern (Rutstein 1984). This is probably due primarily to sociological causes, but there is evidence that at younger maternal ages some infant health problems are also biological (Bongaarts 1987). Our age measure is divided into six age classes, beginning with mothers under age 20 and ending with mothers age 40 and above.

Parity, birth spacing, and multiple-birth status of the index birth. There are biological reasons for expecting first children to be at greater risk (Bongaarts 1987). However, these can be offset by social, cultural, and political factors. For example, the one-child policy created special circumstances placing higher-parity infants at greater risk (Coale and Banister 1994). In addition, higher-parity infants enter families in which circumstances may be straitened relative to those experienced by the firstborn. A shorter interval between the previous birth and the index birth increases the chance that the index birth will be competing for parental care with the preceding birth. Maternal depletion may also be a factor, as maternal health is undermined by childbirth (Palloni and Millman 1986; Koenig et al. 1990). Multiple births are at increased risk for biological and social reasons. There is increased risk at birth, and there is more intense competition for parental care. Parents unwilling to care for two or more infants simultaneously may neglect one or both. We have constructed a polytomous variable that encompasses several distinct circumstances. First, we distinguish between singleton births and multiple births, with the expectation that multiple births will experience higher risk of death. For singletons, we distinguish between first, second, third, and fourth and higher-parity births, with the expectation that first-parity births may be at higher risk of death. Finally, we distinguish between singleton births that occur within 24 months of a previous birth or 24 months or more after a previous birth, with the expectation that shorter birth spacing increases the risk of mortality.[14]

Sex of the index birth. All other things equal, male births are at greater risk of infant death (Bittles et al. 1991). As noted below, the ceteris paribus condition is not additive. Furthermore, there is the added problem, especially for births in the 1980s, of substantial underreporting of female births that became infant mortalities for whatever reason. In the present instance, and at the microlevel, we can analyze only *reported* births. Because of the complexities introduced by the sex of the index birth, we analyze infant mortality separately by sex for rural births, but the size of the Sichuan sample of urban births, as noted earlier, precludes similar treatment. For the urban logistic regressions, sex of index birth is included as a covariate.

Sibset composition at the time of the index birth. Numerous studies have described son preference and demographic behavior that is contingent on the number and sex of previous births (e.g., Arnold and Liu 1986; Muhuri and Preston 1991; Hull 1990; Yi et al. 1993). Because of the conditions imposed by China's birth planning program, we expect infants born in the 1980s with more surviving elder siblings to be at greater risk, and we expect female infants born in the 1980s with an elder female sibling to be at particular risk.

Table 6.7, which also serves other purposes, presents the distributions of the covariates described above (see the columns headed "observed"). Because the units of analysis are births, the interpretation (for example) of the distribution of mother's educational level for rural births is that 47 percent of rural births were to mothers who described themselves as illiterate.[15]

Results Based on Binary Response Models

Using the covariates described above (except sibset composition) and including them as dummy variable classifications, we have estimated binary response models of the form given by equation 2 separately for rural male and rural female births.[16] The period covered is the same as that shown in Figure 6.1—the years 1950–1988. For urban births, the logistic regression is of the form

$$\omega_{it} = \beta_0 + \beta_1 \ln(Year_{it} - 1949) + \beta_2 GLF + \sum_{k=1}^{k=K} \gamma_k X_{ik}, \qquad (3)$$

where $Year_{it}$ is the year of birth of the ith child and $GLF = 1$ if the birth year is in the period 1958–1961, and 0 otherwise.[17] The results of the computations are presented in Table 6.3.

The patterns of the relationships of the covariate dimensions to infant mortality are largely in the substantively expected direction. For example, across residence-sex combinations we find that the more years of schooling the mother has the lower the risk of infant death. Maternal age shows some of the expected ∪-shaped relation to the risk of infant death—generally lowest for mothers in their 30s.[18] Short spacing between the prior birth and the index birth increases the risk of infant death for the index child. Infants born as one of several are at substantially greater risk. Year of birth is also related to the risk of death for male and female rural births, as well as for urban births. The coefficient for sex of child, for urban births, is in the theoretically expected direction for a gender-neutral society (which China is not) but does not approach statistical significance. Based on a likelihood ratio test, the set of paternal occupation contrasts does not achieve statistical significance at any conventional level for rural male births and urban births. For female births, the statistically significant peasant-other contrast is uninteresting, while the remaining contrasts with the peasant category do not achieve statistical significance.[19] Although not discernible from the raw contrasts in Table 6.3, the rural and urban patterns seen in Figure 6.1 do not disappear in the presence of the covariates, as will be clear in later displays.

As Table 6.3 shows, there are small differences between the regressions for rural male and rural female births. Similarly, there are differences between the rural and urban regressions. Perhaps most notably, the maternal education effect is strongest for urban births. As we next show, not only are there differences between the mortality functions for rural and urban births, there are also interactions involving selected covariates within a sex-residence combination.

Results Based on Survival Models

Although it is straightforward to analyze interaction in the binary response formulation used to obtain the results presented in Table 6.3, we prefer to extend that formulation to cast a wider net. In particular, we modify equations 1–2 to become survival models. The approach used thus far treats the first year of life as a single undifferentiated period. This is a simplification—possibly without consequence—because infant mortality is concentrated in the first hours and weeks of life. It could be that the covariate effects will change upon the introduction of a hazard specification or that the hazard is nonproportional (i.e., the covariates interact with the hazard). This is worth checking at the same time that we con-

TABLE 6.3 Logistic Regressions of Infant Mortality, Separately by Sex for Rural Births, and for Urban Births, Sichuan, 1950–1988

Covariates	Rural Male	Rural Female	Urban
Intercept	−2.807	−2.884	−1.136
Parity–birth spacing			
Parity 1			
Parity 2, < 24 months	.382[d]	.427[d]	.414[a]
Parity 2, ≥ 24 months	−.112	−.157	−.108
Parity 2, < 24 months	.572[d]	.784[d]	.386
Parity 3, ≥ 24 months	−.116	.085	.044
Parity 4, < 24 months	.862[d]	1.129[d]	.933[d]
Parity 4, ≥ 24 months	.118	.104	−.059
Member of multiple birth	2.227[d]	2.090[d]	2.828[d]
Maternal age at birth			
< 20 years	.313	.618[b]	−.665
20–24	.096	.319	−.997
25–29	−.117	−.041	−.869
30–34	−.267	−.096	−1.472[a]
35–39	−.314	.024	−1.511[a]
≥ 40			
Male			.181
Maternal education			
Illiterate			
Protoliterate	−.094	−.191[b]	−.256
Primary school	−.142[b]	−.243[d]	−.437[b]
Lower middle school	−.546[d]	−.376[c]	−.631[c]
≥ Upper middle school	−.484	−.519	−.949[d]
Paternal occupation			
Peasant			
Worker	−.283	−.138	.195
Cadre	−.402	−.338	−.100
Other	−.096	−.183[b]	.251
Log (birth year−1949)			−.364[c]
Great Leap Forward (1958–1961)			.709[d]
Birth year			
1950	1.583[d]	.737	
1951	.934[b]	1.069[b]	

(continued)

TABLE 6.3 (continued)

| | Rural | | |
Covariates	Male	Female	Urban
1952	1.163c	.984b	
1953	.508	.852b	
1954	1.113c	.671a	
1955	.881b	.539	
1956	1.200d	1.078c	
1957	1.235d	.408	
1958	1.516d	1.022d	
1959	1.868d	1.790d	
1960	1.657d	1.401d	
1961	1.470d	1.383d	
1962	.968c	.939c	
1963	.697b	.589a	
1964	.806b	.580a	
1965	.797b	.349	
1966	.307	.364	
1967	.578a	.197	
1968	.351	−.011	
1969	.229	.131	
1970	.408	−.232	
1971	.291	.113	
1972	.387	−.104	
1973	.198	.041	
1974	.342	−.010	
1975	.185	.074	
1976	.318	−.336	
1977	.029	−.192	
1978	.575a	−.104	
1979	.227	.280	
1980	.248	.217	
1981	.467	−.234	
1982	.192	−.202	
1983	−.242	−.184	
1984	.262	−.171	
1985	.307	−.307	

(continued)

The Decline of Infant Mortality in China: Sichuan, 1949–1988   171

TABLE 6.3 (continued)

| | Rural | | |
Covariates	Male	Female	Urban
1986	−.349	−.104	
1987	−.062	−.557	
1988			
Likelihood ratio test statistic	722	697	223
Degrees of freedom	57	57	22

[a] $p < .10$; [b] $p < .05$; [c] $p < .01$; [d] $p < .001$.

Note: See Table 6.1 for group Ns. See Table 6.2 for Ns specific to year and group. See Table 6.7 for distributions of other covariates. With the exception of Log (Birth Year–1949), all covariates are binary or polytomous. Polytomous variables are treated as dummy variable classifications, from which the categories omitted for normalization are: parity 1; ≥ 40 years; illiterate; peasant; 1988. The likelihood ratio test statistic compares the null and current models and is asymptotically chi-square distributed with the indicated degrees of freedom.

Source: National Survey of Fertility and Contraception (NSFC).

sider the possibility of interactions among the covariates. In the discussion that follows, we present the results of our explorations.

For the survival model formulation, we retain separate equations for rural male and rural female births and for urban births. In order to examine interactions between year of birth and other covariates, we employ smooth functions of time in conjunction with the dummy variable for the Great Leap Forward. Based on exploratory data analysis, these smooth functions are nothing more than year of birth as a linear term ($Year_{it}$ – 1949) for rural male and female births. For urban births, the time function remains as it was ($ln\ (Year)_{it}$ – 1949). In addition, sibset composition is introduced and allowed to interact with period. A final difference between the binary response and survival model formulations is that terms are introduced to characterize the hazard, which in this instance is not constrained by the commonly employed proportionality assumption.

For the first twelve months of life (separately for rural female, rural male, and urban births), Figure 6.2 presents the observed proportions dying within the first month, and then observed proportions dying at each successive month, conditional on having survived the preceding month.[20]

FIGURE 6.2 Proportion of Male and Female Infants Dying by Month, with Piecewise Linear Spline Approximation

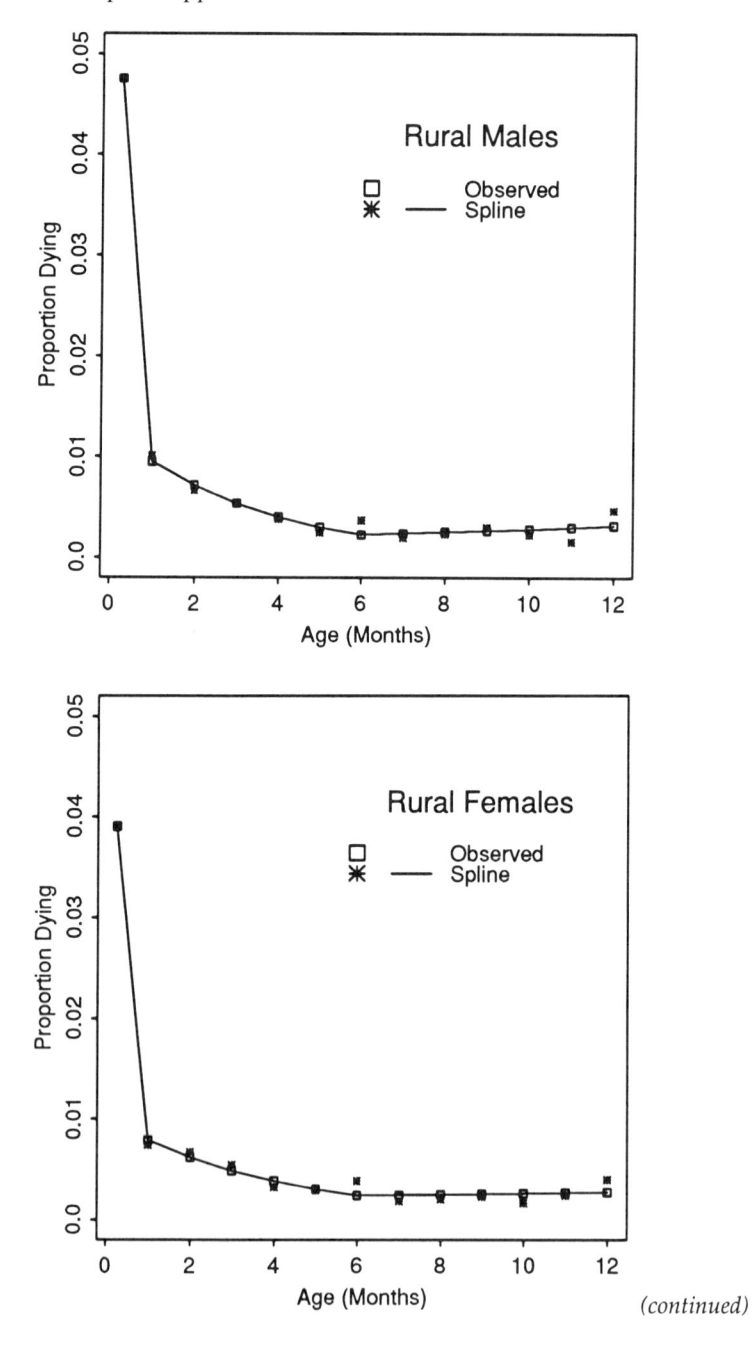

(continued)

FIGURE 6.2 (continued)

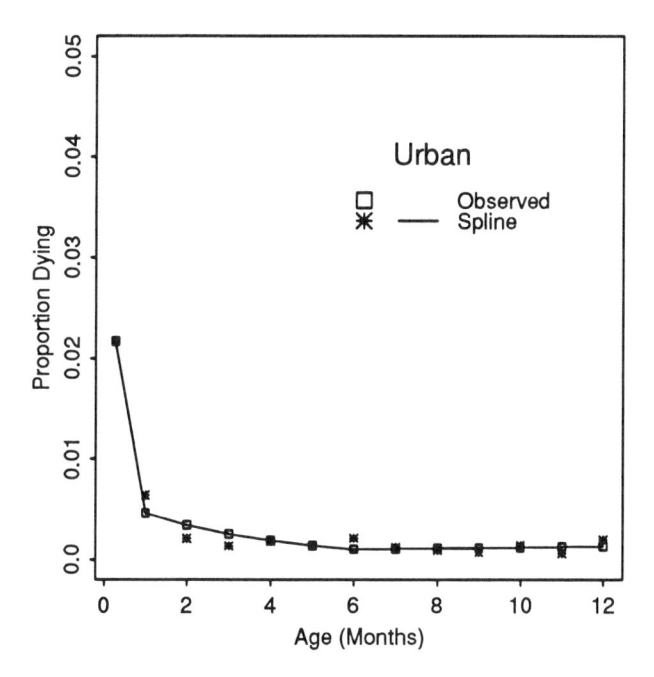

[Figure: Plot of Proportion Dying vs Age (Months) for Urban, showing Observed and Spline]

As the figure clearly indicates, the hazard can be described well by three line segments knotted at months one and six. In the logit metric the segments are straight lines. (The slightly elevated proportions at months six and 12 are the result of age heaping.) We incorporate these findings into the survival model framework. Thus to take into account the changing risk of death over the first year of life, we fit logistic regressions in which the hazard function is captured by piecewise linear splines.[21] In its additive form, this is (for rural births):

$$\omega_{ijt} = \beta_0 + \lambda_1 S_{ij1} + \lambda_2 S_{ij2} + \lambda_3 S_{ij3} + \beta_1 (Year_{it} - 1949) + \beta_2 GLF + \sum_{k=1}^{k=K} \gamma_k X_{ik}, \quad (4)$$

where S_1, S_2, and S_3 are the splines and j denotes month (0, 1, 2, ..., 12).

Tables 6.4A–C present the piecewise linear spline logistic survival regressions for rural male, rural female, and urban births. Each table contains three regressions—an additive fit that parallels the logistic regressions in Table 6.3, a fit that allows for interactions between the hazard and period, and a fit that in addition allows for interactions between sibset composition and period. The additive fit is included to indicate that no real surprises have been introduced by the minor changes in the functional forms of the covariates or by the hazard formulation—which itself reproduces what may be seen in Figure 6.2. We focus on the most detailed interactive model, which we present as the result of our explorations for interactions among the covariates as well as between the hazard and the covariates.

Maternal education, paternal occupation, maternal age at birth, and the parity-spacing-multiple-birth-status classification are included as additive covariates in the regressions presented in Tables 6.4A–C, no interactions involving these dimensions having been found within the residence-sex groupings. The results for these variables are comparable to those presented in Table 6.3. Maternal education is inversely related to infant mortality, with the gradient steepest for urban births. Paternal occupation as included here does not affect infant mortality. Again, maternal age at birth has the somewhat ∪-shaped relation to the risk of infant death seen earlier. Infants born as twins, triplets, and quadruplets are at greatest risk; at somewhat lower risk are singletons born less than two years after the birth of an older sibling (the risk increases with parity). First births and those born two years or more after their preceding sibling are least at risk; there is no parity effect for infants born more than 24 months after a preceding sibling.

We have found some indications of interaction between year of birth and age at death (within the first 12 months of life), as well as between sex of the index child, sibset composition, and period. Tables 6.5 and 6.6 provide conditional coefficients derived from Tables 6.4A–C.

To assess whether the mortality decline was more salient at any particular duration after birth, the piecewise linear spline is multiplied by the birth-year function. Table 6.5 shows the year and *GLF* coefficients conditional on survival times within the first year of life.

For both urban and rural births, the secular decline of infant mortality is larger in the outer months of the first year than it is in the neonatal period. This result parallels Dankert and van Ginneken's (1991:482) finding that the ratio of neonatal to infant mortality increased from the 1960s to the 1980s in Shaanxi, Hebei, and Shanghai. Neonatal mortality is inherently less amenable to public health interventions.

In the case of the famine, for urban and rural male births, the influence of the Great Leap Forward was greater in the post-neonatal period than in the neonatal. For rural female births, the famine effect is lowest in the first week after birth and elevated thereafter, with little indication of sustained increase as duration lengthens. In general, these results are consistent with the hypothesis that infants are protected from disease and famine by

TABLE 6.4A Piecewise Linear Logistic Hazard Regressions of Infant Mortality, Rural Male Births, Sichuan, 1950–1988

Covariates	Model 1	Model 2	Model 3
Intercept	−.241	−1.190[a]	−.819
Parity–birth spacing			
Parity 1			
Parity 2, < 24 months	.339[d]	.340[d]	.390[d]
Parity 2, ≥ 24 months	−.129	−.125	−.070
Parity 3, < 24 months	.486[d]	.488[d]	.604[d]
Parity 3, ≥ 24 months	−.149	−.144	−.019
Parity 4, < 24 months	.757[d]	.762[d]	1.008[d]
Parity 4, ≥ 24 months	.066	.073	.308[b]
Member of multiple birth	2.040[d]	2.046[d]	2.184[d]
Maternal age at birth			
< 20 years	.305	.297	.109
20–24	.106	.103	−.063
25–29	−.079	−.079	−.230
30–34	−.264	−.262	−.376[a]
35–39	−.350	−.348	−.378
≥ 40			
Maternal education			
Illiterate			
Protoliterate	−.095	−.093	−.079
Primary school	−.153[b]	−.152[b]	−.134[b]
Lower middle school	−.517[d]	−.523[d]	−.507[d]
≥ Upper middle school	−.444	−.457	−.476
Paternal occupation			
Peasant			
Worker	−.278	−.270	−.262
Cadre	−.406	−.397	−.387
Other	−.091	−.091	−.091
Birth year	−.032[d]	−.018[c]	−.021[c]
Great Leap Forward (1958–1961)	.699[d]	.291	.259
Child's age spline			
0–1 month	−2.215[d]	−1.644[b]	−1.667[b]
1–6 months	−.289[d]	.165	.151
6–12 months	.058[b]	.059	.060

(continued)

TABLE 6.4A *(continued)*

Covariates	Model 1	Model 2	Model 3
Spline • year of birth interactions			
0–1 month • birth year		–.008	–.008
1–6 months • birth year		–.007[b]	–.007[b]
6–12 months • birth year		.000	.000
0–1 month • GLF		.188	.192
1–6 months • GLF		.165[b]	.168[b]
6–12 months • GLF		–.061	–.060
Born in the 1980s			–.017
Number of older brothers			–.056
Number of older sisters			–.158[d]
Sibset composition • 1980s			
Number of older brothers • 1980s			.248[b]
Number of older sisters • 1980s			.137
Likelihood ratio test statistic	3,212	3,286	3,310
Degrees of freedom	24	30	35

[a] $p < .10$; [b] $p < .05$; [c] $p < .01$; [d] $p < .001$.

Note: See Table 6.1 for group Ns. See Table 6.2 for Ns specific to year and group. See Table 6.7 for distributions of other covariates. Polytomous variables are treated as dummy variable classifications, from which the categories omitted for normalization are: parity 1; ≥ 40 years; illiterate; peasant; 1988. Birth year is coded as (*Year* – 1900). Child's age spline is a piecewise linear spline knotted at months 1 and 6. The likelihood ratio test statistic compares the null and current models, and is asymptotically chi-square distributed with the indicated degrees of freedom.

Source: National Survey of Fertility and Contraception (NSFC).

TABLE 6.4B Piecewise Linear Logistic Hazard Regressions of Infant Mortality, Rural Female Births, Sichuan, 1950–1988

Covariates	Model 1	Model 2	Model 3
Intercept	−.469	−.087	.328
Parity–birth spacing			
Parity 1			
Parity 2, < 24 months	.387d	.390d	.444d
Parity 2, ≥ 24 months	−.188b	−.187b	−.114
Parity 3, < 24 months	.676d	.679d	.805d
Parity 3, ≥ 24 months	.021	.027	.168
Parity 4, < 24 months	.978d	.985d	1.212d
Parity 4, ≥ 24 months	.034	.041	.270
Member of multiple birth	1.899d	1.901d	2.000d
Maternal age at birth			
< 20 years	.597b	.584b	.362
20–24	.335	.331	.126
25–29	.032	.034	−.161
30–34	−.059	−.056	−.206
35–39	−.010	−.008	−.067
≥ 40			
Maternal education			
Illiterate			
Protoliterate	−.189b	−.188b	−.180b
Primary school	−.233d	−.232d	−.227d
Lower middle school	−.327b	−.337	−.343b
≥ Upper middle school	−.442	−.456	−.478
Paternal occupation			
Peasant			
Worker	−.197	−.189	−.178
Cadre	−.413	−.408	−.396
Other	−.178	.179b	.182b
Birth year	−.035d	−.040d	−.043d
Great Leap Forward (1958–1961)	.699d	.247	.215
Child's age spline			
0–1 month	−2.191d	−4.772d	−4.682d
1–6 months	−.239d	.580c	.553c
6–12 months	.024	.092	.090

(continued)

TABLE 6.4B *(continued)*

Covariates	Model 1	Model 2	Model 3
Spline • year of birth interactions			
0–1 months • birth year		.036c	.035c
1–6 months • birth year		−.012d	−.011d
6–12 months • birth year		−.001	−.001
0–1 months • GLF		.748b	.732a
1–6 months • GLF		−.079	−.075
6–12 months • GLF		.088	.089
Born in the 1980s			.073
Number of older brothers			−.140c
Number of older sisters			−.057
Sibset composition • 1980s			
Number of older brothers • 1980s			−.126
Number of older sisters • 1980s			.224b
Likelihood ratio test statistic	2,497	2,546	2,563
Degrees of freedom	24	30	35

[a] $p < .10$; [b] $p < .05$; [c] $p < .01$; [d] $p < .001$.

Note: See Table 6.1 for group Ns. See Table 6.2 for Ns specific to year and group. See Table 6.7 for distributions of other covariates. Polytomous variables are treated as dummy variable classifications, from which the categories omitted for normalization are: parity 1; ≥ 40 years; illiterate; peasant; 1988. Birth year is coded as (*Year* – 1900). Child's age spline is a piecewise linear spline knotted at months 1 and 6. The likelihood ratio test statistic compares the null and current models, and is asymptotically chi-square distributed with the indicated degrees of freedom.

Source: National Survey of Fertility and Contraception (NSFC).

TABLE 6.4C Piecewise Linear Logistic Hazard Regressions of Infant Mortality, Urban Births, Sichuan, 1950–1988

Covariates	Model 1	Model 2	Model 3
Intercept	−1.405	−1.913[a]	−1.780[a]
Parity–birth spacing			
Parity 1			
Parity 2, < 24 months	.411[a]	.413[a]	.524[b]
Parity 2, ≥ 24 months	−.091	−.087	.005
Parity 3, < 24 months	.394	.397	.614[a]
Parity 3, ≥ 24 months	.070	.078	.289
Parity 4, < 24 months	.933[d]	.939[d]	1.293[d]
Parity 4, ≥ 24 months	−.029	−.024	.330
Member of multiple birth	2.654[d]	2.655[d]	2.773[d]
Maternal age at birth			
< 20 years	−.612	−.599	−.662
20–24	−.994	−.987	−1.013
25–29	−.864	−.856	−.861
30–34	−1.465[a]	−1.459[a]	−1.432[a]
35–39	−1.513[a]	−1.505[a]	−1.329
≥ 40			
Male	.172	.173	.173
Maternal education			
Illiterate			
Protoliterate	−.254	−.263	−.246
Primary school	−.399[b]	−.400[b]	−.384[b]
Lower middle school	−.591[c]	−.596[c]	−.600[c]
≥ Upper middle school	−.886[d]	−.893[d]	−.910[d]
Paternal occupation			
Peasant			
Worker	.205	.205	.220
Cadre	−.088	−.086	−.065
Other	.242	.244	.256
Log (birth year–1949)	−.347[c]	−.141	−.195
Great Leap Forward (1958–1961)	.675[d]	.324	.318
Child's age spline			
0–1 month	−2.086[d]	−1.356	−1.393[a]
1–6 months	−.299[d]	−.320	−.319
6–12 months	.040	.123	.119

(continued)

TABLE 6.4C *(continued)*

Covariates	Model 1	Model 2	Model 3
Spline • year of birth interactions			
0–1 months • birth year		−.289	−.275
1–6 months • birth year		.006	.006
6–12 months • birth year		−.051	−.050
0–1 month • GLF		.253	.264
1–6 months • GLF		.037	.038
6–12 months • GLF		.161	.161
Born in the 1980s			.075
Number of older brothers			−.118
Number of older sisters			−.153
Sibset composition • 1980s			
Number of older brothers • 1980s			.699[b]
Number of older sisters • 1980s			−.069
Likelihood ratio test statistic	638	650	656
Degrees of freedom	25	31	36

[a] $p < .10$; [b] $p < .05$; [c] $p < .01$; [d] $p < .001$.

Note: See Table 6.1 for group Ns. See Table 6.2 for Ns specific to year and group. See Table 6.7 for distributions of other covariates. Polytomous variables are treated as dummy variable classifications, from which the categories omitted for normalization are: parity 1; ≥ 40 years; illiterate; peasant; 1988. Birth year is coded as *(Year − 1900)*. Child's age spline is a piecewise linear spline knotted at months 1 and 6. The likelihood ratio test statistic compares the null and current models, and is asymptotically chi-square distributed with the indicated degrees of freedom.

Source: National Survey of Fertility and Contraception (NSFC).

breastfeeding and put at risk by supplementary feeding or weaning that would begin later in the first year of life (Coale, Li, and Han 1988).

In Table 6.6 we question whether the influence of sibset composition on mortality varied by historical period. This hypothesis arises from the observation that the birth-planning policy, particularly the one-child policy that was put into place in the 1980s, put additional pressures on families with particular sex preferences for children, leading to neglect of children of the unwanted sex.

Table 6.6 shows the effect of male and female sibs on mortality contingent on whether the birth was before or during the 1980s, separately for rural male and rural female births and for urban births. For rural births, over the entire 1950–1988 period infant mortality is inversely related to the number of opposite-sex siblings alive at the time of the birth of the index child. For same-sex siblings, we find no effect during the 1950–1979 period. In the 1980s, however, infant mortality is directly related to the number of same-sex siblings alive at the time of the birth of the index child. The risk pertaining to gender redundancy is essentially symmetric for males and females, suggesting that male preference coexists with a desire for familial gender balance, and sex provides only minor protec-

TABLE 6.5 Birth Year Coefficients by Residence, Sex, and Age of Infant, Sichuan, 1950–1988

Age of Infant	Rural Male Year	Rural Male GLF	Rural Female Year	Rural Female GLF	Urban Year	Urban GLF
< 1 month	−.023	.309	−.034	.404	−.266	.386
1 month	−.028	.451	−.008	.948	−.470	.582
2 months	−.035	.619	−.019	.873	−.464	.619
3 months	−.042	.787	−.031	.798	−.458	.657
4 months	−.049	.954	−.042	.723	−.452	.695
5 months	−.056	1.122	−.053	.648	−.446	.732
6 months	−.063	1.289	−.065	.573	−.440	.770
7 months	−.063	1.229	−.066	.662	−.489	.931
8 months	−.062	1.169	−.067	.751	−.539	1.092
9 months	−.062	1.108	−.069	.839	−.589	1.254
10 months	−.062	1.048	−.070	.928	−.639	1.415
11 months	−.062	.988	−.071	1.016	−.689	1.576
12 months	−.062	.927	−.072	1.105	−.738	1.735

Note: Coefficients are derived from Table 6.4A (rural males), Table 6.4B (rural females), and Table 6.4C (urban births).

TABLE 6.6 Sibset Composition Coefficients by Residence, Sex, and Period, Sichuan, 1950–1988

	Rural Male		Rural Female		Urban	
Period	Number of Older Brothers	Number of Older Sisters	Number of Older Brothers	Number of Older Sisters	Number of Older Brothers	Number of Older Sisters
1950–1979	−.056	−.158	−.140	−.057	−.118	−.153
1980–1988	.192	−.021	−.266	.167	.581	−.221

Note: Coefficients are derived from Table 6.4A (rural males), Table 6.4B (rural females), and Table 6.4C (urban births).

tion for redundant males. The proximate mechanisms remain unknown, but these findings suggest differential treatment that is deleterious to infants of the "wrong" sex. This kind of pattern has been observed for reported sex ratios at birth (e.g., Li 1993), about which it can be plausibly presumed that some of the omitted births are in fact infant deaths. The pattern is also detected by Choe, Hao, and Wang (1995), who restricted their focus to ages one to five. Thus there is evidence that in rural China the discrimination against females that is evident in elevated sex ratios at birth continues from birth through at least the first five years of life.

Owing to the relatively small number of urban infant deaths, especially during the 1980s, the full set of interactions involving sex, sibset composition, and period is not estimable in the urban birth sample. The interactions involving sibset composition and period can, however, be estimated. The strong response according to the number of male sibs may be indicative of the varying nature of birth-planning policy in urban and rural areas. Across most of rural China in the 1980s, while the one-child ideal was nominal policy, two children per family emerged as the policy "norm." In urban China, by contrast, the one-child limit was more strictly enforced, and heavy penalties were extracted for a second birth. The desire to have a son is strong in China. Urban families who already have a son have attained this fundamental goal, and any additional child, male or female, can be considered "redundant." Those with a female infant who resist the considerable pressure of policy in order to have another child do so in order to have a son. At least half of them succeed, and thus only half of the urban infants with an older female sib would be considered redundant. Together with the relatively small urban sample, this would help to explain the absence of increase in the risk to urban infants with a female sibling in the 1980s.[22]

The interactions we have detected and discussed, though informative, have few implications for the temporal variance we are most interested in. That the decline of infant mortality appears to have been greatest in months two through 12 (with some inconsistency across sex-residence groupings) and that the *GLF* effect is likewise greatest in months two through 12 (again, with some inconsistency) does not negate the basic features of the time series: decline from the 1950s into the 1970s, with a major departure from that trend caused by the Great Leap Forward. The same conclusion holds for the period-sibset-composition interaction. Comparison of the two interaction specifications within each of Tables 6.4A–C shows that inclusion of the period-sibset-composition interaction does not affect the temporal pattern of infant mortality as measured by the year and *GLF* terms.

We also opt for simplicity with respect to the hazard formulation. As can be seen by comparing the additive specifications for urban births in Tables 6.3 and 6.4C, allowing for the month-by-month survival detail within the first year of life makes no appreciable difference to the year and *GLF* coefficients. Examination of parallel regressions for rural male and female births, not shown here, yields the same conclusion.

For all of the above reasons, then, the remaining analysis is based on the simpler additive binary response formulation of equations 2–3, for which Table 6.3 provides the basic results.

The Decline of Infant Mortality

We consider next whether it is possible to explain the decline in infant mortality. First, we examine the influence of change in population composition on the decline. This is accomplished through a decomposition based on regression standardization. Second, we juxtapose time series plots of the decline with a selected set of variables that embody major families of explanations—income, nutrition, and public health.

Sociodemographic Composition Effects

As noted in the introduction, since 1950 China has undergone a revolution in social structure and demography. Levels of female education have risen. Birth-planning campaigns have driven up the age at marriage and reduced fertility, concentrating childbearing in a narrower age range (Coale 1989; Coale et al. 1991). Birth spacing has been encouraged. All of these trends are favorable to infant survival. How much of the infant mortality decline is attributable purely to the effects of the changing microdemography of the Chinese family? To answer this question we identify three patterns of family demography representing conditions prevailing in the 1950s and early 1960s ("early"), in the 1980s ("late"), and the observed demography in the NSFC ("observed"), which is intermediate.

The values for the early, observed, and late patterns are contained in Table 6.7. The observed pattern consists of the univariate distributions of the covariates in Table 6.3, for births in all years (1950–1988). The late pattern consists of the univariate distributions for births in the years 1980–1988. Because of the inherent selection bias of the study design, the early pattern is based in part on the univariate distributions for the years 1950–1965 and in part on external evidence. In general, for the early pattern we have chosen values at the extreme range to reflect the maximum possible effect of composition change from "early" to "late." Thus we have set maternal illiteracy to 98 percent in 1950, although this rate exceeds other estimates of female illiteracy in Sichuan in the period (Lavely et al. 1990). The intent is to err on the side of compositional explanations. By substituting these values into the logistic regressions presented in Table 6.3, we can derive time series of infant mortality based on the three compositional regimes. These time series, for rural male births, rural female births, and urban births, are portrayed in Figures 6.3, 6.4, and 6.5. Figures 6.3 and 6.4 present the series using both discrete and smooth time functions.[23]

The graphs appear to tell a common story about the infant mortality decline in Sichuan. The range of values represented by early and late compositions is narrow relative to the magnitude of the decline itself, although the composition spread appears larger relative to the overall decrease for urban than rural births. To crystallize these perceptions, using the smooth birth-year functions (with the *GLF* dummy) we partition actual decline into the proportion due to compositional change and the proportion due to mortality change net of composition.

Let E_{50} denote infant mortality in 1950 estimated with "early" composition; E_{88} denote infant mortality in 1988 likewise estimated with "early" composition; and L_{88} denote infant mortality in 1988 estimated with "late" composition. Then the proportion of change due purely to mortality change net of composition so defined is

$$\frac{E_{50} - E_{88}}{E_{50} - L_{88}}$$

and the complement is due to compositional change. For rural Sichuan, only 8 percent of the IMR decline is due to compositional change; for urban Sichuan, 15 percent. Of course, these calculations are a function of the single cross-sectional sample of mothers surveyed in 1988. Given

TABLE 6.7 Early, Observed, and Late Covariate Composition, from the Perspective of the NSFC Birth Sample

	Rural			Urban		
Covariates	Early	Observed	Late	Early	Observed	Late
Parity-birth spacing						
Parity 1	25%	34%	57%	27%	47%	86%
Parity 2, < 24 months	4	7	8	7	7	3
Parity 2, ≥ 24 months	15	17	21	15	16	8
Parity 3, < 24 months	4	4	2	10	4	1
Parity 3, ≥ 24 months	15	12	6	15	10	1
Parity 4, < 24 months	5	6	1	8	4	0
Parity 4, ≥ 24 months	30	19	4	15	11	0
Member of multiple birth	2	1	1	3	1	1
Total	100%	100%	100%	100%	100%	100%
Maternal age at birth						
< 20 years	20%	7%	6%	15%	6%	2%
20–24	20	41	53	25	38	46
25–29	25	30	27	30	39	44
30–34	20	15	10	20	13	7
35–39	10	6	2	8	3	1
≥ 40	5	1	1	2	0	0
Total	100%	100%	99%	100%	99%	100%
Maternal education						
Illiterate	98%	48%	22%	45%	14%	1%
Protoliterate	1	13	10	20	7	1
Primary school	1	30	39	25	30	16
Lower middle school	0	8	25	8	30	46
≥ Upper middle school	0	1	4	2	19	36
Total	100%	100%	100%	100%	100%	100%
Paternal occupation						
Peasant	90%	84%	94%	5%	4%	6%
Worker	6	2	1	60	31	49
Cadre	2	1	0	25	31	23
Other	2	14	5	10	34	22
Total	100%	101%	100%	100%	100%	100%
Male					53%	
Sibset composition						
Number of older brothers		.62			.48	
Number of older sisters		.65			.45	

Note: Some distributions do not sum to 100 percent because of rounding. Entries for sibset composition are averages. Early composition is constructed and refers to univariate distributions for births in the 1950s and early 1960s that have been subsequently modified (notably, education) to be more extreme. Observed composition refers to univariate distributions for all births (1950–1988). Late composition refers to univariate distributions for births in the 1980s.

Source: National Survey of Fertility and Contraception (NSFC).

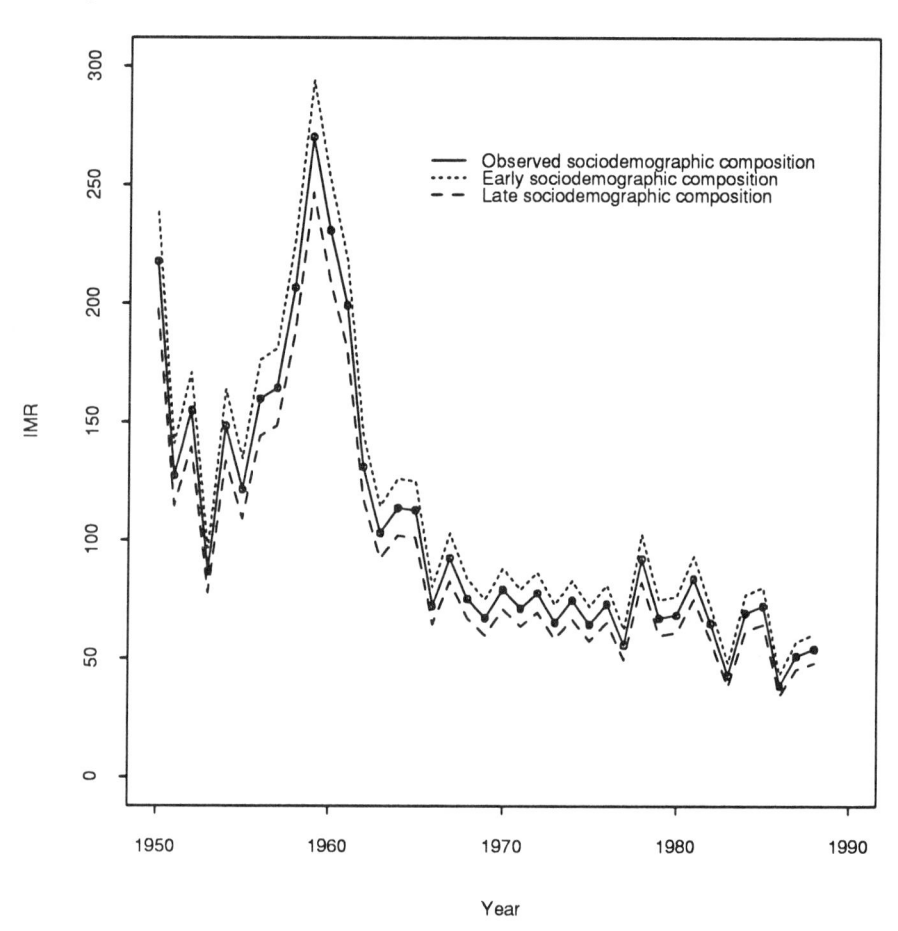

FIGURE 6.3A Sichuan Rural Male IMR (1950–1988), Adjusted (NSFC Sichuan Composition), Discrete Time

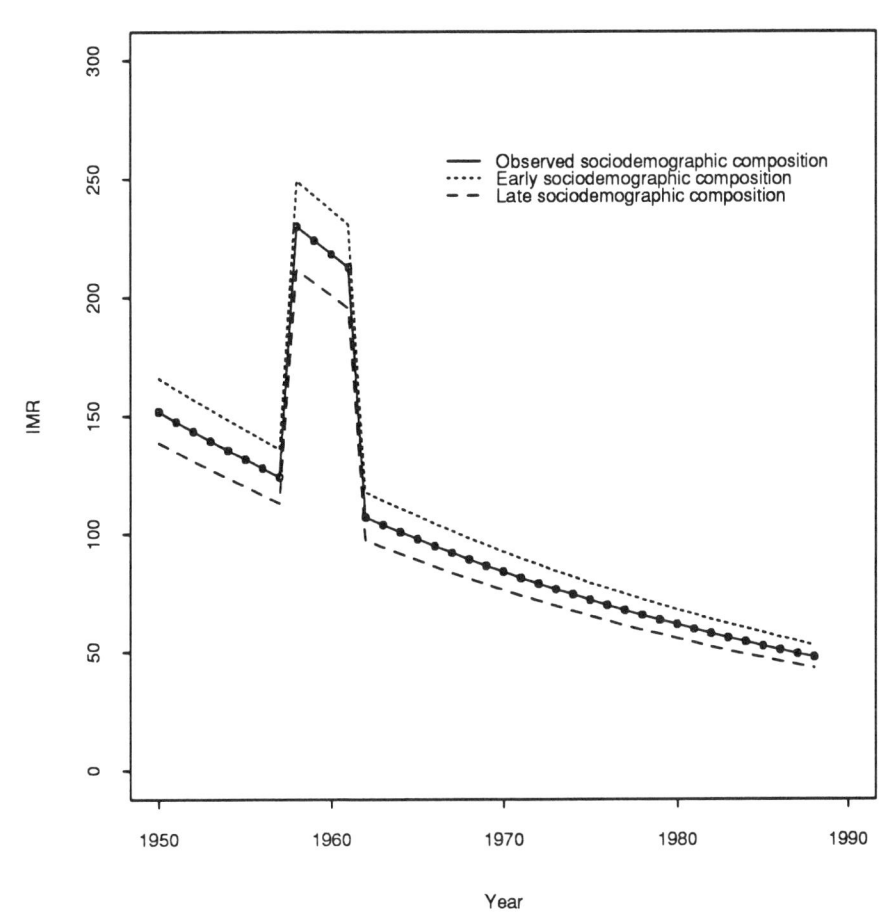

FIGURE 6.3B Sichuan Rural Male IMR (1950–1988), Adjusted (NSFC Sichuan Composition), Smoothed

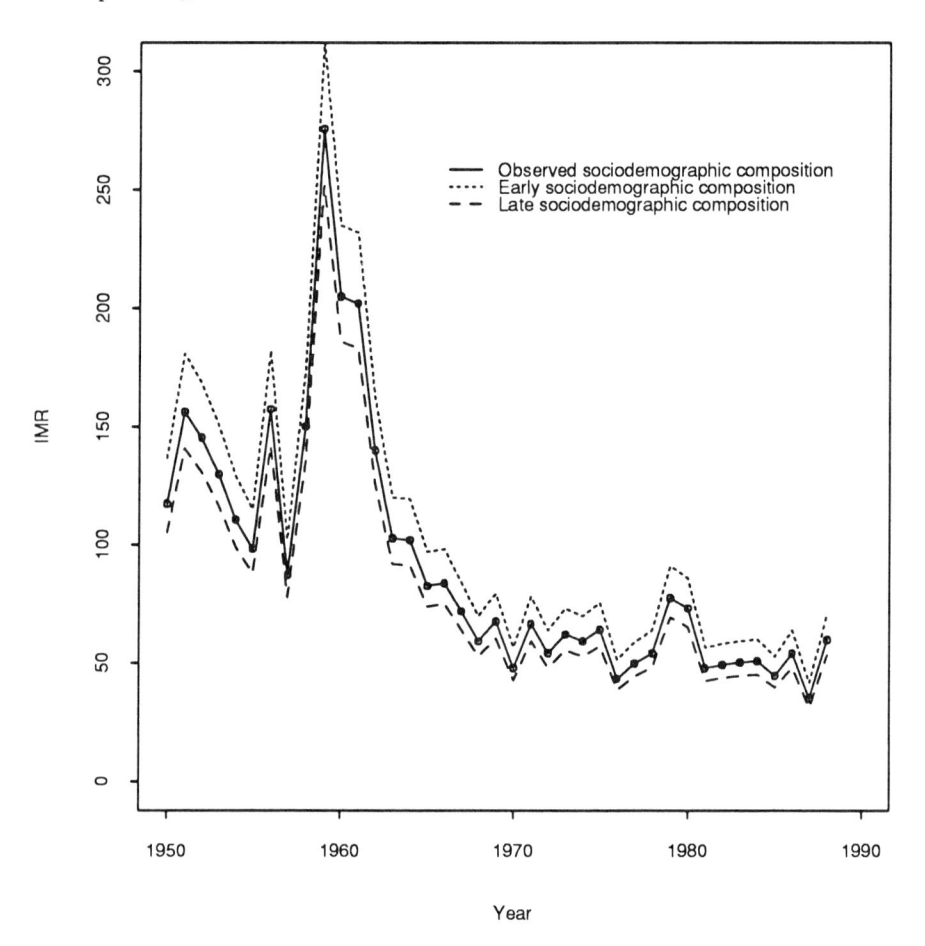

FIGURE 6.4A Sichuan Rural Female IMR (1950–1988), Adjusted (NSFC Sichuan Composition), Discrete Time

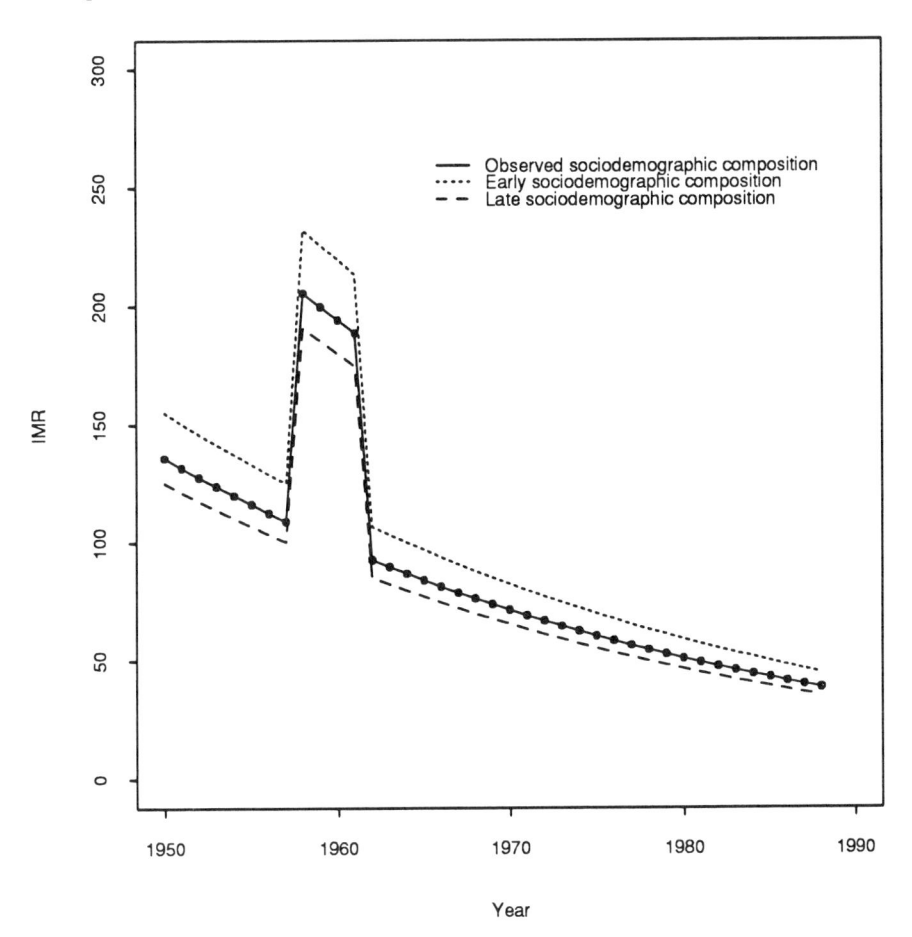

FIGURE 6.4B Sichuan Rural Female IMR (1950–1988), Adjusted (NSFC Sichuan Composition), Smoothed

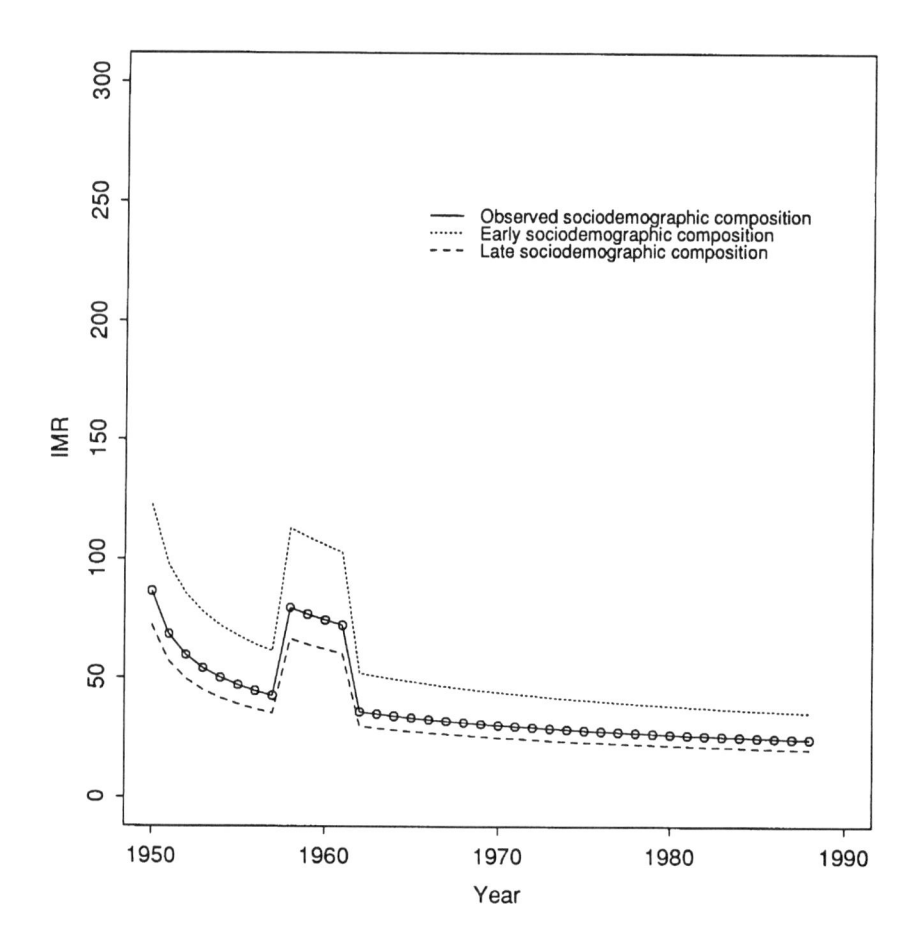

FIGURE 6.5 Sichuan Urban IMR (1950–1988), Adjusted (NSFC Sichuan Composition), Smoothed

that, assuming different initial compositions would produce somewhat different results. But such tinkering would not alter the main conclusion: The effect of sociodemographic compositional change in the decline of infant mortality in Sichuan was modest if not marginal.

If changing sociodemographic composition does not explain the decline of infant mortality, what does? Public health innovations, rising incomes, and improved nutritional levels have been hypothesized to influence infant mortality in China and elsewhere. We next consider these possible explanations.

Public Health, Income, Nutrition

Public health innovations. Although a great deal is known about China's public health and medical system (e.g., Chen and Zhu 1984) and although China's massive rural public health campaigns of the 1950s and 1960s have received worldwide attention (e.g., Lampton 1977; Sidel and Sidel 1982; Wilenski 1976), there is very little published data with which direct assessments can be carried out. We have been able to locate directories of hospitals and epidemiological stations administered at the county level or above (NDCHHED 1985; NDCHHEOEB 1988) that contain a variety of indicators. Most important, for each organization listed the founding date is published. The directories permit construction of an annualized count of the number of hospitals and epidemiological stations, as well as an annualized pervasiveness measure. We thus operationalize two measures of prevalence: number of extant hospitals and epidemiological stations per year and prevalence per million population per year. The spread of hospitals and epidemiological stations administered at the county level or above, though tapping only certain dimensions of public health and medical work in China, is taken as a proxy for a wide variety of public health initiatives.[24] Figures 6.6A–B juxtapose the institutional data against rural and urban mortality.[25]

Looking first at Figure 6.6A, it is clear that the number of hospitals and epidemiological stations administered at the county level or above increased monotonically from the 1950s to the 1960s, even if there was a slowing in the rate of growth for epidemiological stations during the latter 1960s. By the mid-1960s much of the decline in infant mortality had taken place, the Great Leap Forward notwithstanding. The trends displayed in Figure 6.6B, which adjust the hospital and epidemiological station series for population growth, enable the same observation perhaps even more clearly. After an initial period of rapid expansion, the hospital counts per million population actually decline for roughly a decade, while those for epidemiological stations remain stable, again with some decline during the years of the Cultural Revolution. It is possible that the per capita decline in the number of county-level hospitals was

FIGURE 6.6A Sichuan IMR (1950–1988) and Number of Extant Hospitals and Epidemiological Stations (1950–1984) (NSFC Sichuan Composition)

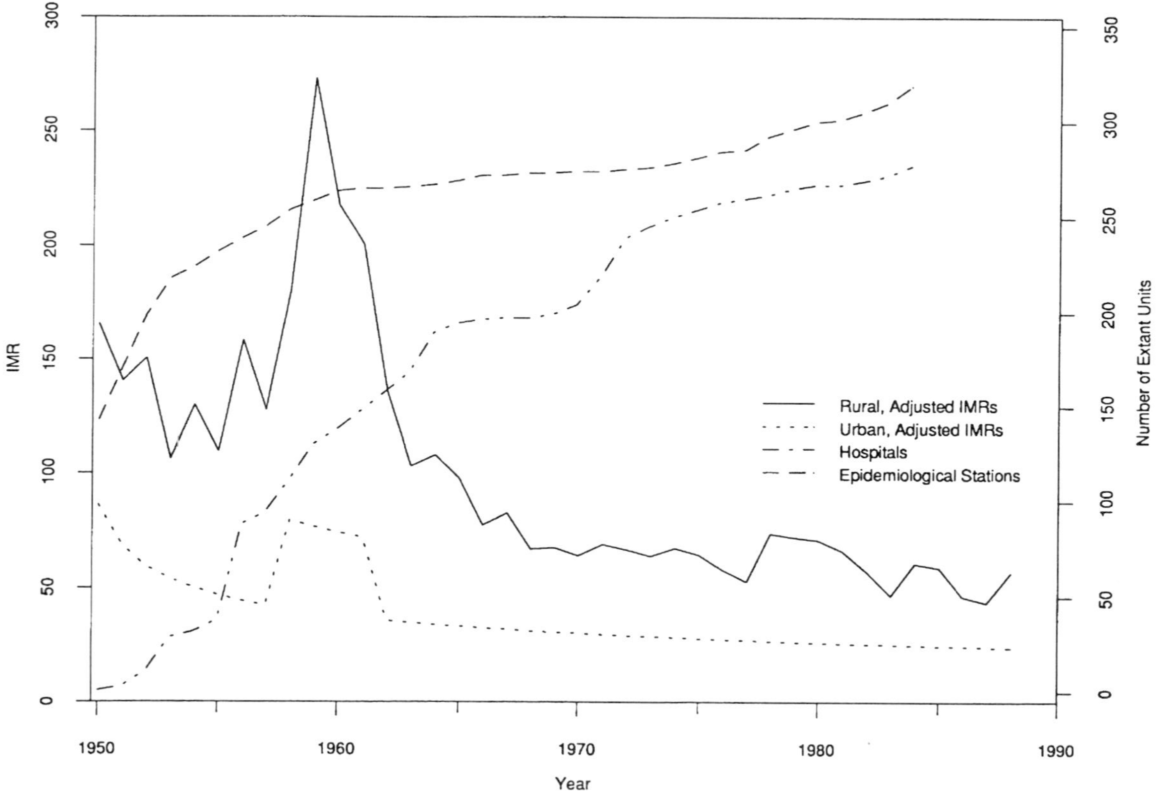

FIGURE 6.6B Sichuan IMR (1950–1988) and Hospitals and Epidemiological Stations per Million Population (1950–1984) (NSFC Sichuan Composition)

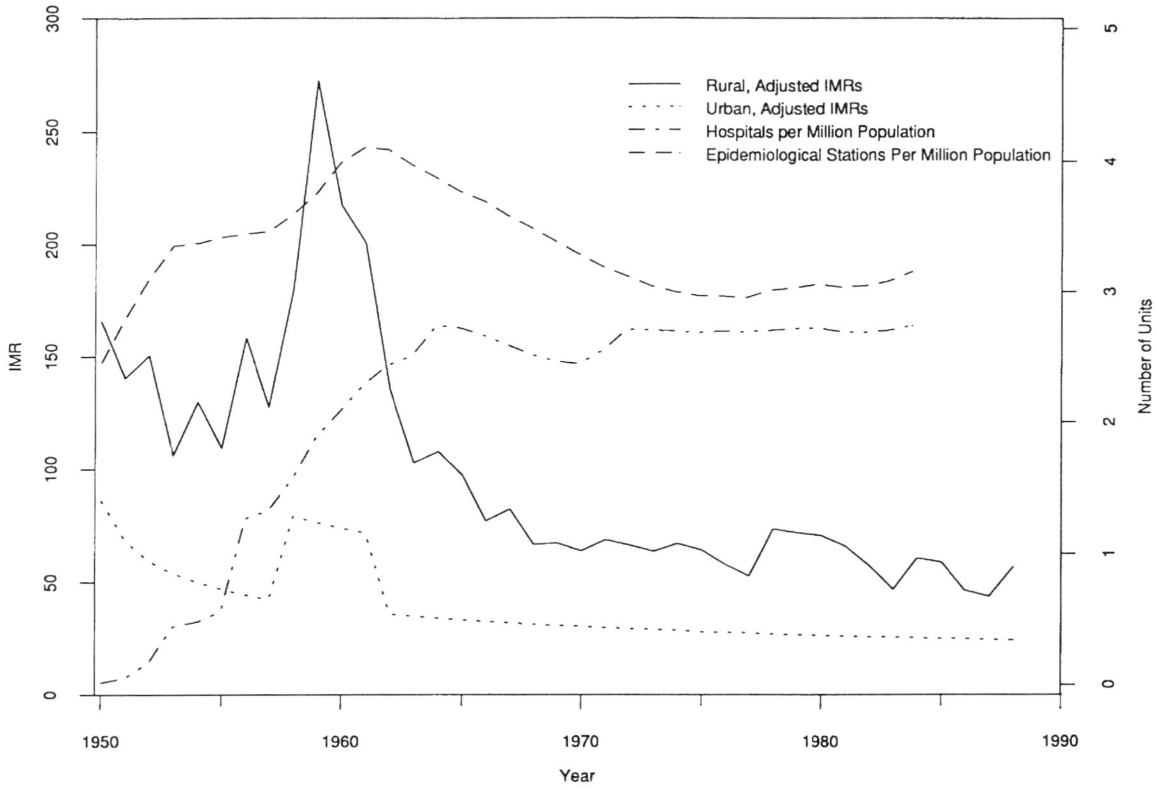

offset by growth in village clinics and by other public health expenditures at the subcounty level for which we do not have data. Nevertheless, increased investment in hospitals and epidemiological stations is inversely associated with the trend in infant mortality during the period that matters most—the 1950s and the early 1960s. The proximate linkages between infant mortality and the public health movement remain a subject for investigation.

Income. Only in recent years has it become possible to collect information on the income of China's population at the microlevel (e.g., Griffin 1993; Griffin and Zhao 1993). Even at aggregated levels, there is very little published information for the period of interest here. In particular, we have been unable to locate any on income distribution. However, there is a compendium of historical time series data for provinces (State Statistical Bureau General Department 1990), and from those series we have extracted a measure of per capita income.[26]

The meaning of an aggregated income measure in a largely rural, socialized economy with low levels of commodity exchange is not wholly obvious. Moreover, we are not aware of income data published separately for the urban and rural sectors. The conceptual ambiguities surrounding the per capita income measure used here are unlikely to be resolved in the near future, and we know of no better data for our purpose.

Figure 6.7 plots income against infant mortality. The explosion in per capita income that occurred at the end of the 1970s as a result of decollectivization and other policy changes comes much too late for it to be considered as a cause of the decline of infant mortality. Given what is already known about the enactment of political, social, and public health policies during the 1950s and early 1960s, there is no reason to suppose that the extremely modest rise of aggregate income prior to Mao's death, and prior to the ascendence of Deng Xiaoping's economic growth and privatization policies, could have played a socially significant role in the infant mortality decline. Moreover, although the social, political, and institutional reforms wrought by the Chinese Communist Party must have influenced infant mortality in various ways, these transformations are too multifaceted to be thought of usefully as "income transfers"—whether in the absence or presence of aggregate income growth. The evidence at hand, limited though it is, does not favor the hypothesis that either economic growth or economic redistribution in a conventional sense combined to form the engine of public health improvement in China during the early years of the PRC.

Nutrition. Change in nutrition has been linked to change in infant mortality, as Jamison and colleagues (1984) and Martorell and Sharma (1985), using nutrition series developed by Piazza (1985), suggest for China. Here we question not whether starvation affects growth, morbid-

FIGURE 6.7 Sichuan IMR (1950–1988) and Per Capita Income (1952–1988) (NSFC Sichan Composition)

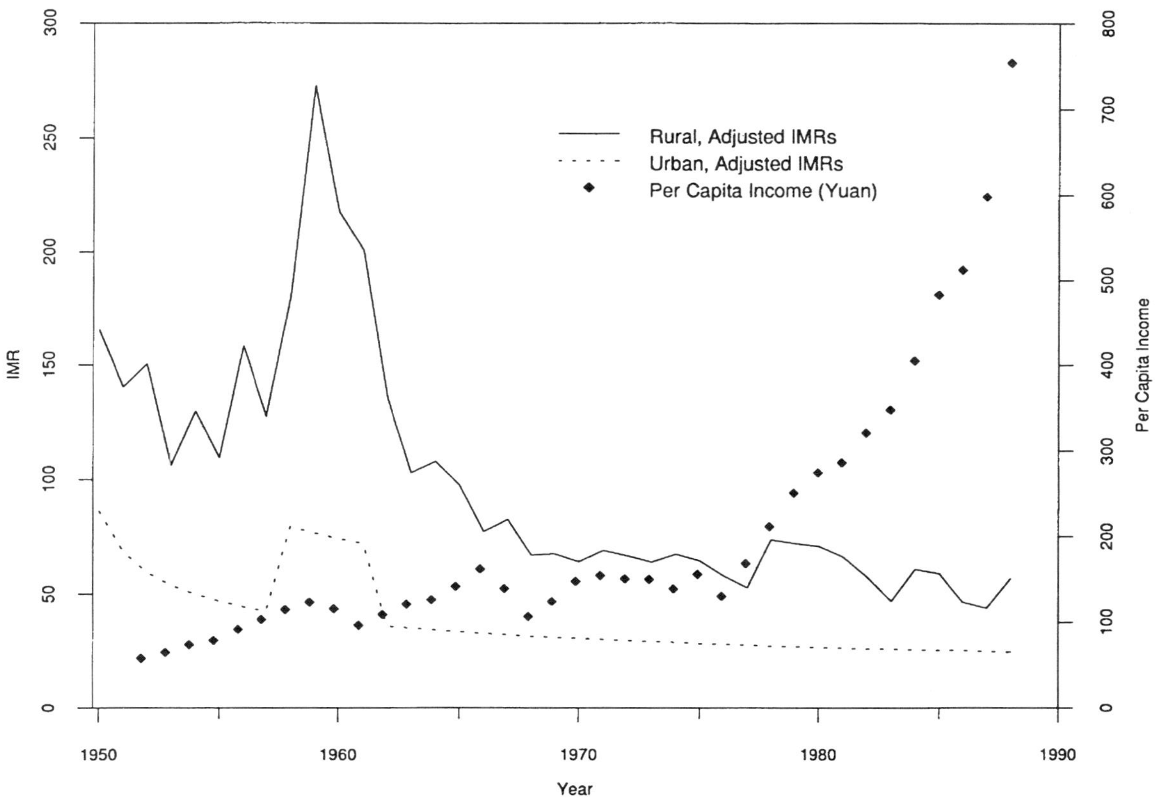

ity, and survival but whether the aggregated, quantitative data available demonstrate nutritional inadequacy effects on infant mortality in China post-1949. Figure 6.8A juxtaposes rural and urban infant mortality with a time series of Sichuan grain output measured in kilograms per capita (State Statistical Bureau 1990). We have no information on any adjustments to the grain series, such as, for example, whether wastage or temporally specific misreporting has been taken into account. Moreover, not only is there no information on the way in which the allocation of grain to the rural and urban sectors may have varied over time, there is also no temporally specific information on grain or other food shipments in or out of Sichuan. These are crude data.

Using the famine period as a point of reference, the Sichuan grain output series is not without face validity as a measure of sustenance, as there is an obvious plummet of grain output and a concomitant rise in infant mortality during the Great Leap Forward.[27] Moreover, prior to the *GLF* grain output increases as infant mortality declines, and after the *GLF* grain output rebounds. Yet after the "interruption" of the *GLF*, rural infant mortality continues on a downward trajectory, while grain output does no more than regain its former putative level (or fluctuate below it). Not until decollectivization does grain output again increase.

Much the same pattern can be observed in Figure 6.8B, which uses national grain output per capita as well as a national food energy measure: increase prior to the *GLF*, a devastating drop during the *GLF*, and subsequent rebound. Even for the national series, the peaks for recorded grain output and available food energy prior to the *GLF* are not substantially exceeded until after decollectivization.[28]

On balance, the grain output and nutrition data do not provide unambiguous evidence for the view that increased nutrition literally fueled the engine of mortality decline. Although increased nutritional levels almost surely played such a role (albeit of unspecified magnitude), the failure of post-*GLF* grain output and nutritional levels to *exceed* those of the pre-*GLF* period during years when infant mortality "resumed" the decline begun before the *GLF* must be explained if the nutrition argument is to be sustained.

Discussion

By our calculation a major reduction in fertility, a contraction of the range of maternal age at birth away from the youngest and oldest extremes, and a vast reduction of female illiteracy—all occurring simultaneously—do not explain the decline of infant mortality over the post-1949 period. Sociodemographic composition in this sense played a modest role at best in the decline of infant mortality. The increase in aggregate

FIGURE 6.8A Sichuan IMR (1950–1988) and Sichuan Grain Output Per Capita, (1950–1988) (NSFC Sichuan Composition)

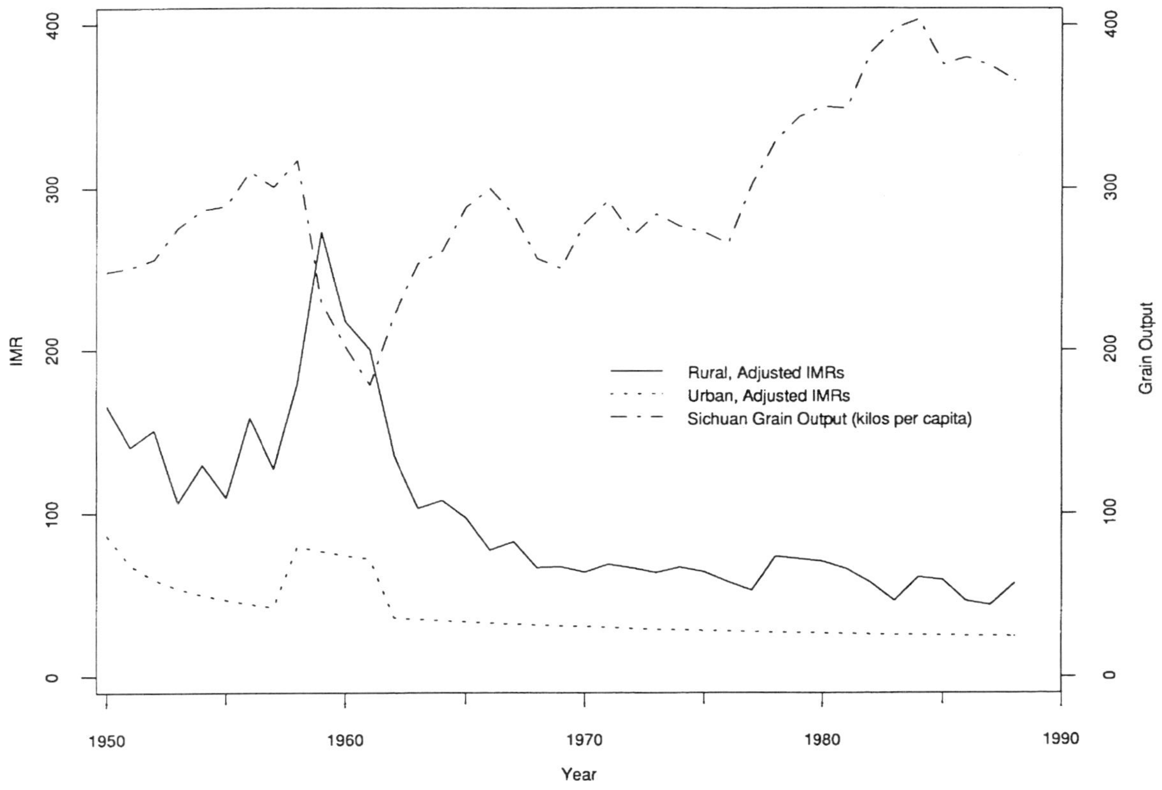

198

FIGURE 6.8B Sichuan IMR (1950–1988) National Grain Output Per Capita, National Food Energy in KCal/10 (1950–1982) (NSFC Sichuan Composition)

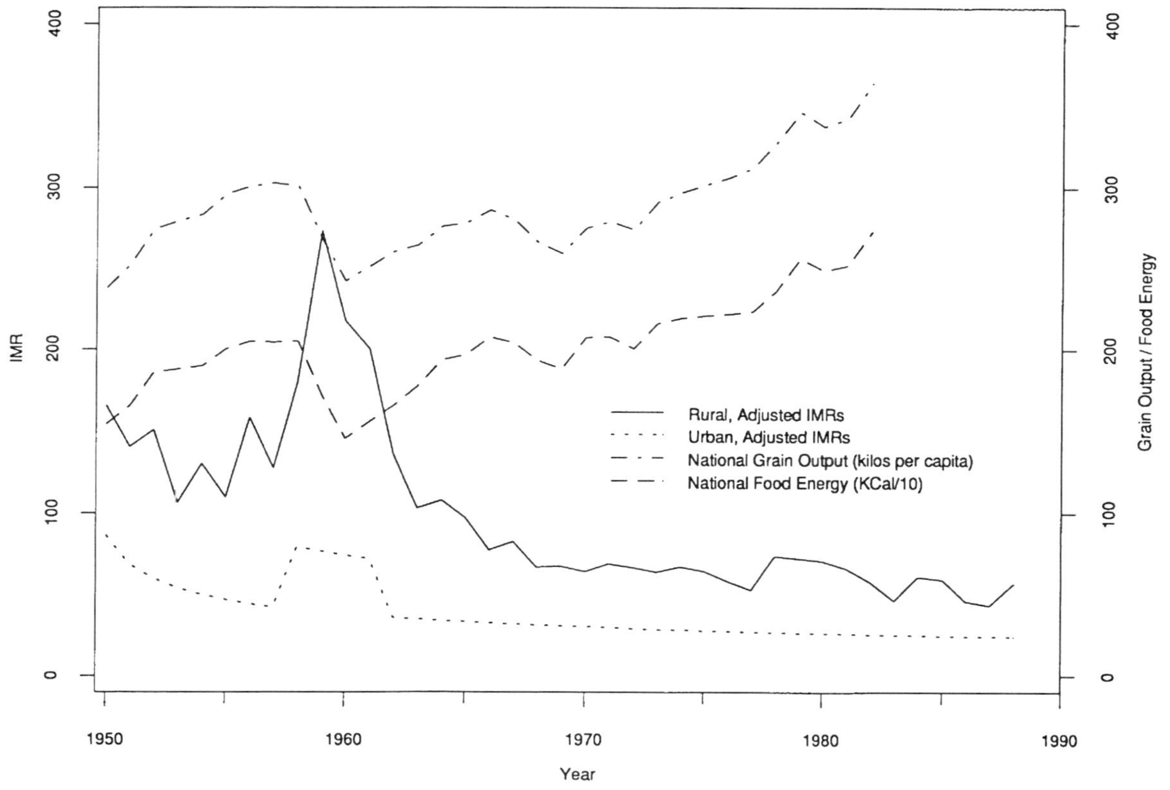

income came too late to affect the mortality decline. The evidence in support of a nutrition argument is weak. Thus "development" as this term is usually construed appears not to have been a major factor. Yet the data *suggest* that investment in public health may have been crucial for the decline of infant mortality.

Although an exploration of the possible sources of mortality decline has been our primary goal, other aspects of our analysis have also been revealing. That mortality decline in the first year of life was steepest for the post-neonate months was to be expected but had not been demonstrated. The importance for infant mortality of sibset composition, especially after the implementation of the one-child policy, is consistent with recent results concerning the rise during the 1980s (and subsequently) of the sex ratio at birth as computed from reported births (Li 1993; Mason, Lavely, and Ono 1994; Yi et al. 1993), but to our knowledge this has never before been documented, nor would it necessarily have been expected from a data base of reported births. Viewed from the perspective of the overall decline of China's infant mortality over the 40-year period, these sibset composition effects are small. They are, nevertheless, important not only as yet another indication of the veracity of the NSFC birth histories but also as markers of the unintended consequences of the one-child policy interacting with strongly held preferences for family composition.

Finally, the present analysis also speaks to the social differentiation of infant mortality. As in most societies, there is an urban-rural differential favoring infants born into urban families. In addition, although maternal education is inversely related to infant mortality, the relationship is much stronger for urban births. This interaction is plausible, since the range of opportunities is presumably greater in urban than rural settings.

The present research has focused on Sichuan. Subsequent reports will describe infant mortality for China as a whole, as well as by province. With the data presently available to us, we can describe for each province the impact of investment in public health, changes in nutrition, the growth of income, and changes in sociodemographic composition on infant mortality. Although we expect to replicate the Sichuan results, that this will happen is not a foregone conclusion.

Notes

We thank Don Treiman for excellent comments on an earlier draft of this chapter, and gratefully acknowledge support from the UCLA Academic Senate Committee on Research, Social Sciences Computing of UCLA, the University of Washington Graduate School Research Fund and China Program, and RAND.

1. Choe, Hao, and Wang (1995) exclude years we consider especially important (1950–1964) and analyze mortality between the ages of one and five—

explicitly excluding the first year of life (i.e., infant mortality). These choices are consonant with their goals, which differ from ours. However, they also reflect a perspective about the likely outcome of an analysis such as ours. For example, with respect to infant mortality they assert that "before age one, the most frequent causes of deaths are associated with genetic conditions: the quality of parental care does not have a large impact." Despite the differences between our approach and that of Choe, Hao, and Wang (1995), their findings and ours are complementary and largely consistent.

2. The infant mortality rate is specific to the first 12 months of life and refers to the number of deaths per 1,000 births. When reported for a specific time interval such as one calendar year, infant mortality rates are period rates and are based on deaths to children under one year of age in the time interval and the number of births in that same interval. Thus, when computed for a period, infant mortality rates are not proportions multiplied by 1,000. For a thorough discussion of the basic infant mortality rate as a period construct, and various adjustments to it, see Shryock, Siegel, and Associates (1973).

3. Even allowing for underreporting, China's infant mortality rate is low relative to comparison countries. For example, the World Bank (1984) estimated China's 1982 IMR at 67, which implies an adjustment for undercount. Nevertheless, among 34 low-income economies, only Sri Lanka and Vietnam had lower infant mortality.

4. This must be qualified: To our knowledge, no researcher in or out of China has full access to these surveys, and it is not even known whether those using the data outside of China are working with identically constructed releases of the data.

5. The oldest women in the sample could have been no more than age 57 at the time of the interview in 1988, and could have turned 58 later that year. These women were no more than age 29 or 30 in 1960, for example. Therefore, for 1960 we have no information on births to women who were 31 or older. These same women were no more than age 19 or 20 in 1950. Therefore, for 1950 we have no information on births to women who were 21 or older. And so on.

6. The counts for 1950 contain some births from the latter 1940s. We have included these cases to increase the *N*s at the beginning of the time series. The *N*s are too small to support points earlier than 1950.

7. As indicated in Table 6.2, we have been unable to discover the explanation for the lack of births in 1977. The interpolated values shown in the table and used in Figure 6.2 are derived from a logistic regression of infant mortality on the natural logarithm of year ($ln(year-1949)$) plus a dummy variable for the years 1958–1961, the functional form for time used for urban births throughout the analyses presented here.

8. That is, from the birth and death histories contained in the Sichuan sample, we compute the proportion of deaths occurring within 12 months from the date of birth in a given year (multiplied by 1,000). Some of these deaths will occur in the calendar year following the year of birth. Proportions (multiplied by 1,000) so computed are cohort rates. Period rates, however constructed, are intended to be understood as referring to deaths within a calendar year.

9. A disparity between Banister's reconstruction and the Sichuan data occurs for female infant mortality from the latter 1970s into the 1980s. Banister's series indicates a nontrivial rise—even before institution of the one-child policy. Although the discrepancy is important, we are unable to investigate its causes in the present chapter.

10. Equation 2 is not formulated to allow for a between-family heterogeneity component. We have, however, examined the data from this perspective and have found that allowing for heterogeneity does not alter the conclusions we draw from the data in this analysis (Mason and Chan 1994; Chan 1995).

11. The RAND Indonesian Family Life Survey provides an excellent illustration of the richness of conceptualization and data collection now possible in the study of infant and child health. The 1994 Luoping County Survey conducted in Yunnan Province (William Lavely, principal investigator) provides another example of contemporary formulation adapted to rural China (Lavely 1993).

12. We use the "peasant" and "worker" terminology for consistency with the NSFC source documentation (SFPC 1988). The peasant-worker distinction is not equivalent to the manual-nonmanual or blue-collar-white-collar distinction. The classification we use was also employed by Streatfield, Kane, and Ruzicka (1991).

13. Specifically, "'state cadres' refers to administrative cadres and intellectuals at various levels of party organizations, technical, and business units" (SFPC 1988:15). The "business units" referred to are state-owned rather than private sector. We have found no satisfactory explanation for the large size of the cadre category relative to the others, for the fathers of urban births (see Table 6.7). In particular, according to the survey protocol (SFPC 1988), white-collar workers in the private sector were to be coded into a separate category.

14. There are too few instances of close spacing to examine fruitfully the effect of a *subsequent* birth on a singleton index birth's chance of surviving its first year.

15. The distributions of covariates for rural male births and rural female births are so similar that they are combined here.

16. Sibset composition could logically be included here. Instead, we include it in the hazard model regressions discussed later. As will be shown, sibset composition interacts with period. In the time series analysis, based on the additive binary logistic response formulation, we do not adjust for sibset composition.

17. We explored other functional forms for trend—always including the *GLF* dummy. The natural log performs well for urban Sichuan births and is a familiar smooth function. We prefer it for these reasons.

18. When expressed as a quadratic, both terms for age so scaled are statistically significant ($p < .05$) in all three groups.

19. For all three residence-sex groups, the peasant-cadre contrast is the lowest (negative and largest in absolute value): For the period we consider, it is plausible that children born to fathers who either were or became cadres had a mortality advantage. A more refined analysis of paternal occupation may yet tease this result out of the data.

20. The granularity of the time scale is a function of the way the NSFC collected death information. The survey did not obtain child's age at death. Rather, it recorded date of death to the nearest month. Thus only an approximate calculation of age at death is possible. For example, those born in the month of

June and dying in that same month could be anywhere from zero to 30 days old at death. Those born in June and dying in July could be anywhere from one to 61 days old at death. For analytic purposes we assume that the risk of death is spread homogeneously over the first month and derive the average length of life in the first interval to be .258 months. Since death is in reality concentrated in the first hours and days of life, the average length in the first interval must be something less than one week.

21. In our exploratory analyses we found that this particular spline formulation of the hazard fits the data better than the Gompertz and Weibull formulations. In addition, we prefer this approach to Cox regression here because we are interested in the form of the hazard and the possibility that it is not proportional. Computationally, we fit "stacked" logistic regressions with a constraint on the intercepts. (See Fienberg and Mason 1978 or Allison 1982 for the basic idea.)

22. We can pursue this question with the pooled urban sample for all provinces.

23. For both rural male births and rural female births, the smooth birth-year function is ($Year$ −1949) plus the *GLF* term.

24. Four health policy guidelines enunciated at the founding of the People's Republic in 1950 were: "(1) Medicine should serve the workers, peasants and soldiers; (2) preventive medicine should take precedence over therapeutic medicine; (3) Chinese traditional medicine should be integrated with Western scientific medicine; (4) health work should be combined with mass movements" (Sidel and Sidel 1982:28). In the first major public health campaign in 1952, the emphasis was on vaccination, sanitation, and elimination of the "four pests"(originally flies, mosquitoes, rats, and grain-eating sparrows) through mass participation (Sidel and Sidel 1982; Wilenski 1976). A degree of success in teaching germ theory in the countryside is claimed for this campaign, through positioning it as a response to an alleged germ warfare plot by the United States directed against China (Wilenski 1976).

25. Rural infant mortality is the pooling of the discrete-time rural male and rural female series based on "observed" composition, weighted in accordance to the sex-year-specific frequencies displayed in Table 6.2. The same series are used in Figures 6.7 and 6.8.

26. We examined a number of possible measures and concluded that conceptually and empirically the per capita income variable is the most readily interpreted and understandable of the choices, which are not described in detail in the source document.

27. Here, as elsewhere, the offset between the NSFC and exogenous series is due to the difference between period and cohort rates.

28. The two national series are correlated .96; the Sichuan grain series is correlated with each of the national series at .90.

References

Allison, Paul. 1982. "Discrete-Time Methods for the Analysis of Event Histories." Pp. 61–98 in Samuel Leinhardt (ed.), *Sociological Methodology 1982*. San Francisco: Jossey-Bass.

Arnold, Fred, and Zhaoxiang Liu. 1986. "Sex Preference and Fertility in China." *Population and Development Review* 12:221–46.

Ashton, Basil, Kenneth Hill, Alan Piazza, and Robin Zeitz. 1984. "Famine in China, 1958–61." *Population and Development Review* 10:613–46.

Baddeley, A. 1979. "The Limitation of Human Memory: Implications for the Design of Retrospective Surveys." Pp. 31–41 in Louis Moss and Harvey Goldstein (eds.), *The Recall Method in Social Surveys*. London: University of London, Institute of Education.

Banister, Judith. 1987. *China's Changing Population*. Stanford, CA: Stanford University Press.

———. 1989. "A New Survey of Infant Morality in China. A Research Note." Manuscript, Center for International Research, U.S. Bureau of the Census.

———. 1992. "Implications and Quality of China's 1990 Census Data." Paper presented at the International Seminar on China's 1990 Population Census, Beijing, October 19–23.

Bittles, A. H., W. M. Mason, J. Greene, and N. A. Rao. 1991. "Reproductive Behavior and Health in Consanguineous Marriages." *Science* 252:789–94.

Bongaarts, John. 1987. "Does Family Planning Reduce Infant Mortality Rates?" *Population and Development Review* 13:323–34.

Caldwell, John C. 1979. "Education as a Factor in Mortality Decline: An Examination of Nigerian Data." *Population Studies* 33:395–413.

Caldwell, John, and P. Caldwell. 1985. "Education and Literacy as Factors in Health." In Scott B. Halstead, Julia A. Walsh, and Kenneth S. Warren (eds.), *Good Health at Low Cost*. New York: Rockefeller Foundation.

Chan, Angelique Wei Ming. 1995. "Reported Infant Mortality in China, 1950–1988: Gender, Socioeconomic Basis, Family-Level Heterogeneity, and Regional Variability." Ph.D. dissertation, Department of Sociology, University of California, Los Angeles.

Chen Haifeng and Zhu Chao (eds.). 1984. *Modern Chinese Medicine*, Volume 3: *Chinese Health Care*. Hingham, MA: MTP Press, and Beijing: People's Medical Publishing House.

China National Collaborating Group on Birth Defect Surveillance (CNCGBDS). 1991. *Zhonghua Fuchanke Zazhi* (Chinese Journal of Obstetrics and Gynecology) 26:338–41, 387.

Choe, M., and N. Tsuya. 1989. "Trends and Covariates of Infant and Child Mortality in Rural China: The Case of Jilin Province." Paper presented at the annual meeting of the Population Association of America, Baltimore, Maryland, March.

Choe, M. K., H. Hao, and F. Wang. 1995. "Effects of Gender, Birth Order, and Other Correlates on Childood Mortality in China." *Social Biology* 42:50–63.

Coale, Ansley J. n.d. "Nuptiality and Fertility from 1982 to 1987 in China: Data from the 2 per Thousand Sample Survey Taken by the State Family Planning Commission in 1988." New York: Rockefeller Foundation.

———. 1989. "Marriage and Childbearing in China Since 1940." *Social Forces* 67:833–50.

Coale, Ansley J., S. Li, J. Han. 1988. "The Distribution of Interbirth Intervals in Rural China, 1940s to 1970s." *Papers of the East-West Population Institute*, No. 109. Honolulu: East-West Center.

Coale, Ansley J., F. Wang, N. E. Riley, and F. D. Lin. 1991. "Recent Trends in Fertility and Nuptiality in China." *Science* 251:389–93.

Coale, Ansley J., and Judith Banister. 1994. "Five Decades of Missing Females in China." *Demography* 31:459–80.

Dankert, G., and J. van Ginneken. 1991. "Birth Weight and Other Determinants of Infant and Child Mortality in Three Provinces of China." *Journal of Biosocial Science* 23:477–89.

Fienberg, Stephen E., and William M. Mason. 1978. "Identification and Estimation of Age-Period-Cohort Models in the Analysis of Discrete Archival Data." Pp. 1–67 in Karl Schuessler (ed.), *Sociological Methodology 1979*. San Francisco: Jossey-Bass.

Gao, E. 1991. "Analysis of Accidental Death Among Children and Teenagers in Shanghai." *Zhongguo Renkou Kexue* (Chinese Journal of Population Science) 3:179–91.

Griffin, Keith. 1993. "Chinese Household Income Project, 1988 (Computer File)." Ann Arbor, MI: Inter-university Consortium for Political and Social Research.

Griffin, Keith, and Zhao Renwei (eds.). 1993. *The Distribution of Income in China*. New York: St. Martin's Press.

Groves, Robert M. 1989. *Survey Errors and Survey Costs*. New York: Wiley.

Gu, J., Y. Shi, E. Gao, and X. Gu. 1991. "Analysis of IMR and its Influencing Factors in China." Paper presented at the International Seminar on Fertility and Contraception, Beijing, August 26–29.

Haaga, John G. 1988. "Reliability of Retrospective Survey Data on Infant Feeding." *Demography* 25:307–14.

Hayase, Y., and S. Kawamata (eds.). 1991. *Population Policy and Vital Statistics in China*. I.D.E. Statistical Data Series No. 56. Tokyo: Institute of Developing Economies.

Hill, Kenneth. 1984. "Demographic Trends in China, 1950–81." Manuscript, World Bank.

Horn, Joshua S. 1969. *Away with All Pests: An English Surgeon in Peoples' China, 1954–1969*. New York: Monthly Review Press.

Hull, Terrence H. 1990. "Recent Trends in Sex Ratios in China." *Population and Development Review* 16:63–84.

Jamison, Dean T., J. Evans, T. King, I. Porter, N. Prescott, and A. Prost. 1984. *China: The Health Sector*. Washington, DC: World Bank.

Kitagawa, Evelyn M. 1955. "Components of a Difference Between Two Rates." *Journal of the American Statistical Association* 50:1168–74.

Koenig, Michael A., J. Phillips, O. Campbell, and S. D'Souza. 1990. "Birth Intervals and Childhood Mortality in Rural Bangladesh." *Demography* 27:251–65.

Lampton, David M. 1977. *The Politics of Medicine in China: The Policy Process, 1949–1977*. Boulder: Westview Press.

Lavely, William. 1993. "Infant Survival in Rural Yunnan: A Three-Year Research Program." Proposal to the Luce Foundation.

Lavely, William, William M. Mason, and Hiromi Ono. 1991. "Chinese Infant Mortality, 1950–1987: An Assessment of Data from the IDFS and the 2 per 1,000 Survey." Paper presented at the International Seminar on Fertility and Contraception, Beijing, August 26–29.

Lavely, William, Z. Xiao, B. Li, and Ronald Freedman. 1990. "The Rise of Female Education in China: National and Regional Patterns." *China Quarterly* No. 121 (March):61–93.

Li, Y. 1993. "Sex Ratios of Infants and Relations with some Socioeconomic Variables: Results of China's 1990 Census and Implications." *Population and Economics* 4:3–13 (in Chinese).

Lucas, An Elissa. 1982. *Chinese Medical Modernization: Comparative Policy Continuities, 1930s–1980s.* New York: Praeger Press.

Martorell, Reynaldo, and Ramesh Sharma. 1985. "Trends in Nutrition, Food Supply and Infant Mortality Rates." Pp. 199–213 in Scott B. Halstead, Julia A. Walsh and Kenneth S. Warren (eds.), *Good Health at Low Cost.* New York: Rockefeller Foundation.

Mason, William M., and Angelique Chan. 1994."Gender Differences in Reported Infant Mortality in Sichuan: Does Family Heterogeneity Matter?" Paper presented at the annual meeting of the Population Association of America, Miami, May.

Mason, William M., William Lavely, and H. Ono. 1993. "Can We Explain the Decline of Infant Mortality in China Under Mao?" Paper presented at the quadrennial meeting of the International Union for the Scientific Study of Population, Montreal, August.

———. 1994. "Son Preference in China: 1950–88." Paper presented at a conference sponsored by the International Union for the Scientific Study of Population, Kyoto, October.

Muhuri, Pradip K., and Samuel H. Preston. 1991. "Effects of Family Composition on Mortality Differentials by Sex Among Children in Matlab, Bangladesh." *Population and Development Review* 17:415–34.

National Directory of County-level and Higher Health and Epidemiological Organizations Editorial Board (NDCHHEOEB). 1988. *National Directory of County-level and Higher Health and Epidemiological Organizations.* Beijing: People's Health Press.

National Directory of County-level and Higher Hospitals Editorial Board (NDCHHED). 1985. *National Directory of County-level and Higher Hospitals.* Beijing: People's Health Press.

Neter, J., and J. Waksberg. 1964. "A Study of Response Errors in Expenditures Data from Household Interviews." *Journal of the American Statistical Association* 59:18–55.

Palloni, Alberto, and Sara Millman. 1986. "Effects of Inter-birth Intervals and Breastfeeding on Infant and Early Childhood Mortality." *Population Studies* 40:215–36.

Peng, Xizhe. 1987. "Demographic Consequences of the Great Leap Forward in China's Provinces." *Population and Development Review* 13:639–70.

Piazza, A. 1985. "Food Consumption and Nutritional Status in the People's Republic of China." Ph.D. dissertation, Stanford University.

Potter, Joseph E. 1977. "Problems in Using Birth-History Analysis to Estimate Trends in Fertility." *Population Studies* 31:335–64.

Ren, Xinhua S. 1994. "Infant and Child Survival in Shaanxi, China." *Social Science and Medicine* 38:609–21.

Rutstein, Shea O. 1984. *Infant and Child Mortality: Levels, Trend and Demographic Differentials*. WFS Comparative Studies No. 24. The Hague, International Statistical Institute.

Shryock, Henry S., Jacob S. Siegel, and Associates. 1973. *The Methods and Materials of Demography*, 2nd Edition. Washington, DC: U.S. Government Printing Office.

Sidel, Ruth, and Victor W. Sidel. 1982. *The Health of China*. Boston: Beacon Press.

Som, Ranjah K. 1973. *Recall Lapse in Demographic Inquiries*. Bombay: Asia Publishing House.

State Family Planning Commission of China (SFPC). 1988. "Quanguo Shengyu Jieyu Chouyang Diaocha Jishu Wenjian" (National Sample Survey of Fertility and Contraception Technical Documentation). Translated by W. Lavely and N. Gu. Seattle: University of Washington Population Research Center Working Paper No. 3, 1991.

State Statistical Bureau. 1988. *Zhongguo Tongji Nianjian 1988* (China Statistical Yearbook 1988). Beijing: China Statistics Publishing House.

———. 1990. *Zhongguo Renkou Tongji Nianjian 1989*. (China Population Statistics Yearbook 1989). Beijing: The Science and Technology Document Publishing House.

State Statistical Bureau General Department. 1990. *Quanguo Gesheng Zizhiqu Zhixiashi Lishi Tongji Ziliao Huibian* (National Compendium of Historical Statistical Data on Provinces, Autonomous Regions, and Municipalities (1949–1988)). Beijing: State Statistical Bureau Press.

Streatfield, K., P. Kane, L. Ruzicka. 1991. *Infant and Child Mortality in Hunan Province of China*. Australian National University Division of Demography and Sociology, Child Survival Research Note Number 37CS.

Sudman, Seymour, and Norman M. Bradburn. 1973. "Effects of Time and Memory Factors on Response in Surveys." *Journal of the American Statistical Association* 68:805–15.

Tu, P. 1989. "The Effects of Breastfeeding and Birth Spacing on Child Survival in China." *Studies in Family Planning* 20:332–42.

Tu, P., and Z. Liang. 1992. "An Evaluation of the Quality of Enumeration of Infant Deaths and Births in China's 1990 Census." Paper presented at the International Seminar on China's 1990 Population Census, Beijing, October 19–23.

Wilenski, Peter. 1976. *The Delivery of Health Services in the People's Republic of China*. Ottawa: International Development Research Centre.

World Bank. 1984. *World Bank Development Report 1984*. New York: Oxford University Press.

Yi, Zeng, P. Tu, B. Gu, Y. Xu, B. Li, and Y. Li. 1993. "Causes and Implications of the Recent Increase in the Reported Sex Ratio at Birth in China." *Population and Development Review* 19:283–302.

Zhang, E., and L. Lu. 1991. "Evaluation of Adult Mortality Estimated from the China National Sampling Survey on Fertility and Contraception." Paper presented at the International Seminar on Fertility and Contraception, Beijing, August 26–29.

Zhang, J., W. Cai, and D. Lee. 1991. "Perinatal Mortality in Shanghai." *International Journal of Epidemiology* 20:958–63.

———. 1992. "Occupational Hazards and Pregnancy Outcomes." *American Journal of Industrial Medicine* 21:397–408.

Zhou, Y., K. Rao, D. Zhang. 1989. "Analysis of China's Infant Mortality Rates." *Zhongguo Renkou Kexue* (Population Science of China) 3:35–46.

PART FOUR

Gender and Social Differentiation

7

Vive la Différence! Continuity and Change in the Gender Wage Gap, 1967–1987

Martina Morris

Sixty cents on the dollar. Few social science statistics have become as well known as this estimate of the gender wage gap, in part because it remained unchanged for close to half a century, despite women's progress on social, political, and legal fronts. When the wage gap finally began to narrow in the 1980s, this was interpreted by many as a sign that full gender equality might be moving within reach (Hartmann, in Nasar 1992). Now, more than a decade later, estimates of the earnings ratio range from a low of 0.65 to a high of 0.72, with the media often citing the figure of 0.70.[1] The trend in the median earnings ratio can be seen in Figure 7.1, which shows the ratio of female to male median earnings from 1967 to 1987 for workers who will be the focus of this chapter: white, full-time, full-year, male and female workers.[2] For this group of workers, the narrowing of the gender gap during the 1980s is evident.

Current explanations for the convergence in wages typically focus on increases in women's qualifications, especially experience, education, and related skills. Initial findings suggest that women's human capital and the monetary returns to their capital have grown relative to men's, particularly with respect to work experience. These factors may explain on the order of 30 to 50 percent of the reduction in the wage gap (Blau and Beller 1988; O'Neill and Polachek 1993; Wellington 1993). It is mainly a cohort effect, with new generations of women bringing higher skill levels to the marketplace as older generations are leaving. Women are entering the workforce in greater numbers with more education and work experience;

FIGURE 7.1 Ratio of Women's to Men's Median Earnings, 1967–1987: Full-time, Full-year, White Workers

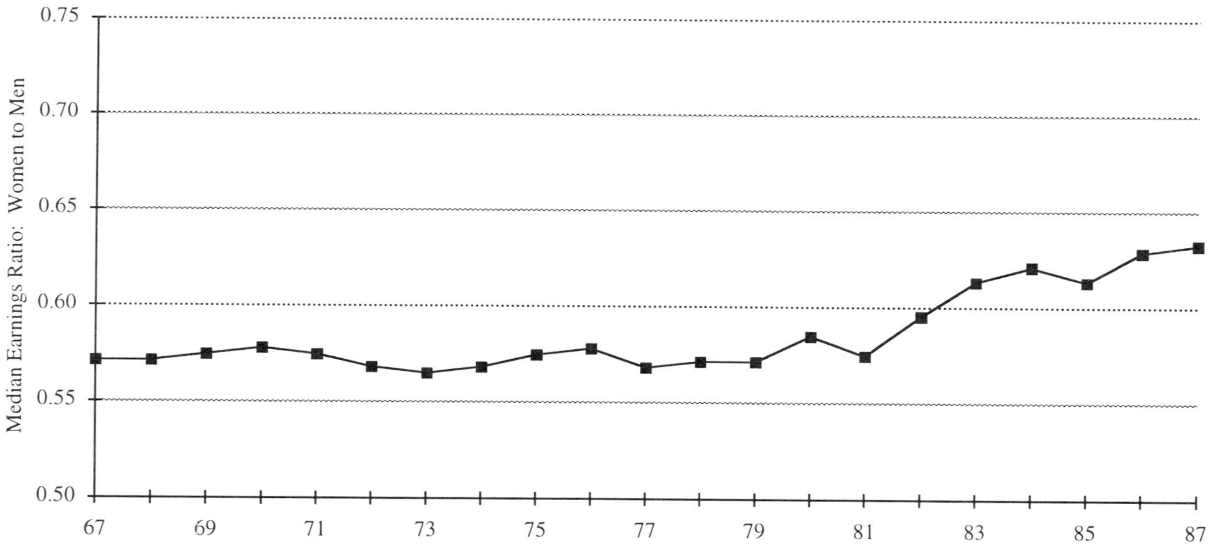

Source: Current Population Survey, March Uniform Series, 1967–87; see text for details.

fewer drop out of the labor market and then for shorter periods of time; more are entering formerly male-dominated occupations. The impact of other factors, such as declining discrimination in the workplace (due perhaps to comparable worth and other legislative efforts) and differential effects of industrial restructuring, remains to be assessed (O'Neill and Polachek 1993). Yet with new cohorts of women possessing ever-improving qualifications, the trend toward equalization of wages seems assured, leading the *New York Times* to conclude that "today's gains in women's pay reflect solid, enduring trends" (Nasar 1992).

The gender wage gap is not the only thing to have changed in the past two decades. In the wake of massive economic restructuring, major changes have also occurred in the overall distribution of earnings, with substantial attendant rises in inequality (Morris, Bernhardt, and Handcock 1994). The growing gap between rich and poor since the 1970s is by now well established and widely publicized (Harrison and Bluestone 1988; Kuttner 1983). Between 1979 and 1987 the income of the top tenth of American families grew by 10.1 percent, while that for the bottom tenth fell by 8.7 percent (Karoly 1993); measures of earnings inequality rose by 20 to 30 percent since the early 1970s, after decades of stability or decline (Levy and Murnane 1992); and low wage jobs rose from 20 to 40 percent of all new jobs from the 1970s to the 1980s (Harrison and Bluestone 1988). Coupled with the effects of deindustrialization and high unemployment rates, the experience of many American workers during the past 20 years has been bleak. Many observers therefore see the recent economic gains by women as both anomalous and promising: If women have managed to swim upstream in the context of 20 years of rising inequality, the future can only be better (Blau and Kahn 1994). Just the opposite may be true, however. If women's gains have simply been a by-product of men's losses, what will happen when the changes in male earnings begin to stabilize?

To answer this question, it is necessary to move beyond average earnings differentials to full distributional comparisons. Only then is it possible to identify the origins of the declining wage gap—whether it is improvement in women's relative earnings or worsening of men's earnings that is the driving force. This analysis recasts our understanding of what women's economic progress really means and also dampens expectations that the trend will continue.

This chapter will devote substantial space to the exposition of methods needed to answer this and other similar questions. While the preliminary results presented here are novel and thought-provoking, they also raise many issues that cannot be addressed in this space (the reviewers provided numerous examples). The sociology lies in these issues, and in their absence it may appear that the substance has gotten short shrift. Perhaps for now, but not for later work. These methods open up new areas to research and enhance our ability to answer questions that interest us.

Data

The data used here are the March Uniform Series of the *Current Population Survey*, for the years 1967 to 1987.[3] The variable analyzed is yearly earnings, and the sample is restricted to full-time, full-year workers aged 16–65, not in school, the military, or farming. The full-time, full-year restriction is a common method of limiting the variation in hours worked, so that differences in earnings are not confounded by differences in amount of work performed. The analysis here is limited to a comparison between white men and white women (designated as "men" and "women" here). Focusing on trends within race is necessary because previous research has shown that changes in earnings distributions over time vary considerably by race, both across and within gender groups. The methods developed below, however, can easily be applied to comparisons of any other working groups. The size of the resulting samples are roughly 20,000 per year for white males, 10,000 per year for white females.

The *Current Population Survey*, like many employment data sets, has some problems in the data on yearly earnings. First, there is the presence of reported earnings that fall below the minimum amount a worker could legally earn. As the percentage of low reports declines over time, either keeping or deleting the cases introduces bias across years. In keeping with the common convention in this field, these cases are not deleted or recoded here.

Second is the well-known "heaping" problem in reported wages: Respondents tend to round yearly earnings to whole figures. For this analysis, the heaping is removed by an imputation scheme that reallocates earnings reported in round numbers within a range of values. A report of $10,000, for example, is assumed to be a rounded version of yearly earnings between $7,500 and $12,500. Earnings reported in round figures are replaced in the analysis by an imputed value chosen randomly from an appropriate range. The resulting distribution has the basic statistical characteristics of the original reported distribution (for additional information, see Handcock 1994). Imputation is also used to eliminate topcoding. The census uses a single code ("topcode") for earnings above a certain threshold, for example, in 1987 all cases above $99,999 were coded as $99,999. The imputation scheme imputes this upper tail using a Pareto distribution. The resulting mean for the topcoded values is very close to 1.45 times the topcode, which is consistent with the value commonly used to recode such observations.

Methods 1: Defining the Relative Distribution

The approach taken here seeks to capture and compare the distributional differences in earnings in a more complete way. Shifting the focus from simple averages to full distributions creates new problems for data display and analysis, as it is easy to move from too little information to too much. To summarize patterns of distributional change and difference, this analysis makes use of *relative distributions* (Morris, Bernhardt, and Handcock 1994).

The relative distribution can be thought of as a generalized ratio. It compares the density of two groups of earners at each earnings level, where the groups can be defined by year, sex, race, or any category of interest. One group forms the baseline (or reference) earnings distribution, and another forms the comparison distribution. The relative distribution is then the ratio of comparison-group earners to baseline-group earners at each level of the earnings distribution. Like any ratio, it takes the value 1 when the numerator and denominator are equal, which happens when the fraction of earners at that level of the earnings distribution is the same for both groups. When the fraction of earners is higher or lower than the reference group, the relative distribution rises or falls. The value taken by the relative distribution can be interpreted either as the number of comparison-group earners per reference-group earner at each earnings level if the groups were the same size, or, by subtracting 1, as the percentage difference in the fraction of workers at that earnings level. When the earnings distributions for both groups are exactly the same, the relative distribution is flat, taking the value 1 over the entire earnings scale.

For notation, let

y_0, y_1 = reference-group and comparison-group earnings
$f_0(\cdot), f_1(\cdot)$ = density functions for each group's earnings distributions,

then the relative distribution of group 1 to group 0 earnings may be defined as follows:

$Rd(y_1, y_0)$ = the distribution of y_1 relative to y_0

$$= \frac{f_1(y_0)}{f_0(y_0)}. \tag{1}$$

Note that the numerator uses the density function of the comparison group, f_1, but gives it the argument y_0, the earnings level of the reference group. The effect is to compare the earnings density functions of the two groups at the same point on the scale, defined here by y_0.[4] Relative distributions can also be used for analyzing changes in a population's earnings over time. Using a baseline year's earnings to define the reference distribution and subsequent yearly earnings to define the comparison distributions, the result is a time series of relative distributions that tracks the changing distribution of income by year.

The differences revealed by the relative distribution can be decomposed into two parts: median and shape differences. The intuition behind the decomposition is straightforward and easy to motivate using the image of changes in one group's earnings over time:

- A pure median shift would occur if every income were multiplied by the same factor, for example, if every earner received the same cost-of-living adjustment. The entire earnings distribution would then be moved up (or down) on the dollar scale, but the underlying shape of the distribution would remain constant. The median earner's percentage increase (or decrease) in this case would summarize the experience of the entire workforce.
- A shape shift, by contrast, would occur if earners were redistributed along the earnings scale. The "declining middle class" scenario provides one example of such a redistribution, with earners moving from the middle of the distribution into the upper and lower tails. But other scenarios are also possible, with growth occurring in the upper tail (a pattern consistent with the job-skill mismatch hypothesis), the lower tail (a pattern consistent with the deskilling hypothesis), or the middle of the distribution (a pattern consistent with a more egalitarian restructuring of wages). In all of these cases, the change in the median earner's income would not necessarily represent the experience of earners in other sections of the distribution.

One or both of these changes may be operating over time. As the relative distribution is a ratio, the natural decomposition is multiplicative. To formalize the definitions of the two components, let

$Rd\ (y_t, y_0)$ = distribution of earnings at time t relative to time 0

$$= \frac{f_t(y_0)}{f_0(y_0)} \ . \tag{2}$$

This relative distribution can be decomposed into the two components:

$$= \frac{f_t(y_0)}{f_t^d(y_0)} \cdot \frac{f_t^d(y_0)}{f_0(y_0)}, \qquad (3)$$

where

$f_t^d(y)$ = the density of year t earnings deflated by the median ratio,

$$\frac{\text{median}(y_0)}{\text{median}(y_t)}.$$

The first term in equation 3 can be interpreted as the median shift effect. The numerator and denominator differ only in the median of the density functions: The ratio holds the distributional shape constant, isolating the effects of the median shift. The second term can be interpreted as the effect of the shape shift. Median deflation equalizes the medians of the baseline and comparison distributions. As a result, the numerator and denominator differ only in the shape of the earnings densities: the ratio holds the medians constant, isolating the effects of the shape shifts. It is important to understand that these effects are recalculated at each point of the earnings scale—they do not simply take two values for the entire distribution but two sets of values that change across the earnings scale.

A simple example of median and shape shifts can be seen in the panels of Figure 7.2. The top two panels show the impact of a median shift. The earnings distribution for blue earners is left-shifted relative to the red earners, but it has the same basic shape. The relative distribution of blue to red earners in the right panel thus displays a simple monotonic decline. At the bottom of the earnings scale, there are relatively more blue earners than red. The relative distribution shows this, as it is well above 1, and the value it takes can be interpreted to mean that there are 3.5 times as many blue earners as red earners at the bottom of the scale. At about 60 on the earnings scale, the fraction of blue and red earners is the same. This is where the earnings distributions cross on the left panel and where the relative distribution takes the value 1 on the right panel. At the top of the earnings scale, there are more red earners than blue, and the relative distribution drops below 1. The value it takes indicates that there are only about 40 percent as many blue earners as red earners at the top earnings level. In the bottom two panels, a shape shift is depicted. Here, blue earners have a more "polarized" distribution of earnings than red earners: There are more blue earners at the top and bottom of the earnings scale, and fewer in the middle. The relative distribution for this kind of

FIGURE 7.2   Examples of Median and Shape Shifts and Their Effects on the Relative Distribution

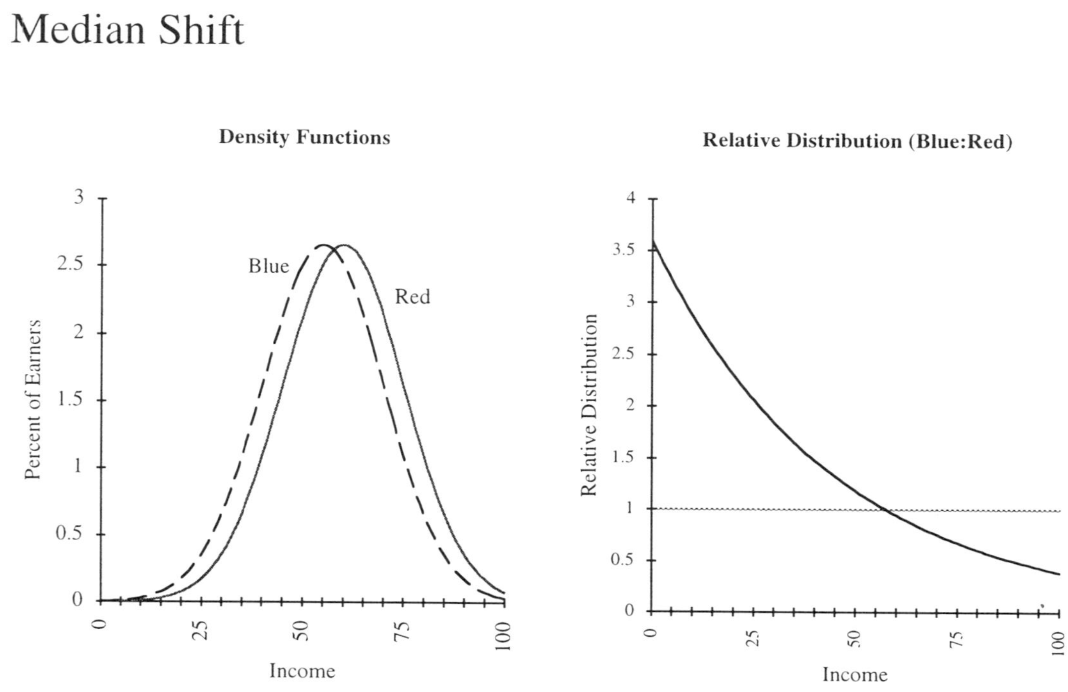

Median Shift

FIGURE 7.2 *(continued)*

Shape Shift

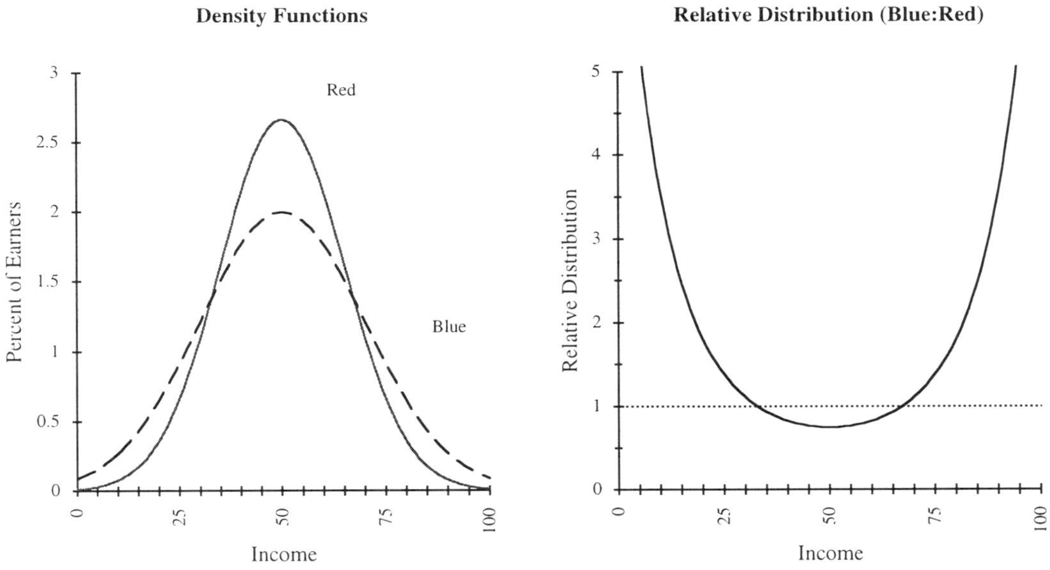

shift takes a simple U-shape. At the top and bottom of the earnings scale, there are about five times as many blue earners as red. In the middle there are only about 70 percent as many blue earners as red.

The relative distribution thus provides a simple and intuitive comparative picture of the earnings distributions between groups. For between-group analyses, both median and shape shifts are of interest. For within-group analyses over time, shape shifts are generally more important. Median shifts as defined here largely represent the effects of inflation and are of little substantive interest. If desired, one can separate out the inflationary component from the total median shift using the same logic as above:

$$\frac{f_t(y_0)}{f_t^d(y_0)} = \frac{f_t(y_0)}{f_t^{cpi}(y_0)} \cdot \frac{f_t^{cpi}(y_0)}{f_t^d(y_0)} \qquad (4)$$

The first term on the right-hand side represents the effects of inflation, using an earnings deflator based on the consumer price index (CPI). The remaining term then represents the relative constant dollar wage and would show whether workers were relatively better or worse off over time. While this is an important issue, it is not directly of interest here for assessing the relative gains of men and women. To ease exposition below, it is left implicit.

As Figure 7.2 demonstrates, this approach readily lends itself to graphical methods, simplifying exploration of the data and reducing the likelihood of errors in interpretation. For visualizing time series, it is helpful to break the earnings distribution into deciles and plot the series as a three-dimensional bar chart. In this case the baseline earnings distribution is partitioned into deciles (so the denominator of the relative distribution always takes the value 0.10), and the fraction of the comparison earners falling into each of these deciles is used to form the numerator. The ratio of the two determines the relative distribution and the height of the bar. This decile-based relative distribution ($\times$ 10) is adopted for all of the figures below.

Initial Findings

In this section, I examine two sets of relative distributions. The first is within-sex over time, focusing on the shape shifts only, and the second is between-sex over time. Both men and women experienced a growth in earnings inequality from 1967 to 1987, but the timing and magnitude of the rise has been sex-specific. White men were the first group of workers to experience the increase, through a steady polarization in their earnings. The first panel of Figure 7.3 tracks the shape shifts in the men's distribution and shows just how striking this trend has been.[5] The relative fraction of men in both the upper and lower earnings deciles increased over the 21-year period, with the growth in the lower deciles being especially pronounced after 1980. The relative fraction of men in the middle of the earnings distribution steadily decreased. It is this polarization in earnings that has generated the widespread concern over a "declining middle class."

The second panel of Figure 7.3 tracks the corresponding shape shifts for women and shows that the earnings of white women underwent a somewhat different set of changes during the same time period. Their earnings upgraded at first, with most of the growth in the middle and top of the distribution. A distinct polarization then set in and continued through the 1980s. By 1987 the inequality in women's earnings was significant, but it remained smaller in magnitude than the men's.

The converging median wage differential shown in Figure 7.1 has thus been complemented by a more complex set of changes at the *distributional* level. The distribution of men's earnings has grown significantly more unequal, and the timing and magnitude of this growth has not been matched by the changes in women's earnings. The reason could be that deindustrialization and economic restructuring have disproportionately affected the wage distribution of men, who were more dependent on traditional manufacturing jobs. Whatever the reason, however, this difference in distributional shifts could, in and of itself, have resulted in an improvement in women's economic standing relative to men. Women may not have gained economic ground on men so much as men lost more ground than women did.

To begin to answer this question, it is necessary to examine the between-group trends, using the relative distribution to compare women's earnings directly to men's. The full decile-based relative distribution of women's to men's earnings from 1967 to 1987 is plotted in Figure 7.4; both median and shape components are included. Men's earnings form the reference distribution, with the deciles reset in each year to capture 10 percent of the current male earners. Women's earnings form the comparison distribution in each year. The relative distribution thus tracks the fraction of women falling into each decile of the men's earnings scale over time.

The immediate impression conveyed by the graph is how dramatically less women earn relative to men. Nearly all the mass in the women's distribution is concentrated in the lower tail of the men's distribution. In 1967 nearly half of all women earners were in the bottom *decile* of the men's distribution, and over 90 percent (the cumulative sum of all those in deciles 1-5) earned less than the median male worker. By 1987 this had changed somewhat, but over a quarter of the women still remained in the

FIGURE 7.3   Shape Changes in the Relative Distribution of Earnings Within Sex over Time: Full-time, Full-year White Workers, 1967-1987

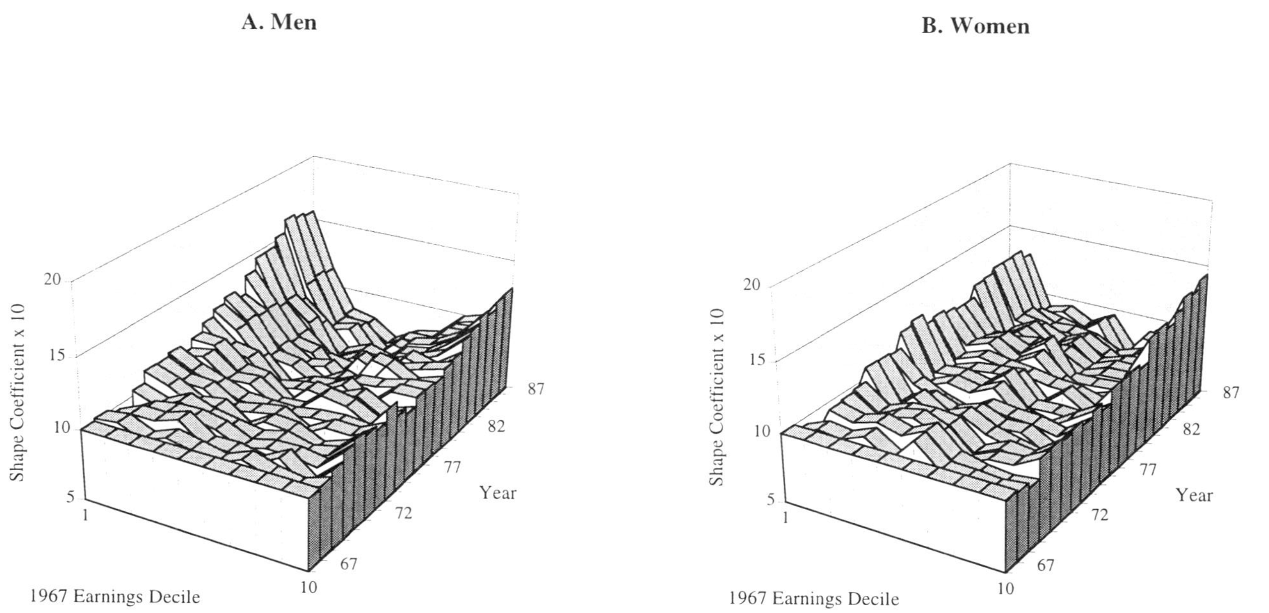

A. Men

B. Women

Note: The vertical axis represents the percent of earners whose median-deflated earnings fall into each decile over time. See equation 3 in the text for definition.

Continuity and Change in the Gender Wage Gap

FIGURE 7.4 Relative Distribution of Women's to Men's Earnings: Full-time, Full-year White Workers, 1967–1987

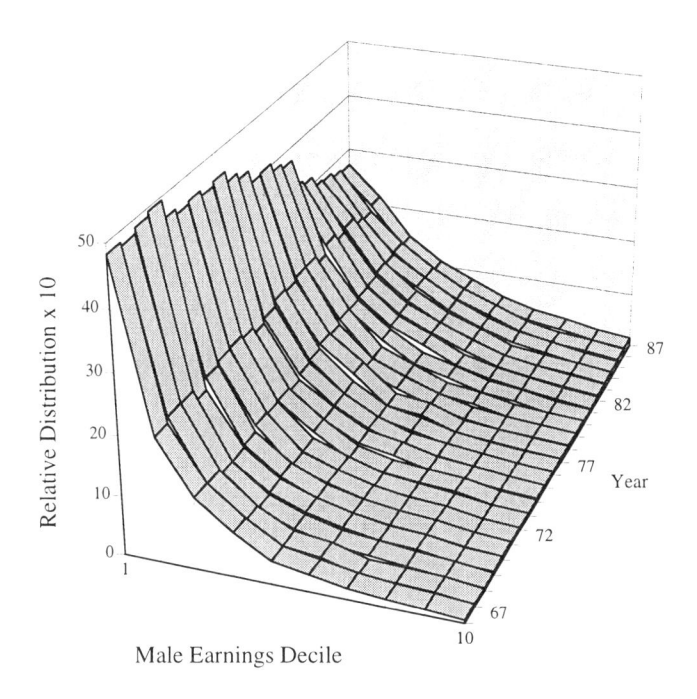

Note: The vertical axis represents the percent of women wage earners in each of the male earnings deciles. See equation 1 in the text for definition.

bottom decile of the men's distribution, and 83 percent still earned less than the median male worker. The persistent absence of women in the upper tail of the men's earnings distribution is equally striking. Less than 1 percent of women fell in the top decile in 1967, and less than 2 percent in 1987.

While the median ratio graphed in Figure 7.1 suggests that women made real progress during this period, the relative distribution makes it clear that progress was limited to women at the bottom end of the earnings distribution: Three-quarters of the changes occurred below the male earnings median, half in the lowest decile alone.

The simple median wage trends in Figure 7.1 thus provide a poor picture of the changes in earnings for men and women. The patterns revealed by the relative distribution in Figure 7.4 provide substantially more information but are complicated to interpret because they represent the combined outcome of several factors: a baseline median earnings differential between the two groups, changes in this differential over time (the information conveyed by the median ratio in Figure 7.1), and the two shape shifts (changes in the shape of the men's and women's distribution shown in Figures 7.3A and 7.3B, respectively). The next section develops a method for separating these effects.

Methods 2 : Decomposing Relative Distribution Changes

The goal here is to decompose mathematically the changes in the relative distribution into within- and between-group shifts in median and shape. The basic principle is similar to that used in the decomposition for a single group over time. To compare the amount of change in real terms (percentage point rather than percent), an additive analogue to the multiplicative decomposition is derived. Methods for statistical inference have not yet been developed.

Multiplicative Decomposition

Changes between two groups over time can be decomposed into four components: two median shifts and two shape shifts. Like ANOVA and dummy-variable regression, these effects can be parameterized in more than one way, depending on the reference point chosen for the "constant" term.[6] A natural choice here is the original base-year relative distribution between the two groups. The remaining terms will then represent the incremental change in that distribution due to each effect. Let

m_t, w_t = men's and women's earnings in year t, respectively,

m_t^d, w_t^d = earnings deflated by the men's median ratio for both groups,

$g_t(\cdot)$ = the density function for men's earnings in year t,

$h_t(\cdot)$ = the density function for women's earnings in year t,

$g_t^d(\cdot), h_t^d(\cdot)$ = density functions for each group based on earnings deflated by the men's median ratio, $\dfrac{\text{median }(m_t)}{\text{median }(m_0)}$,

$g_t^{wd}(\cdot)$ = density function for women's earnings deflated by the women's median ratio, $\dfrac{\text{median }(w_t)}{\text{median }(w_0)}$.

Then, with men as the reference group and women as the comparison group,

$Rd(w_t, m_t) =$ distribution of women's earnings relative to men's at time t

$$= \frac{h_t(m_t)}{g_t(m_t)}$$

$$= \frac{h_t^d(m_t^d)}{g_t^d(m_t^d)}. \tag{5}$$

This is the relative distribution that, in its decile version, is graphed in Figure 7.4. The equality follows because the relative density of the two earnings distributions is unchanged when both (and their common scale, m_t) are multiplied by the same constant (here, deflated by the men's median ratio).[7] Median deflation is useful here because it eliminates the estimation difficulties described above. Note, however, that while the overall median inflation is removed from each distribution, the *relative* median shifts between the two groups are preserved. Changes in the median earnings ratio are therefore retained.

Using the same logic as the within-group decomposition, the relative distribution in equation 5 can be decomposed into a series of terms isolating relative median and shape shift effects, with a few additional terms needed for rescaling.

$$\frac{h_t^d(m_t^d)}{g_t^d(m_t^d)} = \frac{h_0(m_0)}{g_0(m_0)} \cdot \frac{h_t^d(m_t^d)}{h_t^{wd}(m_t^d)} \cdot \frac{h_t^{wd}(m_t^d)}{h_0(m_t^d)} \cdot \left[\frac{g_t^d(m_t^d)}{g_0(m_t^d)}\right]^{-1}$$

$$\cdot \frac{h_0(m_t^d)}{h_0(m_0)} \cdot \left[\frac{g_0(m_t^d)}{g_0(m_0)}\right]^{-1}. \tag{6}$$

The first term in the expression, $\frac{h_0(m_0)}{g_0(m_0)}$, is the constant term: the base-year relative distribution of women's to men's earnings. The next three terms index the *relative* median shift, the women's shape shift, and the men's shape shift, respectively. The relative median shift takes the women's density deflated by the men's median ratio, h_t^d, and compares it to the women's density deflated by their own median ratio, h_t^{wd}. This holds the basic distributional shape (h_t) constant, thus isolating the effects of the relative gains women made in median income. The female and male shape shifts compare current within-group median-deflated densities to their baseline densities and are thus analogous to the within-group shape shift effects identified in equation 3 above.

The two terms on the second line of the decomposition can be seen as rescaling effects but also as part of the male shape shift. Mathematically, they rescale the base-year earnings (m_0) used in the constant term into the current-year median-deflated dollars m_t^d, which are used in the reference distribution. Substantively, however, the medians of the earnings scale and the density functions are the same within each term, so these ratios isolate another part of the male shape shift effect for men and women, respectively. For the purposes of this study, I will combine the effects of these two rescaling terms and the within-group male shape shift term to represent the total male shape shift effect.

For notational simplicity, denote the multiplicative coefficient at earnings level m_t at time t by:

$$RM(m_t) = \frac{h_t^d(m_t^d)}{h_t^{wd}(m_t^d)}, \text{ the relative median shift coefficient,} \quad (7)$$

$$FS(m_t) = \frac{h_t^{wd}(m_t^d)}{h_0(m_t^d)}, \text{ the female shape shift coefficient,} \quad (8)$$

$$MS(m_t) = \left[\frac{g_t^d(m_t^d)}{g_0(m_t^d)}\right]^{-1} \cdot \frac{h_0(m_t^d)}{h_0(m_0)} \cdot \left[\frac{g_0(m_t^d)}{g_0(m_0)}\right]^{-1},$$

the male shape shift coefficient, $\quad (9)$

and in general by $k_i(m_t)$, where i represents the specific component. Then the decomposition from equation 6 can be reexpressed as:

$$Rd(w_t, m_t) = Rd(w_0, m_0) \cdot MD(m_t) \cdot FS(m_t) \cdot MS(m_t). \quad (10)$$

This multiplicative decomposition makes it possible to compare the strength of median and shape shifts on the relative distribution of earnings at each level of the earnings distribution. The coefficients have a simple interpretation. In terms of function, they act as a multiplier, either incrementing or decrementing the fraction of women at each level of the men's earning scale, depending on whether the value of the coefficient is above or below 1. In terms of value, the coefficient can be interpreted as the percentage change in the fraction of women at each level: $k_i(m_t) - 1$ is the percentage change attributable to the ith component.

There is one other decompositional approach in the literature that is worth briefly mentioning here for comparison. Like the approach presented above, it is aimed at separating the effects of changes in average wages from changes in the shape of the wage distribution. The method was developed by Juhn, Murphy, and Pierce (1991) in the context of racial earnings differences and has been applied recently to the gender earnings gap by Blau and Kahn (1994). This approach uses classical linear regression to partial out a series of terms representing changes in mean human capital, mean returns to that capital, changes in the mean residual earnings gap between men and women, and changes in the standard deviation of the men's residual earnings variation:

$$D_t - D_0 = (\Delta X_t - \Delta X_0)\beta_t + \Delta X_t (\beta_t - \beta_0) + (\Delta \theta_t - \Delta \theta_0)\sigma_t + \Delta \theta_t (\sigma_t - \sigma_0).$$

Here, $D_t - D_0$ is the change in the mean wage gap between men and women between year t and year 0, ΔX represents the gender difference in mean human capital (typically a vector of means), β represents men's returns to human capital, $\Delta \theta$ represents the gender difference in the average standardized residual (effectively the intercept difference for the male and female equations), and σ represents the standard deviation in the men's residual wage distribution. Interested readers are referred to the papers cited above for a more detailed explication. While taking account of the human capital component is an important feature of this approach, there are two problems with this type of decomposition. First, it works only with average differences. Even though the residual wage distribution and the men's standard deviation are included, both distributions are collapsed into a single-number summary: the average residual wage gap and the standard deviation in the men's residual wage distribution. This makes it impossible to examine how changes in the distributions affect men and women at different levels of the earnings scale (a more general discussion of the drawbacks of average wage comparisons can be found in Morris, Bernhardt, and Handcock 1994:206–7). Second, this decomposition does not separately identify and estimate the effects of the male and female shape shifts. Instead, the two are summarized and combined in the third term, which reflects simply the changes in the mean residual wage gap multiplied by the men's standard deviation. This has the effect of confounding the two shape shifts, again removing the level of detail needed to answer the most interesting questions—such as whether women's gains were due mainly to upgrading in their own wage distribution or to downgrading of men's earnings.

Additive Decomposition

In some cases it may be preferable to express the effect of a specific shift in terms of the *amount* of change it generates. The multiplicative coefficients in equations 6–10 do not represent change in this way: A coefficient of 1.6 operating at the lowest decile, for example, generates more change than the same coefficient at the top decile, because more women are located in the lowest decile. To represent the fraction of women affected by each component, an additive decomposition is necessary. The goal is to take the total change in the relative distribution from the baseline year to year t, $Rd\ (w_t, m_t) - Rd\ (w_0, m_0)$, and decompose it into the change contributed by each component. Using the general notation for the multiplicative coefficients, $k_i\ (m_t)$, the additive effect for each component is most naturally defined as

$$C\ (k_i\ (m_t)) = Rd\ (w_0, m_0) \bullet (k_i\ (m_t) - 1). \tag{11}$$

In this form $C\ (k_i\ (m_t))$ represents the percentage-point change in the baseline relative distribution at earnings level m_0 that is due to component i at time t— in simple terms, the fraction of women who moved into (or out of) this earnings level as a result of this effect. To form a complete decomposition, the effects must sum to the total change from the baseline to the current relative distribution:

$$\sum_i \text{effect}\ (i) = Rd\ (w_t, m_t) - Rd\ (w_0, m_0)$$

$$= Rd\ (w_0, m_0) \bullet (RM\ (m_t) \bullet FS\ (m_t) \bullet MS\ (m_t) - 1).$$

The three main effects defined by equation 11 sum instead to:

$$\sum_i C\ (k_i\ (m_t)) = Rd\ (w_0, m_0) \bullet (RM\ (m_t) + FS\ (m_t) + MS\ (m_t) - 3).$$

The difference is a residual "interaction effect" that emerges because each coefficient multiplies the effects of the others (see equation 10). This interaction effect is most easily defined by subtraction:

$$C(\text{int}(m_t)) = Rd(w_t, m_t) - Rd(w_0, m_0) - \sum_i C(k_i(m_t)). \quad (12)$$

It tends to be quite small.

Decomposition Findings

Decomposition can help to pinpoint the origins of the changes in the distribution of women's to men's earnings observed in Figure 7.4. It is useful to begin by graphing the multiplicative coefficients for each of the components over the full 21-year series. This shows how each component independently affected the relative distribution over time. The additive decomposition can then be used to summarize the amount of change from 1967 to 1987, and will show which components had the strongest impact in real terms at each level of the earnings scale.

Panel A in Figure 7.5 graphs the constant term of the decomposition, representing the effect of the baseline 1967 relative distribution. Although this graph is rather mundane, it highlights the logic of the decomposition: The median and shape shifts independently act on the starting relative distribution and change it over time. The baseline relative distribution does not contribute to the *change* observed in Figure 7.4, but as we can see here, it is the component that gives the graph its fundamental shape. In addition, because the baseline distribution is so skewed, a large coefficient at the upper deciles will have little net impact, because so few women earn at that high a level. By the same token, even a small coefficient at the bottom deciles will have a large effect, because most of the female earners are located there. The reader should continue to refer back to this panel to interpret the multiplicative effects of each coefficient in the following panels of the figure.

Panel B in Figure 7.5 shows the impact of the changing median ratio between men and women, the *relative* median shift. As we saw in Figure 7.1, this component does not really come into play until the early 1980s. It then begins to reduce the fraction of women in the lowest decile, by roughly one-fifth at the end of the period. Corresponding increases are found in the middle and upper ranges of the distribution, with the fraction of women in the top decile ultimately increased by half. As the gender gap in median earnings has narrowed in the past decade, it should come as no surprise that the median effect would serve to pull women out of the lower deciles and push them into the higher ones.

The effect of the women's shape shift is shown in panel C of Figure 7.5. Net of other changes, this shift strongly pulls women earners toward the middle and top of the relative distribution, and it does so from the

FIGURE 7.5 Multiplicative Decomposition of the Change in the Relative Distribution of Women's to Men's Earnings, 1967–1987

A. Base Year Relative Distribution

B. Relative Median Shift

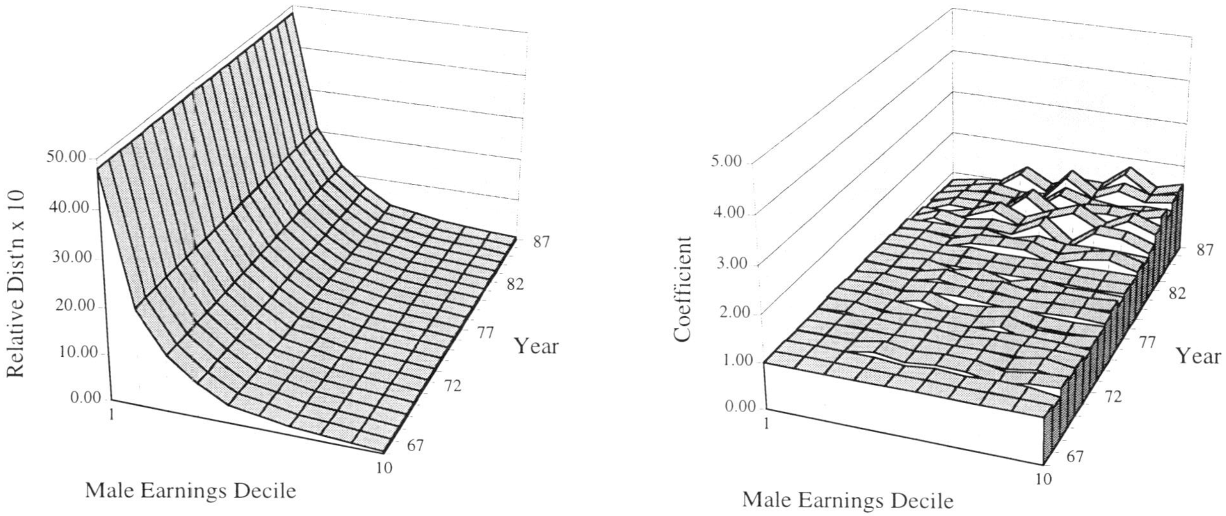

Note: See equations 6–9 in the text for definitions of the multiplicative coefficients.

FIGURE 7.5 *(continued)*

C. Women's Shape Shift

D. Men's Shape Shift

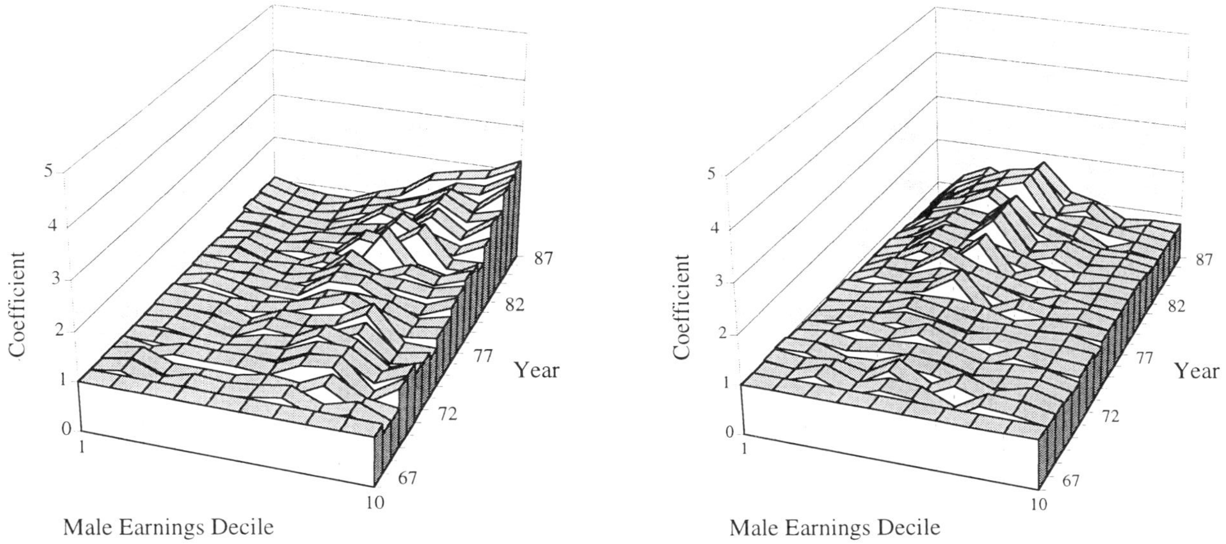

Note: See equations 6–9 in the text for definitions of the multiplicative coefficients.

beginning of the series. By 1987 the percentage of women in the top decile has more than doubled. Recall from Figure 7.3, however, that women's earnings began to polarize in the 1980s. Thus the women's shape shift predicts some late growth in the fraction of women in the bottom decile, while deciles 3 and 4 are predicted to decline by roughly one-fifth.

Panel D of Figure 7.5 isolates the shape shift effect for men. The polarizing trend that was so striking in Figure 7.3 is evident again in Figure 7.5 (because it is expressed here in terms of its effect on women's relative earnings, the shape is inverted relative to Figure 7.3). The marked increase in both low- and high-wage earners among men predicts that women will be "pushed" out of both the lower and upper deciles, toward the lower middle of the earnings scale. This trend begins in the early 1970s, but by the 1980s the stronger effect is clearly in the lower tail: The percent of women in the lowest decile is reduced by more than one-third. If no other changes had taken place, this polarization in men's earnings alone would have raised the relative economic standing of women.

These components provide evidence of a complex set of interconnected changes. The effects sometimes work in different directions and often are manifested in different parts of the earnings scale. This complexity underlines the importance of analyzing gender wage inequality at a distributional level. But the multiplicative coefficients still leave some questions. Overall, the male shape and the relative median shifts correspond most closely to what is observed in Figure 7.4: substantial movement of women out the lowest male earnings decile, with much weaker gains above the male median. The question remains, however: Did women gain economic ground partly at the expense of men—that is, because men's earnings became more polarized and unequal? Or was most of the gain a result of the narrowing gender gap in median earnings, as is commonly held? Answering this question in real terms requires moving to the additive decomposition.

A summary of the changes in each decile of the relative distribution over the 21-year period is provided in Table 7.1.

The additive effects defined in equation 11 can be used to identify the percentage-point change in each decile that is due to each component.[8] Figure 7.6 summarizes these effects by decile.

The male shape shift clearly dominates in the lower half of the earnings scale. As expected, the largest effects are observed in the first (lowest) decile. The percentage of women in this decile fell by a total of 21 percent (see Table 7.1). The shape shift of men was the strongest factor in this change, contributing a 15 percent decline. The median ratio shift added a further 9 percent decline. The women's shape shift for this decile has the opposite effect: Operating alone, this shift would actually have *increased* the fraction of women in the lowest male earnings decile. For

TABLE 7.1 Change in the Distribution of Women's to Men's Earnings: Full-time, Full-year White Workers, 1967–1987

Men's Earnings Decile	Percent of Women Falling in Men's Earnings Deciles		Change from 1967 to 1987
	1967	1987	
1 (low)	48.22	27.08	−21.14
2	20.79	21.69	0.90
3	12.06	14.92	2.86
4	7.38	10.84	3.46
5	3.85	8.28	4.43
6	2.90	5.82	2.92
7	1.83	4.22	2.39
8	1.38	3.36	1.98
9	1.02	2.21	1.19
10 (high)	0.58	1.59	1.01

deciles 2, 3, and 5, the male shape shift is the largest and dominant effect, offsetting the declines predicted by both the median and women's shape shifts. In decile 4 the median ratio shift again becomes important.

In the upper half of the distribution, a very different pattern emerges. The male shape shift no longer dominates. Along with the median ratio shift, the female shape shift now consistently comes into play, especially in generating the gains in deciles 7, 9, and 10. In terms of the amount of change, however, these effects are still relatively small.

The additive effects leave little question as to which factor generated the largest changes in women's relative economic standing: It was the male shape shift. Between 1967 and 1987, the changes in the relative distribution of women's to men's earnings totaled 42.3 percentage points (summing over the absolute value of the change in each decile). Close to half of this was generated by the male shape shift (48 percent), with the median ratio shift contributing 26 percent and the female shape shift 19 percent. The remaining 10 percent was due to the interaction of these effects. The median and women's shape shifts were responsible for the small gains that women made in the upper earnings deciles. But the male shape shift had the largest impact because its effects were strongest where the largest fraction of women workers are located—in the bottom decile of the men's earnings scale. By preserving the full distributional

FIGURE 7.6 Additive Effects of Each Component on the Total Change in the Percentage of Women in Each Male Earnings Decile, 1967–1987

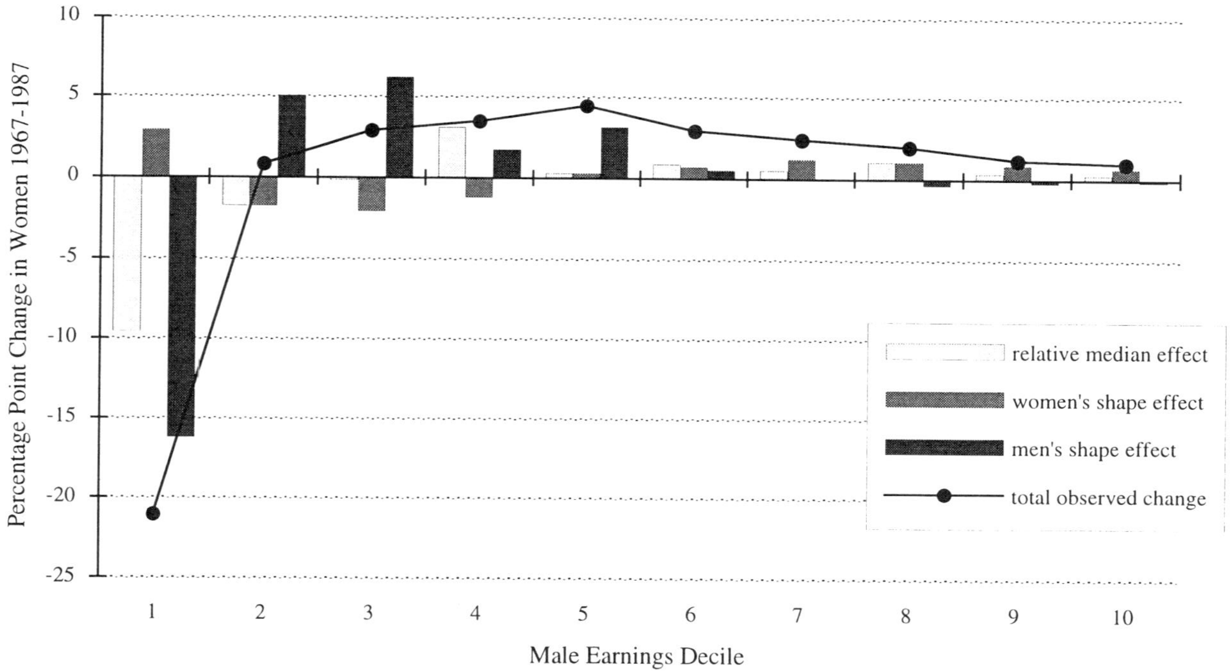

Note: See equation 11 in the text for definition of the effects.

information, we can also see that each of these effects operated differentially at different points of the earnings scale. To try to summarize these effects by their impact on the "average" woman earner, or the average wage gap, would be to lose the details that provide insight.

Discussion

There are several stories to be told about the recent progress in women's economic position. The convergence in median earnings is certainly one of them, but it appears not to be the most important.

Stated in the strongest terms, it is the trends in men's earnings that account for most of the recent improvement in women's relative earnings. Men's earnings have worsened and become more unequal since the early 1970s. This polarization of men's earnings "pushed" significant numbers of women out of the lowest male earnings level. Because most women's earnings fall in this section of the men's earnings scale, these changes had the single largest impact on women's relative gains: 48 percent of the total change in relative earnings was generated by the male shape shift. The median ratio shift, the next largest effect, generated only 26 percent of the change.

A second important point is that *distributional* changes in women's earnings rather than median growth generated their high-end gains. While the relative gains that women have made at higher earnings levels play a much weaker role in their recent improvement, to many these are the substantively important gains because they indicate entry into the most prestigious and best-rewarded occupations. Thus it is interesting that the distributional or shape changes in women's earnings generated these gains. This runs somewhat counter to popular thinking. The shrinking gender gap in average earnings is often assumed to be the result of a leading edge of women entering high-end, well-paid, high-visibility jobs, followed by a mass of women whose median wages are pulling even with men's. In fact, however, the leading edge is not being followed: It is not the shrinking median differential but rather the growing polarization in women's earnings that accounted for the gains made in the higher earnings levels. The women's distributional shift is very much a two-edged sword; it has enabled some women to move into well-paid jobs, but it has also generated greater wage polarization and inequality among women.

These results compel us to reexamine how we analyze and interpret women's recent economic progress. The prevailing approach in the current literature draws on the tradition of research in social stratification: The focus is on the explanatory role of changes in women's human capital—women investing in more education, acquiring more work experience, and making longer commitments to the labor force. Such improvements in women's human capital may have had a significant effect, but they form only part of the picture. The other part is the changing morphology of the American job structure. Women's progress has taken place in the last two decades as men's earnings have suffered; both deindustrialization and America's move to a service economy have played an important role in this. Ultimately, then, how women make economic progress relative to men is a complicated dynamic, with both stratification and morphology playing a role. An important area for further research is to quantify the relative contribution made by each.

The results suggest that optimistic predictions about the future of gender equality may be premature: The convergence of women's and men's wages may be a trend of the past, not the future. Two empirical observations generate this prediction. First, the growing inequality in men's earnings, which has been so beneficial to women, has begun to stabilize (Morris, Bernhardt, and Handcock 1994, esp. figure 5). One of the causes for this trend was deindustrialization, which is by now pretty much played out. Second, women's earnings began to polarize in the 1980s, and this trend does not show any sign of lessening. The analysis above suggests that in the absence of a strong male shape shift, a polarization of women's earnings will increase the percentage of women earners in the lowest deciles of the male earnings scale. Both factors thus suggest that progress will be tougher in the future. Women's recent economic gains can be interpreted in part as an act of structural ventriloquism; the worsening of men's earnings both improved their relative standing and mitigated the effects of growing inequality in their own earnings. In coming years, as the male earnings distribution stabilizes, it remains to be seen whether other forces will emerge to produce continued economic progress for women.

Notes

1. The variation in the estimates stems from the use of different data sets, sample definitions, and summary measures (for a detailed review, see Marini 1989).

2. Median, rather than average, earnings will be used throughout this chapter for statistical purposes that will become clear below.

3. The author would like to thank Annette D. Bernhardt, Robert D. Mare, and Christopher Winship for the use of the uniform series of the March *Current Population Survey* files, created with financial support from the National Science Foundation through grant SOC-7912648.

4. Technically, the relative distribution is a proper probability density function and takes as its arguments the densities of each group at each percentile rank of the reference earnings level. It represents the density of comparison-group earners at each percentile of the reference-group earnings scale. The precise

technical definition of the relative distribution is given in the appendix to this chapter.

5. Decile 1 is the lowest earnings level, 10 the highest. The baseline year throughout these analyses is 1967 because this is the first year in the data series that permits exact tracking of the earnings measure over time. Choosing an alternative baseline year would change the view provided by the decile graphs, but it would *not* change the central trends or year-to-year comparisons that one would infer from the graphs.

6. Though one must keep in mind that the parameters are indexed by the earnings scale.

7. Technically, the relative distribution is invariant to any monotonic transformation, while the components of the decomposition are invariant to multiplicative transformations.

8. The definition of these effects also yields an interaction term, but in this case it is relatively small. For deciles 1 through 10, respectively, it is 1.87, −0.68, −1.14, −0.20, 0.61, 0.64, 0.48, 0.10, 0.05, and 0.10.

References

Blau, Francine D., and Andrea H. Beller. 1988. "Trends in Earnings Differentials by Gender, 1971–1981." *Industrial and Labor Relations Review* 41:513–29.

Blau, Francine, and Lawrence Kahn. 1994. "Rising Wage Inequality and the U.S. Gender Gap." *American Economic Review* 84:23–8.

Handcock, Mark. 1994. "Imputation Methods for Coarse Income Data." Technical Report, Department of Statistics and Operations Research, New York University, New York.

Harrison, Bennett, and Barry Bluestone. 1988. *The Great U-Turn: Corporate Restructuring and the Polarizing of America*. New York: Basic Books.

Juhn, Chinhui, Kevin M. Murphy, and Brooks Pierce. 1991. "Accounting for the Slowdown in Black-White Wage Convergence." Pp. 107–43 in Marvin H. Kosters (ed.), *Workers and Their Wages: Changing Patterns in the United States*. Lanham, MD: AEI Press.

Karoly, Lynn. 1993. "The Trend in Inequality Among Families, Individuals, and Workers in the United States: A Twenty-Five Year Perspective." Pp. 19–97 in S. Danziger and P. Gottschalk (eds.), *Uneven Tides*. New York: Russell Sage Foundation.

Kuttner, Robert. 1983. "The Declining Middle." *Atlantic Monthly* 252:60–72.

Levy, Frank, and Richard Murnane. 1992. "U.S. Earnings Levels and Earnings Inequality: A Review of Recent Trends and Proposed Explanations." *Journal of Economic Literature* 30:1333–81.

Marini, Margaret M. 1989. "Sex Differences in Earnings in the United States." *American Sociological Review* 15:343–80.

Morris, Martina, Annette D. Bernhardt, and Mark S. Handcock. 1994. "Economic Inequality: New Measures for New Trends." *American Sociological Review* 59:205–19.

Nasar, Sylvia. 1992. "Women's Progress Stalled? Just Not So." *New York Times*, October 18, 1992, Sec. 3.

O'Neill, June, and Solomon Polachek. 1993. "Why the Gender Gap in Wages Narrowed in the 1980s." *Journal of Labor Economics* 11:205–28.

Wellington, Allison J. 1993. "Changes in the Male/Female Wage Gap, 1976–85." *Journal of Human Resources* 28:383–411.

Appendix to Chapter 7

The notation in this chapter is designed for simplicity, clarity, and brevity. The precise definition of the relative distribution requires this notation to be unpacked to make explicit the rescaling from the original earnings scale to the percentile rankings that form the basis of the distributional comparison.

Let Y_0 and Y_t be random variables representing income in the baseline year and year t, respectively. We define the cumulative relative distribution of Y_t to Y_0 by:

$$G_t(r) = F_t(F_0^{-1}(r)), \qquad 0 < r \leq 1$$

where $F = \inf_y \{y : F_0(y) \geq r\}$ is the inverse cumulative distribution function of Y_0, and r is the percentile rank of y in the earnings distribution, F_0. Note that G is defined even when the income distributions are not continuous.

The relative distribution in equation 1 is then the probability density function defined by:

$$\text{Rd}(y_1, y_0) \equiv G'(r)$$

$$= \frac{f_1(F_0^{-1}(r))}{f_0(F_0^{-1}(r))}.$$

If the income distribution is aggregated into quantiles, the relative distribution remains well defined but the relative density does not exist. Consider a group-level income distribution with Q groups. The ith cut point, $c(i)$, specifies the income level for which the cumulative proportion of the income distribution is $\dfrac{i}{Q}$:

$$F_0(c(i)) = \frac{i}{Q}$$

or

$$c(i) = F_0^{-1}\left(\frac{i}{Q}\right), \qquad i = 0, 2, \ldots, Q.$$

In this case the analogue to the relative density function is the proportion of the comparison group whose earnings fall between each pair of quantile cut points, divided by the proportion in the reference group.

8

Gender Inequalities in the Distribution of Responsibility

Carol A. Heimer

The distinction between compassion and corruption, Wuthnow (1991:279–80) argues, is a distinction between two forms of overcommitment. Both entail exercising discretion in the application of rules, going beyond a job description, the letter of the law, or the fine print of a contract. But while corruption entails bending the rules for personal benefit, compassion involves going beyond what is required in the opposite direction—overconforming, overperforming for the benefit of others. One of these poles, corruption—or "moral hazard," as it is often called in the social science literature—has been studied extensively; the other, which I call responsibility, has only recently received much attention, though I believe it is crucial to our understanding of the abiding inequalities between the sexes. I use the term "responsibility" rather than "compassion" because one may pursue the goals of an organization, a profession, or world peace using reason and calculation, and such sane pursuit of the goals of institutions would ordinarily be called responsibility. Similarly, one may pursue goals through empathy that is well rewarded and treat patients well because a professional reputation is to one's advantage, but such reasoned going beyond the bare minimum would not usually be called compassion.

Here I make the case for why social scientists should be interested in responsibility. Sociologists have been accused of believing that social structure and norms are so determinative of human action that there is little room for human agency (e.g., Wrong 1961). It is clear that people do make choices, and real choices at that. My premise is that many such choices are oriented to the welfare of others, of social groups, of values.

Choices and agency are "responsible" only when they are social. But how much people really *choose* varies from one situation to another; we have knee-jerk responses in some situations, while in others we think long and hard before deciding what to do or how to do it. To develop sociological theories that incorporate human agency, we need to examine situations that require agency—situations in which people must use their human capacities to reflect, strategize, and choose. Variations between situations or roles that require responsibility and those that do not provide the raw materials for theories that take account of human agency. That kind of agency I call "responsibility" since that is the core meaning of the word as it is usually used. For example, in saying that some jobs should be paid more because they require more responsibility (Jaques 1972; Soltan 1987), people mean that occupants of those positions have to think, strategize, and choose on behalf of a complicated system of social values.

The most important parts of social structure cannot be created or managed without agency, and responsibility is the core of what we try to achieve through incentive systems, the design of the legal system, teaching our children values, and other devices to get others to take a larger view or to consider the relation between action and a complicated set of purposes. We want social arrangements that make people look beyond themselves to consider the needs and interests of the organizations, families, friendship groups, or societies in which they are embedded. When we try to get someone to "take responsibility," for instance, by assigning a task or mandating some behavior, we are disappointed if we get legalism rather than thoughtful compliance. In giving their children chores, parents hope to instill a sense of obligation for the collective welfare and to teach that many rules are guidelines for coordinating the activities of a group of people. Even if the work gets done, parents are disappointed when their child repeatedly chooses the easiest jobs or fails to notice when a task needs to be done, insisting that no rule specifies *when* it has to be done.

Responsibility is also fundamental to caring. Gilligan (1982) argues that moral development can proceed along two different paths, one guided by the ethic of justice, the other by the ethic of care. One can either reason deductively from principles of justice or attempt to decipher and balance the needs of various parties. Gilligan suggests that those guided by the ethic of care are more likely to feel responsible for finding a solution that works well for everyone. At the highest level of development, though, the ethic of justice and the ethic of care tend to converge. Paying attention to the spirit as well as the letter of the law and attending to the rights as well as the needs of concrete people would, by my argument, often lead to the same outcome.

This connection between responsibility and caring is especially strong when responsibilities are fates rather than opportunities, as I explain below. Gender differences in distributions of caring work encumber women with responsibilities not easily shifted to others, leaving men freer to invest in responsibilities that are both more likely to lead to rewards and easier to escape should they become burdensome.[1] To anticipate my conclusion, for men responsibilities are more likely to be taken on as strategic opportunities or investments, while for women responsibilities are more likely to be fates that limit their capacity to strategize and to invest outside the family.

What Do We Mean by "Responsibility"?

Roles requiring more responsibility can be differentiated from those requiring less along five dimensions.[2] (1) More responsible roles tend to require a person to take account of others' interests as well as his or her own. The utility function[3] being maximized is that of another person or some institution rather than the person's own, or at the very least it includes arguments describing others' interests as well. (2) More responsible roles tend to carry more diffuse obligations. That is, a person is required to maximize a utility function rather than a single value. (3) More responsible roles require that a person think about long-term outcomes and maximize the utility function over a longer time horizon. (4) More responsible positions have more discretion. The person chooses *how* to maximize the utility function rather than following a rule or prescribed procedure. And (5) more responsible roles entail an obligation to deal with whatever contingencies arise. The person accepts the obligation to maximize the utility function under conditions of uncertainty about what exactly is entailed and what costs and benefits will accrue to him or her. I discuss these dimensions in more detail below, highlighting factors that support or undermine the acceptance of responsibility. Of course one or another of these attributes may characterize many roles requiring little or no responsibility; roles requiring substantial responsibility are distinctive in *simultaneously* requiring a person to take account of others' interests, accept a diffuse definition of the job, think about the long term, use discretion, and accept resulting variations in his or her own welfare.

Taking Others' Interests Seriously

While to be rational is to choose trade-offs among values according to one's own preferences and tastes, to be responsible is to be rational on someone else's behalf (or at least not only on one's own behalf).[4] Behaving rationally and behaving responsibly may conflict; people are probably more likely to behave responsibly when rationality and responsibility coincide.[5] Being responsible (being rational on someone else's behalf) means thinking about the costs and benefits to the other party as well as to oneself and agreeing to bear some costs to achieve the other's purposes. Being responsible may not entail complete self-sacrifice, but it often requires some compromise between others' interests and one's own. If responsibility involves taking others' interests into account, then correspondingly it is irresponsible to define too narrowly the group on whose behalf one is supposed to make choices and select trade-offs.

In some instances a legal requirement reinforces the fiduciary obligation to make sacrifices in one's own welfare for the sake of others to whom one has a responsibility. Laws against insider trading make it clear that the board of directors is to defend stockholder interests and that board members cannot use inside connections and information in ways that would harm stockholder interests (Zey 1993). Similarly, professional privileges are partly justified by claims that professionals are altruistically oriented to their clients' needs and interests. But though some (e.g., Parsons 1968) believe such claims are legitimate, others (e.g., Friedson 1970; Starr 1982) are skeptical. Professionals may generally believe that they and their colleagues protect client interests, but they may nevertheless disagree about limits on the obligation to sacrifice their own interests. Bosk and Frader (1990), for instance, find that some medical students deny any obligation to care for AIDS patients if providing such care jeopardizes their own health.

Mechanisms that increase information about others' interests or make them more salient increase the chance that a person will take responsibility for others' welfare. Such mechanisms may create a community of fate in which the interests of the two parties are partially fused (Heimer 1985:201–6). An insurance contract, for instance, specifies that a policyholder cannot be compensated for a loss if he or she caused the loss or did nothing to prevent it. Because a policyholder's outcome depends on taking account of the insurer's interests, the policyholder will be more likely to take both sets of interests into account in deciding how much to spend on loss prevention (Heimer 1985); it is just such mechanisms that bring self-interest and responsibility into alignment. More generally, contracts make the outcomes of one person or organization dependent on the outcomes of the other, though, as Stinchcombe (1990:194–239) argues, such interdependence is produced more easily in hierarchies and in contracts that incorporate hierarchical features. Similarly, pressure groups try both to inform policymakers of their members' interests and to remind them that their welfare depends to some degree on the goodwill of the pressure group.

Defining Obligations Diffusely

Taking responsibility typically means accepting a broad definition of one's obligations. Parsons and Shils (1951), for instance, distinguished between roles judged by diffuse standards and roles with specific obligations. A central difficulty with getting people to accept diffusely defined obligations is that if rewards are attached to more narrowly defined achievements, attention and effort are easily deflected from ultimate goals.

Drawing on Merton's (1949/1968:253–4) discussion of the displacement of goals, Blau (1963:44–7) showed how instrumental values became terminal values. Workers would complete easier interviews in order to meet their monthly quotas, in the process undermining the official priority system for cases. They would also occasionally inflate measures of referrals by listing as referrals cases in which an employee was merely returning to an earlier placement after an illness. In both examples workers used official indicators to claim to have met organizational goals they had not actually met.

Similarly, Bardach and Kagan (1982) provide innumerable instances of the perverse effects of narrowly focused regulations. In some cases otherwise admirable regulations were enforced in contexts where they were unnecessary or even harmful. At a large aluminum plant with a good burn-prevention program, the Occupational Safety and Health Administration (OSHA) required workers to wear protective clothing even though such garb increased the risk of heat exhaustion (1982:87). Elementary school teachers processed endless bureaucratic forms (absence slips, lesson plans, ethnic surveys, permissions for field trips) though they lacked paper for lessons and art classes (1982:91). In other cases regulatory intervention ultimately led to *lower* standards than would have been achieved without intervention. After repeated OSHA inspections (to resolve a subordinate question) showing no violation of standards, one large manufacturing plant ultimately reversed its decision to respond to worker complaints by installing a new ventilation system (1982:107–8).

Workers' sense of their obligations may be resistant to change. A job is composed of core tasks strongly associated with the job and a penumbra of tasks more loosely tied to the position.[6] Both the core and the penumbra can shift through negotiation. In describing the division of work between themselves and their bosses, personal secretaries talk about "my work, your work, and our work" (Charlton 1983). Some tasks characterize all secretarial positions; others vary with the occupations of employers. While a boss may hope to convince a secretary that a lot of work is "our work," more negotiation will be required about that sphere than about tasks clearly defined as the secretary's own work. But secretaries who define "our work" and "my work" more liberally will likely be thought more "responsible" by their bosses.[7]

Resistance to diffuse definitions of a job will thus vary with whether proposed changes lie in the core or the penumbra and will increase the more it seems that an employer is attempting to redefine the core by making strategic assignments. A nanny may be quite happy to take on new childcare tasks (such as arranging for a toddler to participate in play groups) that clearly fall into the core, but may resist assignments that suggest that an employer is trying to turn her into a housekeeper. And a secretary's willingness to help select gifts for her boss's children will depend on whether she believes he is attempting to redefine her role from clerical worker to personal servant.

When job descriptions are associated with multiple measures of performance, people will adjust their behavior to produce activities and outputs that are easily measured. A babysitter whose only obligation is to care for the child will be evaluated by the health, happiness, and development of the child; a babysitter whose charge includes housework will be judged at least partly on the cleanliness of the house. Because it is easier to tell whether a house is clean than whether a child is well cared for, the babysitter may concentrate her efforts where her performance can most easily be evaluated. A worker's sense of responsibility is presumably also shaped by such technical considerations, and, as Bardach and Kagan rightly comment in distinguishing between accountability and responsibility, we must worry about whether "everyone will be accountable for everything, but no one will be responsible for anything" (1982:323).

But some flexible rule systems, such as the standard of seaworthiness in marine insurance (Heimer 1985), do encourage responsibility. A ship must be seaworthy for a marine insurance contract to hold, but what constitutes seaworthiness varies with the season, the route, and the trade. In addition, insured vessels must be classed and inspected by classification societies, and these professional bodies modify their rules with the accumulation of information from research about safety, with the development of technology, and the like. Responsibility then arises because there is no fixed standard to hide behind—there is only the ill-defined goal of safety and no authoritative checklist of tasks or standards. When only terminal values are articulated and few rewards are given for the achievement of instrumental goals, goal displacement is less likely to occur. Being responsible, then, means being honest about accomplishment and about the function of any task in the overall system, and continually adjusting measures of accomplishment and definitions of tasks to focus attention on core objectives. It means being true to the spirit rather than the letter of the law (or in this case of the indicator). Assuming a responsibility means only rarely saying "not my job."

Thinking About the Long Term

Jaques (1972) pointed to the intimate connection between long-term performance and hierarchical differences in responsibility in industry. Higher ranks are reviewed at longer intervals, he argued, because short-run measures of performance distract executives from using long-term objectives to set priorities. Thus the more responsible the role, the more the performance measures embedded in the incentive and authority systems of industrial hierarchies will focus on distant outcomes.

Uncertainty about the future makes it hard to think about what would be the best way to arrange a piece of that future, and so makes it difficult to get people to take responsibility for long-term outcomes, particularly long-term outcomes of people with whom they may have only a short-term relationship. The social arrangements connecting one person to another (e.g., as a teacher, physician, therapist, or financial adviser) may have rather short lives, undermining long-term planning. Nevertheless, attention to the future is a core part of responsibility, and failure to plan for the future is regarded as irresponsible. Rules requiring insurance companies to maintain reserves to cover the losses of their policyholders and rules about the management of pension funds place a premium on being able to manage obligations for the future as well as the present.

Whether the sequence is the life cycle of a person or of a firm, others will be especially concerned that those who control the early parts of a sequence feel responsible for the future consequences of present actions. Teachers, for instance, should be concerned about preparing students for subsequent stages in the educational process and, ultimately, for adult life, not just about the quality of the classroom experience. Japanese schools are widely believed to take more responsibility than their American counterparts for launching students into adulthood; nearly half of work-bound graduates find jobs through semiformal contracts between employers and the schools from which they regularly recruit (Rosenbaum and Kariya 1989:1343).

Among physicians, pediatricians are notable for their concern about the future of their patients. Such concern has been manifested in political pressure, for instance, in support of immunization programs and against nuclear testing after strontium 90 was discovered in milk, and by the expansion of the jurisdiction of pediatricians beyond the early childhood years and into psychosocial areas. This broad definition of mission is anomalous. As Halpern notes, while most medical fields establish legitimacy by making narrow claims to expertise, early pediatricians "argued that pediatrics was legitimate precisely because it failed to designate a highly restricted arena of professional practice" (1988:54). In contrast, neonatologists are sometimes faulted for worrying too little about the futures of the infants they save—according to one neonatologist, every infant gets "the best," even when evidence suggests that the child is not neurologically intact (Guillemin and Holmstrom 1986:234). Anspach (1993) points to a central difficulty neonatologists face in taking responsibility: When connections between present indicators and future outcomes are poorly understood, reasonable people will disagree about the responsible course of action even when all agree that the future cannot be ignored. Though intensive-care staff agreed on the principle that life-sustaining treatment should be withheld from infants who would not survive or would survive only with serious neurological deficits, this consensus disintegrated in practice because of disagreements about the prognosis of individual babies (Anspach 1993:58).

Though there are relatively few rewards for taking a long-term perspective, a variety of mechanisms can strengthen the connection between present and future. Annual reviews of a person's work make the tie between present performance and career prospects more real and more predictable in the present. Periodic calculation and release of indicators that will be used in future decisionmaking (e.g., grade point average and rank in class) focus attention on the implications of present courses of action. Planning committees provide some rewards in the present for thinking about the future and coordinate planning so that the schemes of one group do not undermine those of another. Rewards can be arranged so that planners have a personal stake in the adequacy of their planning. When executives are compensated in stock rather than cash, their personal outcomes will vary with how well they have planned for the company's future.[8] Other incentive mechanisms, such as tenure, force people to internalize the long-term consequences of their decisions by forcing them to live with those consequences for the rest of their careers.

Using Discretion to Meet Contingency

Responsible adaptation to contingencies requires, first, adapting action and spending the right resources to deal appropriately with the flow of events and, second, deciding who should pay for the resources used to meet the contingency. Though they have different causes and different effects, the acceptance of responsibility requires that both problems of discretion be solved. These two aspects of adaptation to contingency may shape the experience of responsibility in different ways. For example, many people like the discretion of the housewife role but not the fact that the housewife has to come up with all the extra effort to care for a sick child in the middle of the night.

Maximizing a utility function or choosing trade-offs between values and interests means doing different things under different circumstances. Similarly, taking responsibility will involve monitoring the relation between output and input more or less continuously, adjusting one's own inputs (number of hours, specific activities, level of effort, level of attention, etc.), and using one's authority over a collectivity's fund of resources to produce whatever result is required.

The smaller a person's resources or authority, the more the responsibility can be measured by the variability in the person's own inputs. As resources and authority increase, variations in responsibility are instead reflected in variations in attention and monitoring and variations in how the resources under the person's control are used. The responsible party may either vary his or her own inputs or cause the inputs of others to vary. If accomplishing some result requires more time, more attention, or some particular performance, then those are the inputs that must be supplied. But the time commitment, attention, and activity of some subordinate may vary more than the inputs of the superordinate who holds ultimate responsibility. Such variations in responsibility and authority are illustrated by the differences between working an eight-hour shift as a restaurant employee, where one's obligations are limited to performing prespecified tasks; managing a small restaurant, where one's tasks and working hours depend on what emergencies arise; and managing a large restaurant, in which emergencies are met by juggling others' assignments rather than adjusting one's own.

Formal responsibility in organizations is generally associated with both a high mean and a high variance in hours of work, as I discuss later. Another measure of discretion is whether a worker is considered skilled; skill increases discretion both by increasing a worker's capacity to determine what needs to be done and his or her capacity to do it (Stinchcombe 1990). In contrast, people whose jobs are closely scripted have little discretion to adjust their activity to variations in the situation. As Leidner (1993) shows, the constraint of a script is imposed on McDonald's workers, whose responses to variability are not trusted; the purpose of the script is to curb responsiveness when responsiveness might lead to bad results.

Even relatively skilled workers may be precluded from taking much responsibility. Bosk (1979) shows how attending surgeons curb the discretion of residents, insisting that they rigidly follow the idiosyncratic preferences (the rough equivalent of medical scripts) of the attending they are working with. Such rules facilitate coordination, of course, but they also reinforce the notion that with ultimate responsibility goes the right to make decisions about how subordinates will perform their duties.

Rules intended to solve one problem may limit a person's discretion in solving another. For instance, class assignments designed to curb cheating may not be ideal teaching devices. While organizational rules may have the desired effects of increasing uniformity of outcomes and preventing the most flagrant failures to take responsibility, they may also lead to a ritualistic focus on means rather than ends (Merton 1949/1968) and so undermine responsible adjustment to contingency. Organizations often counter this tendency by arranging an overall assessment of how far the organization has achieved its goals (ignoring for the moment whether it has followed its rules). External examiners, accreditation reviews, site visits, and boards of directors all serve these functions. Parsons (1956) and Stone (1975) both comment on the importance of having a committee with some substantial outside representation to fulfill this function. In general, although accountability is increased by having a single individual on whom to pin the blame, ultimate responsibility for trade-offs between values is often lodged in committees composed of representatives of those values. A single individual is too easily seduced into focusing on following rules rather than on achieving general and vague goals that take account of the interests of several parties.

Responsible and effective adjustment cannot be achieved if discretion is lodged in the wrong place. Chandler (1962) shows how the change from a functional to a divisional form at DuPont improved managers' capacity to adapt responsibly to individual product markets. In effect, managers were adjusting to the wrong things because they had not tied engineering, production, and marketing together in a way that facilitated adjustment to individual product markets. Lodging discretion in the wrong place undermines responsible adjustment by focusing attention and rewards on the wrong things.

Discretion, then, involves the right, the motivation, and the capacity to use appropriate means to respond to situational variations. But others can grant or deny a right to discretion, motivation can be undermined if rewards are not given for responsible behavior, and lack of resources can curtail a person's capacity to respond. Access to resources affects the range of responsibilities that can be accepted and influences a person's tendency to think of responsibilities as costs or investments. The experience of responsibility is fundamentally shaped by whether a person owns or has authority over substantial resources or can call on others for assistance. Plentiful resources make it possible to be rational in one's own interest and responsible to others' interests or to institutional values.

Accepting the Consequences of Contingency and Discretion

While having discretion is important, being willing to accept the consequences is also crucial. In an organization, discretion thus entails having the right to gamble on the company's behalf. Responsible people will "go out on a limb" or "stick their necks out" rather than "passing the buck" and accept that their own outcomes (and even the outcomes of subordinates or family members) depend on the success or failure of the enterprise for which they are responsible. The rewards contingent on success or failure can be small or large—anything from temporary inconvenience to the fortunes of a business empire to the lives of people entrusted to one's care. Often the stake is an ill-defined reputation for competence, probity, or reliability; people with a reputation for responsibility are those whom others would want beside them in a crisis.

But this stake may make some people wish to avoid responsibility. A recently promoted secretary I interviewed, for instance, found her new responsibilities as personnel manager too burdensome because others' fates hinged on her activities; she had carried out the same activities with equanimity when her supervisor bore ultimate responsibility. Others are pleased at the consequential nature of their acts and report that their jobs are satisfying *because* of the responsibility they have. Among my respondents, reports of promotion were often described as "the usual increases in *responsibility* and pay" (Heimer 1984; emphasis added). Presumably, most people are pleased with increases in responsibility at work partly because responsibilities are "experience rated." Because rights to assume important, interesting responsibilities are contingent on having met previous obligations, current responsibilites are investments in future responsibilities and authority.

The "greedy institutions" Coser (1984) describes, for instance, require early heavy investments if a person is to reap the reward of interesting opportunities later. Project work is also greedy, though projects have more limited lives. Kidder (1981), for example, shows how devoted project members worked around the clock (often with little thought to how their schedules affected their families) to develop a new computer. Though they thrived on the excitement of the work, they also fantasized about the reputational effects of being associated with a fundamental breakthrough. Faulkner (1983) similarly argues that the career prospects of musicians producing music for movie projects depend both on the quality of their music and on the success or failure of the film as a whole, and that musicians are keenly aware that everyone listed in the credits gets a reputational payoff if the film is a success. The career boost from being listed in the credits of a successful movie arises partly from having a solid connection with a "hot" director who will be doing more films but partly also from the reputational effects in the market. The investments made by musicians composing the score for a film, by young computer scientists developing a new machine, or by entrepreneurs starting a business lead to failure at least as often as to success. Sometimes investments nevertheless pay off in skills and experience, though such rewards may not compensate for the association with a box-office flop, a machine design that never went to production, or the loss of personal fortune in a bankrupt business. But because opportunities to accept subsequent responsibilities hinge on willingness to devote oneself to projects at earlier career stages, aspiring musicians and computer scientists must make substantial investments and accept heavy responsibilities even though the odds are usually against them.

The five dimensions that differentiate more responsible from less responsible behavior are also the dimensions around which accusations of irresponsibility and rewards for taking responsibility are organized. I have suggested how each of these dimensions renders responsible behavior problematic and what incentives and institutional arrangements increase the likelihood that people will take responsibility. I turn now to a core distinction between responsibilities experienced as fates and responsibilities experienced as opportunities.

Responsibilities as Fates or Opportunities

We need to distinguish between two different ways that people come to have particular responsibilities and their correspondingly different experiences with them. Briefly, responsibilities can be either opportunities or fates. People may come to have particular responsibilities because they choose them, for instance by volunteering for one task rather than another at work or by choosing a line of employment. In choosing one responsibility rather than another, a person might be driven by the chance to do an interesting task, get credit for a job well done, avoid an onerous alternative task, or win the opportunity to undertake an especially attractive job later. Reactions to this first type of responsibility are tapped by survey questions that ask whether respondents would like to take on more responsibility at work or whether they already have as much responsibility as they want. Evidence from surveys suggests that people like their jobs better when those jobs carry more responsibility.[9]

But not all responsibilities are so freely chosen. Some responsibilities are received as accidents of fate and experienced as burdens rather than opportunities, though people may still be able to refuse a responsibility or to limit their obligations. A premature birth or the illness of an aging parent does not lead to fantasies of credit for a job well done or of future opportunities to care for disabled relatives. Instead, people worry about how to balance the new responsibility with preexisting commitments, and how to husband their resources or find new ones. Rather than seeking rewards, people strive to avoid guilt and blame. The best they can hope for is credit for having done their duty despite the unfairness of being dealt a hand of inescapable obligations.

Although in some senses a responsibility is a "fate" whenever one does not freely choose it and cannot escape it, the potential disproportion between obligations and resources is fundamental to the consequential character of fatelike responsibilities. When a responsibility is a fate, one must dip into or even deplete one's own resources even though others do not honor one's acceptance of responsibility enough to pitch in. A responsibility is a "fate," then, whenever one might be stuck in a permanently losing situation, in which the responsibility can be discharged only by exhausting one's resources. It is even more a fate if such a permanently losing position does not leave one with sufficient resources to discharge the responsibility adequately. But fatelike responsibilities are not limited to the arena of personal life. One is confronted with property ownership as a fate when one's business goes bankrupt with unlimited liability, especially if one then feels an obligation to pay all the creditors anyway after the bankruptcy.

Two aspects of responsibility, the inescapability of the obligations and the relation between resources and obligations, predict being stuck in a situation similar to bankruptcy. When resources do vary with the magnitude of an obligation, and when one can escape burdens that have become intolerable or just unattractive in comparison with other responsibilities one might shoulder, one retains the flexibility to strategize about which package of obligations to accept. In contrast, when resources cannot be adjusted in response to contingencies and when one retains responsibility "come hell or high water," one's capacity to maneuver is decreased, and previous obligations act as rigid constraints on one's ability to respond to other opportunities that might arise. It is this constraining aspect of fatelike responsibility that so deeply shapes women's experience of responsibility. In the pages that follow I explore the various mechanisms that bind people, sometimes loosely, sometimes tightly, to their responsibilities and the mechanisms that are only sometimes available to adjust resources to obligations.

Choosing to Accept or Refuse Responsibilities: Positional and Personal Obligations

How much choice a person has about whether to accept or refuse a responsibility depends on whether responsibilities are associated with positions or with persons and on how interchangeable a person is with others who might occupy a position or be assigned a personal responsibility. At one extreme are occupational roles easily filled by others, though at any given point it will be important to be clear about who occupies the position and is assigned the associated responsibilities. At the other extreme are personal obligations, such as those of close kin, where responsibility is uniquely assigned to a single person or group of people bound by long-term, often biological ties. An obligation is somewhat diluted if it is shared by others; a child's obligation to care for an aging parent decreases if he or she has siblings. In between lie obligations that are difficult to shed either because of biography (e.g., firm- or job-specific capital), personal characteristics (e.g., an affirmative action officer must be a member of a minority group [Collins 1988]), or a weak bargaining position (e.g., women cannot as easily as men refuse household responsibilities or dead-end assignments at work).

All responsibility entails some sense of personal obligation, of course, as Latané and Darley (1970) find in their studies of unresponsive bystanders. Unless he or she can be made to feel a special obligation either because of some contact with the "victim" (even a brief conversation creates a tie) or because no alternative helper is available, a bystander is not likely to intervene and provide assistance.

But the sense of personal obligation associated with a job may be fleeting. Even the most conscientious worker's sense of obligation diminishes dramatically the day after leaving a position. When responsibilities are associated with a position rather than a person, credit and blame do not so closely adhere to the person. One can shirk work obligations without compromising one's self-regard; it is more difficult to preserve a sense of oneself as an essentially good person if one shirks family obligations. Though a variety of rewards (both long and short term) are used to induce people to take positional responsibilities, the moral overtone common in personal responsibility is often missing or attenuated in positional responsibilities. But because moral suasion may be cheaper and more reliable than other kinds of incentives, organizations may try to transform positional responsibilities into personal ones. Professional reputation, award ceremonies, and other public praise reinforce an individual's investment in a public identity as a responsible worker and increase a worker's sense that an obligation belongs uniquely to him or her.

If the goal of employers and co-workers is to make an individual feel a personal stake in a responsibility, the goal of the worker should be to invest just enough to acquire a reputation for accepting and meeting important obligations without becoming so identified with a particular responsibility that escape is impossible. Escape becomes impossible if investments are perceived as so task-specific that the person's experience does not qualify him or her for other tasks, or if the task becomes so thoroughly identified with the person that attempts at escape are seen as dishonorable defaulting.

Both acceptance of new responsibilities and rejection of old ones depend on the degree to which a responsibility is personal rather than positional. Though job-related obligations are likely to be recognized as obligations from the start, responsibilities acquired through the formation of a relationship vary in when and whether they are evaluated as responsibilities. While the obvious dependence of an infant may force early recognition that parenthood entails responsibility, the obligations of friendship and love often become apparent only long after binding ties have been formed.

Ironically, then, the obligations undertaken with least forethought and with the slimmest evidence about what is entailed may be the very ones that are hardest to escape. Though parents often undertake childbearing with full knowledge that they are accepting a heavy responsibility, exactly how heavy that burden will be depends on the luck of the draw, and responsibility is accepted long before most of the crucial information is available. Though, as Rothman (1986) argues, couples may make only tentative commitments to babies prior to getting ultrasound and amniocentesis results, once a child is born parental commitment cannot legitimately vary with the traits, health, or behavior of the child. The lapse in time between the acquisition of other personal responsibilities, such as those of friendship and marriage, and when the obligation comes due; the muted emphasis on responsibility in the early stages of relationships; and the inherently unknowable character of distant future obligations all decrease the likelihood that anyone will strategize about which relationships to enter on the grounds that future burdens may be too great.[10]

Negotiating About Resources and Limitations on Responsibility

How one experiences responsibility depends on what resources one has. When one controls many resources or can tap extra resources to meet unexpected burdens, meeting responsibilities is mainly a matter of allocating resources among competing needs, making choices among attractive possibilities, and investing in the hope of even more interesting options later. When one has fewer resources, responsibilities must be met with one's own labor, and there is little point in strategizing about how different allocations of one's effort might shape future opportunities. Three main mechanisms facilitate the adjustment of resources to burdens: limitations on obligations, explicit sharing of responsibilities in some sort of pool, and the provision of extra resources to meet increased obligations.

When resources are fixed, obligations often are limited as well. Many work-related obligations are limited by being confined to the amount of work a person can do in a specified period, such as a 40-hour week. Obligations are also bounded in time at higher levels, though the time periods tend to be longer, as Jaques (1972) would predict. Limits on obligation often are specified in the currency of time or money but can also be imposed by distinguishing among categories of obligations. For instance, a parent who felt responsible for paying a child's college expenses might not feel obligated to support the child's hobbies, and employees willing to devote their time to a job might nevertheless be unwilling to use their own funds to purchase work-related supplies.

Obligations can also be limited through a division of labor, a practice not entirely distinct from the bounding of obligations with time limits. Over time the bundling of tasks into discrete positions may be renegotiated as work is redistributed to take account of inequities or differences in talent. This reassignment of tasks is a more formal version of the sharing of work in a group such as a secretarial pool. While a more formal division of labor with job descriptions and committee assignments makes clear who has what responsibilities for a longer interval and thus requires more adjustment of effort to obligation by individual workers, the assignment of tasks to a group allows more rapid adjustment of resources to the collective obligation. Ideally, no one sits idle while others work, and no one works overtime while others loaf or go home early.

The provision of extra resources to compensate for increases in burden entails drawing resources from outside the group primarily responsible for meeting an obligation. By hiring temporaries, appealing to friends or relatives for help, or applying for special funds, members of a workgroup attempt to draw on a larger store of resources just as insurance companies use reinsurance contracts to spread truly catastrophic losses over a larger group.

Fates and Opportunities: Constrained and Unconstrained Choices

Fates, then, are doubly constraining responsibilities—fatelike responsibilities are constraining both because people have little choice about accepting them and little capacity to refuse them and because acceptance of such obligations often does not entail access to resources commensurate with obligations. In contrast, opportunity-like responsibilities are less constraining both because a person is permitted to choose whether to accept the responsibility and because resources are more likely to match burdens. When resources are inadequate, the person may choose to vacate the role rather than accept an "unreasonable" responsibility. These points are summarized in Table 8.1. My hypothesis, then, is that the experience of responsibility and its effect in shaping a person's future options depend both on the extent to which the obligation is strongly associated with a person rather than with a position temporarily occupied by that person, and on whether resources can be flexibly adjusted to match the burden. And though analytically separable, these two variables are strongly correlated empirically. The more resources one has, and particularly the more resources one can call on when contingencies create large requirements, the more acceptance of responsibility is a matter of choice and strategic calculation. Even when the responsibilities are personal rather than positional, a resource-rich person can pick and choose to find

TABLE 8.1 Differences Between Responsibilities as Fates and as Opportunities

	Responsibility as Fate	*Responsibility as Opportunity*
(1) Entry—acceptance of responsibility	Less choice; no legitimate choice if have personal obligation	Considerable choice
Comparison with alternatives	Comparisons only legitimate at the outset, if then	Comparisons can be made both at the time the responsibility is accepted and later (though may be less legitimate unless comparisons are made because other interesting alternatives arise)
(2) Working conditions	Little room for negotiation either at outset or as situation evolves	More room for negotiation both at outset and as the situation evolves
Limitations on obligations—time, money, or nature of obligation	Limitation more possible if there are others who share the obligation or if a person has legitimate competing obligations	Limitations possible
Sharing of obligations	Obligation may be shared by others who have the same relation to a particular responsibility	Obligations can be shared with subordinates or others willing to take on parts of the work
Adjustment of resources to needs	Resources less likely to be adjusted to meet need (and obligation does not vary much with adequacy of resources)—pool is often small; shallower pockets	Resources often adjusted to meet needs; if resources inadequate, moral obligation decreases and exit becomes more legitimate; deeper pockets
(3) Exit—default on responsibility	Often default is not legitimate option	Exit legitimate, though often must find someone to assume responsibility; acceptable reasons include undertaking other responsibilities and inadequacy of resources; default may be legitimate

the least costly ways of meeting responsibilities and can choose responsibilities that yield the highest payoff in honor, wealth, or future positions for the least cost.

Fates are responsibilities that one is normatively expected to shoulder and for which cost-benefit calculations are regarded as illegitimate. In contrast, for responsibilities that are opportunities cost-benefit analysis is normatively appropriate and choices in either direction (that is, to accept responsibilities or to reject them) are normatively acceptable. There is, nevertheless, a residual element of choice in the acceptance of a fate. While responsibilities themselves may not be chosen, the decision to honor normative expectations about a fatelike responsibility is a choice, though once such a choice is made continuous revision is unacceptable. One may decide whether or not to have an abortion and so whether or not to accept a fatelike responsibility for a child. But once a decision has been made to bear the child rather than abort it, one must live with the consequences. Such choices about whether to honor normative expectations are fundamentally different from choices about whether to honor work-related obligations, where it is normatively acceptable to refuse a responsibility or even to leave the role if costs exceed benefits and to revise choices as circumstances change. But the choice to honor normative expectations even when that means embracing a costly fate is exactly what allows people to feel that they have honorably done their duty.

Responsibility as a Constraint: Implications for Gender Inequality

Because responsibilities carry contingent obligations, assuming one responsibility tends to limit one's capacity to accept others. The conflict is more acute for responsibilities that are fates than for those that are opportunities, because fates cannot as easily be shed or reduced to accommodate new possibilities and because they are more likely to be associated with the shallower pockets of families than the deeper pockets of organizations. I argue that gender inequality in the distribution of fatelike responsibilities is a deep and abiding constraint on the capacity of women, who disproportionately take on such personal obligations as the care of children and the elderly, to seek or accept more highly rewarded responsibilities.

Discussing variations in the periodicity of work and consumption, Douglas and Isherwood comment that women tend to be saddled with chores that must be done at frequent intervals and that this limits their capacity to do other things:

> The most general account of the division of labor between the sexes that fits everywhere would be based on the periodicities of women's work, starting out from the recurring physical services required by small babies, the sick, and the dying. Anyone with influence and status would be a fool to get encumbered with a high-frequency responsibility. ... High-frequency work is not compatible with being available for important tasks of unpredictable occurrence. ... Women tend to join the councils of the state only when they can delegate or dodge the periodicity-constrained parts of the normal woman's role. (1978:120–1)

As they note, "to be poor is to be periodicity-constrained in the process of household management" (1978:121); wealth mitigates some effects of periodicity (some high-frequency tasks can be delegated to hired help, and periodicity can be reduced by stocking more goods). Here I make a parallel point about responsibility: Women tethered to fatelike responsibilities cannot easily pursue wealth, fame, or power. Abundant resources at least lengthen the tether, but offers of assistance, relief from excessive workloads, or resources to purchase labor-saving devices are more likely to be available to mitigate the burdens of positional responsibilities than of personal ones.

Gender and Personal Responsibility

We need not dig very deep to find evidence that women disproportionately shoulder the burdens of caring for small children or aged, ailing, or disabled family members. Clearly, maternal responsibilities are less often shed than paternal ones.[11] In 1992, 23 percent of children under 18 lived with their mother only, 71 percent with both parents, 3 percent with their father only, and 3 percent with neither parent (U.S. Bureau of the Census 1993:64; people under 18 who maintained their own households or family groups were excluded). Racial and ethnic differences are substantial: In 1992, 54 percent of black children under 18, but only 18 percent of white children and 28 percent of children of Spanish origin, lived with their mothers only (U.S. Bureau of the Census 1993:64). But though groups differ in whether children live with both parents or with their mother, they do not differ in the likelihood that fathers will care for children alone. For all groups, only 3–4 percent of children live with only their father. Groups vary more in the likelihood that children will live with someone other than their parents. While only 2 percent of white children and 3 percent of Hispanic children lived with neither parent, 7 percent of African American children lived with neither parent (U.S. Bureau of the Census 1993:64).

Over the life course, women's ties with kin are stronger than men's, and their sense of normative obligation to kin is also stronger (Rossi and Rossi 1990). Women spend more hours per day on childcare and household work whether or not they are employed, and women with children at home have fewer hours of leisure than men. Daughters are more likely than sons to assist aging parents (Spitze and Logan 1990). Women also do the kin work of maintaining ties across households (DiLeonardo 1987). And women shoulder obligations to others even when it hurts—Simmons, Klein, and Simmons (1977) found that controlling for the type of relationship (parental, sibling, etc.) women are more likely than men to donate kidneys.

But the argument that women are disproportionately *constrained* by being assigned a large share of fatelike obligations depends both on showing that women accept more than their share of such burdens and on demonstrating that they have little choice in the matter. To understand apparent gender differences in the extent to which responsibilities are inescapable and constraining personal obligations, we need to look at (1) whether women are more likely than men to define obligations as theirs rather than someone else's, (2) whether *others* see obligations as belonging to particular women but not to particular men, (3) whether women are more likely than men to believe that a relationship is at stake and whether gender differences in expressivity then shape the sense of obligation, (4) whether women are more likely than men to be embedded in ongoing exchange relations and whether these exchange relations then create different obligations for the two sexes, (5) whether men and women differ in the extent to which resources such as money are available to meet obligations and whether such substitutions are acceptable, and (6) whether others (e.g., neighbors or the state) are more likely to provide assistance to men than to women so that familial obligations can be met without substantial changes in a care provider's life. The first two conditions concern how responsibilities are assigned, the second two are about the circumstances under which obligations are incurred, and the third pair focuses on whether other resources give relief from obligation. Although these six conditions are analytically separable, they are not empirically independent. In particular, often it is through relationships that obligations come to feel and be defined as personal, and relationships arise and are sustained through repeated exchange.

To some degree it seems that women accept responsibilities as belonging peculiarly to them because women conceive obligations to be matters of relationship. For instance, LaRossa and LaRossa (1981), studying differences between husbands' and wives' adaptations to the birth of a child, concluded that women found their obligations to babies compelling partly because they conceived of infants as *people*, while men thought of them as objects. It is easier to justify leaving a child in the crib while you read or do housework if you believe that the child is not a person who responds to your attention.

Rossi and Rossi (1990) make similar observations about the links among gender, expressivity, and responsibility. Overall, they find that gender is strongly related to a person's sense of obligation to kin but that nearly all of women's heightened sense of obligation can be accounted for by gender differences in expressivity (measured by the person's own ratings of whether he or she is affectionate, eager to help, concerned to please others, and able to express deep feelings) (Rossi and Rossi 1990:39, 495–6). On the average, women are more expressive than men, but controlling for expressivity men are as likely as women to feel that they owe their relatives instrumental help, should offer them comfort, or are expected to help celebrate major occasions. Explaining the relation between expressivity and obligation, Rossi and Rossi refer to expressivity as an "open, relational quality" (1990:496). It is the possession of this quality that makes it harder for mothers than for fathers to ignore the personhood of an infant.

Whether or not women felt shame or guilt for shirking their responsibilities, they would also face social disapproval. The normative obligations that women acquire through their relationships are policed by others. The social costs to women of shirking their obligations to family members seem to exceed the costs to men for similar misbehavior. Noting the continued commitment of women to disabled husbands, Oliver (1983) commented that women worried that their children would disapprove if they abandoned their husbands. In a study of unmarried care givers of both sexes, Wright (1983) found that daughters were more likely than sons to be pressured both by elderly parents themselves and by other people (such as managers and welfare workers) to give up their jobs and stay home. In a study of men's and women's commitment to critically ill infants, I found that hospital staff members were more likely to note and evaluate the behavior of mothers than of fathers (even controlling for the substantial differences in their presence in the unit), to blame mothers who were "inappropriate," and to hound mothers to accept responsibility for their infants (Heimer and Staffen 1995). Mothers could not escape obligations as easily as fathers.

What makes fatherhood a more positional responsibility and motherhood a more personal one? While mothers themselves may feel obligated when fathers do not, others also assign mothers responsibilities that they would not assign fathers. The social expectations associated with motherhood and fatherhood, and therefore the standards by which others judge individual enactments of parental roles, are very different. A good father could easily be a negligent mother, and one might, for instance, expect to find different standards applied to men and women accused of abandoning or endangering their children. Both extrinsic and intrinsic rewards for attentiveness to children differ for men and women, and even children apply different standards to mothers than to fathers.[12] To be a good father requires something different (less) than to be a good mother (LaRossa and LaRossa 1981; Heimer and Staffen 1995).

Responsibilities are also created through exchange networks. DiLeonardo (1987), for example, argues that in addition to its altruistic purposes the kin work of holiday celebrations and gift and card exchanges also has the instrumental purpose of creating obligations. Hogan, Eggebeen, and Clogg find that in American families women are more likely than men to be involved in a high level of intergenerational exchange or to live with an aging parent (1993:1442–3). They argue, rather circularly, that women's higher level of intergenerational exchange occurs because women are more likely than men to be "high exchangers." But the circularity of their argument is decreased if the point is that one incurs inescapable obligations by being embedded in a system of repeated exchange. Each obligation, then, also carries the moral weight of reciprocation and routine—a person is more morally obliged when a relative's dependence arises in the context of a long and reliable history of interdependence and exchange.

Men are more able than women to escape responsibility by substituting someone else's labor for their own. Women are less able than men to buy substitutes and less likely to have others volunteer to substitute for them. But even when substitutes are available, women more than men continue to retain responsibility for locating, supervising, and perhaps rejecting substitutes. Wright, for instance, found that in Britain the local government more often supplied a "home help" for unmarried male care givers than their female counterparts; 53 percent of employed single male care givers but only 35 percent of single employed female care givers received this service (1983:96). Men are also more likely than women to put their elderly parents into nursing homes, partly because neither sons nor their parents consider the possibility that a son might stay home to provide care, while both parties consider this option when the caregiver is a daughter (Wright 1983; note that all care givers in this study were unmarried).[13]

Though it is considered legitimate to hire substitutes to watch her children, a mother is by no means relieved of her parental obligations by having a regular babysitter. Hertz argues that the birth of children brings a "resurrection of an asymmetrical relationship" in dual-career couples because housekeepers and babysitters are the working wife's responsibility (1986:189). "Housekeepers and sitters are not," she stresses, "simply performing the traditional role of wife and mother" (Hertz 1986:188);

mothers are not therefore as free as fathers to pursue careers unfettered by parental obligations. The outcome, she concludes, is that "wives ... are the ones who really provide their husbands with continuous flexibility. And, in turn, the housekeeper provides the wife with flexibility" (1986:189). But while a father has two buffers to protect his work schedule, a mother has only one, and to have even that one she must invest considerable effort in finding and supervising a babysitter or housekeeper.

It is clear, then, that women feel that the burdens of children and family are *theirs* and cannot be laid down without incurring shame, guilt, and disapproval. It matters little that women might find other options attractive or that they pay considerable personal cost in continuing to bear such burdens. Even the most privileged of women, many argue, continue to accept and be assigned responsibilities as personal obligations that they must either meet themselves or at the very least share with others by supervising those substitutes. Because responsibilities more often are assigned to them as persons, and often must be met with their own labor, women are much more constrained than men in their capacity to adjust to the demands of positional obligations. They cannot as freely choose among opportunities and so cannot as fully treat other responsibilities as investments.

Gender and Positional Responsibilities at Work

To say that women are disproportionately saddled with the burdens of fatelike responsibilities says little about how these "personal" responsibilities shape men's and women's capacities to take on responsibilities outside the home. Pleck (1977) long ago suggested that the boundary between work and home was asymmetrically permeable for men and women—that for men work intruded into the time and space allocated to family life while for women family life intruded on work time and space. Men then use the resources of the home to provide the flexibility needed to make a go of their careers—working weekends when necessary, entertaining a visiting dignitary for the evening, working an extra shift because a colleague is ill. In contrast, women use whatever flexibility can be wrung from a job to handle the uncertainties of family life—they make deals with bosses about making up hours so they can stay home with a sick child, rank potential jobs by how tolerant the supervisor is of obligations to children, and refuse offers of extra hours or chances to entertain the visiting dignitary because such tasks are incompatible with household obligations (Freeman 1982). In all occupations men average longer hours than women and are more likely than women to work 60 or more hours per week (U.S. Bureau of the Census 1970:747–74); even when both spouses are employed, women spend more time than men on housework and childcare (Hochschild 1989; Szalai 1972; Robinson 1977).[14]

For both men and women, these statistical differences in hours spent on household versus work obligations are produced by processes that are often uncomfortably constraining. But though both sexes are constrained, we must not overlook the differences in how behavior is shaped and in the long-term consequences of these patterns. For men and women alike, hours of labor very likely go up in response to increases in the demand for their labor. For both sexes, increases in hours are at least partly an attempt to reduce costs—for instance, by providing more attention for a troubled child at home or by placating an angry supervisor at work. But when men placate angry supervisors or put in extra hours because of a bulge in the flow of work, they anticipate that such investments will yield returns in stability of employment, increases in wages, or opportunities for advancement. Women have no similar expectations about changes in returns at home. Because some family obligations are accepted almost unconditionally, the economy of family life does not require as close a tie between investment and return.

Further, men's contributions to housework and childcare and women's contributions on the job are not evaluated in a parallel fashion. At work women are compared with other potential employees and are seen as uncommitted compared with men; at home men are compared with other potential husbands and so may not seem so bad. The standard at work is either sex-neutral or male, but no one truly expects a husband to be like a wife. Women can then be judged unworthy workers because of their family obligations, but men's work obligations are unlikely to make them be perceived as unworthy spouses.

What, then, are the consequences of women's fatelike personal responsibilities for their capacity to invest in work outside the home? To adjust flexibly outside the home, to accept outside responsibilities, or to strategize about responsibilities as investments requires that women control the time and other personal resources they might invest. They must be able to make binding commitments that their families will honor, and they must be able to subordinate some other obligations to newly acquired obligations at work.

One crude indicator of whether people have the flexibility to take on major work responsibilities is whether they can relocate to take a good job. Bielby and Bielby (1992) show that in dual-earner couples, wives are more reluctant than husbands to relocate for a better job, apparently because of gender differences in concern about the costs of such a relocation to the spouse and family. Gender-role ideology explains some of these differences, but even among less traditional men and women the gender gap remains large. If husbands are reluctant to take account of their wives' jobs in their own decisions to relocate, women have less capacity to make binding commitments to their careers. If women feel they must consider their husbands' jobs when deciding about their own job opportunities, then women's capacity to make binding commitments is further reduced. Women are thus *doubly* constrained—by their husbands' decisions and by their own inclination to take account of their husbands' careers—while men are essentially unconstrained. Not surprisingly, geographic moves usually increase the earnings of dual-career husbands and decrease those of wives (Mincer 1978).

Gerstel and Gross (1984) examine the consequences of women's reluctance to ask men to relocate. In their study of commuting marriages, they found that couples are especially likely to opt for commuting as a solution to dual-career problems when they have few responsibilities for children. Further, a commuting arrangement is usually adopted to expand the wife's (not the husband's) career opportunities. Typically, the husband's career was already well established, and the wife had spent the early years of the marriage making whatever adjustments were necessary for his career. But when the wife decided to have a career as well, couples did not decide that it was now the husband's turn to make career sacrifices. Instead, they adopted a commuting pattern.

The costs of women's careers are paid differently than the costs of men's, and the resources to pay such costs are more available at some lifecycle stages than others.[15] The flexibility required for a woman to have a career comes from her family, not from her husband's career. Either her career investment occurs when family obligations decrease, or family work is cut back. As Hochschild explains, "The latent deal between husband and wife is 'I'll share, but we'll do less,'" and couples "capitulate to a workaholism à deux, each spouse equitably granting the other the right to work long hours, and reconciling themselves to a drastically reduced conception of the emotional needs of a family" (1989:209).

Women's constraints also shape the *kinds* of jobs that they can take. Because wives and mothers have less flexibility than husbands and fathers in their day-to-day schedules, we might expect that married women and mothers would be grossly underrepresented in especially demanding occupations. Only by forgoing marriage and family can women gain the flexibility to invest in serious careers. Caplette (1982) notes that women in publishing, a demanding and time-consuming field, are considerably less likely than their male counterparts to be married or to have children. Epstein (1981) makes the same observation about lawyers.

Hours of work can serve as a crude proxy for capacity to invest in a job. On the average in 1970, employed men worked 42.2 hours per week, while employed women worked 34.8 hours.[16] In every major occupational category, employed men worked more hours per week than did employed women. Women tended to work full time or less, whereas men worked full time or more. While 9.45 percent of employed men worked 60 or more hours per week, only 2.11 percent of employed women worked that many hours.

Jobs that carry a lot of responsibility, and therefore offer high wages and chances to move up, are disproportionately likely to require long and somewhat variable hours. For both men and women, having supervisory or managerial responsibility or being self-employed increased hours of work. Men who were nonfarm administrators and managers, for instance, on average worked 47.5 hours per week, and 17.84 percent of them worked 60 or more hours per week; women in this category worked 41.7 hours per week, and 11.2 percent of them worked 60 or more hours per week.

More detailed breakdowns show the same pattern—as responsibility increased, hours of work went up and proportions of workers working 60 or more hours a week also rose. But striking differences remained between men and women in mean hours and in the proportions working 60 or more hours. For example, in retail trade male salesclerks worked an average of 40.0 hours per week, while women worked 30.5 hours per week; 10.53 percent of men but only 1.98 percent of women worked 60 or more hours per week. Hours rose substantially for salaried managers and administrators in retail trade: On the average, men worked 51.2 hours and women 43.2 hours, but 23.96 percent of men and only 9.74 percent of women worked 60 or more hours per week. Finally, self-employed managers and administrators in retail trade worked even longer hours and were even more likely to work 60 or more hours per week, though the gender differences remained. In this group, men worked on the average 56.9 hours and women 49.1 hours; 50.18 percent of men and 31.53 percent of women worked 60 or more hours per week. The patterns reported here held for the range of occupations for which the census table reports variations in responsibility: farm work; construction work; manufacturing; transportation; communications, utilities, and sanitary services; wholesale trade; school teaching; and clerical work.

As one rises in an organization, whether it be a firm, political party, religious group, or voluntary association, the variability of demands increases. People who have other responsibilities are less able to adapt quickly to new demands unless a staff of assistants can carry much of the load. But fatelike responsibilities typically must be met with resources from the flexibility of small groups of people and the shallow pockets of families and friends rather than the large staffs and deep pockets of organizations. Further, family work is more constraining than many commitments at work. Family life is more variable in its demands—only really exceptional work situations call for round-the-clock work as sick children occasionally do in every family—and therefore calls for more adaptability than most other occupations. Anyone assigned the primary responsibility for a home and family will have little capacity to take on responsibilities in other settings. As long as such responsibilities are perceived as *personal* and women lack the resources to decrease the burden, they will be unable to invest equally with men in the world of positional responsibilities. The fateful consequence of being the gender that shoulders fatelike responsibilities is that women are less able to invest strategically in responsibilities that are also opportunities.

Conclusion

The facts are not new, and indeed they have been pithily presented before: Wives provide their husbands with continuous flexibility (Hertz 1986); the boundary between work and family life is asymmetrically permeable for men and women (Pleck 1977); because of gender differences in the "second shift" employed women with children in effect work an extra month of 24-hour days (Hochschild 1989); women are more likely than men to be assigned the high-periodicity household tasks that then preclude their joining the councils of state or business (Douglas and Isherwood 1978). As Hochschild (1989), Hertz (1986), and Gerson (1985) argue, changes in the workplace have outstripped changes in the home. Women continue to do more than their share at home despite participation in the labor force, and this inequality both in labor and in responsibility stunts or distorts women's careers. The link between the domestic sphere and the public sphere, between the more complete revolution at work and the stalled one at home (Hochschild 1989) continues to pose a puzzle.

I have tried to construct the microfoundations for a theory of responsibility that clarifies what it is about women's domestic commitments that precludes strategic investment in opportunities outside the home. Gerson (1985) shows how women's decisions about work, parenthood, and careers are shaped as much by their current experiences and opportunities as by childhood socialization. Here I move a step further to show what it is about family obligations that makes them so uniquely constraining. I argue that in whatever setting they occur, roles that carry a lot of responsibility differ from other roles in requiring a person to look out for the interests and needs of others, to define obligations diffusely, to think about both long- and short-term consequences, to use discretion in adapting to contingencies, and to accept the consequences come hell or high water. But when responsibilities are tied to *persons* (as family obligations are especially tied to mothers, daughters, wives, and sisters) rather than to positions (as responsibilities at work often are), it is difficult to escape responsibilities that have become losing propositions. Further, one is more likely to have to meet personal obligations with one's own time, skill, and money. Because one must meet whatever obligations life brings along from one's own reserves and because the responsibilities of family life are quite variable compared with the demands imposed by the world of work, women cannot as easily invest their reserves in pursuing high-powered careers.

Neither family life nor high-powered careers come packaged in limited-liability, 40-hour weeks with prespecified tasks. But having a wife makes family life more like a "job" for men; the bulk of the uncertainty is absorbed by a woman, leaving the man free to make strategic investments in his career. The complaint that husbands are willing to "help out" at home but don't accept responsibility is then not a petty gripe but a key element of the persistence of gender inequality.

Notes

For helpful comments on earlier drafts of this essay, I thank James Baron, Howard Becker, Kennette Benedict, James Coleman, Andrew Gordon, Christopher Jencks, Robin Leidner, Margaret Levi, Jane Mansbridge, Susan Shapiro, Donald Treiman, and R. Stephen Warner. It was Arthur Stinchcombe's fate to comment on the essay more than once; I am grateful that he did not shirk his duty.

1. It is important to keep in mind that there are also intragender differences in the constraints of family roles. Childless women will usually be less constrained by family roles than other women. But sometimes other siblings will assume that the unmarried or childless sister is the obvious caretaker for their aging mother.

2. My argument is about variations among roles rather than about variations among incumbents of roles. But of course some differences we observe are instead differences among incumbents in the orientations, personality traits, or talents they bring to roles. By analyzing roles rather than incumbents, I do not mean to suggest that variations among individual occupants of roles are trivial.

3. By a utility function, economists mean a system of trade-offs among different values or among the interests of different people. To "maximize a utility function," then, one must decide how much of one value (e.g., happiness of a child for whom a trust has been set up) to trade to get more of another value (e.g., reserving resources for adulthood).

4. We speak of people acting irresponsibly when they are shortsighted about their own future interests. In making this accusation, we may be charging them with rationality on behalf of current selves at the expense of responsibility for future selves. The bitter tone of such comments suggests that shortsightedness about the future seems particularly irresponsible when people are setting up situations in which others will later have to take responsibility for them or are squandering opportunities responsibly created by others.

5. Mansbridge similarly argues that self-interested and altruistic motives can reinforce one another and that we err in suggesting that any hint of self-interest contaminates altruism:

Conceptually we distinguish among motivations by opposing them to one another. ... Empirically, we demonstrate that people are acting for unselfish reasons by devising situations in which they are demonstrably acting against their self-interest.

Yet in practice we often try hard to arrange our lives so that duty (or love) and interest coincide. (1990:133)

6. The penumbra is analogous to Barnard's (1938) zone of indifference. But while Barnard argues that workers are willing to do anything that falls within the zone of indifference, I argue that there are variations in consent even within that zone. Consent will be more precarious the further a task lies from the core of the job.

7. Some attempts to assign tasks or to set performance standards may be undermined or modified by worker resistance (Burawoy 1979), which in turn may vary with how fairly management plays the incentive game. In other cases the penumbra (and perhaps even the core) will be substantially defined by informal training, and conceptions of responsibilities will then vary with whether or not particular groups are excluded from some parts of professional socialization (White 1970). Worker resistance to more diffuse job definitions may then indicate fear of exploitation or variations in conceptions of the job rather than objections to diffusely defined jobs per se.

8. No doubt stock options are sometimes simply devices to provide higher incomes for top managers than stockholders would ordinarily approve. The complexity of schemes to encourage "responsibility" may make them especially vulnerable to corruption.

9. These surveys do not usually measure *actual* responsibility. Instead, they ask about numbers of superiors and subordinates, ownership of the business, frequency of supervision, and sometimes whether the respondent is happy with current responsibilities or would like to have more or less. As one example, Jencks, Perman, and Rainwater's (1988) index of job desirability includes some items that could be construed as measures of responsibility.

10. Early detection of degenerative diseases (such as multiple sclerosis) and diseases with long latency periods (such as AIDS) and the increasing availability of information about genetically based diseases (such as Huntington's disease or sickle-cell disease) certainly increase the incentive for people to strategize about future responsibilities and so pose interesting questions about how people reconcile current self-interest and potential future obligations. Does one inquire whether a potential partner is a sickle-cell carrier if one is a carrier oneself? How ethical is it to consider a person's sero status in making decisions about embarking on a relationship?

11. It may be somewhat easier to give up motherhood by refusing the role at the start, for instance by relinquishing a child for adoption. Still, the lore that "birth mothers" (but not "birth fathers") need to compensate for having given up babies or worry about how their children have fared suggests some residual sense of personal obligation.

12. Hochschild provides a poignant example of a child applying different standards to her two parents. Alexandra, who had school friends but no "home friends," explained that "in order to invite friends home, you need a *mother* at

home" (1989:89; emphasis in the original). The child, teacher, father, and even the mother herself assumed that the mother should be responsible for solving the problem. Ultimately, the mother drastically cut her work hours, with very serious career effects.

13. An important consideration here is that a nursing home might provide better care than a son but worse care than would be provided by a daughter. Wright finds that parents living with daughters were more likely than those living with sons to need help with going to bed and getting up, dressing and undressing, and using the toilet—despite relatively small differences in incontinence and need for assistance in bathing (1983:98). Further, even quite disabled elders helped sons with housework; elderly parents were less likely to help out when they lived with daughters (Wright 1983:97).

14. Bielby and Bielby find that "compared with men with similar household responsibilities, market human capital, earnings, promotion opportunities, and job responsibilities, women allocate substantially more effort to work activities" (1988:1055). But while this says that women work harder than equally situated men, it ignores other important questions, such as gender differences in labor force participation (especially during the months after childbirth), in likelihood of working part time, in hours worked, and even in decisions about what kinds of jobs to accept. Household and family obligations do not make women shirk once they accept paid employment, but they make them more reluctant to take on employment obligations that they would be unable to meet.

15. The conventional economic argument about household career dynamics is that it usually makes sense to give priority to the husband's career because the husband typically earns more than the wife, partly because he is likely to be older and more advanced in his career. The problem with this argument is that what is rational for the *household* may not be rational for all members of the household considered as individuals. Though income can be pooled and shared among members of the household (and economic arguments usually forget that income is not always shared), other rewards from jobs (e.g., prestige, contacts, experience) accrue to individuals. When couples favor husbands' careers in order to maximize household income, they then systematically disadvantage wives, who are less able than husbands to accrue such individual rewards as status, experience, or opportunities to accept interesting assignments.

16. The figures discussed in the text come from table 45 (pp. 747–74) of the 1970 Census of the Population (U.S. Bureau of the Census 1973).

References

Anspach, Renée R. 1993. *Deciding Who Lives*. Berkeley: University of California Press.

Bardach, Eugene, and Robert A. Kagan. 1982. *Going by the Book*. Philadelphia: Temple University Press.

Barnard, Chester I. 1938. *Functions of the Executive*. Cambridge: Harvard University Press.

Bielby, Denise D., and William T. Bielby. 1988. "She Works Hard for the Money: Household Responsibilities and the Allocation of Work Effort." *American Journal of Sociology* 93:1031–59.

Bielby, William T., and Denise D. Bielby. 1992. "I Will Follow Him: Family Ties, Gender-Role Beliefs, and Reluctance to Relocate for a Better Job." *American Journal of Sociology* 97:1241–67.

Blau, Peter M. 1963. *The Dynamics of Bureaucracy.* Revised Edition. Chicago: University of Chicago Press.

Bosk, Charles L. 1979. *Forgive and Remember.* Chicago: University of Chicago Press.

Bosk, Charles L., and Joel E. Frader. 1990. "AIDS and Its Impact on Medical Work: The Culture and Politics of the Shop Floor." *Milbank Quarterly* 6:257–79.

Burawoy, Michael. 1979. *Manufacturing Consent.* Chicago: University of Chicago Press.

Caplette, Michele. 1982. "Women in Book Publishing: A Qualified Success Story." Pp. 148–74 in Lewis A. Coser, Charles Kadushin, and Walter W. Powell (eds.), *Books: The Culture and Commerce of Publishing.* New York: Basic Books.

Chandler, Alfred D., Jr. 1962. *Strategy and Structure.* Cambridge: MIT Press.

Charlton, Joy Carol. 1983. "Secretaries and Bosses." Unpublished Ph.D. dissertation, Northwestern University, Evanston, IL.

Collins, Sharon. 1988. "Pathways to the Top." Unpublished Ph.D. dissertation, Northwestern University, Evanston, IL.

Coser, Lewis A. 1974. *Greedy Institutions.* New York: Free Press.

DiLeonardo, Micaela. 1987. "The Female World of Cards and Holidays: Women, Families, and the Work of Kinship." *Signs* 12:440–53.

Douglas, Mary, and Baron Isherwood. 1978. *The World of Goods.* New York: Basic Books.

Epstein, Cynthia F. 1981. *Women in Law.* New York: Basic Books.

Faulkner, Robert R. 1983. *Music on Demand.* New Brunswick, NJ: Transaction Books.

Freeman, Caroline. 1982. "The 'Understanding Employer.'" Pp. 135–53 in Jackie West (ed.), *Work, Women, and the Labour Market.* London: Routledge and Kegan Paul.

Friedson, Elliot. 1970. *Professional Dominance: The Social Structure of Medical Care.* New York: Atherton.

Gerson, Kathleen. 1985. *Hard Choices.* Berkeley: University of California Press.

Gerstel, Naomi, and Harriet Gross. 1984. *Commuter Marriage.* New York: Guilford.

Gilligan, Carol. 1982. *In a Different Voice.* Cambridge: Harvard University Press.

Guillemin, Jeanne Harley, and Lynda Lytle Holmstrom. 1986. *Mixed Blessings.* New York: Oxford University Press.

Halpern, Sydney A. 1988. *American Pediatrics.* Berkeley: University of California Press.

Heimer, Carol A. 1984. "Organizational and Individual Control of Career Development in Engineering Project Work." *Acta Sociologica* 27:283–310.

———. 1985. *Reactive Risk and Rational Action.* Berkeley: University of California Press.

Heimer, Carol A., and Lisa R. Staffen. 1995. "Interdependence and Reintegrative Social Control: Labeling and Reforming 'Inappropriate' Parents in Neonatal Intensive Care Units." *American Sociological Review* 60:635–54.

Hertz, Rosanna. 1986. *More Equal Than Others*. Berkeley: University of California Press.

Hochschild, Arlie Russell, with Anne Machung. 1989. *The Second Shift*. New York: Viking.

Hogan, Dennis P., David J. Eggebeen, and Clifford C. Clogg. 1993. "The Structure of Intergenerational Exchanges in American Families." *American Sociological Review* 98:1428–58.

Jaques, Elliott. 1972. *Measurement of Responsibility*. New York: Wiley.

Jencks, Christopher, Lauri Perman, and Lee Rainwater. 1988. "What Is a Good Job? A New Measure of Labor Market Success." *American Journal of Sociology* 93:1322–57.

Kidder, Tracy. 1981. *The Soul of a New Machine*. New York: Avon Books.

LaRossa, Ralph, and Maureen Mulligan LaRossa. 1981. *Transition to Parenthood*. Beverly Hills, CA: Sage.

Latané, Bibb, and John M. Darley. 1970. *The Unresponsive Bystander*. New York: Meredith Corporation.

Leidner, Robin L. 1993. *Fast Food, Fast Talk*. Berkeley: University of California Press.

Mansbridge, Jane J. 1990. "On the Relation of Altruism and Self-Interest." Pp. 133–43 in Jane J. Mansbridge (ed.), *Beyond Self-Interest*. Chicago: University of Chicago Press.

Merton, Robert K. (1949) 1968. *Social Theory and Social Structure*. Enlarged Edition. New York: Free Press.

Mincer, Jacob. 1978. "Family Migration Decisions." *Journal of Political Economy* 86:749–75.

Oliver, Judith. 1983. "The Caring Wife." Pp. 72–88 in Janet Finch and Dulcie Groves (eds.), *A Labour of Love: Women, Work, and Caring*. London: Routledge and Kegan Paul.

Parsons, Talcott. 1956. "A Sociological Approach to the Theory of Organizations." *Administrative Science Quarterly* 1:63–85, 225–39.

———. 1968. "Professions." Pp. 536–47 in *The International Encyclopedia of the Social Sciences*. New York: Macmillan.

Parsons, Talcott, and Edward A. Shils. 1951. "Categories of the Orientation and Organization of Action." Pp. 53–109 in Talcott Parsons and Edward A. Shils (eds.), *Towards a General Theory of Action*. New York: Harper and Row.

Pleck, Joseph H. 1977. "The Work-Family System." *Social Problems* 26:417–27.

Robinson, J. P. 1977. *How Americans Use Time*. New York: Praeger Press.

Rosenbaum, James E., and Takehiko Kariya. 1989. "From High School to Work: Market and Institutional Mechanisms in Japan." *American Journal of Sociology* 94:1334–65.

Rossi, Alice S., and Peter H. Rossi. 1990. *Of Human Bonding*. New York: Aldine de Gruyter.

Rothman, Barbara Katz. 1986. *The Tentative Pregnancy*. New York: Viking Penguin.

Simmons, Roberta G., Susan D. Klein, and Richard L. Simmons. 1977. *Gift of Life*. New York: Wiley.
Soltan, Karol E. 1987. *The Causal Theory of Justice*. Berkeley: University of California Press.
Spitze, Glenna, and John R. Logan. 1990. "Sons, Daughters, and Intergenerational Social Support." *Journal of Marriage and the Family* 52:420–30.
Starr, Paul. 1982. *The Social Transformation of American Medicine*. New York: Basic Books.
Stinchcombe, Arthur L. 1990. *Information and Organizations*. Berkeley: University of California Press.
Stone, Christoper D. 1975. *Where the Law Ends*. New York: Harper and Row.
Szalai, Alexander (ed). 1972. *The Use of Time*. The Hague: Mouton.
U.S. Bureau of the Census. 1973. *1970 Census of the Population, Subject Reports: Occupational Characteristics*. Washington, DC: U.S. Government Printing Office.
———. 1993. *Statistical Abstract of the United States: 1993*. 113th Edition. Washington, DC: U.S. Government Printing Office.
White, Martha S. 1970. "Psychological and Social Barriers to Women in Science." *Science* 170:413–6.
Wright, Fay. 1983. "Single Carers: Employment, Housework and Caring." Pp. 89–105 in Janet Finch and Dulcie Groves (eds.), *A Labour of Love: Women, Work, and Caring*. London: Routledge and Kegan Paul.
Wrong, Dennis. 1961. "The Oversocialized Conception of Man in Modern Sociology." *American Sociological Review* 26:183–93.
Wuthnow, Robert. 1991. *Acts of Compassion*. Princeton, NJ: Princeton University Press.
Zey, Mary. 1993. *Banking on Fraud*. New York: Aldine de Gruyter.

9

Currents and Anchors: Structure and Change in Australian Gender Role Attitudes, 1984–1989

M.D.R. Evans and Karen Oppenheim Mason

This chapter focuses on two attitudes central to women's place in society: (1) the norm supporting the traditional gender-based division of labor in the family, in which women stay at home full time while men support the family financially; and (2) the perception that the extradomestic employment of mothers harms the well-being of their children and family life in general. The choice between staying home and working for pay outside the family defines women's ties to the economy, with implications for their financial independence, sources of life satisfaction, self-concept, and role within the family. These choices are changing rapidly in Australia and most other industrial nations, with women's labor force participation rising sharply in recent decades. Whether married women choose to work outside the home has major implications not only for a woman herself but also for her family. A working wife increases family income, with all the advantages that brings, but working competes with domestic activities and may consequently harm the emotional well-being of children and other family members. In the gender role ideology dominant in the West during most of the nineteenth and twentieth centuries, the perception that the absence of mothers from the home for appreciable periods of the day would damage the well-being of their children (especially their young children) was a major reason for people to withhold moral support from the employment of married women.

The current chapter specifically focuses on four issues: (1) the size of recent changes in public support for the norm that married women's employment is legitimate and for the perception that maternal employment harms family life; (2) the extent to which their interrelation—so important in traditional gender role ideology—persists; (3) the sources of continuity and change in these attitudes; and (4) the extent to which women's and men's attitudes differ. To assess these issues we use data from the 1984 and 1989 National Social Science Surveys (NSSS), large, nationally representative samples of Australian citizens aged 18 and over.

Theory

Theories of continuity and change in gender role attitudes rely on two main mechanisms of change. The *cohort replacement* mechanism leads attitudes to become more feminist as younger cohorts having attitudes more supportive of gender equality replace older, more traditional cohorts. Changes in attitudes due to cohort replacement may also reflect structural changes across cohorts—for example, gains in educational attainment or the increasingly common experience of having grown up in a family with the mother working outside the home. The *changing relationships* mechanism refers to the changing relationship between structural or attitudinal factors and gender role attitudes. For example, Christian beliefs are a well-known "anchor" for gender role attitudes: They are enduring and they have traditionally bolstered gender-differentiated family arrangements. Nonetheless, the increasing profeminist orientation of many mainstream religious elites—reflected in expanded roles for women in worship services and in new gender-neutral liturgies—might well be loosening the links between Christian beliefs and endorsement of traditional family roles. Both cohort replacement and changing relationships mechanisms are posited by the three theories of gender role attitude change we consider here: postmaterialist values theory, marital exchange theory, and a theory of feminism as a social movement.

Postmaterialist Values

The theory of postmaterialist values argues that as societies become increasingly affluent and ensure nearly universal provision of basic material needs, their dominant values shift up the hierarchy of basic needs from material survival to luxuries such as individual fulfillment and self-actualization (Inglehart 1977, 1990; Lesthaeghe 1983; Lesthaeghe and Meekers 1986; Lesthaeghe and Surkyn 1988). Such shifts toward postmaterialist values erode beliefs about the necessity or value of the family arrangements that were historically important for survival, for example, lifelong marriage and a gender-based division of labor. Instead, there is increasing support for individual freedom and choice, including the right of women to choose nontraditional roles.

The theory of postmaterial values thus suggests that in affluent welfare states like Australia, support for traditional gender roles should decline over time. The individualism of the postmaterialist worldview should undermine women's traditional obligations to the family and hence should ultimately destroy the perception that a mother's presence in the home is necessary to her children's well-being. Postmaterial value shift appears to be gradual, occurring largely through cohort succession (Inglehart 1990); the theory of postmaterialist values thus suggests that changes in gender role attitudes should likewise occur largely through cohort succession. The theory of postmaterial values predicts few, if any, gender differences in attitudes toward women's roles, since the source of attitude change is society-wide affluence generated by economic growth. Finally, postmaterial values' emphasis on individual fulfillment leads to the hypothesis of a weakening of the traditional ideological link between the perception that maternal employment harms children's well-being and moral support for the traditional familial division of labor.

Marital Exchange Theory

Marital exchange theory (Becker 1981; Huber and Spitze 1983; Morgan and Walker 1983) argues that gender role attitudes reflect women's and men's rational self-interests and therefore change as new conditions alter those interests. The traditional arrangement in which the husband's lifelong economic support was exchanged for the wife's domestic services met the self-interests of both sexes so long as the divorce rate was low and women's education and consequent earning power were also low. Conditions have changed, however. Rising divorce rates mean that wives can no longer rely on their husbands' lifelong support; at the same time, gains in women's educational attainment and earnings during the postwar period make solo living a viable option for many women. As a result, the traditional "deal" has become less attractive to women, leading them to support more similar roles for husbands and wives.[1] Exchange theory thus predicts more rapid gender role attitude change among women than among men and a consequent gender "gap" during periods of attitude transition. It also suggests that women's attitudes can change very rapidly; hence as much attitude change may occur within as across cohorts. According to exchange theory, with time, more women will view employment as legitimate and fewer will think that maternal employment harms children's well-being. Marital exchange theory does not, however, suggest a necessary weakening of the link between moral support for married women's employment and perceived costs of women's careers to their families, because it bases its prediction of increasing support for married women's employment on a rejection of the entire traditional marital/gender arrangement.

The Theory of Mass-Movement Feminism

The theory of second-wave feminist movements explains changing attitudes incidentally as part of a broader explanation for the rise of so-called second-wave feminist movements after World War II (Chafetz and Dworkin 1986). It argues that mass-based feminist movements raise ordinary women's (and some men's) consciousness about changing gender realities and purvey new ideologies of gender to the grassroots level, processes that accelerate gender role attitude change. The theory thus predicts rapid gender role attitude change, hence change within as well as across cohorts of the population. This theory also implies that there may be a gender gap in attitude change, although the extent of it will depend on the feminist movement's particular ideological appeal. Whether beliefs about maternal employment's effects on children's well-being become disconnected from moral support for nontraditional gender roles in the family also depends on the message purveyed by the mass feminist movement.

Predictions from the Three Theories

What do these three theories predict about Australian gender role attitude change during the 1980s (and earlier)? The postmaterialist values theory implies gradual attitude change brought about by cohort replacement. Australia, like the other industrial democracies, has experienced rising incomes and the development of a full-blown welfare state during much of this century, including in the 1970s and 1980s. Certainly, it qualifies as the kind of affluent society in which a shift to postmaterialist values is predicted and in which rising support for women's rights and individual opportunities can consequently be expected through a gradual process of cohort replacement. The 1970s and 1980s in Australia also saw changes in the realities of women's work and family circumstances that, according to the marital exchange theory, should have increased women's support for gender equality. For example, the divorce rate rose, especially after changes in the divorce law in 1974 (McDonald 1990), women's educational attainment levels increased (Yates 1987), and married women's labor force participation rates rose as well (Eccles 1984; Evans 1988b). This theory thus predicts rapid attitude change in Australia during the 1980s.

The theory stressing the role of feminist movements as agents of change would predict slower changes because Australia's elite feminist movement, although achieving substantial bureaucratic and legislative change, appears to have had less mass involvement than the second-wave feminist movements in some other Western countries. Thus, if mass feminist movements produce rapid attitude change, Australia's attitude change may be relatively slow compared to countries like the United

States, where the second-wave feminist movement achieved considerable mass penetration. As is summarized in Table 9.1, predictions for Australia vary among the theories.

Data and Methods

The NSSS is a periodic, multipurpose sample survey of the adult Australian population that covers a variety of social, political, and economic issues. Both the 1984 and 1989 surveys were based on nationally representative probability samples of Australian citizens aged 18 and over.[2] The 1984 and 1989 surveys were collected somewhat differently. The 1984 NSSS (N = 3,012) combined household interviews in urban areas with a mail survey in rural areas (Kelley, Cushing and Headey 1988).[3] The 1989 NSSS (N = 4,513) was conducted in late 1989 and early 1990 entirely as a mail survey.[4] A comparison of these surveys with the 1986 Australian census shows that both samples closely resemble the population as a whole on basic demographic and socioeconomic variables such as age, gender, education, and employment patterns (Bean 1991). The use of a mail survey rather than personal interviews seems not to have affected responses in any serious way: Comparison of demographic and attitudinal variables from an earlier NSSS based on personal interviews with subsequent mail surveys asking the same questions showed no appreciable differences (Bean 1991).

The 1984 and 1989 surveys contain two sets of gender role attitude items that were intended to form scales measuring, respectively, moral support for married women's employment (as opposed to a traditional

TABLE 9.1 Summary of Predictions Made by the Three Major Theories of Gender Role Attitude Change

Prediction	Postmaterialist Values	Marital Exchange	Mass Feminist Movements
Gender differences in attitudes?	No	Yes	Depends
Attitude change?	Yes, small	Yes	Maybe
Change predominately due to cohort replacement?	Yes	Maybe	No
Does the link weaken between norms supporting careers and perceptions of conflict with the family?	Yes	No	Depends

gender division of labor between husband and wife) and perceptions of whether the nonfamilial employment of mothers is harmful to their children or to family life. Both scales were pretested and proved to be reliable in the 1984 survey (Kelley 1988). As the correlations and factor analysis results shown in Table 9.2 suggest, the two sets of items form distinct and reliable scales when the 1984 and 1989 NSSS are combined. In the combined data set, intercorrelations between the individual items in the "legitimacy of married women's employment" scale range from .37 to .45, while those in the "perceived costs to family" scale range from .44 to .51. In the factor analysis a two-dimensional solution had a significantly better fit than did a one-dimensional solution (χ^2 = 179, 8 df, versus χ^2 = 968, 9 df), thereby confirming that the two scales tap distinct underlying dimensions. The χ^2 for the two-factor solution is also less than 2 percent of its value in the baseline independence model (11,759 with 15 df); the standardized root mean square residual is .053, the normed goodness-of-fit index is .959, and the goodness-of-fit index is 0.988. These scales form the dependent variables for our analysis.

Also included in the two surveys are a variety of background and sociodemographic variables relevant to gender role attitudes. In this chapter we focus on five of these variables (plus survey year): gender, age, educational attainment, maternal employment while the respondent was growing up, and religious beliefs. Past studies in Australia and other industrialized countries have found these variables to be strong and theoretically plausible predictors of gender role attitudes, with women, the young, the well-educated, those whose mothers worked while they were young, and the less religious generally being the most supportive of married women's employment and the least likely to believe that such employment harms children or family life (Evans 1988b; Herzog and Bachman 1982; Huber and Spitze 1981; Mason and Bumpass 1975; Mason and Lu 1988; Mason, Czajka, and Arber 1976; Molm 1978; Morgan 1987; Morgan and Walker 1983; Spitze and Waite 1980; Thornton and Freedman 1979). We omitted from our analysis some variables commonly used to predict gender role attitudes (marital status, number of children, current employment status) because theory and prior research into their links to gender role attitudes suggest they are jointly endogenous with attitudes.[5] Their inclusion as predictors would therefore be likely to produce upwardly biased estimates of their true causal impact on gender role attitudes.[6] Definitions of the predictor variables, along with their means and standard deviations, are given in Table 9.3.

Our hypotheses about sources of approval of married women's employment and perceptions of costs to the family of such employment are graphically represented in the path diagram in Figure 9.1. This model treats legitimacy of married women's work as the ultimate dependent

TABLE 9.2 Means, Correlations, and Factor Loadings (Completely Standardized Lambdas) of Items in Gender Role Attitude Scales: 1984 and 1989 NSSS Combined Sample[a]

Scale and Items	Mean	a	b	c	Factor Loading [b]
Support for married women's work scale					
a. I approve of a married woman earning money in business & industry even if she has a husband capable of supporting her	64	1.00			.60
b. A woman should devote almost all her time to her family (reversed scoring)	55	.42	1.00		.73
c. A married woman should not attach much importance to a career (reversed scoring)	59	.37	.45	1.00	.60
Perceived costs to family scale					
a. A working mother can establish just as warm and secure a relationship with her children as a mother who does not work (reversed)	42	1.00			.70
b. All in all, family life suffers when the woman has a full-time job	56	.55	1.00		.79
c. It is more difficult to raise children successfully when both parents work full time	66	.44	.51	1.00	.64

[a] Based on the combined 1984 and 1989 NSSS ($N = 7{,}252$). All items had four- or five-point "strongly agree" to "strongly disagree" response categories, which were scored in even intervals from zero to 100.

[b] Factor loadings are lambdas from the completely standardized solution estimated by LISREL (version 8e) on the pooled sample.

TABLE 9.3 Variable Definitions, Means, and Standard Deviations Used to Predict Gender Role Attitude Scales: 1984 and 1989 NSSS Combined Sample

Variable Definition	Mean	SD
Survey year (1984 = 0; 1989 = 1)	.60	.49
Gender (female = 0; male = 1)	.48	.50
Age in 1984 (in years)[a]	40.0	16.5
$(Age - 44)^2$	88.3	288.0
Mother worked? (full-time = 100; part-time = 50; stayed home = 0)	25.0	34.2
Education (equivalent full time years of study completed)	10.6	3.1
$(Education - 10)^2$	9.7	16.7
Religious beliefs (multiple-item scale scored 0–100, with high score indicating strongest religious beliefs)[b]	55.8	29.5

[a] We experimented with dummy specifications to capture nonlinearities, but they performed no better than the quadratic specification for this variable.

[b] Based on four items asking about (1) belief in God (with six answer categories ranging from "I don't believe in God" to "I know God really exists, and I have no doubts about it"), (2) belief in life after death, (3) belief in heaven, and (4) belief in hell. The inter-item correlations ranged from .54 to .73, with factor loadings for a single factor solution ranging from .72 to .93. The scale appears to be highly reliable.

variable, with perceptions about the costs of such work for family life being its first proximate determinant. Because one could make a plausible argument against this causal ordering (positing instead the "wishful thinking" hypothesis that people first develop views about the legitimacy of women's employment, then shape their perceptions of the cost of careers to the family according to these views), we ran two parallel analyses, using the same model to predict both employment approval and costs to the family. We also, however, include a final model that allows for a causal effect of perceived costs to the family on employment legitimacy.

The ultimate exogenous variables in the model are cohort and gender. The first block of intermediate variables consists of mother's employment while the respondent was young and respondent's education. The last intermediate variable is Christian religious beliefs. There is little question that mother's employment is causally prior to current beliefs and moral

FIGURE 9.1 Causal Model of the Determinants of Gender Role Attitudes

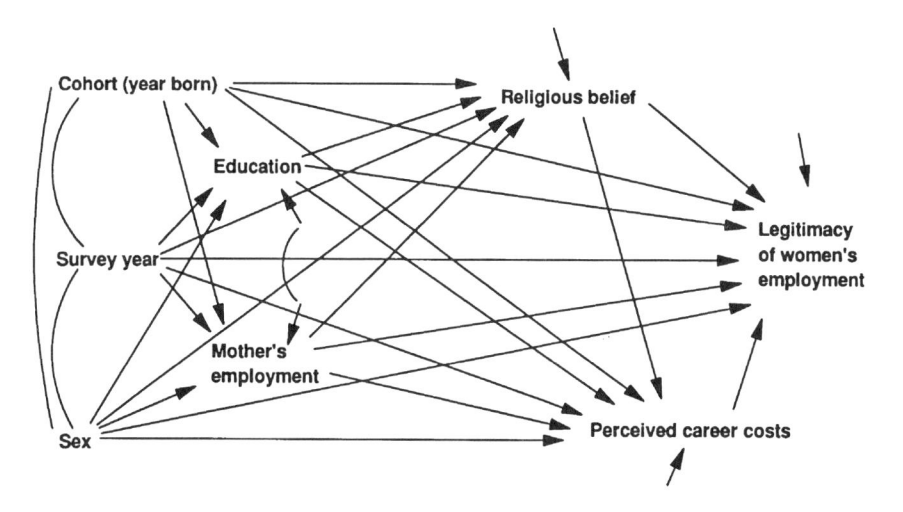

attitudes. Our placement of education as a cause of gender role attitudes is somewhat more contentious because liberal gender role attitudes formed early in life might encourage girls to go further in education and to hold liberal gender role attitudes as adults. Such an effect should not hold for boys, however. It also seems dubious even for girls, given the evidence from longitudinal studies that education tends to liberalize social attitudes, especially those involving self-actualization (Newcomb 1943; Feldman and Newcomb 1969; Hyman and Wright 1979). That we find no significant gender difference in the link between education and support for married women's employment (see Appendix) is consistent with our assumption that education is causally prior to the attitudes measured in this study.

Religious belief is assumed to be the last intermediate variable in the causal sequence for two reasons: first, because adults' beliefs are in part a product of childhood and adolescent socialization, including parental practices (such as mother's employment) and experiences outside the home (such as education); and second, because most adults' religious beliefs are enduring and provide global orientations that shape other, more specific attitudes and values, including gender role attitudes and perceptions.

In the analysis that follows, we begin by examining responses to the individual attitude items, separately by gender and survey year, in order to understand the extent to which the specific items that constitute the two attitude scales show gender differences and change over time. We then turn to a series of ordinary least-squares (OLS) regression models predicting support for married women's employment and perceived costs to the family of married women's work. In both series of models, the first equation makes the attitude scales a function of age in 1984, gender, and time only (plus an interaction between age and gender). We interpret the age effects as cohort effects rather than as representing life-course variation in attitudes. We strongly suspect, however, that past sea changes, or period effects, have muted the original cohort differences in attitudes. The next model includes the variables in the first equation plus mother's employment and education, while a third set of equations adds religious belief. Finally, for the models predicting support for married women's employment only, we also estimate a "full" model that includes all of the exogenous and intermediate variables plus beliefs about the costs to the family of married women's employment.

Assessing interactions is complicated because we are working with a range of models for which we seek a consistent specification. To arrive at the specifications used here, we first used the LISREL "multiple groups" procedure to bring to light possible differences among the four groups formed by crossing gender and year (women in the 1984 sample, men in the 1984 sample, women in the 1989 sample, and men in the 1989 sample). In that analysis we used linear specifications of education and age, although, based on previous findings (e.g., Evans 1988b), we planned to include quadratic terms in the final analysis. We then also estimated the simple linear models using OLS and tested pairwise for differences in coefficients among the four groups mentioned above (the Appendix gives the significance tests). A parsimonious summary of the interaction effects revealed through these exploratory analyses is that: (1) the effect of perceived career costs on employment legitimacy differs between 1984 and 1989; and (2) birth-year/cohort differences differ between women and men. We have allowed for both of these interactions in the models discussed in the text. To clarify discussion of the interactions and quadratics, we compute predicted values on the attitudes for the predictors in question (setting all other variables equal to their means in the post-1960 cohorts) and then present these predicted values graphically.

Results

Descriptive Results

As is the case in other Western countries, Australian opinion is divided on whether married women's employment has deleterious consequences for their families. This is shown in Table 9.4, which gives the percentages of people who agree and disagree with the individual items in our scales, separately by year and gender. A majority believe that a working mother can establish as warm and secure a relationship with her children as can a mother who does not work outside the home (Table 9.4, first question), but only a small minority—slightly more than one-third—doubt that family life suffers when the woman works full time, and a mere one-fifth doubt that it is more difficult to raise children successfully under these conditions (Table 9.4, second and third questions). Thus, Australian opinion seems to be that married women's employment, although not an insurmountable barrier to good mother-child relationships, creates problems for families.

Nonetheless, the legitimacy of married women's employment is widely endorsed. By the end of the 1980s, more than two-thirds of Australians approved of a married woman's working (Table 9.4, fourth question), and roughly one-half disagreed with the traditional precept that a wife should devote all her time to her family and not attach any importance to a career outside the home (Table 9.4, fifth and sixth questions). Australians are thus more likely to support a married woman's right to work than they are to perceive that such employment is without undesirable consequences for family life, especially if the woman works full time.[7]

Change between 1984 and 1989 was moderate on most of the items in Table 9.4; over all items, it averaged approximately four percentage points among women and five among men, or roughly one point per year. There was considerable variation across individual items in the amount of attitude change, however. For example, among women, perception of a working mother's ability to have a good relationship with her children (question 1) and approval for married women's work (question 4) grew by eight or nine points; in contrast, endorsement of the idea that a woman should devote all her time to her family (question 5) and not attach much importance to having a career (question 6) hardly changed.

On almost all the items in Table 9.4, women hold less traditional attitudes than men. Moreover, gender differences in the items tapping perceived career costs to the family tend to be larger than the changes over time, although the picture is more mixed on the items tapping legitimacy of married women's employment. Thus, as marital exchange theory predicts, perceptions of married women's careers as having deleterious consequences for the family appear to have declined faster among women than among men. However, the absence of a significant interaction between gender and year in the exploratory analysis described earlier suggests that this tendency is, at most, weak. To understand the underlying nature of the changes over time and gender differences shown in Table 9.4 requires that we turn to the multivariate analyses of the two gender role attitude scales.

TABLE 9.4 Percentages Agreeing or Disagreeing with Six Gender Role Attitude Items, by Year and Gender: Australia, 1984 and 1989

		Women			Men			Gender Diff	
Item		1984	1989	Diff	1984	1989	Diff	1984	1989
Perceived costs to family									
1. A working mother can establish just as warm and secure a relationship with her children as a mother who does not work (agree)		55%	63%	8*	43%	51%	8*	12*	12*
2. All in all, family life suffers when the woman has a full time job (disagree)		31	38	7*	24	32	8*	7*	6*
3. It is more difficult to raise children successfully when both parents work full time (disagree)		21	23	2	15	18	3*	6*	5*
Legitimacy of women's employment									
4. I approve of a married woman earning money in business and industry even if she has a husband capable of supporting her (agree)		61	69	8*	63	68	5*	−2	1
5. A woman should devote almost all her time to her family (disagree)		52	51	−1	44	46	2	8*	5*
6. A married woman should not attach much importance to a career (disagree)		55	55	0	47	52	5*	8*	3
Number of cases[a]		1,524	2,271		1,438	2,139			

* $p < .05$

[a] Varies slightly across questions because of missing data; the numbers shown are the smallest for any item.

Structure and Change in Australian Gender Role Attitudes

TABLE 9.5 Ordinary Least-Squares Metric Regression Coefficients Predicting Legitimacy of Married Women's Employment Scale: 1984 and 1989 NSSS Combined Sample

Predictor variable	(1)	(2)	(3)	(4)	(4a)[a]
Survey year (1=1989, 0=1984)	1.95*	1.88*	1.93*	−7.39*	.08*
Gender (1=male, 0=female)	−.66	−.96	−2.08	−.16	−.03*
Age in 1984 (cohort)	−.33*	−.19*	−.19*	−.13*	−.11*
$(Age^2) \times 10$	−.03*	−.03*	−.03*	−.03*	–
Gender × age	−.04	−.05*	−.05*	−.03	–
Education (years)	–	1.63*	1.59*	1.29*	.20*
$Education^2$	–	.11*	.11*	.08*	–
Mother worked? (0–100)	–	.05*	.05*	.02*	.02*
Religious beliefs (0–100)	–	–	−.11*	−.07*	−.10*
Perceived career costs	–	–	–	−.49*	−.46*
Career costs × year	–	–	–	.15*	–
Constant	73.4*	48.5*	55.5*	81.8	76.1
R-squared	.09	.16	.19	.38	.37

* $p < .05$
[a] Standardized slopes for a simple linear version of model 3, omitting quadratic and interaction terms

Multivariate Analysis

Period Changes, 1984–1989. Table 9.5 reports OLS results for the "legitimacy of married women's employment" scale, and Table 9.6 reports results for the "perceived costs to family" scale. As indicated by the coefficients for survey year shown in the first row of each table, during the 1980s a growing number of Australians perceived married women's employment as morally legitimate, while a declining number perceived it as costly to the family. Because these results are estimated net of birth cohort, education, and other variables that have changed over time, they represent true period effects, rather than cohort replacement effects. The content of the attitudinal shift is consistent with the rise of

TABLE 9.6 Ordinary Least-Squares Metric Regression Coefficients Predicting Perceived Costs to Family Scale: 1984 and 1989 NSSS Combined Sample

Predictor variable	(1)	(2)	(3)	(3a)[a]
Survey year (1=1989, 0=1984)	−2.37*	−2.26*	−2.30*	−.05*
Gender (1=male, 0=female)	3.66*	3.94*	4.92*	.15*
Age in 1984 (cohort)	.25*	.14*	.14*	.11*
(Age^2) × 10	.00	.01	.04	−
Gender × age	.04	.05	.05	−
Education (years)	−	−.76*	−.72*	−.10*
Education^2	−	−.07*	−.06*	−
Mother worked? (0–100)	−	−.09*	−.08*	−.12*
Religious beliefs (0–100)	−	−	.09*	.12*
Constant	43.8*	58.4*	52.3*	51.3*
R-squared	.05	.08	.09	.09

* $p < .05$
[a]Standardized slopes for a simple linear version of model 3, omitting quadratic and interaction terms.

postmaterialist values, because it represents a more individualistic view of women's roles; however, the fact that it occurs within cohorts rather than only via cohort replacement contradicts postmaterialism. Some aspects of the change over time also contradict marital exchange and feminist movement theories. That they are common to both men and women is contrary to the prediction of marital exchange theory, and that they occur during a period when the Australian feminist movement focused more on the bastions of power than on grassroots consciousness-raising is contrary to feminist movement theory. The mechanism underlying this change is consequently unclear. Nevertheless, as the descriptive results first suggested, in the 1980s Australians were adopting an increasingly egalitarian view of women's roles.

Effects of Cohort and Gender. In order to clarify the OLS results for gender and cohort shown in Tables 9.5 and 9.6, we have computed predicted values on the attitude scales associated with these variables and have graphed them in Figure 9.2.[8] Panels A–C in that figure show the values on the "legitimacy of married women's employment scale" that are predicted by models 1, 3, and 4 in Table 9.5. Panel D shows the values on the "perceived costs to family" scale that are predicted by model 3 in Table 9.6.

Younger people are much more likely than the elderly to view married women's employment as legitimate, as panels A-C of Figure 9.2 indicate. Indeed, in our base model predicting the employment legitimacy scale from cohort, gender, and survey year only (Table 9.5, model 1), the difference between the oldest and youngest cohorts is 24 points out of 100 (panel A). Although controlling for the intermediate variables (especially for the perception of career costs to the family) markedly reduces the cohort difference, it remains significant even after all the controls have been introduced. Thus, although cohorts differ in their perceptions of the consequences of women's work for the family, even when these differences are taken into account, the older cohorts remain morally more traditional than the younger ones.

This difference among cohorts is generally consistent with the theory of postmaterialist values, although the decreasing size of the difference after World War II—the prosperous era when Australia achieved full status as an affluent welfare state—contradicts that theory. Sizable cohort differences in attitudes are less consistent with marital exchange theory and the theory of mass feminist movements, both of which imply rapid change in attitudes within cohorts rather than large differences between them. If we can assume that the cohort differences seen in Table 9.5 and panels A-C of Figure 9.2 are enduring, then they suggest that considerable change in support for married women's employment has occurred during this century via the process of cohort succession. What has caused this difference in outlook among cohorts is, however, unclear.

Panels A-C of Figure 9.2 also show that there is a gender difference in support for married women's employment, with women endorsing wives' employment more frequently than men do. This gender difference is rapidly diminishing, however, and in the full model (panel C) disappears entirely. The existence of a gender difference is consistent with marital exchange theory, but its disappearance during a period when divorce rates and women's employment were rising is not.[9] Because postmaterialist values theory predicts rising support for married women's employment among both sexes, the disappearing gender gap may indicate that during the 1980s the shift toward support for married women's work in Australia was part of a broader shift from materialist to postmaterialist values.

Turning to the "perceived costs to family" scale, the coefficients in Table 9.6 and the graph in panel D of Figure 9.2 make clear that there is, again, a difference among birth cohorts in attitudes, although a somewhat

FIGURE 9.2 Predicted Values on the "Legitimacy of Women's Employment" Scale and "Perceived Costs to Family" Scale, by Birth Cohort and Gender

291

FIGURE 9.2 *(continued)*

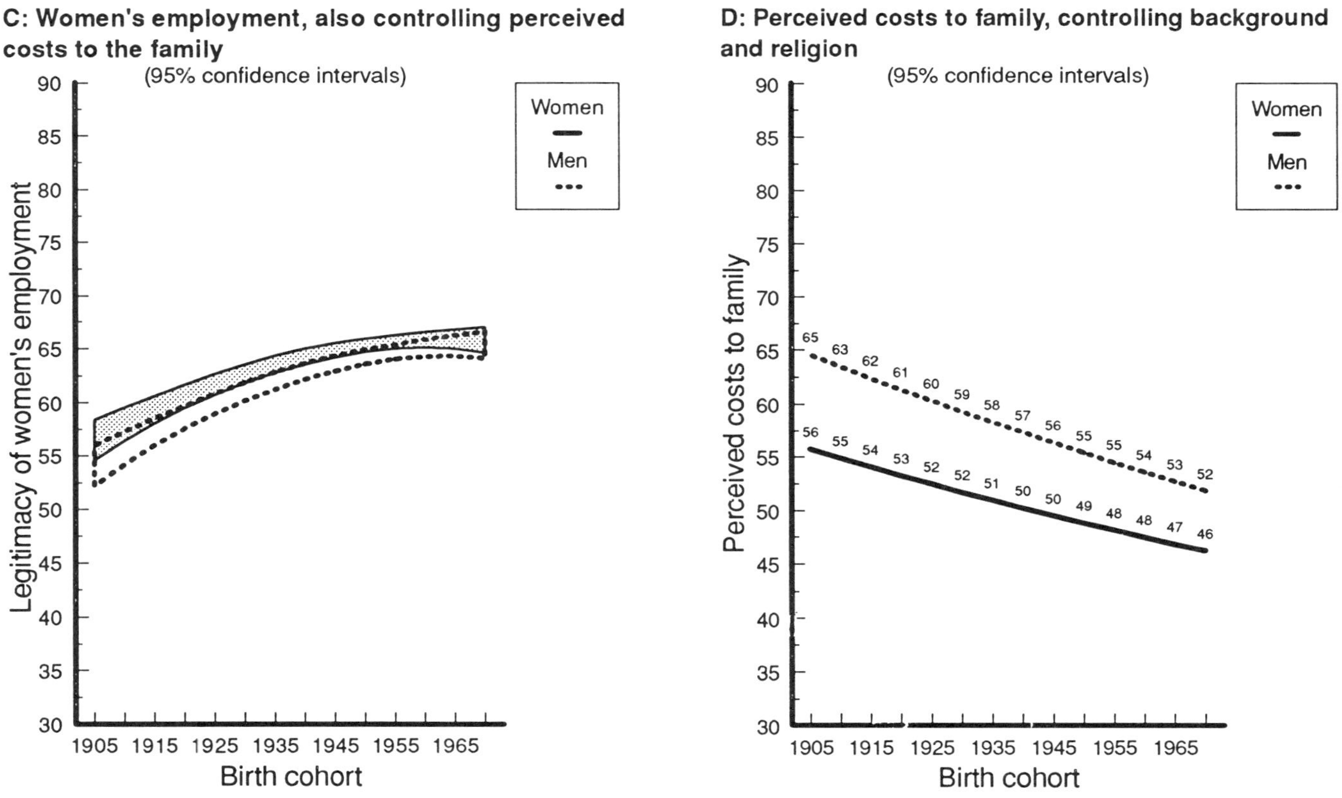

C: Women's employment, also controlling perceived costs to the family
(95% confidence intervals)

D: Perceived costs to family, controlling background and religion
(95% confidence intervals)

Source: Table 9.5, models 2–4, and Table 9.6, model 3.

smaller one than exists for the "legitimacy of married women's employment" scale. There is also a sizable gender gap that persists in the most recent cohorts (perhaps slightly diminished, although the interaction between cohort and gender is not statistically significant). These results are consistent both with postmaterialist values theory, which predicts cohort differences, and with marital exchange theory, which predicts the gender gap. Men, more than women, see wives' employment as risky to the family's well-being, perhaps because it poses a threat to their own freedom to pursue a remunerated career (Presser 1995). Moreover, as a comparison of panels B and C in Figure 9.2 reveals, this gender difference in perceived costs to the family completely accounts for the apparent gender difference in the legitimacy of married women's employment. If women and men agreed about the consequences of wives' employment for the family, then they would be equally likely to endorse the legitimacy of wives' working.

Effects of Education, Maternal Employment, and Religious Beliefs. As Figure 9.3 makes clear, the well-educated are much more likely than the poorly-educated to feel that it is legitimate for married women to work. They are also much less likely to think that doing so is costly to family life. This result is similar to results from studies in a number of other countries (Evans 1988b; Huber and Spitze 1981; Mason and Bumpass 1975; Molm 1978; Morgan and Walker 1983; Spitze and Waite 1980). In Australia university education is especially likely to foster tolerance for married women's employment (which is true as well in the United States; see Mason and Lu 1988). This is consistent with all three theories, because the university-educated are more economically secure and hence sympathetic to postmaterialist values; the occupations available to university graduates are particularly rewarding and hence more desirable in rational marital exchange calculations; and the women's movement in Australia has been much stronger in universities than among the population at large and thus would be expected to have its main impact among the well-educated.

We do not graph the results for maternal employment because they are so straightforward. As model 2 in both Tables 9.5 and 9.6 indicates, having had a mother who worked outside the home while one was growing up leads to slightly greater support for women's employment and substantially undermines the belief that women's work is bad for the family. Thus, the practical example of a woman both raising a family and working outside the home has enduring effects on the gender role attitudes of her children. Note that controlling for perceived costs to the family reduces the effects of maternal employment on norms concerning women's employment by about one-half (compare models 2 and 4 in

Structure and Change in Australian Gender Role Attitudes 293

FIGURE 9.3 Predicted Values on the "Legitimacy of Women's Employment" Scale and "Perceived Costs to Family" Scale, by Education

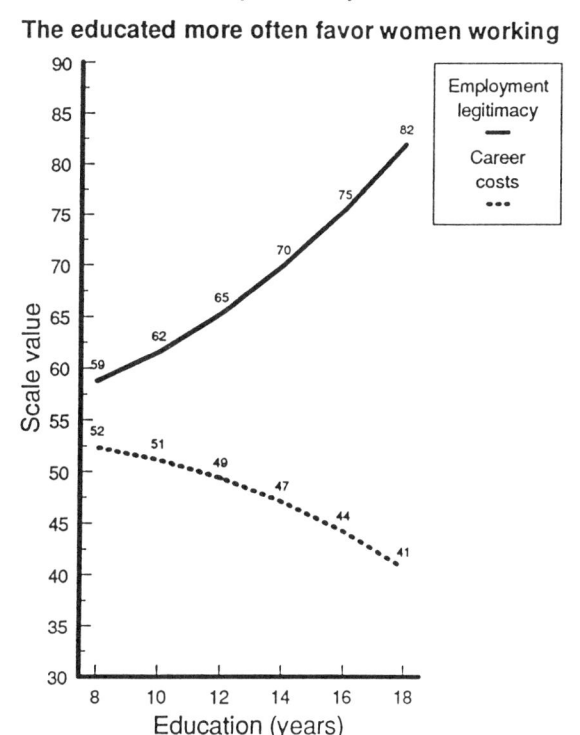

The educated more often favor women working

[Figure: Line graph showing Scale value (y-axis, 30–90) versus Education in years (x-axis, 8–18). Employment legitimacy (solid line) rises from 59 at 8 years, 62, 65, 70, 75, to 82 at 18 years. Career costs (dotted line) declines from 52 at 8 years, 51, 49, 47, 44, to 41 at 18 years.]

Source: Tables 9.5, model 4, and Table 9.6, model 3.

Table 9.5). This suggests that the primary reason that maternal employment eventuates in moral support for a married women's right to work is because it undermines the traditional belief that a working mother is bad for family life. When generalized to the macrolevel, results of this form indicate why rising rates of labor force participation among married women are likely to lead eventually to stronger moral support for that participation. A process of this kind may ultimately explain the cohort differences in support for married women's employment seen earlier.

The results for Christian beliefs are also straightforward. Those holding strong Christian beliefs are substantially more likely than those with a secular worldview to perceive women's work as harming family life (Table 9.6, model 3). Partly for this reason, devout Christians are substantially less likely than others to endorse married women's right to work outside the home (see Table 9.5, models 3 and 4). This result is similar to findings for the United States, where religiosity enforces a traditional outlook toward gender roles (Herzog and Bachman 1982; Mason and Bumpass 1975; Molm 1978; Morgan 1987) and inhibits change in gender ideology (Thornton, Alwin, and Camburn 1983). Note that the exploratory analysis (see Appendix) detected no diminution of the conservative impact of Christian beliefs on gender role attitudes during the 1980s. This is contrary to what might be expected in light of pervasive, apparently feminist, changes in liturgies and gender roles in worship services in most mainstream Christian denominations in Australia during that period. Thus, no evidence of a changing relationship to attitudes is found for Christian beliefs.

Effects of Perceived Costs to the Family on Norms About Women's Working. As model 4 in Table 9.5 indicates, people who believe that a married woman's working harms her family tend to withhold moral support from a family division of labor in which wives as well as husbands work outside the home. Those who perceive great conflict exhibit scores of only 40 or 50 points (out of 100) on the employment scale, while those who perceive little or no conflict score 80 or 90 points (Figure 9.4). Indeed, if one accepts the causal assumption implicit in this model—namely, that perceived costs form one basis on which people develop their attitudes toward the legitimacy of married women's employment rather than vice versa—these perceptions are by far the strongest determinant of norms about married women's working (see the standardized results in Table 9.6, model 4a). Moreover, the strong relationship between perceptions of costs to the family and moral support for married women's employment holds equally for women and men.

Figure 9.4 makes clear, however, that the link between perceived costs and moral support for women's work has weakened appreciably over time. In the few years between 1984 and 1989, the slope of the relationship dropped by about one-third. This decline is consistent with the postmaterialist theory of increasing individualism but not with marital exchange theory's prediction of a continued strong link.

The apparent weakening of the link between perceptions of costs to the family and moral support for married women's employment is important. In the gender role ideology dominant in the West during most of the nineteenth and twentieth centuries, the perception that mothers' absence from the home would damage their children's well-being was perhaps the major reason for people to withhold moral support from the employment of married women and to endorse a continuation of the traditional division of labor between husbands and wives. If the link continues to weaken in the future as quickly as it did during the 1980s, within a few decades this bulwark of traditional norms will be entirely a matter of history in Australia.

FIGURE 9.4 Predicted Values on the "Legitimacy of Women's Employment" Scale, and "Perceived Costs to Family" Scale, by Year

Perceived costs to the family are tremendously important, but less so in recent years

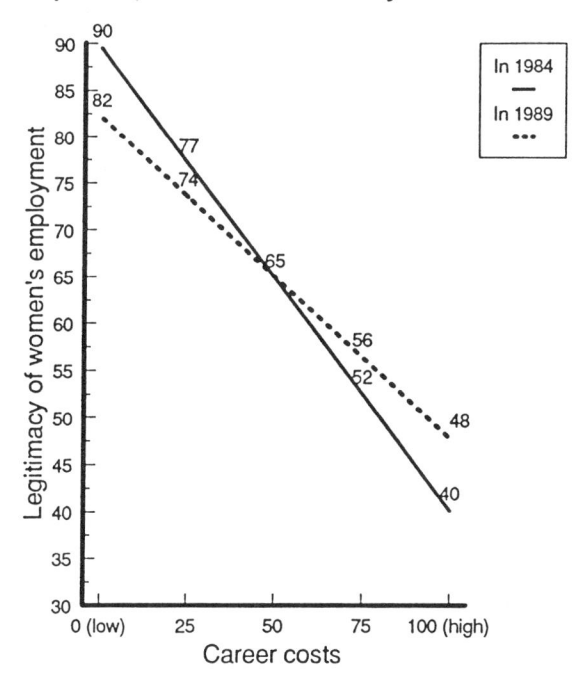

[Graph: Legitimacy of women's employment (y-axis, 30 to 90) vs. Career costs (x-axis, 0 low to 100 high). In 1984 (solid line): 90, 77, 65, 52, 40. In 1989 (dotted line): 82, 74, 65, 56, 48.]

Source: Table 9.5, model 4.

Summary and Conclusions

This chapter has presented the first rigorous analysis of change over time in Australian gender role attitudes. Using data from the 1984 and 1989 National Social Science Surveys, we have explored the structure of gender role attitudes, the extent of change in these attitudes, and the nature of their determinants. In the 1980s gender role attitudes were organized around at least two distinct dimensions: a perceptual one concerned with the impact of married women's work on family life and a moral dimension concerned with the legitimacy of a married woman's working outside the home. Change in a feminist direction has occurred in both dimensions. Importantly, the ideological link between them has weakened, albeit remaining strong in 1989. We also found that gender role attitudes in Australia have changed both through a process of cohort succession (as predicted by postmaterialist value theory) and through period shifts (contrary to postmaterialist value theory). In the older cohorts men and women differ sharply in their gender role attitudes, but in more recent cohorts the difference in perceptions of career costs to the family shrinks slightly and the difference in legitimacy of employment of married women disappears completely.

What do our results suggest about the future of gender role attitudes in Australia? Our analysis has shown that education, maternal employment, and religious beliefs all have a strong bearing on gender role perceptions and norms. If educational levels and rates of maternal employment continue to rise in Australia (as seems likely), then we would expect greater support for nontraditional gender role arrangements than is seen today. A decline in the strength of religious beliefs (which is not seen today) would also have this effect. According to the marital exchange theory, support for nontraditional gender role arrangements will also rise if divorce rates continue to rise and marriage rates fall. Full support for similar roles for husbands and wives seems unlikely to be forthcoming, however, so long as both women and men—especially men—continue to perceive that rearing children and having a happy family life is made difficult when mothers go out to work. Australia, however, like other countries of the West, seems well on the road to redefining the traditional roles of women and men in the family.

What do our results imply about the theories of gender role attitude change reviewed in this chapter? Parts of our results are consistent (and other parts inconsistent) with two of the three theories considered here: postmaterialist value change and marital exchange theories. Only the theory of feminism as a mass movement does not seem to apply to Australia: We find no distinctive traces of change in people's attitudes when this movement was building momentum in the 1970s.

Marital exchange theory plausibly accounts for the existence and persistence of a gender gap in perceptions of whether maternal employment has deleterious consequences for family life. This theory, however, also makes at least two incorrect predictions: first, that women's gender role attitudes should liberalize faster than men's in the 1970s and 1980s, leading to a growing gender gap; and second, that men's and women's normative outlooks should be identical in the oldest cohorts because the divorce risks in these cohorts were minimal. Marital exchange theory correctly draws our attention to the role of self-interest in gender role attitudes but may overstate the scope and size of self-interest in determining gender role attitudes or may misinterpret gender differences in self-interest. In particular, in Australia and elsewhere, as women's earnings have risen and as married women have taken up employment in increasing numbers, they have continued to take major responsibility for homemaking and child rearing. Whether men's self-interests are threatened by women's employment is therefore unclear. If anyone's self-interests are threatened, it would appear to be women's only.

Both the liberalization of gender role attitudes across cohorts and the apparent partial or complete convergence of women's and men's attitudes over cohorts are consistent with the predictions of postmaterialist value theory. Also consistent with what this theory would suggest is the strong impact of education, especially the fact that the impact is identical for women and men. Finally, perhaps most in line with this theory is the gradual delinking of the legitimacy of married women's employment from perceptions about the costs of women's employment to their children. Because postmaterialist value theory attributes rising support for the legitimacy of married women's employment to a general rise in individualism rather than to changes in the actual roles and opportunities of the sexes, it posits a weakening of the link between norms and the perceptions that have traditionally provided a rationale for these norms. Inconsistent with the predictions of postmaterialist value theory, however, is the timing of cohort change observed in our results. Postmaterialist value theory predicts little or no change among cohorts growing to adulthood before World War II and dramatic change among subsequent cohorts. By contrast, our results suggest change already in progress among cohorts born shortly after the turn of the century and a slowing of change in postwar cohorts. Thus it would appear that many processes contribute to changes in gender role attitudes in Australia. Recent changes in these attitudes follow along the lines of rising employment for women, a destabilization of traditional family arrangements, and perhaps most of all the rise of individualistic values that are characteristic of postmaterialist society.

Notes

Support for the 1984 National Social Science Survey (NSSS) from the Australian Research Grants Committee and the Research School of Social Sciences in the Australian National University, and for the 1989 NSSS from the Australian Institute for Family Studies, the Standing Committee of Attorneys General, and the Research School of Social Sciences in the Australian National University is gratefully acknowledged.

1. According to some theorists (e.g., Becker 1981), the traditional deal has also become less attractive to men because they have lost their wives' full-time domestic services. This, however, ignores the gain in family income that arises when wives enter the labor force, something that may compensate husbands for the loss of wives' domestic services. Wives, in contrast, cannot be said to have gained much of anything with rising divorce and employment rates that might compensate them for the higher risk of losing access to their husband's income.

2. The restriction to citizens should not bias our results on the issues considered here, because prior research finds that the only substantial differences between citizens and non-citizens are that: (1) immigrants who enter as refugees take out citizenship faster than do other immigrants; (2) immigrants who have been in the country longer are more likely to have become citizens; and (3) immigrants from other English speaking countries are less likely to become citizens; see Evans 1988a; Kelley and McAllister, 1982.

3. In the most urban three-quarters of Australia, respondents were chosen using an area probability sample to select dwellings and a randomizing device (the Kish grid) to select individuals within chosen households; data were collected through face-to-face interviews. In rural areas selection was by simple random sample from the (compulsory) electoral register; data were collected via a postal questionnaire. The rural sampling frame necessarily omits those who had moved from the address they gave on the electoral roll and excludes noncitizens, except those of British origin who arrived in past years when Commonwealth citizens were eligible to vote in Australia. Extensive previous research indicates that these citizens differ little from noncitizens; duration of residence increases the probability of citizenship, but citizens do not differ from noncitizens in socioeconomic status, social integration, or political attitudes (Evans 1988a; Kelley and McAllister 1982). The response rate for the 1984 survey, defined to be completions as a percentage of completions plus refusals, was 67 percent (63 percent for urban interviews and, after five follow-ups, 79 percent in rural areas).

4. It used a simple random sample drawn by the electoral office from the (compulsory) electoral rolls. Sampled individuals were sent a questionnaire, addressed to them personally, followed about 10 days later by a thank-you/reminder letter. Nonrespondents were sent up to four more mailings over the next six months, including two mailings with fresh copies of the questionnaire, one by certified mail. The sampled population is thus persons who could be reached through the address they gave to the electoral register at some point over that six-month period. This excludes noncitizens, citizens who had moved without updating their address with the electoral register, individuals who left Australia for the entire survey period, unoccupied dwellings (Australian Bureau of Statistics figures indicate about 9 percent of dwellings are unoccupied at any one time), and dwellings occupied but not by the sampled individual. The (few dozen) respondents who were unable to complete a questionnaire because of lack of knowledge of English were also excluded (see Evans and Kelley 1991 for a description of Australian immigrants, their language skills, and their socioeconomic position). The 4,513 respondents to the 1989 NSSS represent a final response rate of 68 percent.

5. For example, in an instrumental variables analysis, Evans (forthcoming) shows that attitudes about married women's work are a key predictor of women's actual labor force participation.

6. We are unable to estimate the strength of the reciprocal pathways between these variables and the attitude scales because we lack the appropriate instrumental variables, that is, variables that are unambiguously exogenous to only one of the two jointly endogenous variables.

7. According to data from the International Social Survey Program (Evans 1990:4–48), at the end of the 1980s Australian perceptions of the cost to families of women's employment were middle-of-the-road among developed countries. Percentages agreeing with the statement "A working mother can establish just as warm and secure a relationship with her children ..." ranged from 52 percent in Hungary to 66 percent in the United States, compared to 57 percent in Australia; percentages disagreeing with or remaining undecided about whether "family life suffers when the woman has a full-time job" ranged from 37 percent in Hungary to 65 percent in the United States, with 50 percent in Australia.

8. In computing the predicted values, we set the value of all other variables in the equation at the sample mean for the post-1960 cohorts.

9. If close to 100 percent of Australian women viewed wives' working as morally legitimate, then the shrinking gender gap might be consistent with marital exchange theory because men's attitudes could be catching up with women's at the "end" of the gender role revolution. In 1989, however, although Australian women's support for married women's working was fairly high (69 percent), it remained a good distance from 100 percent.

References

Bean, Clive S. 1991. "Comparison of National Social Science Survey Data with the 1986 Census." *National Social Science Survey Report* 2:12–19.

Becker, Gary S. 1981. *Treatise on the Family.* Cambridge: Harvard University Press.

Chafetz, Janet Saltzman, and Anthony G. Dworkin. 1986. *Female Revolt: Women's Movements in World and Historical Perspective.* Totowa, NJ: Rowman and Allanheld.

Eccles, S. 1984. "Women in the Australian Labour Force." Pp. 80–93 in Dorothy Broom (ed.), *Unfinished Business.* Sydney: Allen & Unwin.

Evans, M.D.R. 1988a. "Choosing to be a Citizen: The Time Path of Citizenship in Australia." *International Migration Review* 22:243–64.

———. 1988b. "Working Wives in Australia: Influences of the Life Cycle, Education, and Feminist Ideology." Pp. 147–62 in Jonathan Kelley and Clive S. Bean (eds.), *Australian Attitudes.* Sydney: Allen & Unwin.

———. 1990. "Australian Family Values in International Perspective." Melbourne: Australian Institute for Family Studies.

———. Forthcoming. "Ideological, Economic, and Life-Course Influences on Women's Employment." *British Journal of Sociology.*

Evans, M.D.R., and Jonathan Kelley. 1991. "Prejudice and Discrimination in the Labor Market." *American Journal of Sociology* 97:721–59.

Feldman, Kenneth A., and Theodore M. Newcomb. 1969. *The Impact of College on Students.* San Francisco: Jossey-Bass.

Herzog, A. R., and Jerald G. Bachman. 1982. *Sex Role Attitudes Among High School Seniors.* Ann Arbor, MI: Institute for Social Research.

Huber, Joan, and Glenna Spitze. 1981. "Wife's Employment, Household Behaviors, and Sex-Role Attitudes." *Social Forces* 60:150–69.

———. 1983. *Sex Stratification: Children, Housework, and Jobs*. New York: Academic Press.
Hyman, Herbert H., and Charles R. Wright. 1979. *Education's Lasting Impact on Values*. Chicago: University of Chicago Press.
Inglehart, Ronald. 1977. *The Silent Revolution: Changing Values and Political Styles Among Western Publics*. Princeton, NJ: Princeton University Press.
———. 1990. *Culture Shift in Advanced Industrial Society*. Princeton, NJ: Princeton University Press.
Kelley, Jonathan. 1988. "Political Ideology in Australia." Pp. 58–80 in Jonathan Kelley and Clive S. Bean (eds.), *Australian Attitudes*. Sydney: Allen & Unwin.
Kelley, Jonathan, Robert G. Cushing, and Bruce Headey. 1988. *National Social Science Survey, First Round: 1984*. Canberra: Australian National University, Department of Sociology.
Kelley, Jonathan, and Ian McAllister. 1982. "The Decision to Become an Australian Citizen." *Australian and New Zealand Journal of Sociology* 18:428–39.
Lesthaeghe, Ron. 1983. "A Century of Demographic and Cultural Change in Western Europe: An Exploration of Underlying Dimensions." *Population and Development Review* 9:411–35.
Lesthaeghe, Ron, and Dominique Meekers. 1986. "Value Changes and the Dimensions of Familism in the European Community." *European Journal of Population* 2:225–68.
Lesthaeghe, Ron, and Johan Surkyn. 1988. "Cultural Dynamics and Economic Theories of Fertility Change." *Population and Development Review* 14:1–45.
Mason, Karen Oppenheim, and Larry Bumpass. 1975. "U.S. Women's Sex-Role Ideology, 1970." *American Journal of Sociology* 80:1212–9.
Mason, Karen Oppenheim, and Yu-hsia Lu. 1988. "Attitudes Toward Women's Familial Roles: Changes in the United States, 1977–1985." *Gender and Society* 2:39–57.
Mason, Karen Oppenheim, John L. Czajka, and Sara Arber. 1976. "Change in U.S. Women's Sex-Role Attitudes, 1964–1974." *American Sociological Review* 41:573–96.
McDonald, Peter. 1990. "The 1980s: Social and Economic Change Affecting Families." *Family Matters* 26:13–18.
Molm, Linda D. 1978. "Sex Role Attitudes and the Employment of Married Women." *Sociological Quarterly* 19:522–33.
Morgan, Carolyn Stout, and Alexis J. Walker. 1983. "Predicting Sex Role Attitudes." *Social Psychology Quarterly* 46:148–51.
Morgan, Mary. 1987. "The Impact of Religion on Gender-Role Attitudes." *Psychology of Women Quarterly* 11:301–10.
Newcomb, Theodore M. 1943. *Personality and Social Change*. New York: Dryden.
Presser, Harriet B. 1995. "Are the Interests of Women Inherently at Odds with the Interests of Children or the Family?" In Karen Oppenheim Mason and An-Magritt Jensen (eds.), *Gender and Family Change in Industrialized Countries*. Oxford: Clarendon Press.
Spitze, Glenna D., and Linda J. Waite. 1980. "Labor Force and Work Attitudes: Young Women's Early Experiences." *Sociology of Work and Occupations* 7:3–32.

Thornton, Arland, Duane F. Alwin, and Donald Camburn. 1983. "Causes and Consequences of Sex-Role Attitudes and Attitude Change." *American Sociological Review* 48:211–27.

Thornton, Arland, and Deborah Freedman. 1979. "Change in Sex Role Attitudes of Women." *American Sociological Review* 44:831–41.

Yates, Lyn. 1987. "Australian Research on Gender and Education." Pp. 241–68 in John P. Keeves (ed.), *Australian Education: Review of Recent Research.* Sydney: Allen & Unwin.

Appendix to Chapter 9

TABLE 9A.1 Significance Tests (T-Values) for Interactions: Men and Women, 1984 and 1989 NSSS, Treated Separately, with Linear Models

Independent Variable	Women 1984 vs. Men 1984	Women 1984 vs. Women 1989	Women 1984 vs. Men 1989	Men 1989 vs. Women 1989	Men 1984 vs. Men 1989	Women 1989 vs. Men 1989
Panel A. Dependent variable: Legitimacy of women's employment						
Education	−0.516	0.450	0.804	1.074	1.445	0.443
Mother worked	0.333	0.875	0.436	0.504	0.074	−0.472
Age	−0.507	1.535	3.846*	2.013*	4.253*	2.409*
Christian beliefs	−0.768	0.688	−0.397	1.475	0.413	−1.134
Career costs	0.186	−6.321*	−7.861*	−5.991*	−7.437*	−2.057*
Constant	0.935	0.763	0.933	−0.293	−0.131	0.194
Panel B. Dependent variable: Perceived career costs						
Education	−1.344	−1.691	−3.576*	−0.300	−2.334*	−2.186*
Mother worked	0.653	1.913	1.373	1.318	0.737	−0.619
Age	−0.604	−0.944	−3.179*	−0.366	−2.636*	−2.184*
Christian beliefs	−1.100	−2.149*	0.337	−1.220	1.532	2.586*
Constant	−0.110	2.471*	2.540*	2.792*	2.895*	−0.052

*$p < .05$

10

The Social Construction of Modern Intelligence: An Exploration of Gender-Differentiated Boundaries

William Tudor

The conceptualization of human intelligence as a product of sociocultural as well as psychobiological forces is well established. It is known that mental development occurs within socially structured environments; that these environments vary systematically in complex societies; that such variability is associated with variation in the levels and (arguably) types of intelligence produced. As Berger (1978:31–2) suggests, what is known as "intelligence" in the modern world is a "manifestation of a collective configuration of consciousness." As such, it coexists with other formations in the history of modern *mentalités*, an element of collective consciousness anchored in the structures of a given time and place.

This chapter explores one feature of the environments in which intelligence takes shape: the threshold level of social acceptance described by normative boundaries. It attempts to document a meaningful correspondence between patterns of variability in these boundaries and parallel patterns in the socioeconomic organization of late modern societies. The patterns on which it focuses are defined by the simple dichotomy of gender.

My guiding hypothesis is that gender-differentiated norms of intellectual development are related to gender-differentiated roles in the modern economy. The population on which I test this hypothesis may be identified roughly with the American baby boom. This population is treated not as an aggregate of individuals but as an organized grouping conceived collectively in terms of cultural configurations and institutional structures, including normative boundaries identifiable at societal and regional levels of analysis.

Gender and Norms of Mental Development

Assuming the mental development of a population is subject to social control through the definition of performance norms, I begin by examining the process by which such norms are defined and maintained in popular consciousness. Following Durkheim (1938), I look to the boundaries between "normal" and "deviant" behavior for insight into this process. In doing so, I focus on mental "retardation" as a label for the particular form of deviance marking the boundary between acceptable and unacceptable rates of intellectual development. Institutional reactions to retardation thus present themselves as elements of a boundary-maintenance process with potential to affect the development of normal as well as subnormal intelligence.

Boundary-Maintaining Rituals

Erikson (1966), Goffman (1961), and "societal reaction" theorists suggest that modern deviant-processing rites function in ways comparable to the religious rituals Durkheim (1915/1965) describes. These authors focus on deviant frames of mind conventionally attributed to "illness," but the insight seems applicable to "retardation" as well. From this point of view, the diagnosis and treatment of retardation provide occasions for the affirmation of cultural norms concerning intelligence. Through ambivalent identification with both authorities and deviants, participants in such rituals (including "the public" as audience) are presumed to experience vicariously both antisocial inclinations and their legitimate control.

Seen in this light, the periodic screening of marginal performers at school, the institutional sequestration of identified "retardates," even playground torments, become interpretable as ritual processes. As such, they may function to maintain minimal levels of commitment to the goals and established procedures of intellectual development.

There seems little doubt that the boundary between "normal" and "retarded" is known to most children. Goodman (1990) reports that a majority in her sample of normal third-graders had learned to distinguish the category "retarded" from that of merely "dumb." Most of her sample attributed some capacity for improvement through personal effort to the latter category but denied this to the retarded. Although children express feelings of sympathy (Budoff and Siperstein 1982; Kyle and Davies 1991), several studies document the low status, even stigma, assigned retarded children by their peers, as well as negative attitudes toward academic incompetence (Budoff and Siperstein 1978, 1982; Goodman 1990; Levinson and Starling 1981). Popular attitudes among both children and adults are evident in the pejorative evolution of formerly clinical labels such as "moron," "imbecile," and "idiot."

Thus in everyday understandings and experiences one finds the makings of a meaningful if mundane degradation ceremony: an identifiably degraded status, concerning which children demonstrate both knowledge and social distance; an authoritative apparatus of status assignment, extending from the classroom teacher upward through layers of increasing medicoscientific expertise; certified theoreticians, evaluative instruments, technical terminology; buildings and inmates, licensed by the state. In theory, at least, the ritual process constituted from these elements seems capable of giving collective expression to developmental norms. Theoretically, such expressions may become internalized, contributing shape and import to the generalized others in relation to which children form images of self.

Modern Industrial Intelligence

It is a commonplace that the details of this process describe specifically modern phenomena.[1] Writers as diverse as Braverman (1975:181) and Parsons (1971:110) suggest that socialized competence becomes increasingly defined as a generalized resource in modern societies. Predictable supplies of such competence, including "abstract labor" at lower class levels and abstract "intelligence" at higher levels, may depend on the maintenance of formalized screening procedures, involving the quantitative measurement and evaluation of school-age populations by technical specialists.

Giddens (1991:20) regards such procedures as constitutive of the institutional reflexivity distinguishing "high modernity" from other forms of social organization. Through the routine surveillance of their populations amid other productive resources, modern societies create self-referential knowledge at the system level, resulting in distinctively modern capacities for social planning and change. Thus if abstract "intelligence" describes an especially salient resource for modern societies, the institutional surveillance of intelligence seems peculiarly modern, too. And reactions to perceptible retardation in the development of this resource take the typically modern form of a process of quality control.

At the heart of this process lies a bookkeeping function whose residues include official records of subnormal development. These may be interpreted as straightforward tallies of deviant mentalities or, as Kitsuse and Cicourel (1963:136-7) note, "in terms of the deviant-processing activities of [specifiable] organizations." In this chapter I presume that relevant records describe both population attributes and sociocultural processes. They will be analyzed below as reflections of a compound phenomenon created through the interaction of psychobiological populations with boundary rituals of surveillance and social control.

Gender Differences in Reported Rates

Reports from a variety of advanced capitalist societies consistently describe more retarded males than females. This disparity characterizes the epidemiological literature (see Lapouse and Weitzner's 1970 review of older studies; McLaren and Bryson's 1987 review of more recent ones); the literature describing teacher referrals for clinical evaluation (Berk, Bridges, and Shih 1981; Mercer 1973); studies of actual placement into programs for the retarded following clinical evaluation (Berk, Bridges, and Shih 1981; Mercer 1973; Richardson, Katz, and Koller 1986); and summaries of institutional statistics describing the clientele of various types of treatment facility (Singer and Osborn 1970; Tudor, Tudor, and Gove 1979). The consistently repeated fact of this difference provides the central empirical datum to be elaborated below.

While males are generally thought to be more vulnerable to psychobiological causes of retardation (e.g., chromosomal abnormalities and maturational problems, whether biological or psychological), the data are difficult to explain entirely in terms of sex-linked differences in individual attributes. Several studies note that the overrepresentation of males is more pronounced at milder levels of retardation, with sex ratios among the severely retarded approaching those of the normal population (McLaren and Bryson 1987). This is hard to explain as the simple result of a presumed constitutional weakness and generalized vulnerability of the male organism. Similar complications are presented by reports that IQ scores among the retarded are higher for males than for females (Richardson, Katz, and Koller 1986).

One clue to interpreting these reports can be found in the definition of retardation provided by the American Association on Mental Deficiency (Heber 1961; Grossman 1973). For purposes of administrative classification, retardation is defined in terms of two interdependent qualities: clinically measured intelligence, and adaptive behavior. "Measured intelligence" is operationally defined by IQ tests constructed with the specific aim of neutralizing sex differences. "Adaptive behavior" is conceptualized as the degree to which one meets "the standards of personal independence and social responsibility expected of his age and cultural group" (Grossman 1973:11). Appraisals of this quality thus depend on the definition of performance standards for relevant reference groups, as well as on individual capacities. In practice and at the milder levels that account for most cases, these appraisals are strongly colored by classroom performances at school (Richardson, Katz, and Koller 1986).

Richardson, Katz, and Koller (1986) report that several studies defining retardation solely in terms of IQ fail to describe higher rates for males, while studies including "adaptive behavior" in their definition generally do.[2] They conclude that sex differences in these rates reflect appraisals of school performance or adaptive behavior defined relative to "the standards of ... [one's] group." Although the evidence is equivocal, others, too, have speculated that reported rates reflect gender-specific standards of intelligence (McLaren and Bryson 1987; Richardson, Koller, and Katz 1986; Tudor, Tudor, and Gove 1979). The complex interaction effects reported by Singer and Osborn (1970) seem difficult to interpret otherwise. In a study of all first admissions to inpatient treatment in southwestern Ontario over a five-year period, these authors found that sex differentials in the IQ scores of retarded children were greater among those of school age; and that at this age, but not earlier, social class was positively related to the IQ scores of retarded boys, but not to the scores of retarded girls. They interpret these findings in terms of childhood normative environments rather than psychobiological traits, speculating that greater performance expectations lead to higher thresholds of minimally acceptable competence (1) at higher socioeconomic levels, (2) in the school system, (3) for males.

It is tempting to summarize these data in Berger's (1978) terms: The more closely one approaches central structures of modernity, the greater the expectation that one should display the configuration of consciousness called modern "intelligence."[3] On the assumption that proximity to the modern core varies by gender, social class, and involvement in modern school systems, the corollary would explain Singer and Osborn's (1970) findings: The closer to the core, the greater the degree of deviance attributed to any given level of psychobiological retardation. In terms of the conceptual framework outlined above, one might expect modern forms of boundary maintenance, effected through modern screening processes, to be more rigorous in social settings and strata where intelligent behavior is thought to be more consequential for modern society.

Interpreted in this light, the literature on retardation suggests the following research expectations, presented here in the language of one-tailed hypotheses.

(1) Hypothesis: Higher standards of "normal intellectual development" are associated with more strategically located strata, operationally defined here by the stratum of males.

(2) Hypothesis: Different standards of development for different genders may be explained by gender-differentiated access to the central structures of modernity.[4]

Although these hypotheses derive from the literature reviewed above, other interpretations of the same empirical regularities have been advanced with equal plausibility. If the rates under discussion were presumed to reflect a simple mapping of psychobiological capacities into the record books, sex differences might be interpreted as straightforward reflections of complex psychological and/or biological differences. It seems unlikely but nevertheless conceivable, as Vandenberg (1987) suggests, that the entire surplus of retarded males in these statistics is due to X-linked genetic retardation. Others hypothesize that male populations exhibit greater variability in cognitive capacities more generally, which might explain higher rates of male retardation even in the absence of any difference in central tendency (Shields 1982; Feingold 1992). The variety of psychobiological interpretations for these rates is remarkable and cannot be dismissed simply because interpretive underpinnings are non-sociological.[5]

Method of Analysis

Without denying the force of biological and psychological explanations, the following analysis attempts to hold those forces constant statistically. Only then can reported rates be assumed to measure the impact of normative expectations with any accuracy. The analytic strategy will be to model the process by which these rates are produced, and to do so in a manner such that a fit between model and data depends on an index of boundary maintenance defined independently of psychobiological attributes. If the rate-producing process can be modeled in this way, then the residue it leaves in the record books may yield information about gender-differentiated intellectual boundaries disentangled from the organic and mental developments ostensibly measured by reported rates.

Empirical Data

The research focuses on a range of diagnostic events involving the authoritative labeling of patients as "mentally retarded" by licensed medical facilities. Such facilities keep track of different types of events, depending on whether service is provided on an inpatient or outpatient basis and whether provided in a general hospital or not.[6] Data describing "first admissions" are used where available here, in order to maximize the degree to which these events reflect levels of symbolism comparable to the "degradation ceremonies" Goffman (1961:139) portrays in his discussion of admission rituals in mental hospitals.

Relevant data from a total of 2,646 public and private facilities of various types are aggregated below to form a rough measure of annual incidence in the population overall.[7] Data were reported to the National Institutes of Mental Health (NIMH) by a self-selecting sample of all known U.S. institutions, hospitals, and clinics treating mental retardation in 1968.[8] Age-specific rates for the U.S. population are calculated from these reports, on the basis of which the hypothetical experience of an artificial cohort is described as if it were aging in time.[9] The youth of this cohort is a synthetic construction based on a cross-section of the baby boom's school years: Children entering kindergarten in 1968 were born before Kennedy's assassination, while those in college were born with Levittown. This generation, aged five to twenty at the time of data collection, accounted for roughly 60 percent of the 23,084 diagnostic events to be analyzed here.

Table 10.1 estimates the incidence of these diagnostic events for various segments of the U.S. population specified by age, sex, and level of measured intelligence.[10] As indicated by male-to-female ratios in this table, rates of diagnosis for males generally exceed those for females. This is true at both levels of severity, for nearly all age groups. The analytic problem presented by this finding is that various possible causes of the disparity are commingled here, confounding all attempts to distinguish gender-differentiated norms of intellectual development, for example, from sex-linked differences in organic or cognitive growth.

Modeling the Rate-Producing Process

In attempting to circumvent this problem and isolate a measure of normative boundaries, the data of Table 10.1 are employed below to estimate parameters for a model describing the lifetime of a hypothetical cohort subject to age-specific rates of diagnosis like those in the table. This model decomposes the rate-producing process into analytically separable parts: a "developmental" component and a "constant" one.

The developmental component describes a medical model of retardation conceived as a psychobiological phenomenon. Following numerous others (Fisher and Zeaman 1970; Lapouse and Weitzner 1970; Lemkau and Imre 1969; Scott, Greenfield, and Partridge 1989), the design of this component assumes that the prevalence of relevant symptoms in the population changes during some developmental period, independently of the labeling process through which symptoms become recognized, diagnosed, and reported to agencies like the NIMH.[11] For reasons of parsimony, the model assumes a constant rate of change.[12] Although the American Association on Mental Deficiency (AAMD) describes a span extending 16 to 18 years from birth, no constraint is imposed on the

TABLE 10.1 Diagnoses of Retardation in the United States by Age, Sex, and Severity, 1968

Severity	0–4	5–9	10–14	15–17	18–19	20–24	25–34	35–44	45–54	55+	Age Stdzd.
Mild											
Male											
Number	385	1,212	1,553	1,033	496	703	680	419	268	166	
Rate[a]	66	190	258	281	210	138	82	50	34	14	106
Female											
Number	256	572	918	713	317	521	556	422	264	170	
Rate[a]	40	94	151	203	138	96	66	51	33	12	69
M/F (rate)	1.65	2.02	1.71	1.38	1.52	1.44	1.24	0.98	1.03	1.17	1.54
Severe											
Male											
Number	551	1,128	578	285	123	179	172	117	67	72	
Rate[a]	107	153	85	73	49	35	20	14	8	6	49
Female											
Number	447	771	454	194	83	113	135	122	87	48	
Rate[a]	92	109	67	50	34	22	15	14	10	3	38
M/F (rate)	1.16	1.40	1.27	1.46	1.44	1.59	1.33	1.00	0.80	2.00	1.30
All levels											
Both sexes											
Number	2,554	4,691	4,647	2,863	1,337	1,968	1,996	1,422	941	665	
Rate[a]	195	314	327	354	260	177	115	82	56	24	160

[a] Rates per million are calculated from the aggregation of first admissions to institutions for the mentally retarded and mentally ill, discharges from general hospitals, and terminations after treatment in outpatient psychiatric clinics, after adjusting for under-reporting to the NIMH.

Sources: NIMH 1968:6, 29, 56–8, 153–5, 250–2, 302, 306; Tudor, Tudor, and Gove 1979: table 2.

model, which estimates the duration of this period from the data.[13] In later years the model assumes a constant prevalence rate.[14]

Thus the developmental component of the model, conceived to represent a minimalist version of the clinical perspective, rests on three parameters to be estimated from empirical data: (1) the length of the developmental period, (2) the rate of change in prevalence during that period, and (3) the level of presumably constant prevalence afterwards. Figure 10.1 portrays this component of the model schematically. Given numerical values for the three parameters indicated there, hypothetical prevalence rates for any cohort may be calculated at each age of its lifetime.[15]

Figure 10.1 models the prevalence of retardation conceived independently of any social recognition or labeling. If the rate-producing process consisted of a transparent translation of population attributes into government statistics, Table 10.1 would measure no more than this. On the assumption that a sociocultural "screening function" operates on psychobiological prevalence, however, an additional process must be described. This is the process through which traits become recognized, labeled, and treated as symptoms of retarded development.

FIGURE 10.1 Age Distribution of Psychobiological Prevalence as Assumed by Model

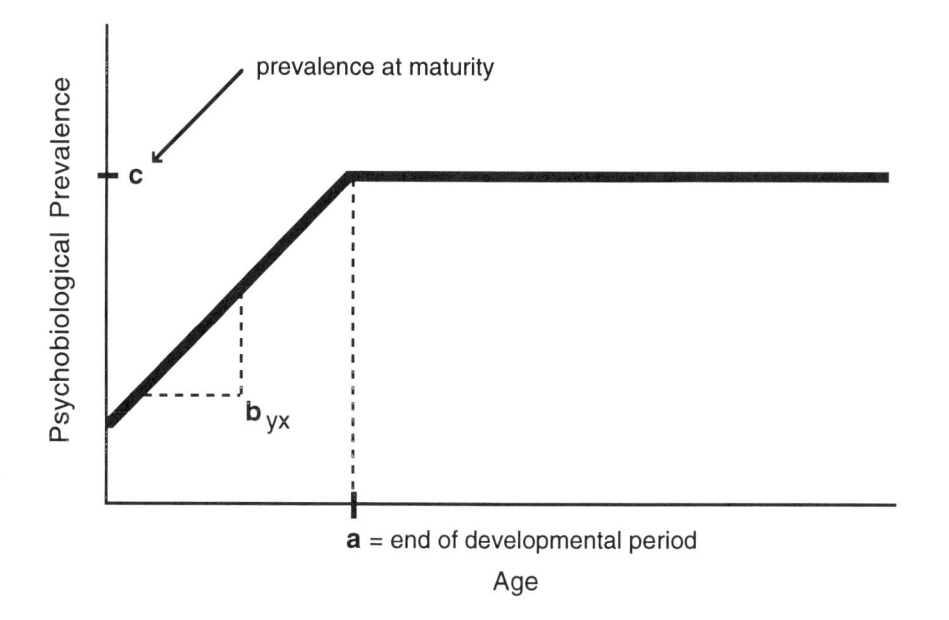

A minimal model of this process consists of the assumption that institutional reactions to deviant behavior take the form of a filter operating at constant intensity throughout a cohort's lifetime. One might picture a developing pool of psychobiological properties interacting with an age-blind screening process, such that some constant proportion of previously unlabeled "clinical retardation" gets diagnosed during any given year.[16] A fourth parameter, consisting of a constant screening rate, may thus be added to those above, providing a connecting link between the developmental process modeled in Figure 10.1 and the data described by Table 10.1. As a measure of boundary rituals distinguishing normal from subnormal intelligence, this rate describes the focus of the following analysis.

Societal Reactions to Retardation

Estimating National Screening Rates

Given values for all four parameters described above, hypothetical rates of diagnosis may be predicted for any given period of a cohort's life. Table 10.2A compares empirically observed rates from Table 10.1 with expected rates derived from the model's best fit to the data. The first row of this table presents best-fitting estimates for observations described in the second row.[17] As can be seen in the third row, these estimates are consistently lower than observed rates at conventional ages of entry into the school system and the labor force, and in older age groups.[18] Overall, however, the model explains more than 90 percent of the variability observed in age-specific rates of diagnosis.[19]

Table 10.2B describes values for the four parameters on which the fit between data and model is based. If one assumed a population in which each birth cohort included some initial pool of "psychobiological retardation" which subsequently expanded at the rate of 466 per million per year until age 15; that this pool remained at a constant prevalence of 9,029 per million in the population beyond that age; and that during each year of the cohort's lifetime, 7.25 percent of those in the pool who had not yet received institutional treatment became diagnosed in one of the facilities represented in Table 10.1—then rates of diagnosis observed in annual cohorts by those facilities would be as described by the prediction line in Figure 10.2. Applying these annual rates to a population with the age structure of the United States in 1970, age-specific rates for larger groupings would be as predicted in Table 10.2A. These predictions closely approximate the actual rates calculated from NIMH data for those age-groups in the U.S. population at that time.[20]

Although Table 10.2 permits rejection of the null hypothesis that rates of diagnosis are unrelated to age, that is not the primary interest here.

TABLE 10.2 Decomposition of Observed Rates of Diagnosis for Mental Retardation: U.S. Total, Both Sexes, All Levels of Severity

A. Age-Specific Rates (per million)

Rates	0–4	5–9	10–14	15–17	18–19	20–24	25–34	35–44	45–54	55+
Predicted	206	288	343	327	271	210	123	57	27	9
Observed	195	314	327	354	260	177	115	82	56	24
Difference	11	−26	16	−27	11	33	8	−25	−29	−15

B. Parameters

Developmental Period	Annual Rate of Change	Prevalance at Maturity	Annual Screening Rate	Adjusted R^2	p
15 yr.	466/yr.	9,029	7.25%	.93	.001[a]

[a] $F_{(3,6)} = 51.928$

FIGURE 10.2 Observed and Predicted Rates of Diagnosis for Mental Retardation: Both Sexes, All Levels of Severity

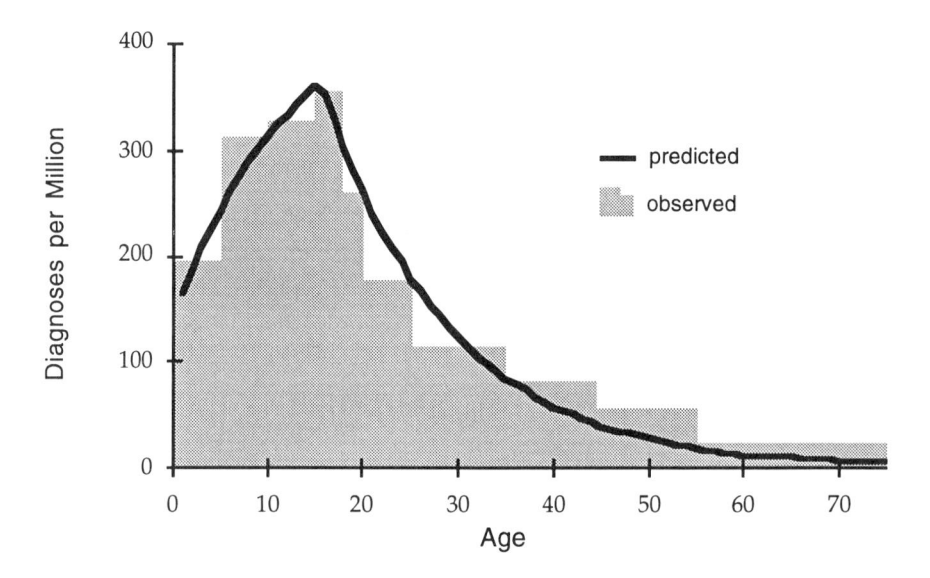

Essentially, the significance level ($p < .001$) tells us that the model provides better predictions of age-specific incidence than would a crude rate of incidence for the population as a whole. Beyond meeting this threshold condition, the analysis aims to construct an index measuring the rigor of boundary maintenance while holding constant a variety of developmental phenomena.

On its face, the screening rate of 7.25 percent in Table 10.2B provides such an index, with potential values ranging between zero and 100 percent. Whether this index as an empirical measure has the meaning ascribed to it by virtue of its role in the model above is a question that reaches beyond tests of significance. A brief consideration of its validity may be found in Appendix B.

Estimating Gender-Specific Screening Rates

Assuming the screening rate does tap sociocultural constancies associated with normative boundaries, and assuming measurement error is randomly distributed across comparison groups, a comparison of screening rates for different genders should permit evaluation of the hypothesis that boundaries of "normal intellectual development" are gender-specific. Speculation in the literature has suggested that standards for males may be more rigorous. If so, then ratios of male-to-female screening rates should be greater than unity.

Previous research also suggests that if gender-differentiated screening does exist, the difference should be more pronounced near the boundaries of normality. Theoretically, this is where marginal differences in minimal expectations would have their greatest impact. Empirically, it is where differences are most frequently reported in the literature. The expectation would be that the ratio of screening rates should be higher in the case of "mild" as opposed to "severe" retardation.

These expectations find support in Table 10.3, which describes the model's application to rates of diagnosis calculated separately for each gender and level of severity.[21] In three out of four independent applications, the model explains over 97 percent of the variance in reported rates across age groups. The remaining application (mild retardation among females) produces a looser fit but still attains statistical significance.

Best-fitting parameters in Table 10.3 describe a clear difference between male and female screening rates in the case of mild retardation, and in the expected direction. The table indicates that if 1,000 clinically retarded but as yet untreated males were subject to the societal screening that best predicts the rates reported in Table 10.1, then on an annual basis over the course of a lifetime, roughly 86 would be diagnosed as "mildly retarded" in an average year. And if 1,000 similarly retarded females were similarly screened, roughly 62 (or an average 6.18 percent annually) would be diagnosed each year. It should be noted that these rates are defined independently of whatever difference might exist between male and female prevalence rates. The disparity between gender-specific probabilities of diagnosis is quantified in the male-to-female ratio of screening rates (M/F = 1.39).

It is notable that among the severely retarded, no such disparity exists between screening rates. The sex ratio of 1.00 suggests that the probability of being diagnosed "severely" retarded is unrelated to gender, once differences in prevalence are controlled. Thus for both mild and severe retardation, the configuration of screening rates is consistent with prior expectations.

Table 10.3 also describes parameters designed to reflect the prevalence of retardation conceived in terms of a medical model. At both levels of measured intelligence, the model describes more males than females among those possessing the clinical indicia of retardation. This is consistent with speculation concerning sex-linked biological anomalies, learning disabilities, and other maturational abnormalities.[22] Growth in the prevalence of these disparate sources of deviance appears to be more rapid for males, and more so among the severely retarded, as indicated by rates of change in Table 10.3. But by the end of childhood, sex ratios of

TABLE 10.3 Decomposition of Observed Rates of Diagnosis, U.S. Total Specified by Sex and Severity

	Age								
Severity	0–4	5–9	10–14	15–17	18–19	20–24	25–34	35–44	45–54	55+

Severity	0–4	5–9	10–14	15–17	18–19	20–24	25–34	35–44	45–54	55+
Mild										
Male										
Predicted	68	186	260	269	214	158	84	33	14	4
Observed	66	190	258	281	210	138	82	50	34	14
Female										
Predicted	32	104	157	172	146	118	75	39	21	8
Observed	40	94	151	203	138	96	66	51	33	12
Severe										
Male										
Predicted	107	150	95	65	51	38	20	8	3	1
Observed	107	153	85	73	49	35	20	14	8	6
Female										
Predicted	92	108	68	47	37	27	14	5	2	1
Observed	92	109	67	50	34	22	15	14	10	3

	Developmental Period	Annual Rate of Change	Prevalence at Maturity	Annual Screening Rate	Adjusted R^2	p
Mild						
Male	15.5 yrs.	393/yr.	5,962	8.62%	.97	.001
Female	15.5 yrs.	299/yr.	4,413	6.18%	.88	.001
M/F		1.31	1.35	1.39		
Severe						
Male	5 yrs.	483/yr.	2,555	8.85%	.98	.001
Female	5 yrs.	294/yr.	1,919	8.85%	.97	.001
M/F		1.64	1.33	1.00		

prevalence rates for both mild and severe retardation have stabilized at roughly four males per three females.

The remaining parameter described in Table 10.3 shows no difference between sexes but obvious differences between mild and severe retardation. The developmental period for mild retardation extends into the sixteenth year, while for severe retardation it ends at age five. In essence, the model implies that a five-year-old who is not yet retarded might subsequently become "mildly" retarded but not "severely" so. This fits common conceptions of etiology.

While these developmental parameters describe extraneous influences to be held constant here for analytic purposes, they provide evidence of the model's capacity to capture relevant features of the real world. This lends credence to its description of screening rates. In this context it may be noted that the pattern of sex ratios in Table 10.3 displays theoretically meaningful differences between screening and prevalence rates. Differential screening is a function of distance from normative boundaries in this analysis (as indicated by differences between screening sex ratios at mild versus severe levels of retardation), while differential prevalence is not. This makes sense if "screening" refers to normative boundaries, and "prevalence" does not.

Table 10.4 pursues the primary finding of Table 10.3, which is that probabilities of diagnosis near the margins of normality differ by gender. The table tests the null hypothesis that this difference reflects random variability among the mildly retarded rather than systematically more rigorous screening for males. This is a one-tailed test of the central hypothesis emerging from literature reviewed earlier.

The test here consists of a comparison of two versions of the general model above.[23] These are distinguished from one another by the fact that one version assumes gender-differentiated screening, while the other does not. They are identical otherwise. Both versions assume the same developmental period for males and females and the same prevalence rate at birth.[24] Both versions assume sex-differentiated rates of prevalence at maturity. Model 1 in this table, which estimates a single screening rate whether male or female, explains a significant proportion of variability in the age-specific rates described by Table 10.1.[25] Model 2, which estimates gender-specific screening rates as well as separate prevalence rates, explains an additional 21 percent of the residual variability not explained by Model 1.[26] This represents a statistically significant increase in explanatory power, permitting rejection of the null hypothesis that the ratio of screening rates is less than or equal to unity.

In sum, this analysis demonstrates that gender differences in reported rates at the national level may be decomposed into component parts. There is a developmental difference that culminates in different rates of

TABLE 10.4 Comparison of Two Models for Decomposing Observed Rates of Mild Retardation

	Model 1	Model 2
Prevalence at Maturity		
Male	6,159	5,953
Female	3,968	4,441
M/F	1.55	1.34
Annual Screening Rate		
Male	7.87%	8.64%
Female	7.87%	6.13%
M/F	1.00	1.41
Explained Sum of Squares	122,551	123,485
(df)	(5)	(6)
Residual Sum of Squares	4504	3570
(df)	(15)	(14)
Adjusted R^2	.95[a]	.96[a]
Model 1 versus Model 2		
Incremental PRE	–	.21
$t_{(14)}$	–	1.914[b]

[a] $p < .001$ ($F > 80.0$)
[b] one-tailed $p < .05$

Note: Both models assume sex-differentiated prevalence rates at maturity. Model 1 assumes a single unisex screening rate, while Model 2 does not.

"prevalence at maturity." And there is a difference between constant "screening rates." The developmental difference is found at both levels of retardation. Among the severely retarded, it explains essentially all the difference between male and female rates in Table 10.1. At milder levels, however, gender differences exist that cannot be explained by the developmental processes modeled here. Holding constant all variation explicable in terms of different prevalence rates, significant gender differences remain to be explained by screening rates.

The interpretation of these findings relies on the assumption that cultural definitions of gender exhibit important constancies across all ages, while bodies and minds (especially for children) are essentially developing. Given this assumption, age-invariant differences between male and female screening rates are interpreted as reflections of gender-specific norms, while differing prevalence rates are isolated analytically in an effort to control psychobiological differences.[27]

So interpreted, the data provide evidence of gender-differentiated boundaries to normal intelligence. Males in this analysis appear more likely to become the focus of societal reactions that function, in theory, to reinforce popular commitment to established norms of intellectual development. This finding stands independently of the differences measured by prevalence rates.

Subsocietal Reactions

In pursuing possible explanations for this finding, the following analysis applies the model above to NIMH data organized within separate census divisions.[28] These are conceived as geographically circumscribed systems, differently situated with respect to the central structures of modernity. While limitations imposed by sample size and the quality of regional data are severe, these systems possess a critical advantage over the national system as units of analysis: They highlight regional variability in the rates under examination, permitting an interpretation informed by the analysis of structural correlates.[29]

In compensating for the loss of information at this level, only two parameters are estimated from regional data: prevalence and screening rates. The length of the developmental period, together with the rate of prevalence at the beginning of this period, remains fixed for all regions at national levels determined from analysis of more finely grained data.[30] Table 10.5 describes values for the parameters estimated from 18 independent applications of this modified model to regional data.[31] Over all nine regions, this set of parameters explains 98 percent of sample variability in age-specific rates among males and 97 percent among females.[32]

Consistent with the analysis of national data above, both prevalence and screening rates are higher for males in this table. Weighted averages of these two rates across all regions are comparable to the rates estimated from national data in Table 10.2; and sex ratios computed from these averages deviate only slightly from the ratios for mild retardation in Table 10.3. Regional data thus appear capable of supporting informative comparisons at the lower bounds of normal development, despite occasionally poor fits between an abbreviated model and coarsely grained data.[33]

Explaining Regional Variation in Screening Rates

Within the conceptual framework introduced earlier, gender describes one among several structures mediating relationships between normative

TABLE 10.5 Decomposition of Regional Rates by Sex, All Levels of Severity Combined

A. Age-Standardized Rates of Diagnosis (per million)[a]

	N. Eng.[b]	Mid. Atl.	ENC	WNC	S. Atl.	ESC	WSC	Mtn.	Pac.	U.S. Total
Male	192	143	124	238	210	136	217	161	137	167
Female	155	96	93	162	150	115	162	98	114	122
M/F	1.24	1.49	1.33	1.47	1.40	1.18	1.34	1.64	1.20	1.37

B. Parameters

	N. Eng.[b]	Mid. Atl.	ENC	WNC	S. Atl.	ESC	WSC	Mtn.	Pac.	Wtd. Avg[c]
Prevalence										
Male	10,324	8,124	7,012	12,167	11,760	9,120	12,624	8,289	6,895	9,978
Female	9,424	5,594	5,260	8,858	9,392	7,632	10,280	5,242	5,429	7,120
M/F	1.10	1.45	1.33	1.37	1.25	1.20	1.23	1.58	1.27	1.40
Screening										
Male	7.91%	7.26%	6.80%	9.25%	6.24%	4.47%	6.33%	8.14%	12.0%	7.47%
Female	4.93%	5.69%	5.07%	6.43%	4.57%	4.23%	4.47%	6.74%	12.2%	5.80%
M/F	1.61	1.28	1.34	1.44	1.37	1.06	1.42	1.21	0.98	1.29

[a] Observed and predicted age-specific rates for each region may be found in Appendix C, Table 10A.2.
[b] Regions are defined by the standard U.S. Census divisions: N. Eng. (Maine, New Hampshire, Vermont, Massachusetts, Rhode Island, Connecticut; Mid. Atl. (New York, New Jersey, Pennsylvania); ENC (Ohio, Indiana, Illinois, Michigan, Wisconsin); WNC (Minnesota, Iowa, Missouri, North Dakota, South Dakota, Nebraska); S. Atl. (Delaware, Maryland, District of Columbia, Virginia, West Virginia, North Carolina, South Carolina, Georgia, Florida); ESC (Kentucky, Tennessee, Alabama, Mississippi); WSC (Arkansas, Louisiana, Oklahoma, Texas); Mtn. (Montana, Idaho, Wyoming, Colorado, New Mexico, Arizona, Utah, Nevada); and Pac. (Washington, Oregon, California, Alaska, Hawaii).
[c] Weights for calculating average prevalence rates consist of the estimated numbers of psychobiologically retarded people aged 16+ in each region (i.e., the sex-specific regional population, age 16+, multiplied by the sex-specific regional prevalence rate). Weights for calculating average screening rates consist of regional populations of a given sex, age 16+, in 1970.

boundaries and the institutional underpinnings of modernity. If that conceptualization is appropriate here, other structures than gender might explain regional differences in boundary maintenance. By doing so, they could provide external validation for the operationalization of boundary maintenance employed in this analysis. And the conceptualization of gender as an instance of some more general class of mediating structures might be clarified.

In describing the structural correlates of IQ, Berger (1978:40) speculates that "upper-middle-class homes mediate to children the consciousness appropriate to [modernity] in much better ways than do working-class or even lower-middle-class homes." Her focus on stratification in this context is supported by the work of Kohn and his associates, who describe "intellectual flexibility" as one among several psychological variables correlated with socioeconomic status. Although they do not investigate standards of intellectual development directly, Kohn and Schoenbach (1983) examine both cognitive functioning and associated performance norms as related to various dimensions of socioeconomic status. It is not a far step from their findings to speculate that standards of cognitive development might accompany the psychological complex of self-concept, cognitive style, and parental values they describe (see their table 7.2).

If developmental norms are reflected in screening rates, then variability in these rates at the regional level might be related to the same dimensions of stratification Kohn and Schoenbach (1983) emphasize. Taking the individual as their unit of analysis, they focus on educational attainment and occupational complexity. Extrapolated to the system level, thir work suggests the one-tailed hypothesis that regional screening rates in Table 10.5 are *positively* correlated with regional concentrations of higher education and occupational complexity.

Variation in prevalence rates can also be observed in Table 10.5. These rates, too, may be correlated with socioeconomic indexes. Tarjan (1970:749) notes considerable geographic variability in mild retardation during the period under analysis, estimating that 80 percent of all cases are found in impoverished areas. Possible explanations include substandard nutrition and medical care; exposure to toxic substances; familial, neighborhood, and educational degradation; and subcultural variability in configurations of collective consciousness. Thus if the parameters in Table 10.5 correctly distinguish psychobiological attributes from normative expectations, prevalence may be *negatively* correlated with regional concentrations of socioeconomic resources.

In short, there is reason to expect that the two major components of recorded rates (i.e., screening and prevalence rates) will be oppositely correlated with relevant socioeconomic variables. In regions where more modern institutional forms and resource levels prevail, the prevalence of deviant mental development (measured by modern standards) should be lower. But in those same regions, intellectual expectations phrased in modern terms should be higher; inclinations and capacities to consult and pay for modern diagnostic services should be more widespread; and modern forms of surveillance and screening should be more rigorous.

Table 10.6 describes ecological correlations between selected socioeconomic indexes and the regional rates described by Table 10.5. Occupation here describes proportions of the regional labor force in managerial, technical, and professional positions, thus providing an index of engagement with modern technology and bureaucracy at strategic levels. Education describes regional concentrations of human capital at post-secondary school levels. Median income provides a crude measure of access to the material and cultural resources of a capitalist society. As system properties, these variables describe the articulation of regional populations and structures with supra-regional systems of modernity, not individual statuses. Like the dependent variables for this table, they are measured in gender-specific terms.

Correlations between the age-standardized rates of Table 10.5A and these socioeconomic indexes are generally weak in the left-hand columns of Table 10.6, and they fail to reach conventional levels of significance. Correlations between the component parts of observed rates and the same socioeconomic indexes, however, reveal more complex interrelations. Screening rates are strongly correlated with regional concentrations of the typically modern capital resources described by Table 10.6. As expected, these relationships are positive, and in opposite direction to the negative relationships with prevalence rates.[34] The greater the density of higher-status occupations, college certification, and personal income in a region, the higher its screening rates—and the lower its prevalence rates. Although correlations with prevalence rates are generally insignificant, they are in the direction hypothesized.

Not surprisingly, given these findings, further analysis reveals negative correlations between prevalence rates and screening rates. Although the relationship is spurious for males, presumably reflecting the hypothesized impact of socioeconomic forces on both prevalence and screening rates, the situation for females is less clear-cut.[35] In recognition of the possibility that relationships between socioeconomic variables and screening rates above may be contaminated by mutual relations with prevalence rates, Figure 10.3 summarizes the more significant findings of Table 10.6 after adjusting for regional differences in prevalence. The dependent variable here describes regional screening rates in terms of residual deviations from the prediction lines defined by gender-specific regressions on regional prevalence rates.[36] The independent variable is a composite index

TABLE 10.6 Correlations of Regional Indicators with Rates of Diagnosis and Their Component Parts

Socioeconomic Indicator (1970)	Age-Standardized Rates		Prevalence Rates		Screening Rates	
	Male	Female	Male	Female	Male	Female
% prof./tech./mgr.[a]						
Male	-.17	-.24	-.43	-.43	.72*	.63*
Female	.14	.01	-.09	-.20	.70*	.65*
% 16+ yrs. education[b]						
Male	-.07	-.13	-.32	-.31	.73*	.63*
Female	.02	-.07	-.24	-.27	.76*	.69*
Median income[c]						
Male	-.39	-.42	-.62*	-.58	.61*	.47
Female	-.38	-.34	-.54	-.44	.50	.44

* one-tailed $p < .05$
[a] Base for % professional/technical/managerial occupations = those of a given gender, age 16+, in the labor force.
[b] Base for % with 16+ years of education = those of a given gender, age 25+.
[c] Median income is calculated for those of a given gender, age 18+, with income.

Source: U.S. Bureau of the Census 1973: tables 156, 157, 161, 165, 166, 344.

FIGURE 10.3   Screening Rates by Education and Occupational Structure

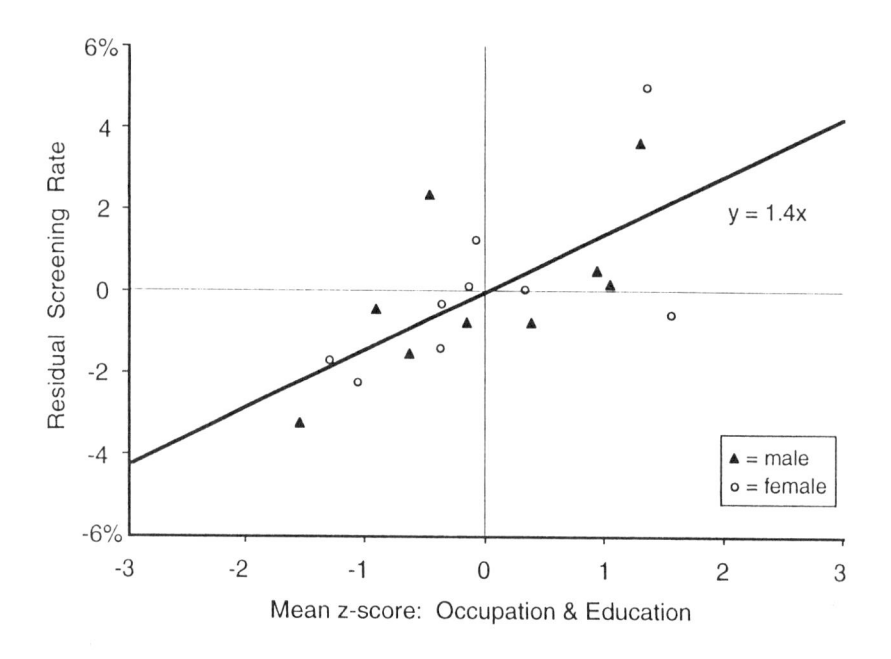

Note: Screening rates are measured in terms of residual deviations from regressions on gender-specific prevalence rates. Occupation and education are measured in terms of standard deviations from gender-specific means. See Appendix C, Table 10A.1.

formed from standardized z-scores describing the educational and occupational variables of Table 10.6 in terms of regional deviations from gender-specific means.[37]

The units of analysis plotted in this figure consist of 18 mutually exclusive populations specified by region and gender, each characterized by some unique combination of prevalence and screening rates and by a particular distribution of socioeconomic status attributes. Populations with positive scores on the vertical axis are subject to higher screening rates than predicted from their prevalence rates. Positive scores on the horizontal axis indicate higher than average concentrations of education and occupational status. The regression equation indicates that with prevalence held constant, annual screening rates increase by 1.4 percentage points, on average, for every increase of one standard deviation in the index measuring concentrations of occupational status and human capital (semipartial $r = .65; p < .01$). This equation describes both genders.

These data support the interpretation of screening rates as measuring something not simply different from prevalence rates, but different in ways predictable from the interpretation of screening as a boundary process independently associated with the socioeconomic core of modernity. The intensity of this process is greater in regions whose populations control more sociocultural "capital" defined in modern terms. Since genders, too, differ with respect to the positioning of their members in a capitalist economy, these findings encourage a search for socioeconomic explanations of gender-differentiated screening rates.[38]

Explaining Gender-Differentiated Screening Rates

As indicated by sex ratios in the bottom row of Table 10.5, regions differ not only in the overall intensity of their screening for retarded development. They also differ in the degree to which their screening procedures distinguish between different genders. In the first case, the issue is one of boundaries between normal and subnormal intellect; in the second case, of boundaries between masculine and feminine intellect.

The variables explaining overall levels of screening for either gender above do not explain their *differences*. For that, one must explore dimensions of social organization on which the difference between genders is more pronounced. Such a dimension is defined by rates of participation in the long-term labor force.[39] During the period under examination, more than twice as many American men as women were employed for 50+ weeks of the year (72 percent of men vs. 27 percent of women). Further analysis indicates that gender differences on this dimension explain notable differences in screening rates.

Figure 10.4 presents the relationship between gender-differentiated work roles and boundary maintenance as it emerges from this analysis. The independent variable here is the difference between male and female rates of participation in the long-term labor force. The dependent variable is the difference between male and female screening rates, calculated after adjusting for prevalence levels—that is, the difference between gender-specific rates as described by the vertical axis in Figure 10.3.[40] It may be noted that while the independent variable describes people above the age of 25, the dependent variable is constructed from data concentrated in a younger generation (e.g., 78 percent of those in Table 10.1 are younger than 25). The relationship thus describes a system transcending the domain of any single generation.

It is clear that the distribution of gender-differentiated screening rates in Figure 10.4 closely parallels the distribution of gender-differentiated

FIGURE 10.4 Gender-Differentiated Screening Rates by Gender-Differentiated Employment

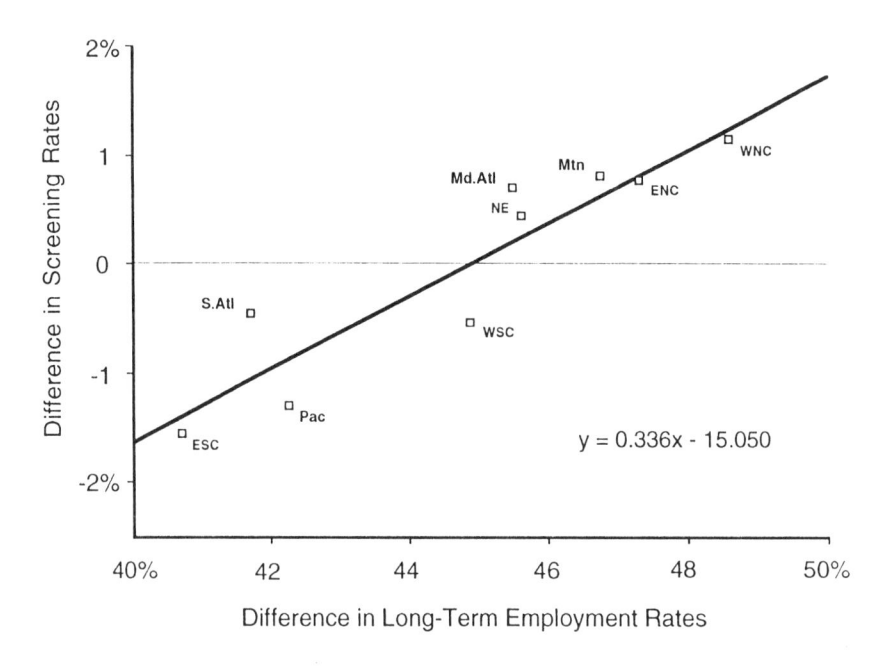

Note: Screening rates are measured in terms of residual deviations from regressions on gender-specific prevalence rates. See Appendix C, Table 10A.1.

work.[41] Where the difference between genders is greater vis-à-vis their long-term, stable participation in the labor force, the difference between screening rates is greater as well ($r = .92; p < .01$).[42]

Thus the analysis of regional data indicates that socioeconomic variables explain both the overall intensity of screening in a region and the degree to which males are distinguished from females in the process. While the intensity of screening overall is best predicted by the distribution of essentially middle-class occupations and certifications, the degree of gender differentiation is best predicted by differences in the extent to which work of any sort is commodified in packages of 50 weeks' employment or more. For both regions and genders in this analysis, screening is more intense for populations more strategically placed in the modern economy.[43]

Conclusion

With minor qualifications, these findings support hypotheses emerging from the literature reviewed earlier. Assuming screening rates describe the implementation of developmental norms, more vigorous implementation is associated with (a) males and (b) regions in which typically modern forms of human and social capital are more densely concentrated. The difference between genders, as between regions, can be explained by different levels of involvement in institutional structures at the core of modern life. For regions, these are defined in the present study by the organization of modern technology and bureaucracy; for genders, by the market for work as a "durable" commodity. In either case the explanation of differences consists in a specific formulation of the more general finding: Operative definitions of intellectual subnormality in the modern world are keyed to the organization of work.

The findings thus describe an institutional complex spanning occupational structures on the one hand and authoritative reactions to deviant development on the other. The significance of this complex lies less in its impact on those called "retarded" than in its implications for the social whole. Reactions to deviance are classically interpretable in terms of boundary maintenance. If screening rates reflect a process reaching beyond the definition of subnormality to include the tacit celebration of normality as well, then these findings describe a linkage between occupational structures and what might be interpreted as boundary rituals. In regions where the occupational structure facilitates access to the administrative and technical core of modernity, such rituals appear to be more rigorous.[44] Where the difference between genders is greater re their long-term involvement in that structure, the ritual distinction between genders is more pronounced.

It is a central feature of this complex that it spans generations as well as institutional spheres. The labor force in this analysis was born before the atom bomb, while reported diagnoses are concentrated among those born afterwards. Thus in relating occupational structure to screening rates, these findings relate the work performed by an earlier generation to the mental development of a later one.

The ramifications of this relationship lie beyond the scope of the data at hand. It is presumed here that definitions of self and its relations to normative order become articulated and enlivened through involvement in boundary rituals. Interpreted from this perspective, the data describe one aspect of a larger process by which childhood commitments to the modern reification of intelligence might be reinforced from time to time for selected audiences. Assuming the intellectual development of a population is not automatic but rather motivated by commitments of this sort, the apparent linkage between developmental standards and occupational expectations implies an economic basis for the social construction of intelligence on more than one level. Both as reified cultural form and as 'self' enhancing cast of mind, modern intelligence may rise above a floor determined in part by the organization of modern work.[45]

While the intergenerational nature of relationships suggests a certain dynamic, these findings are essentially cross-sectional. Extrapolating from cross-sectional to temporal dimensions of variability, one might predict that regions or genders exhibiting an increase in modern forms of human and social capital would exhibit an increase in the rigor of screening rituals. And where the differentiation of work by region or gender declines, anticipated differences in screening rates should decline concurrently. Whether such predictions hold for the American system remains a question for further research. Since the period analyzed here, significant changes have occurred both in the organization of services for the mentally retarded and in the integration of peripheral populations into the national economy. The theoretical significance of present findings is not dependent on their temporal location. But as a cross-sectional description of "modernity," they may best be viewed as a historically located baseline from which subsequent change might be assessed.

Notes

1. The first American institution for the feebleminded (sic) was established in 1848, while Binet's intelligence test and its derivatives are twentieth-century phenomena.

2. Meaningful sex differences are reported only for the mildly retarded in the studies they review. Among the severely retarded, such differences are reported to be much attenuated or nonexistent.

3. Although the language derives from Berger's (1978) discussion, it should be noted that she focuses neither on gender nor on normative expectations. Rather, she discusses variation in IQ scores across racial, ethnic, and social class boundaries.

4. Among the central structures identified by Berger, Berger, and Kellner (1973:55), technological production and bureaucratic organization are described as primary carriers of specifically modern cognitive styles. Specific themes in the "symbolic universe of modernity" associated with these carriers include "rationality," "componentiality," "multi-relationality," and others that on the face of it seem relevant to modern notions of intelligence (Berger, Berger, and Kellner 1973:110–2).

5. Such explanations apply to both aspects of retardation identified by the AAMD, that is, to "adaptive behavior" as well as "IQ." Given recurrent attempts to reduce IQ scores to genetics, it should be emphasized that the distinction between "psychobiological" and "sociocultural" is not the same distinction as

that between IQ and adaptive behavior. Tests of either dimension of retardation may be interpreted as measuring either psychobiological or sociocultural phenomena (or both).

6. Roughly two-thirds of the sample consists of "first admissions" either to institutions for the mentally retarded or to psychiatric hospitals. First admissions probably carry greater weight symbolically and best exemplify the process modeled below. Roughly 20 percent of reported diagnoses are produced by outpatient psychiatric clinics, which have no admissions to report, describing "terminations" of service after treatment instead. Another 15 percent of the sample was diagnosed in psychiatric wards of general hospitals, which describe "discharges" rather than admission statistics. Statistics from the latter facilities are included in the analysis because the error thus introduced seems preferrable to that which might result from their omission.

7. As indicators of "incidence," the rates created by aggregating statistics from these disparate institutions will obviously be inflated to some unmeasured degree, depending on (1) the extent to which inpatient admissions or discharges are preceded by prior diagnoses at outpatient clinics; and (2) the extent to which the diagnoses reported by outpatient clinics and general hospitals are preceded by prior admissions to residential facilities for the mentally ill or retarded.

8. The choice of this year is a pragmatic one based on the availability of data, but it may be noted that in 1968 the number of discharges from public institutions for the retarded surpassed the number of admissions for the first time, ending a half century of stability in resident movement statistics and beginning a period of "deinstitutionalization" that continues to date (Lakin, Blake, Prouty, Mangan, and Bruininks 1993:35). The synthetic cohort constructed from these data thus has the merit of mimicking a real-time cohort more closely than might be possible with a less stable empirical base.

9. The life history described for this synthetic cohort will differ from that of any given empirical cohort to the extent that age-specific rates characterizing the U.S. population at the time of data collection differ from the rates experienced by the given empirical cohort during its lifetime. This is the familiar condition of life table analysis, applied in this instance to rates of diagnosis rather than mortality.

10. This table reproduces NIMH data reported by Tudor, Tudor, and Gove (1979: table 2). Rates per million U.S. residents were calculated after correcting for underreporting to the NIMH, assuming that age- and sex-specific rates of diagnosis for reporting and nonreporting institutions of the same type are equivalent. Of a known total 3,921 facilities (including 182 private institutions for the mentally retarded, represented in these data by 73 facilities reporting data for 1966 but not for 1968), roughly two-thirds reported data on admissions, discharges, or terminations. In addition to rates calculated by Tudor, Tudor, and Gove (1979), Table 10.1 describes the number of diagnostic events on which each rate is based, as an indicator of its empirical stability. (Raw numbers are tabulated from NIMH 1966 and NIMH 1968.) Age-standardized rates in this table and Table 10.4 describe a population with the age structure of the total U.S. population in 1968.

11. The present research does not address a central question raised by the medical model: the question of what retardation "is" apart from its social recognition or labeling. For analytic purposes, the model simply assumes the existence of

some phenomenon not reducible to the diagnostic process itself but nonetheless a constitutive part of diagnosed "retardation." The specific content of that phenomenon (which describes an extraneous variable for present purposes) is defined in purely operational terms, through the estimation of parameters in the course of analysis. Operationally, it reflects an unspecified array of developmental attributes that, in interaction with a constant screening process, result in the diagnosis of "mental retardation" by facilities such as those in Table 10.1. The common presumption that such attributes are importantly psychobiological informs the interpretation of results below, but the model itself (formally distinct from its conceptual motivation) is silent on that point.

12. This assumption is supported by the work of Fisher and Zeaman (1970), who develop a measure of "retardate intelligence" that is arguably superior to IQ in low-scoring groups, since on average it does not decline during the developmental period (as do the IQ scores of retarded populations). The "mental ages" associated with typical age-specific scores on this measure differ from those associated with the normal IQ score of 100, and increasingly so as chronological age increases. The extent of this difference, reflecting the degree to which retarded populations typically deviate from normality, is a roughly linear function of age during the developmental period. After that period the difference typically remains fairly constant. While this is not a measure of prevalence but rather of typical age-specific deviations from normality, it is suggestive of the form a measure of deviant prevalence might take if conceived in terms of unit acts rather than individuals and expressed as a function of age.

13. The AAMD Manual (Heber 1961) defined the developmental period as ending at age 16 prior to 1973, when the upper limit was changed to 18 years (Grossman 1973). The model uses the least-squares criterion to estimate a best fit (plus or minus three months) from empirical observations.

14. This assumption ignores the fact that mortality rates for institutionalized populations of the retarded are generally higher than for the population at large, which would reduce their numbers disproportionately as a population aged. These differentials are less pronounced for the mildly retarded, who remain of greatest theoretical interest here (Balakrishnan and Wolf 1976).

15. Since the psychobiological bases of intelligence are commonly described in developmental terms as modeled here, Figure 10.1 is presented as a model of psychobiological prevalence. This is not to say that prevalence rates are independent of sociocultural influence, as is evident when considering the social contexts in which prenatal trauma, childhood malnutrition, toxicity, learning, and a variety of other psychological and biological processes make their mark on intellectual development. The label "psychobiological" is intended to emphasize that the population properties measured by prevalence rates are conceived to be analytically separable from whatever social significance may be attached to those properties.

16. While the assumption of constancy in societal reactions clearly oversimplifies reality, it has the virtue of reproducing a central feature of the phenomena of interest here, that is, the ageless constancy of one's gender identity. To the extent that other constancies interact with developmental processes to influence rates of diagnosis, such constancies (e.g., any psychological or biological properties of an

aging cohort that may remain constant) will be confounded with the sociocultural constancies captured by the model's screening rate. Similarly, one would expect that to the extent societal reactions are not in fact age-blind but rather vary with age, they may be reflected in the developmental component of the model rather than its screening rate. As true of crude rates in general, the notion of a constant screening rate in this analysis is an abstraction useful primarily for comparative purposes.

17. The second row of Table 10.2 is reproduced from the bottom row of Table 10.1. In Table 10.2 and the following analysis, these data are treated as if they describe age-specific rates of "first diagnosis per person-year" for a single hypothetical cohort during different intervals of its lifetime. In Table 10.1, they describe age-specific rates of "first diagnosis per person" for different empirical cohorts during the single year of 1968.

18. The least-squares criterion is used to fit model to data through a computerized iterative process that treats all reported diagnoses as "first" diagnoses (see Appendix A). The poor fit at older ages may reflect the declining adequacy of this assumption in older age groups, where an increasing proportion of reported diagnoses occurs in outpatient clinics and general hospitals. These institutions, accounting for half of those treated at ages 35+ (versus fewer than a third at younger ages), report all "discharges" and "terminations" rather than first admissions. The inclusion of readmissions as well as first admissions in these reports creates an inflated index of first diagnosis, and increasingly so at older ages.

19. Although the data represent essentially the entire U.S. population in 1968, Table 10.2 and following tables report R^2 values adjusted for bias due to small N, and tested for statistical significance on the assumption that the universe of theoretical interest extends beyond this time and place.

20. In predicting expected rates for larger age groups during any given year, the expectations for single-year cohorts are weighted to reflect the age structure of the larger category. Weighted averages then describe each larger grouping as a whole. Appendix A outlines the algorithm for producing age-specific predictions from given values of the model's four parameters.

21. The level labeled "mild" throughout this analysis includes those diagnosed more precisely at mild, moderate, and borderline levels in 1968. The category labeled "severe" includes diagnoses at both severe and profound levels.

22. See Halpern (1992:59–97) for a review of relevant literature on cognitive differences. To the extent that sex differences in aggression and other problem behaviors are developmental, whether genetically or socially scripted, and to the extent that such differences are reflected in rates of diagnosis for mental retardation, they, too, should be captured in the developmental component of this model.

23. Both versions estimate age- and sex-specific rates of diagnosis for males and females considered simultaneously—that is, they each provide a simultaneous fit to the 20 data points described in rows 2 and 4 of Table 10.1.

24. These assumptions are supported by Table 10.3. The developmental period for mild retardation is identical for males and females in that table; and the implied prevalence at birth takes a numerical value slightly less than zero for both sexes. (It may be noted parenthetically that "negative" prevalence rates are set equal to zero by the model before calculating expected rates of diagnosis.)

25. Given the assumption of identical screening rates, the disparity in age-standardized admission rates (M/F = 1.54 in Table 10.1) must be explained entirely by different prevalence rates (M/F = 1.55 by Model 1).

26. Parameter values estimated by Model 2 are essentially equivalent to those described in Table 10.3.

27. Needless to say, neither type of rate describes a pure measure. As noted above, it seems likely that "prevalence" rates in particular describe a residual category with considerable sociocultural content.

28. Contrary to usage by the Census Bureau, I call these nine divisions "regions" in the discussion below.

29. Rates of diagnosis may be calculated in each of five age categories for each gender and census division, comparable in abbreviated form to the rates presented in Table 10.1 for the nation as a whole. As in Table 10.2, these rates describe all diagnostic levels combined, including "mild," "severe," and "unknown" diagnoses in a single conglomerate category. Synthetic regional cohorts are defined in terms of these data (see Appendix C, Table 10A.2), to be analyzed similarly to the national cohorts above.

30. Values for these "fixed" parameters are determined by applying Model 2 (above) to national data, including all diagnostic categories as described above but excluding data from the 73 private residential facilities for which regional data are not available. On this basis the length of the developmental period is fixed at 15.2 years for both sexes in all regions, and the rate of prevalence at birth (presumably less susceptible to regional variation than the rate of change after birth) is fixed at 1,856 per million. (Given these fixed constants, rates of change during the developmental period are completely determined by prevalence rates at maturity.)

31. As in the analysis of national data, estimates for larger age cohorts consist of weighted averages of the annual estimates for single-year cohorts within each larger grouping. (Weights consist of sex-specific regional populations in one-year groupings as of 1970.)

32. Adjusted $R^2 = .96$ for males and $R^2 = .94$ for females, with $p < .001$ in both cases (H_0: age-specific rates = crude rate). Significance tests consist of F-statistics calculated for each gender with 20 degrees of freedom in the numerator, and $df = 24$ in the denominator. Total $N = 45$ observations for each test.

33. Values for adjusted R^2 at regional levels vary between $.78 < R^2 < .99$.

34. Differences between the correlations of socioeconomic variables with prevalence rates, on the one hand, and with screening rates, on the other, are generally significant only for males (one-tailed $p < .05$ with $t > 1.943$ and $df = 6$ in five out of six comparisons). For five out of six pairs of correlations between female rates, comparable differences are statistically insignificant.

35. Zero-order correlations between screening and prevalence are $r = -.29$ for males, and $r = -.50$ for females ($p > .08$ in both cases). First-order partials with socioeconomic variables controlled are negligible for males (e.g., $r = .04$ with occupation controlled) and insignificant if not negligible for females ($-.50 < r < -.37$ with education, occupation, or income controlled; $p > .10$ in all cases).

The Social Construction of Modern Intelligence

36. Prediction equations are SCREENING = 10.265 − (277.8 × PREVALENCE) for males, and SCREENING = 10.416 − (587.2 × PREVALENCE) for females. PREVALENCE in these equations describes the probability that an individual of the given sex in a given region is psychobiologically retarded, and SCREENING describes the percentage of such individuals who would be diagnosed "retarded" during any given year. That is, PREVALENCE here is scaled by dividing the prevalence rates of Table 10.5 by 1 million.

37. Education and occupation describe essentially the same system property as measured at the regional level here ($r = .99$). The relevant indicators from Table 10.6 are combined into a single index score for each gender by first standardizing each measure, then taking the average of the two resulting z-scores. This might be conceived as a composite measure of human and social capital defined as collective rather than individual properties (cf. Coleman 1990: ch. 12).

38. Males score higher than females on all measures of collective socioeconomic attributes in Table 10.6, in all regions. See Appendix C, Table 10A.1.

39. This dimension was selected following exploratory analysis that eliminated a dozen or more variables of possible relevance but negligible explanatory power. Census data describing men and women are not strictly comparable here, resulting in an operational definition of the male rate as the proportion of men aged 25–65 who worked 50+ weeks in 1969, while the female rate is the proportion of women aged 25–60 who worked 50+ weeks (U.S. Bureau of the Census 1973: tables 156, 157, 175, 176).

40. Positive scores on the vertical axis of Figure 10.4 occur in one of two ways. Where the screening of males is more rigorous than predicted from prevalence rates, positive scores indicate that female screening rates exceed predicted levels to a lesser degree or not at all. Where the screening of males is less rigorous than predicted, positive scores indicate that female rates fall farther than males below the prediction line. Negative scores, on the other hand, indicate either that female rates exceed expectations to a greater degree than do rates for males (e.g., Pacific coast states); or that rates for females fall short, but not so far short as for males (e.g., East South Central states). See Appendix C, Table 10A.1.

41. Although somewhat attenuated, the relationship remains when differences between screening rates are calculated without controlling regional variation in prevalence rates ($r = .70; p < .05$).

42. This relationship remains essentially unchanged when gender differences in rates of juvenile delinquency are controlled (partial $r = .91$). Delinquency describes a form of deviance exhibiting well-known gender differences, held constant here as a proxy for differences in milder forms of problem behavior that might conceivably influence the diagnostic process. Gender differences both in rates of delinquency and in rates of long-term employment are independently predictive of the dependent variable in Figure 10.4. (Multiple $R = .97$, with standardized beta coefficients $\beta = 0.65$ for the gender difference in employment and $\beta = -0.42$ for the difference in delinquency; $3.10 < t < 4.84$ with 5 degrees of freedom and $p < .05$ for either β-coefficient). Data describing delinquency may be found in U.S. Children's Bureau (1967:50). Rates are calculated in Appendix C, Table 10A.1.

43. Although sample sizes on which this conclusion is based are very small, the data describe very stable units of analysis. Each data point in Figure 10.4, for example, summarizes information about massive structures and large numbers of people engaged in them.

44. Whatever the ritual significance of the diagnostic events analyzed here, it is not their overall frequency which screening rates measure, but the institutional propensity to manufacture such events from a given pool of unrealized potential. To say that the process is more "rigorous" is to say that psychobiological indicia of retardation are more likely to be diagnosed as such by facilities reporting to the NIMH.

45. It is worth reiterating that the process tapped by screening rates in this analysis does not distinguish intelligence per se from a lack of intelligence. More precisely, it distinguishes a typically modern configuration, formally defined by technical specialists, from conceivable alternatives. Other configurations, reinforced by other rituals, may find anchorage in structures different from those examined here.

References

Baird, P. A., and A. D. Sadovnick. 1985. "Mental Retardation in Over Half-a-Million Consecutive Livebirths: An Epidemiological Study." *American Journal of Mental Deficiency* 89:323–30.

Balakrishnan, T. R., and Lucille C. Wolf. 1976. "Life Expectancy of Mentally Retarded Persons in Canadian Institutions." *American Journal of Mental Deficiency* 80:650–62.

Berger, Brigitte. 1978. "A New Interpretation of the IQ Controversy." *Public Interest* 50:29–44.

Berger, Peter, Brigitte Berger, and Hans Kellner. 1973. *The Homeless Mind*. New York: Random House.

Berk, Richard A., William P. Bridges, and Anthony Shih. 1981. "Does IQ Really Matter? A Study of IQ Scores for the Tracking of the Mentally Retarded." *American Sociological Review* 46:58–71.

Braverman, Harry. 1974. *Labor and Monopoly Capital: The Degradation of Work in the Twentieth Century*. New York: Monthly Review Press.

Budoff, Milton, and Gary N. Siperstein. 1978. "Low-Income Children's Attitudes Toward Mentally Retarded Children: Effects of Labeling and Academic Behavior." *American Journal of Mental Deficiency* 82:474–79.

———. 1982. "Judgments of EMR Students toward their Peers: Effects of Label and Academic Competence." *American Journal of Mental Deficiency* 86:367–71.

Coleman, James S. 1990. *Foundations of Social Theory*. Cambridge: Harvard University Press.

Durkheim, Emile. 1938. *The Rules of Sociological Method*. Glencoe, IL: Free Press.

———. (1915) 1965. *The Elementary Forms of the Religious Life*. New York: Free Press.

Erikson, Kai. 1966. *Wayward Puritans*. New York: Wiley.

Feingold, Alan. 1992. "Sex Differences in Variability in Intellectual Abilities: A New Look at an Old Controversy." *Review of Educational Research* 62:61–84.

Fisher, Mary Ann, and David Zeaman. 1970. "Growth and Decline of Retardate Intelligence." Pp. 151–91 in Norman R. Ellis (ed.), *Research in Mental Retardation*, Volume 4. New York: Academic Press.

Giddens, Anthony. 1991. *Modernity and Self-Identity*. Stanford, CA: Stanford University Press.

Goffman, Erving. 1961. "The Moral Career of the Mental Patient." Pp. 125–69 in Erving Goffman, *Asylums*. Garden City, NY: Anchor.

Goodman, Joan F. 1990. "Variations in Children's Conceptualizations of Mental Retardation as a Function of Inquiry Methods." *Journal of Child Psychology and Psychiatry* 31:935–48.

Grossman, H. J. (ed.). 1973. *A Manual on Terminology and Classification in Mental Retardation*. Washington, DC: American Association on Mental Deficiency.

Halpern, Diane F. 1992. *Sex Differences in Cognitive Abilities*. Hillsdale, NJ: L. Erlbaum Associates.

Heber, Rick. 1961. *A Manual on Terminology and Classification in Mental Retardation*. 2nd Edition. Monograph Supplement to the *American Journal of Mental Deficiency*.

Kitsuse, John I., and Aaron V. Cicourel. 1963. "A Note on the Uses of Official Statistics." *Social Problems* 11:131–9.

Kohn, Melvin L., and Carrie Schoenbach. 1983. "Class, Stratification, and Psychological Functioning." Pp. 154–89 in Melvin L. Kohn and Carmi Schooler, *Work and Personality: An Inquiry into the Impact of Social Stratification*. Norwood, NJ: Ablex.

Kyle, Catherine, and Katherine Davies. 1991. "Attitudes of Mainstream Pupils Towards Mental Retardation." *British Journal of Special Education* 18:103–6.

Lakin, K. Charlie, Ellen M. Blake, Robert W. Prouty, Troy Mangan, and Robert H. Bruininks. 1993. *Residential Services for Persons with Developmental Disabilities: Status and Trends Through 1991*. Minneapolis: University of Minnesota Center on Residential Services and Community Living.

Lapouse, Rema, and Martin Weitzner. 1970. "Epidemiology." Pp. 197–223 in Joseph Wortis (ed.), *Mental Retardation*. New York: Grune and Stratton.

Lemkau, Paul V., and Paul D. Imre. 1969. "Results of a Field Epidemiological Study." *American Journal of Mental Deficiency* 73:858–63.

Levinson, Richard M., and Debra M. Starling. 1981. "Retardation and the Burden of Stigma." *Deviant Behavior* 2:371–90.

McLaren, Jennifer, and Susan E. Bryson. 1987. "Review of Recent Epidemiological Studies of Mental Retardation: Prevalence, Associated Disorders, and Etiology." *American Journal of Mental Retardation* 92:243–54.

MacMillan, Donald L., Reginald L. Jones, and Gregory F. Aloia. 1974. "The Mentally Retarded Label: A Theoretical Analysis and Review of Research." *American Journal of Mental Deficiency* 79:241–61.

Mercer, Jane R. 1973. *Labeling the Mentally Retarded*. Berkeley: University of California Press.

National Institutes of Mental Health. 1968. *Reference Tables on Patients in Mental Health Facilities: Age, Sex, and Diagnosis, 1968*. American Statistics Index microfiche 4228-1 (1974).

Parsons, Talcott. 1971. *The System of Modern Societies*. Englewood Cliffs, NJ: Prentice-Hall.
Richardson, Stephen A., Mindy Katz, and Helene Koller. 1986. "Sex Differences in Number of Children Administratively Classified as Mildly Mentally Retarded: An Epidemiological Review." *American Journal of Mental Deficiency* 91:250–56.
Richardson, Stephen A., Helene Koller, and Mindy Katz. 1986. "Factors Leading to Differences in the School Performance of Boys and Girls." *Journal of Developmental and Behavioral Pediatrics* 7:49–55.
Schuster, Tonya L., and Edgar W. Butler. 1986. "Labeling, Mild Mental Retardation, and Long-Range Social Adjustment." *Sociological Perspectives* 29:461–83.
Scott, Marcia S., Daryl B. Greenfield, and Mary F. Partridge. 1989. "Classification of Normally Achieving and Mildly Retarded Students on the Basis of Their Oddity Transfer Performance." *American Journal on Mental Retardation* 93:527–34.
Shields, Stephanie A. 1982. "The Variability Hypothesis: The History of a Biological Model of Sex Differences in Intelligence." *Signs* 7:769–97.
Singer, Benjamin D., and Richard W. Osborn. 1970. "Social Class and Sex Differences in Admission Patterns of the Mentally Retarded." *American Journal of Mental Deficiency* 75:160–62.
Tarjan, George. 1970. "Some Thoughts on Sociocultural Retardation." Pp. 745–58 in H. Carl Haywood (ed.), *Social-Cultural Aspects of Mental Retardation*. New York: Appleton-Century-Crofts.
Tausig, Mark. 1985. "Factors in Family Decision-Making About Placement for Developmentally Disabled Individuals." *American Journal of Mental Deficiency* 89:352–61.
Tudor, William, Jeannette F. Tudor, and Walter R. Gove. 1979. "The Effect of Sex Role Differences on the Societal Reaction to Mental Retardation." *Social Forces* 57:871–84.
U.S. Bureau of the Census. 1970. *Current Population Reports Series P–25, No. 441*. Washington DC: U.S. Government Printing Office.
———. 1973. *1970 Census of the Population Volume 1, Characteristics of the Population, Part 1, U.S. Summary*. Washington, DC: U.S. Government Printing Office.
U.S. Children's Bureau. 1967. *Statistics on Public Institutions for Delinquent Children, 1966*. Washington, DC: U.S. Government Printing Office.
Vandenberg, Steven G. 1987. "Sex Differences in Mental Retardation and Their Implications for Sex Differences in Ability." Pp. 157–69 in June M. Reinisch, Leonard A. Rosenblum, and Stephanie A. Sanders (eds.), *Masculinity/Femininity*. New York: Oxford University Press.

Appendix A to Chapter 10:
Algorithm for Estimating Rates of Diagnosis

The following algorithm, written in computer language C, takes four parameters and produces rates of "first recorded diagnosis" for a cohort characterized by a given age structure. The cohort in this example has an age structure described by the total U.S. population, both sexes, comparable to the population described in Table 10.2.

```
#define POP(x)   ( male[x] + fem[x] )

/* Given the following parameter values from Table 10.2 */

dev_period = 15; change = 466; screen = .0725; prevalence = 9029;

/* Calculate prevalence rates at birth and at the midpoints of yearly age
intervals thereafter. */

birthprev = prevalence - (change * dev_period);
for (age = 0; age < 76; ++age)
{
  midpt = age + 0.5;
  if (midpt < dev_period)
    prev[age] = birthprev + (change * midpt);
      else prev[age] = prevalence;
}
```

/* Assuming a cohort's average age to be the midpoint of its age span, calculate the size of the pool of not-yet-diagnosed but psychobiologically retarded persons per million in each single-year age interval. Then calculate age-specific rates of diagnosis for each one-year interval, as determined by the screening rate in Table 2. */

```
prior[0] = 0;                                   /* No diagnoses prior to birth */
for (age = 0; age < 76; ++age)
{
  pool = prev[age] - prior[age];                /* Rate per million */
  if (pool > 0)  diagnos[age] = pool * screen;  /* Rate per million */
    else diagnos[age] = 0;                      /* No negative rates */
  prior[age + 1] = diagnos[age] + prior[age];
}
```

/* Given these age-specific rates of diagnosis for yearly intervals, calculate rates for larger age groupings. For example, consider the group of both sexes bounded by age = 0 and age = 5. Assume an age structure as given by the U.S. Bureau of the Census (1970a: table 50). */
 person_years = 0;

male[0] = 1.778;   fem[0] = 1.707;   /* Population (millions) */
male[1] = 1.722;   fem[1] = 1.656;
male[2] = 1.679;   fem[2] = 1.612;
male[3] = 1.741;   fem[3] = 1.678;
male[4] = 1.826;   fem[4] = 1.756;

total_diagnoses = 0;   /* Initial conditions */
for (age = 0; age < 5; ++age)

{
            /* Calculate the number of diagnoses at each year of age */
number[age] = POP(age) * diagnos[age];

            /* Calculate the cumulative number of diagnoses, ages 0–5 */
total_diagnoses += number[age];

                /* Calculate the cumulative number of person-years */
person_years += POP(age);

              /* Note: POP(age) is defined at the beginning of the program */
}

rate = total_diagnoses / person_years;
printf ("Diagnoses per million person-years = %5.1f", rate);

/* The total number of diagnoses in the age-group, divided by the total number of person-years lived by the group, describes the rate of "first recorded diagnoses" (per million). This is an age-specific rate describing the 0–5 age group in a population with a given structure, assuming the parameter values of Table 10.2. */

Note

The parameter values of Table 10.2 were estimated by means of an iterative process that minimizes the sum (across age groups) of squared deviations between age-specific rates for larger groupings as calculated in this example, and the age-specific rates described by Table 10.1.

Appendix B to Chapter 10:
Considerations of Validity

The validity of the index of screening rates may be considered in the context of other parameters estimated above.

1. The estimated developmental period of 15 years in Table 10.2 is reasonably close to the 16–18-year period described by the AAMD (Heber 1961; Grossman 1973). This estimate rises to 15.5 years when analysis is limited to the mildly retarded in Table 10.3.

2. The estimated prevalence of 9,029 in Table 10.2 falls within the range reported in the epidemiological literature. Studies reviewed by McLaren and Bryson (1987) measure retardation in different ways and span a variety of populations, but they generally report prevalence rates between 6,700 and 9,900 per million, age unspecified, for all levels of severity combined.[1] These studies report the prevalence only of *diagnosed* cases, however, while the model is designed to estimate the prevalence of all cases whether diagnosed or not.

3. Estimated rates of change in childhood prevalence are supported by data from British Columbia. Baird and Sadovnick (1985: figure 1) report age-specific rates of roughly 1,500 diagnosed cases per million at age 0–4 years, and 7,700 per million at age 15–29.[2] This implies a rate of change in the prevalence of labeled cases equivalent to an average 310 per million per year between ages 2.5 and 22.5 years (the midpoints of reported age intervals), which is comparable to that implied by the model.[3] As noted above, however, the model's estimates are conceived to describe all cases whether labeled or not.

4. Of the four parameters estimated here, the screening rate seems most problematic. The annual rate of 7.25 percent estimated in Table 10.2B amounts to a rate of roughly 30 percent over a five-year period. This seems low, but it is a crude rate averaged over a lifetime.

Baird and Sadovnick (1985: 325) provide perhaps the best empirical benchmark for this index. Among 708 cases they describe in three Canadian categories jointly labeled "mildly" retarded in this analysis, the median age of the first diagnosis appears to be around nine or ten years.[4] This is considerably younger than the median implied by the model developed here (using parameters estimated for mild retardation in Table 10.3), when applied to a population with the age structure of British Columbia in 1980. For the Canadian categories jointly labeled "mild" by the NIMH, Table 10.3 implies a median age of 13 years. By that age, roughly 70 percent of Baird and Sadovnick's (1985) sample had been diagnosed.

In assessing the model's estimates in this light, it should be noted that the British Columbia Registry summarizes data from more than 80 different sources, including public health units, special schools, and service organizations not included in the NIMH data on which the research reported here is based. Given these differences, one would expect younger median ages of entry into the Registry when compared to records compiled by the NIMH. And different population attributes as well as health care systems may be relevant.[5] Interpreted judiciously, and acknowledging that the model is designed to provide a crude rate averaged across all ages, the screening index seems serviceable for comparative purposes.

Notes

1. Estimates based on the sum of mild and severe levels of prevalence in Table 10.3 are lower, due to the exclusion of cases diagnosed at unknown levels of severity.

2. These rates derive from the British Columbia Health Surveillance Registry, describing all known cases of retardation in the 1952–1966 birth cohort as of 1981. They do not describe changes in age-specific rates broken down by sex or level of measured intelligence.

3. Table 10.2B describes an increase of 466 × 12.5 yrs. = 5,825 per million between the ages of 2.5 and 15 years, followed by zero increase between 15 and 22.5 years. The average annual increase during this period would be 5,825 / 20 = 291 per million per year. It should be noted that Baird and Sadovnick (1985:328) interpret the change in prevalence as indicative of "lag time" in the diagnosis of presumably pre-existent retardation, rather than as a measure of growth in the size of the psychobiologically retarded population itself.

4. Roughly half of those in the lowest category (labeled "moderate" in the Canadian study) were diagnosed before age eight; half of 212 people in the middle category (labeled "mild") were diagnosed before age ten; and half of the 354 "borderline" cases were diagnosed before age eleven. These figures describe people registered without other known disabilities.

5. The parameters estimated from analysis of Pacific Coast states in Table 10.5 imply a median age of nine or ten years (depending on gender) when applied to the 1980 British Columbia age structure—but the data for Table 10.5 include more severe levels of retardation as well.

Appendix C to Chapter 10:
Regional Measures and Rates

TABLE 10A.1 Variables Used in Table 10.6, Figure 10.3, Figure 10.4, and Note 42

	N. Eng.	Md. Atl.	ENC	WNC	S. Atl.	ESC	WSC	Mtn.	Pac.
Table 10.6									
% prof./tech./mgr.									
M	31.7	28.8	25.8	27.3	26.0	21.6	26.4	30.7	30.1
F	13.6	11.4	11.0	12.9	11.9	10.5	11.6	13.3	13.0
% higher education									
M	15.7	14.4	12.1	12.1	13.1	9.40	12.5	15.9	16.6
F	8.95	7.88	7.22	7.75	8.25	6.28	7.76	10.0	10.1
median income ($)									
M	7221	7381	7743	6358	5721	4918	5614	6532	7499
F	2678	2819	2553	2123	2424	1926	1976	2194	2780
Figures 10.3 and 10.4									
mean z–score (occ. and educ.)									
M	0.95	0.39	−0.63	−0.46	−0.15	−1.55	−0.91	1.05	1.30
F	0.34	−0.37	−1.05	−0.07	−0.36	−1.29	−0.13	1.57	1.36
residual screening rate									
M	0.52	−0.75	−1.52	2.37	−0.76	−3.26	−0.43	0.18	3.65
F	0.05	−1.44	−2.26	1.22	−0.33	−1.70	0.09	−0.60	4.97
diff.	0.47	0.69	0.74	1.15	−0.43	−1.56	−0.52	0.78	−1.32
% long-term employment									
M	74.1	72.5	73.8	76.3	71.7	67.5	71.8	72.8	68.7
F	28.4	26.9	26.4	27.7	30.0	26.9	27.0	26.1	26.5
diff.	45.7	45.6	47.4	48.6	41.7	40.6	44.8	46.7	42.2
Note 42									
institutionalized delinquents (per 1000 pop., age 5–17, ca. 1966)									
M	1.22	0.93	1.24	1.40	1.40	2.63	1.62	0.82	2.88
F	0.43	0.29	0.35	0.44	0.51	0.76	0.45	0.38	0.49
diff.	0.79	0.64	0.89	0.96	0.89	1.87	1.17	0.44	2.39

TABLE 10A.2 Age-Specific Rates of Diagnosis (per million) by Region and Sex: All Levels of Severity Combined

	N. Eng.	Mid. Atl.	ENC	WNC	S. Atl.	ESC	WSC	Mtn.	Pac.
Male									
predicted									
0–17 yrs.	342	260	219	439	334	210	360	284	287
18–24	270	207	176	320	307	215	332	211	149
25–44	99	81	74	100	139	120	149	76	35
45–64	20	19	19	15	39	49	41	14	3
65+	4	5	5	3	12	22	13	3	0
observed									
0–17 yrs.	357	266	226	457	361	206	373	302	292
18–24	245	199	165	286	269	225	316	177	137
25–44	115	84	80	130	155	105	138	109	54
45–64	51	31	26	59	67	47	75	35	22
65+	14	12	16	20	29	39	23	14	13
Female									
predicted									
0–17 yrs.	231	160	140	263	218	171	233	168	231
18–24	229	133	121	228	222	173	243	126	108
25–44	121	63	63	100	123	100	136	53	25
45–64	45	20	23	27	49	42	55	14	2
65+	18	7	9	8	21	20	24	4	0
observed									
0–17 yrs.	248	168	157	285	234	173	248	179	238
18–24	205	120	96	195	201	175	226	109	90
25–44	127	70	78	117	130	91	139	59	58
45–64	64	33	38	52	63	57	68	35	27
65+	13	4	9	18	18	16	27	20	7

PART FIVE

Conclusion

11

Social Differentiation and Inequality: Some Reflections on the State of the Field

James N. Baron, David B. Grusky, and Donald J. Treiman

We believe the various contributions to this volume do justice to their authors' mentor, John C. Pock. Like him, these essays are provocative, innovative, ambitious, careful and sophisticated in their reasoning and inference, and focused on some of sociology's central issues. At the same time, this collection also highlights the obvious fact that our theories and research addressing status attainment provide a decidedly incomplete picture of the social forces involved. In particular, too little emphasis has been paid to both macro- (demographic, structural, and institutional) and micro- (individual and primary group) influences. We sketch the beginnings of a more comprehensive framework here, and we show how a number of the chapters in this volume address issues that fit comfortably within such an expanded view of how the process of status attainment works in modern industrial societies. We also discuss some implications of this broadened conception of the status attainment process for future research.

Macrosocial Underpinnings of Status Attainment

We suggest that a comprehensive theory of status attainment must include an account of both the factors that determine what sorts of opportunities are (differentially) available to individuals and the extent and ways in which individuals are able to exploit the opportunities available to them. Let us first consider the structure of opportunities, which we think of as reflecting macrosocial factors. These are of three kinds: demographic, structural, and organizational-institutional.

Demographic Factors

Changes in birth rates and death rates and changes in the number and social composition of immigrants and emigrants affect the ratio between supply and demand for various kinds of positions. A simple example, close to home, is the impact of changes in the birthrate between the 1930s and 1950s on job prospects for new Ph.D.'s. Those who completed their graduate studies in the 1960s enjoyed favorable job prospects because the birth cohorts of the 1930s (who were the Ph.D. cohorts of the 1960s) were unusually small, while the demand for teaching faculty was expanding rapidly as the baby boom produced larger and larger cohorts of college-aged youths. A decade later the situation was reversed, as the baby boom cohorts began to produce ever larger numbers of Ph.D.'s at a time when the demand for new faculty was weakening because the size of college-entry cohorts was leveling off or even dropping.

As another example, in countries devastated by war there may be large holes in the male age structure, creating special opportunities for the survivors as well as for those in younger cohorts. The destruction of Poland's Jewish population, for instance, must have had a profound effect on the chances for occupational mobility among the remainder of the population given that the Jews, who constituted a large fraction of the population of many Polish cities, were so disproportionately a merchant and professional class (Institute for the Study of Minority Problems 1932; Zielinski 1954; Altshuler 1993). Many other examples of this kind could be cited. But demographic factors of this sort are seldom taken into account in status attainment studies. Although scholars of social mobility have long sought to characterize, in descriptive fashion, the amount of such structurally induced mobility, the models they conventionally deploy can neither distinguish the effects of different types of demographic processes (e.g., differential mortality or fertility) nor readily control for microlevel sources of mobility (Sobel, Hout, and Duncan 1985; Hauser and Grusky 1988).

A welcome exception is the essay by Robert Mare (Chapter 5), which explicitly models the combined roles of differential fertility, differential mortality, and intergenerational educational mobility in generating changes in the distribution of educational attainment among U.S. women during the last half of the twentieth century. Although many scholars have recognized the potential importance of such demographic processes (e.g., Duncan 1966; Vining 1986; Herrnstein and Murray 1994), Mare is one of the first scholars to test these arguments explicitly (see also Preston and Campbell 1993). In doing so, he introduces a one-sex projection model that is frequently used to understand patterns of population redistribution but that is quite distinct from the micro-oriented models commonly employed in status attainment research. His chapter should serve as a model of the kinds of alternative approaches that can serve to broaden our understanding of stratification processes.

Structural Factors

Closely akin to demographic influences are structural factors that affect the demand for different sorts of labor. Paramount among these are changes in the technology of production and macroeconomic changes that affect the demand for various sorts of goods and services. For example, industrial societies are quite different from peasant societies in their mix of jobs, and hence the rate of industrialization of societies creates differences in mobility chances (Treiman 1970). Economic changes can have a similar impact. Students of status attainment have not yet adequately appreciated that the state of the economy may thus have a profound impact on the opportunities and constraints individuals face. By contrast, scholars of social mobility have long recognized and sought to model structurally induced mobility, yet their analytic approach cannot easily be adapted to structural equation models of the sort that scholars of status attainment conventionally estimate. In the context of the latter models, some researchers have attributed over-time or cross-national variability in the intercept to macrolevel factors of the above-mentioned kind (e.g., Grusky and DiPrete 1990). But such interpretations assume that the model being estimated is adequately specified and that the intercept is therefore not attributable to omitted variables at either the individual or macrostructural level. The specter of omitted-variable bias always haunts nonexperimental research; however, it is especially troubling in the present context, if only because the degrees of freedom with which to adjudicate between competing macrolevel effects are perforce limited in over-time or cross-national designs. If structural effects are to be incorporated convincingly, then an analytic innovation of a sort that we cannot now anticipate is likely to be required.

Organizational and Institutional Factors

We here include the way that different units of society are organized, the norms and rules governing social behavior and interaction within these settings, and the way resources are allocated within and between various units. This is a rather comprehensive definition, encompassing what could alternatively be thought of as aspects of structure; however, the present state of theoretical development makes distinctions among these aspects of institutions somewhat difficult, especially within the limited space available here. The need to incorporate institutional factors into models of status attainment has been widely recognized and has helped to fuel the development of the "new structuralism" Neil Fligstein and Haldor Byrkjeflot refer to in Chapter 2 of this volume. In our view a comprehensive institutional framework has yet to be developed, but there is surely evidence of much scholarly interest in building one (see, especially, Kerckhoff forthcoming). We suggest that such a framework will need to include at least four institutions: states, educational systems, employment systems, and the family. Although it is useful for analytic purposes to separate these four institutions, they are strongly interrelated, in the sense that institutional arrangements in one sphere will usually affect other spheres as well.

Our concern here with states is restricted to public policies and practices promulgated by governmental agencies at all levels via legislation, administrative fiat, or judicial decisions that affect stratification systems. These are of two principal kinds: tax and income transfer policies and employment policies. Tax policies, which are virtually never considered by students of stratification, affect the degree of inequality in income and wealth and the level of funding available for public programs. It has been well documented that the degree of income inequality in the United States increased during the 1980s, partly as a consequence of Reagan administration policies that made the federal income tax less progressive (Gramlich, Kasten, and Sammartino 1993; Mishel and Bernstein 1994: ch. 2). To cite another example, local financing of schools via property taxes ensures much larger inequalities in per pupil expenditures across communities than would occur with a more centralized redistribution system such as many European countries have adopted (Wise 1967; Kozol 1991). Tax policies may also affect the level of labor force participation. In Ireland, for example, women are discouraged from entering the labor force by a steeply progressive income tax system that adds the income of husband and wife rather than (approximately) averaging them, as is the case in the United States. For middle-class Irish women, the cost of entering the labor force typically exceeds the net income earned, thus creating a strong disincentive for labor force participation (see Esping-Andersen 1993 for related considerations).

Public regulation of employment policies includes pay equity legislation; laws and regulations pertaining to collective bargaining; laws and regulations governing wages, hours, working conditions, and discharge; affirmative action or other legislation designed to minimize gender- or ethnically-based discrimination in hiring and promotion; and policies that explicitly advantage one ethnic or racial group at the expense of others, such as characterized South African employment policies until a few years ago. Although the impact of such governmental policies in the

United States is widely debated (Sowell 1975; Walker and Block 1982; Burstein 1985, 1994; Grusky and DiPrete 1990; Jencks 1992; Uri and Mixon 1992; Graham 1994), there is quite substantial evidence of a reduction over time in occupational segregation by race (Williams and Jaynes 1989) and some evidence of a corresponding reduction in occupational segregation by gender (Jacobs 1989; Reskin 1993).

Of course governmental regulation affects stratification through a number of other avenues as well. Governmental entities control processes of vocational credentialing and occupational licensure, which in turn shape the supply, demand, and market power associated with particular work roles. Laws and regulations regarding public and private pension plans can have a significant impact on labor market outcomes, including rates of turnover, retirement ages, and the life-cycle patterning of earnings. Governments also promulgate industrial policies and regional development policies that can have profound ramifications for the distribution of opportunity and wealth across sectors and regions of the economy. A less obvious but nonetheless important way in which such policies can affect social stratification is by influencing housing markets, which in recent decades have become more heterogeneous within the United States and represent for many individuals their major source of net worth. National, state, and local government policies (e.g., regarding zoning, growth, and tax breaks for employers) and public sector expenditures (e.g., for education, protective services, infrastructure) serve to make housing more scarce and desirable in some locales than others. As a result, individuals or families owning otherwise equivalent housing in disparate housing markets may experience quite different patterns of wealth accumulation over time as their home equity appreciates or depreciates, and governmental policies that encourage relocation of job opportunities from one region to another can promote massive redistribution of wealth not only through the labor market but also through housing markets.

Finally, as Hannan (1988) has noted, the diversity of career trajectories available to individuals within a given line of work depends enormously on the diversity of organizational forms within which that work role can be carried out. Consequently, governmental policies regarding entrepreneurship, self-employment, and industrial competition can influence the number and types of work organizations within a given sphere, thereby shaping the types and range of labor market opportunities available to individuals. For instance, regulations that broaden the definition of a "financial services" organization permit individuals with training in relevant occupations to fashion careers in many different kinds of organizational settings rather than just in a traditional bank or insurance bureaucracy. According to this perspective, governmental programs that promote *organizational* diversity may be an effective way of promoting *labor force diversity*; a more heterogeneous population of organizations within a given sphere of activity is presumably capable of offering a more diverse menu of employment opportunities and career paths, thereby broadening the pool of individuals who may be well matched to available jobs.[1]

Because of the strong links between educational attainment and occupational qualifications, the provision of education is almost universally regarded as an obligation of government. However, educational systems vary widely in the availability of schools, especially for persons in rural areas; in how selective they are; in the extent to which there are deliberate attempts to create equal opportunity for educational advancement by providing special academic and financial assistance to those from disadvantaged backgrounds; and in the extent to which education is subsidized by the state or financed directly by students or their parents (Archer 1979). Nations also vary enormously in the extent and types of stratification and segmentation among educational institutions and in the tightness of the linkages between specific educational institutions and labor markets. There has recently been increased attention paid to these variations across countries (Shavit and Blossfeld 1993), including a few efforts to document differences across countries in the ways that schools channel students into the labor market (König and Müller 1986; Allmendinger 1989; Rosenbaum and Kariya 1989a, 1989b, 1991; Ishida, Müller, and Ridge 1995). These variations across time and space in the way that education and school systems are organized have obvious implications for stratification and mobility, both within and across generations, but have received too little attention in past research.

The chapter by Fligstein and Byrkjeflot in this volume reminds us that social institutions consist of sets of rules or norms governing social relationships—in their case relationships between employers and employees. They make the important point that the particular rules and norms that come into being within a given sphere of economic activity must be understood as an evolutionary process that depends upon the specific circumstances—in particular the balance of power between contending actors—at the time the institutions were created. Their emphasis on the *institutionalization* of employment systems suggests a resistance to change; consistent with Hannan's (1988) previously cited argument, it may often be the case that a reallocation of opportunities and attainments among social and demographic groups requires the creation of new organizational forms and the death of old ones, given inertial tendencies in firms and employment systems. Again, this is a lesson that needs to be absorbed by researchers in the status attainment tradition.

Chapter 9 by M.D.R. Evans and Karen Mason and Chapter 8 by Carol Heimer document the variability among families with respect to the gendered division of labor and its implications for women's participation in paid employment. The two chapters complement each other nicely. Evans and Mason show that even in late-twentieth-century Australia—a preeminently modern, industrial, secular society—a substantial fraction of both men and women still believe that a woman's place is in the home and that families suffer if women work. Heimer's essay suggests why this might be so: The way that family arrangements are institutionalized in modern industrial society assigns to women family responsibilities that are not easily shifted to others ("fates," in Heimer's terminology). In contrast, men view their responsibilities more in market terms—as opportunities or investments to be treated strategically and modified when superior opportunities or investments become available. If this analysis is joined with Fligstein and Byrkjeflot's arguments about the formation and persistence of institutional arrangements, we can better understand why gender differences in income have been so persistent.

Microsocial Underpinnings of Status Attainment

Most status attainment research to date has focused on the attributes of individuals that lead them to be more or less successful in the attainment of education, good jobs, or high income. Accordingly, we can be relatively brief in considering the microsocial underpinnings of status attainment. It is obvious enough that whatever the opportunities and constraints facing them, some individuals are more successful than others. The simple question is: Why is this so? We think that the advantages (or disadvantages) accruing to individuals may be usefully disaggregated into characteristics of families of origin and characteristics of individual actors. The intergenerational transmission of advantage (or disadvantage) may be seen as a reflection of the extent to which families differentially hold three forms of capital: cultural, material, and social capital. The intragenerational accumulation of advantage (or disadvantage) may be seen as a reflection of the extent to which actors themselves hold those same three forms of capital. Differential accumulation and deployment of these three forms of capital explains how effectively individuals seize the opportunities or overcome the constraints created by macrosocial factors.

"Cultural capital" refers to the stock of information, knowledge, abilities, skills, and motivations held by a family or an individual. The term "cultural capital" is largely synonymous with the term "human capital," widely used by economists and others, except that "cultural capital" is a somewhat broader concept, encompassing all manner of information, knowledge, and the like, not merely that fraction that produces differential income.[2] In status attainment models, family cultural capital is often measured, rather crudely, by father's education or parental education. However, the work of Bourdieu (1984) has inspired attempts to measure cultural capital more directly through such indicators as the number of books available in one's childhood household and the frequency with which parents participated in high culture—going to concerts, the ballet, opera, and so on. (This list might be supplemented with such contemporary sources of cultural capital as opportunities to travel and to use computers.)

The hypothesized linkage between cultural capital and status attainment is quite straightforward: Children from families with abundant cultural capital will do better, go further in school (because they start school with a competitive advantage that accumulates over their school careers), and ultimately enter more lucrative occupations. Because they come from families in which the attributes that facilitate school success—literacy and numeracy, abstract reasoning, and oral discussion and argumentation—are valued and practiced, they become proficient at these skills and are motivated to continue to improve them. Bourdieu argues, secondarily, that family participation in high culture is a status signifier that results in favorable consideration by teachers.

The link between education and occupational attainment is obvious and has been well documented, without exception, in all status attainment studies of the United States and other countries. Whether the trappings of education—an educated style—affect occupational chances above and beyond either the cognitive capacities acquired through education or educational credentials is as yet much less clear, since little work has been done on this topic. There is, however, evidence that education enhances income even among those with occupations of similar status (Sewell and Hauser 1975: ch. 6).

"Material capital," as used in this literature, refers to income, wealth, and property. It is unclear to what extent in societies such as the United States family or individual material capital serves as a resource for status attainment rather than simply as an aspect of the status attained, a return on earlier investments in education and careers. Of course children who have a safety net of family resources not only can delay career beginnings to engage in a longer training regimen but can also search for just the right career or take more substantial risks in the hope of larger payoffs. At the same time, schooling in the United States is essentially free up to the tertiary level, and low-cost tertiary education is widely available, thus suggesting that the direct effects of material capital on years of schooling (if not on the *quality* of schooling) may be modest (see Sewell and Hauser 1975 for relevant evidence). In other societies family material capital may be far more important, especially where schooling requires substantial financial investment. In societies where inheritance or purchase of land or a business is an important avenue of status attainment, family capital will matter far more than it does in the United States, where almost no one inherits a family business or farm.

"Social capital" refers to interpersonal relationships of obligation and influence. Here the claim is that, at least under certain circumstances, individuals may obtain admission to universities, acquire good jobs, secure lucrative contracts, and otherwise profit from their personal connections. The role of social capital has been widely studied, starting with Granovetter's (1974) influential hypothesis regarding the "strength of weak ties." However, the results have generally been somewhat unsatisfactory to date, perhaps because social capital is by its nature quite specific to particular biographical and historical circumstances and therefore cannot be readily measured or understood through such abstract concepts as the number of available contacts or the average power, status, and "strength" of these contacts. More refined studies of social networks within particular work contexts have documented that it is not simply *whom* one knows, but in what capacity, as well as the patterning of relations *among* those whom one knows, that matters for social mobility (Burt 1992; Podolny and Baron 1995). The complex effects of social capital can thus be teased out only by collecting data of a far more subtle sort than labor force survey designs conventionally provide. Moreover, a credible model of influence-wielding through social networks would take into account not only whether the requisite social ties are available to a given individual but also whether there are historical, personal, or organizational reasons for expecting such ties to be activated on particular issues.

Just how micro- and macrolevel factors combine to produce particular labor market outcomes is as yet far from clear, in part because of the difficulty of designing research that explicitly models both sets of factors in a single analysis. Although research methods for estimating simultaneously the impact of macro- and microinfluences are readily available and have been widely applied (e.g., Mason, Wong, and Entwisle 1983; Grusky and DiPrete 1990), all such research is limited by the available number of macrocontexts (firms, countries, etc.) and the consequent difficulty in adjudicating among the effects of highly correlated macrolevel variables. In Chapter 3, for example, Treiman and Lee analyze the attributes of individuals and bring demographic, structural, and institutional factors into the interpretation of the results but not into the analytic design (except insofar as the analysis of a single labor market, the Los Angeles metropolitan area, successfully controls for such factors). Treiman and Lee show that ethnic differences in income are largely attributable to ethnic differences in cultural capital. It is a useful thought experiment to ask how these findings would be modified by an *explicit* attempt to model structural factors, particularly variations in the actual—probably noncompetitive—labor markets available to different ethnic groups.

Directions for Theory and Research

We recognize the pitfalls inherent in enumerating such a long and diverse list of factors that warrant attention in studies of stratification. Whereas stratification researchers might once have held out the goal of constructing a comprehensive model of status attainment (see Featherman 1981), the above comments suggest, if nothing else, that this goal will not be easily achieved and that in the sociological near term no single study is likely to be able to capture even a majority of the possible causal influences we have identified. But we think this conceptual overview is useful in drawing attention to some important limitations in current scholarship and promising directions for the future.

First, the emphasis we have placed on macroinfluences highlights the importance of more comparative and/or historical work that maximizes variation on the relevant demographic, structural, and organizational-institutional influences. Moreover, this kind of work is also likely to sharpen our understanding of the various microinfluences on stratification and inequality, which are themselves likely to vary across macrocontexts (see Baron and Pfeffer 1994). For instance, the most interesting hypotheses about the role of social capital in status attainment concern the institutional arrangements that make social capital more or less important. Those who champion the thesis of universalism and industrialism would posit that in the United States, where jobs increasingly are filled on a bureaucratic basis, social capital is not very important. They suggest that universalism may be an inherent feature of market economies—whoever has the money can buy whatever is for sale—and the norm of universalism may carry over to other realms, such as hiring and promotion. By contrast, particularism may be an endemic feature of command economies, especially economies of scarcity, because in the absence of a market mechanism there is no clear-cut allocation rule (see Stark 1987). The command economies of communist Eastern Europe were widely regarded as bastions of personal influence and the same is true today in China, where to accomplish virtually anything one must exercise one's *guanxi*, that is, one's personal connections (Bian 1994).

It would of course be naive to conclude that informal social ties no longer exert a significant impact on individual advancement within corporations operating in a market context (for relevant evidence, see Burt 1992; Podolny and Baron 1995). In fact, some scholars might argue that the formal pressures for universalism, combined with an increasing emphasis on teamwork, "corporate culture," and minimizing bureaucracy in the workplace, have in fact made social capital *more* important, rather than less. Only systematic comparisons of network effects across a variety of macro contexts will resolve the debate.

Second, we have emphasized the causal paths *from* a variety of macro and micro influences *to* stratification and inequality, but it is important to emphasize that the causal arrows run in the opposite direction as well. Indeed, given our own training as Reed sociologists, we suspect that most of the contributors to this volume were, like us, attracted to the field of stratification in particular because of an interest in the *consequences* of social differentiation and inequality. We sought to understand how social class and socioeconomic status affect a person's behavior and beliefs, and how, at the societal level, the distribution of labor market outcomes affects other features of social systems, such as collective action and the polity, demography, families, deviance, social conflict, and structural change.

Several chapters in this volume pick up on these themes. William Mason and his colleagues document the powerful demographic consequences of socioeconomic stratification (Chapter 6). William Tudor documents how women's subordinate standing within society and the labor market causes them to be differentially labeled as mentally deficient (Chapter 10). As noted previously, other chapters examine how changes in women's educational and/or labor market positions have shaped gender role attitudes (Chapter 9) and the allocation of time and effort within households (Chapter 8).

These efforts to understand the consequences of stratification and inequality are predicated, of course, on various implicit models of the structure of inequality, which we believe merit more attention in future research. As Jesper Sørenson and David Grusky suggest in Chapter 4, sociologists are typically asked to choose between (1) gradational models of stratification, which map disaggregated occupations onto vertical scales of prestige or socioeconomic status, and (2) categorical models of class, which portray the stratification system in terms of mutually exclusive, highly aggregated, and (possibly) interdependent groups. The presumption, then, is that real class structuration will inevitably be found at highly aggregate levels of analysis, whereas the residue of structuration at lower levels is regarded as less fundamental and hence reducible to mere socioeconomic differentiation.

In contrast, Sørenson and Grusky argue that some detailed occupations (especially crafts and professions) take on the characteristics of sociopolitical communities, becoming the principal loci of "stratification effects," whereas social classes of the traditional aggregate sort appear to be less well formed and subjectively less salient to working men and women. Emmison and Western (1990), for instance, reported that only 7 percent of all Australians regarded their social class as a "very important" identity, and other commentators (e.g., Saunders 1989) have stressed that open-ended queries about class identification tend to yield numerous confused responses, refusals to answer, and even explicit denials of the very existence of classes (also see G. Evans 1992; M.D.R. Evans 1995). This type of evidence has led some sociologists to conclude that the class system is no longer the primary basis of identity formation (e.g., Laclau and Mouffe 1985).

Interestingly, when Emmison and Western asked respondents to name the single "identity source" they thought was most important, the most frequently cited identity was the old sociological standby of occupation, suggesting that the alternative statuses of gender, ethnicity, or nationality may attract more academic attention than their salience in the subjective domain merits (Emmison and Western 1990: table 3). Not only are detailed occupations the building blocks of macro level labor markets, but they are also important forces for socialization and acculturation at the micro level, which may explain their salience for workers' identities (see Becker and Carper 1956). As Caplow (1954) noted long ago, occupations also often require of their incumbents prolonged study, which can inculcate and enforce explicit codes of behavior, whereas aggregate classes have no comparable influence or authority over secondary patterns of socialization.

This evidence raises the possibility that the contours of collective action in the contemporary economy reflect the boundaries among specific occupations more than membership in the aggregate class categories that are the traditional fare in research on stratification and mobility. Three primary types of collective action can be found at the detailed occupational level: (1) *downward-directed* closure strategies designed to restrict access to occupational positions (e.g., closed union shops, credentialing, etc.); (2) *lateral* competitive struggles between occupational associations over functional niches in the division of labor (see Abbott 1988), and (3) *upward-directed* collective action oriented toward securing occupation-specific benefits (e.g., monopoly protection) from the state and from employers. In short, not only do real working men and women disavow the importance of social class and emphasize the subjective salience of their particular occupations, but there may also be more prima facie evidence of occupational roles as bases of collective action than there is for highly aggregated classes or occupational categories (e.g., professionals, manual labor, etc.)[3]

Of course the relative importance of occupational versus nonoccupational forms of class structuration itself varies considerably over time and space. As Fligstein and Byrkjeflot emphasize in Chapter 2, employment systems evolve very differently, producing distinctive patterns of social stratification and inequality. In terms of the taxonomy that Fligstein and Byrkjeflot advance, occupational or industrial structuration is especially strong within vocational and professional employment systems, whereas organizational or firm-based structuration is especially strong within systems of managerialism. Kalleberg and Lincoln (1988; see also Lincoln and Kalleberg 1985) similarly have examined how the architecture of inequality varies across contexts, but they focus on differences among countries rather than organizations. Consistent with the argument they develop, their empirical evidence suggests that occupational affiliation is more decisive for objective attainments and subjective identities within America's highly mobile society, whereas Japanese corporatism renders organizational affiliation more salient. The relative salience of occupational versus organizational and institutional identities may vary *within* countries as well as between them. Baron and Pfeffer (1994), for instance, have applied theory from cognitive and social psychology to suggest how and why organizations vary in the classification and valuation of work roles, the matching of persons to those roles, and the extent and consequences of reward differentiation.

This discussion highlights the importance of future research examining the *consequences* of stratification and inequality. Despite some important exceptions (e.g., Lamont and Fournier 1992), there continues to be surprisingly little attention paid to the structural and societal consequences of stratification, inequality, and mobility—that is, how the extent and bases of inequality in the labor market affect firms, families, and other social institutions. Happily, there has been increasing attention paid to some individual-level consequences of stratification and inequality, most notably those pertaining to voting, political behavior, and political attitudes (e.g., Kelley 1992; Weakliem 1993). We might also cite in this context the recent Bourdieu-inspired stream of research on the class-based structuring of lifestyles and consumption practices (e.g., De Graaf 1991; Peterson and Simkus 1992) and the recent resurgence of work on the individual-level effects of social mobility (Sobel 1985; De Graaf, Nieuwbeerta, and Heath 1995).

More work along these lines is likely to prove invaluable in addressing some enduring conceptual and methodological debates to which we referred above. For instance, debates about the extent and bases of class structuration in advanced societies hinge not simply on the magnitude of socioeconomic inequality and how it is structured (e.g., across occupations, social classes, industries, etc.) but also on the extent to which differences in class position (however operationalized) have important social, political, cultural, and cognitive consequences. This requires more studies along the lines of Emmison and Western (1990), comparing the salience of various categorizations (social class, occupation, firm, demographic groups) for workers' identities, attitudes, and behaviors, as well as analyses of how the relative importance of different category memberships may vary across time and space.

Progress along these lines will require overcoming what has until recently been an almost complete segmentation of the field into those who analyze the determinants of socioeconomic differentiation versus those who seek to understand its contours and determinants. That division of labor is fairly evident, for instance, among the contributions to this volume that focus on sex roles and gender inequality. Morris, for instance, adroitly documents temporal changes in the income differentiation between men and women in the United States, whereas Heimer (in Chapter 8), Tudor (in Chapter 10), and Evans and Mason (in Chapter 9) focus on the implications of differences in men's and women's socioeconomic standing for assumption of responsibility, labeling of mental deficiency, and gender role attitudes (respectively).

These essays raise a theoretical and methodological query that their authors no doubt encountered in John Pock's lectures and debated intensely in his seminars but that continues to pervade social science research—namely, what is the role of norms, attitudes, and cognitions in producing and sustaining social inequality? Are the latter fundamental *causes* of social differentiation and social stratification or merely epiphenomenal *outcomes* of a person's social standing? The rigid division of labor between those who study subjective versus objective facets of inequality impedes progress toward answering this query; those who focus on norms and attitudes can allude to their relevance for material outcomes without being required to demonstrate any impact, while social demographers can document trends in social inequality and invoke changes in norms, institutions, attitudes, and the like as explanatory factors or likely outcomes without feeling compelled to substantiate their claims empirically. We hasten to point out that these are not observations about the particular chapters in this volume, which are unusually creative and attentive to the interaction between social structure and attitudes, but rather on the broader sociological literatures concerned with objective and subjective dimensions of social differentiation and inequality.

Space limitations preclude us from giving this issue the attention it deserves, but we wish to note briefly several promising directions of research seeking to integrate social structure and attitudes in accounting for inequality. The first is exemplified by the provocative chapters by Mare and Heimer, which focus on the role of processes within the family for the reproduction of social hierarchies. We suspect that much of the subtle yet profoundly significant interplay between objective and subjective facets of stratification and inequality occurs within the family. Most conventional research has treated the connections between the family and the labor market fairly superficially, concentrating solely on how family roles and constraints influence labor supply and how labor market outcomes influence family formation, fecundity, child rearing, and the like. For instance, we know from studies of intergenerational mobility that family structure and the educational and occupational pursuits of parents influence both the labor market aspirations and attainments of their children (Sewell and Hauser 1975; Blake 1989; Biblarz and Raftery 1993) and that marital status and the number and age of one's children influence the careers of men and women differently (Roos 1983; Peterson 1989).

However, recent studies have provided powerful and more subtle evidence of how the family of destination both influences and is shaped by the activities of men and women in the labor market. Consistent with Heimer's argument, studies have documented how labor market inequalities between the sexes create and reinforce inequalities in the division of labor and the balance of power within the household (Bielby and Bielby 1988a, 1988b; 1989; Hochschild 1989; Bielby 1992). Other research has linked stress and mental health within families to the labor market positions of men and women (Kessler, Turner, and House 1989; Wethington and Kessler 1989). And some studies suggest that family dynamics play an important role in shaping the orientations and interests that men and women bring into the labor market. Wharton and Baron (1987), for example, demonstrated that among men working in gender-integrated work settings, the ones most dissatisfied with their jobs had a working wife, suggesting that a traditional division of labor at home made it easier for men to cope with threats to their dominance in the workplace. It is not simply that what one's paycheck can buy depends on how many people are sharing it; it is also that what it means to perform a given job or to work in a given firm depends on roles, experiences, and the division of labor and power within the family. We believe research examining linkages between the labor market and the family in more detail would not only improve our understanding of the interplay between objective and subjective facets of social differentiation but would also help elucidate the macro- and micro-underpinnings of status attainment.

As noted above, we believe another promising route toward those same ends involves applying social network analysis to studies of stratification and inequality. Researchers have documented important effects of social networks on objective and subjective career outcomes, particularly in studies that have focused on specific work roles and organizations rather than on the labor market as a whole (Granovetter 1974; Burt 1992; Podolny and Baron 1995). Other studies have shown that the structure and content of ties within informal social networks play a crucial role in affecting subjective assessments, including evaluations of how successful one has been and how fairly one has been treated (Dean and Brass 1985; Krackhardt and Porter 1985; Gartrell 1987; Ibarra and Andrews 1993). It therefore seems likely that studies of stratification incorporating information on social networks (including the context, content, and patterning of the social ties comprising the network) could help link the objective and subjective dimensions of attainment and inequality and also provide a bridge between a number of the macro- and micro-forces impinging on attainment that we discussed above.

Conclusion

Pondering and discussing these issues as we drafted this essay has brought the three of us back to our sociological roots and has reminded us that much of what is ultimately interesting and important about studying social stratification has to do with the broad consequences of social differentiation and inequality for individuals and social systems. This is, after all, what attracted us to the discipline of sociology via John Pock in the first place. (And judging from Paul Siegel's personal reminiscence in this volume, we suspect this was also true for most others who studied sociology at Reed under Pock's tutelage.) Accordingly, future research should examine those consequences—both material and symbolic—for individuals, groups, organizations, and social systems, as well as how and why those consequences vary across contexts. Research along these lines will help us better adjudicate among rival accounts emphasizing class, occupation, organization, demographic categories, and other distinctions as the backbone of stratification systems in contemporary societies.

Notes

1. For instance, one might hypothesize that the entry of women into specific industries is positively correlated with the prevalence of women-owned firms and with organizational forms that rely on externalized work arrangements that enable women to balance work and family commitments (see Pfeffer and Baron 1988).

2. For a review and critique of this literature, see Baron and Hannan 1994:1122-4.

3. A weaker variant of the same argument would assert that even if specific occupations do not correspond to agents of collective action or reflect self-conscious identities among incumbents, they nonetheless are proxies for the key outcomes of social stratification, such as working conditions, power or prestige, consumption patterns, and values or attitudes. Such a position is consistent with the implicit, if not explicit, thrust of most stratification research since the 1960s, which regards occupations as the main "connecting link between different institutions and spheres of social life" (Blau and Duncan 1967:6). These "connecting

links" arise through various processes: Functional specialization generates differences in work conditions and in the distribution of power, prestige, and privilege; occupational training, socialization, and association create occupation-based heterogeneity in consumption patterns and attitudes; and the obverse forces of occupational selection produce corresponding variability in the traits and predispositions of occupational incumbents (Treiman 1977:1–24).

References

Abbott, Andrew. 1988. *The System of Professions: An Essay on the Division of Expert Labor.* Chicago: University of Chicago Press.

Allmendinger, Jutta. 1989. "Educational Systems and Labor Market Outcomes." *European Sociological Review* 5:231–50.

Altshuler, Mordechai (ed.). 1993. *Distribution of the Jewish Population of the USSR, 1939.* Jerusalem: Centre for Research and Documentation of East-European Jewry, Hebrew University of Jerusalem.

Archer, Margaret S. 1979. *Social Origins of Educational Systems.* London: Sage.

Baron, James N., and Michael T. Hannan. 1994. "The Impact of Economics on Contemporary Sociology." *Journal of Economic Literature* 32:1111–46.

Baron, James N., and Jeffrey Pfeffer. 1994. "The Social Psychology of Organizations and Inequality." *Social Psychology Quarterly* 57:190–209.

Becker, Howard S., and James Carper. 1956. "The Elements of Identification with an Occupation." *American Sociological Review* 21:341–47.

Bian, Yanjie. 1994. "*Guanxi* and the Allocation of Urban Jobs in China." *China Quarterly* 140:971–99.

Biblarz, Timothy J., and Adrian E. Raftery. 1993. "The Effects of Family Disruption on Social Mobility." *American Sociological Review* 58:97–109.

Bielby, Denise D. 1992. "Commitment to Work and Family." *Annual Review of Sociology* 18:281–302.

Bielby, Denise D., and William T. Bielby. 1988a. "She Works Hard for the Money: Household Responsibilities and the Allocation of Work Effort." *American Journal of Sociology* 93:1031–59.

———. 1988b. "Women's and Men's Commitment to Paid Work and Family: Theories, Models, and Hypotheses." *Women and Work* 3:249–63.

———. 1989. "Family Ties: Balancing Commitments to Work and Family in Dual Earner Households." *American Sociological Review* 54:776–89.

Blake, Judith. 1989. *Family Size and Achievement.* Berkeley: University of California Press.

Blau, Peter M., and Otis D. Duncan. 1967. *The American Occupational Structure.* New York: Wiley.

Bourdieu, Pierre. 1984. *Distinction: A Social Critique of the Judgment of Taste*, translated by Richard Nice. New York: Cambridge University Press.

Burstein, Paul. 1985. *Discrimination, Jobs, and Politics: The Struggle for Equal Opportunity in the United States Since the New Deal.* Chicago: University of Chicago Press.

——— (ed.). 1994. *Equal Employment Opportunity: Labor Market Discrimination and Public Policy.* New York: Aldine de Gruyter.
Burt, Ronald S. 1992. *Structural Holes: The Social Structure of Competition.* Cambridge: Harvard University Press.
Caplow, Theodore. 1954. *The Sociology of Work.* Minneapolis: University of Minnesota Press.
Dean, James W., Jr., and Daniel J. Brass. 1985. "Social Interaction and the Perception of Job Characteristics in an Organization." *Human Relations* 38:571–82.
De Graaf, Nan Dirk. 1991. "Distinction by Consumption in Czechoslovakia, Hungary, and the Netherlands." *European Sociological Review* 7:267–90.
De Graaf, Nan Dirk, Paul Nieuwbeerta, and Anthony Heath. 1995. "Class Mobility and Political Preferences: Individual and Contextual Effects." *American Journal of Sociology* 100:997–1027.
Duncan, Otis Dudley. 1966. "Methodological Issues in the Analysis of Social Mobility." Pp. 51–97 in Neil J. Smelser and Seymour Martin Lipset (eds.), *Social Structure and Mobility in Economic Development.* Chicago: Aldine.
Emmison, Michael, and Mark Western. 1990. "Social Class and Social Identity: A Comment on Marshall et al." *Sociology* 24:241–53.
Esping-Andersen, Gosta. 1993. "Post-Industrial Class Structures: An Analytical Framework." Pp. 7–31 in Gosta Esping-Andersen (ed.), *Changing Classes: Stratification and Mobility in Post-Industrial Societies.* London: Sage.
Evans, Geoff. 1992. "Is Britain a Class-Divided Society? A Re-Analysis and Extension of Marshall et al.'s Study of Class Consciousness." *Sociology* 26:233–58.
Evans, M.D.R. 1995. "Sources of Identity." *Worldwide Attitudes,* June 12, 1995.
Featherman, David L. 1981. "Social Stratification and Mobility: Two Decades of Cumulative Social Science." *American Behavioral Scientist* 24:364–85.
Gartrell, C. David. 1987. "Network Approaches to Social Evaluation." *Annual Review of Sociology* 13:49–66.
Graham, Hugh Davis. 1994. "Race, History, and Policy: African Americans and Civil Rights Since 1964." *Journal of Policy History* 6:12–39.
Gramlich, Edward M., Richard Kasten, and Frank Sammartino. 1993. "Growing Inequality in the 1980s: The Role of Federal Taxes and Cash Transfers." Pp. 225–50 in Sheldon Danziger and Peter Gottschalk (eds.), *Uneven Tides: Rising Inequality in America.* New York: Russell Sage Foundation.
Granovetter, Mark S. 1974. *Getting a Job: A Study of Contacts and Careers.* Cambridge: Harvard University Press.
Grusky, David B., and Thomas A. DiPrete. 1990. "Structure and Trend in the Process of Stratification for American Men and Women." *American Journal of Sociology* 96:107–43.
Hannan, Michael T. 1988. "Social Change, Organizational Diversity, and Individual Careers." Pp. 161–74 in Matilda W. Riley (ed.), *Social Change and the Life Course,* Volume 1. Newbury Park, CA: Sage.
Hauser, Robert M., and David B. Grusky. 1988. "Cross-National Variation in Occupational Distributions, Relative Mobility Chances, and Intergenerational Shifts in Occupational Distributions." *American Sociological Review* 53:723–41.

Herrnstein, Richard J., and Charles Murray. 1994. *The Bell Curve: Intelligence and Class Structure in American Life.* New York: Free Press.

Hochschild, Arlie Russell. 1989. *The Second Shift: Working Parents and the Revolution at Home.* New York: Viking.

Ibarra, Herminia, and Steven B. Andrews. 1993. "Power, Social Influence, and Sense Making: Effects of Network Centrality and Proximity on Employee Perceptions." *Administrative Science Quarterly* 38:277–303.

Institute for the Study of Minority Problems. 1932. *The Polish and Non-Polish Populations of Poland: Results of the Population Census of 1931.* Warsaw: Institute for the Study of Minority Problems.

Ishida, Hiroshi, Walter Müller, and John Ridge. 1995. "Class Origin, Class Destination, and Education: A Cross-National Comparison of Ten Industrial Nations." *American Journal of Sociology* 101:145–93.

Jacobs, Jerry A. 1989. "Long-Term Trends in Occupational Segregation by Sex." *American Journal of Sociology* 95:160–73.

Jencks, Christopher. 1992. *Rethinking Social Policy: Race, Poverty, and the Underclass.* Cambridge: Harvard University Press.

Kalleberg, Arne L., and James R. Lincoln. 1988. "The Structure of Earnings Inequality in the United States and Japan." *American Journal of Sociology* 94 (Supplement): S121–53.

Kelley, Jonathan. 1992. "Social Mobility and Politics in the Anglo-American Democracies." Pp. 21–50 in F. Turner (ed.), *Social Mobility and Political Attitudes: Comparative Perspectives.* New Brunswick, NJ: Transaction.

Kerckhoff, Alan C. (ed.). Forthcoming. *Generating Social Stratification: Toward a New Generation of Research.* Boulder: Westview Press.

Kessler, Ronald C., J. Blake Turner, and James S. House. 1989. "Unemployment, Reemployment, and Emotional Functioning in a Community Sample." *American Sociological Review* 54:648–57.

König, Wolfgang, and Walter Müller. 1986. "Educational Systems and Labour Markets as Determinants of Worklife Mobility in France and West Germany: A Comparison of Men's Career Mobility, 1965–1970." *European Sociological Review* 2:73–96.

Kozol, Jonathan. 1991. *Savage Inequalities: Children in America's Schools.* New York: Harper Perennial.

Krackhardt, David, and Lyman W. Porter. 1985. "When Friends Leave: A Structural Analysis of the Relationship Between Turnover and Stayers' Attitudes." *Administrative Science Quarterly* 30:245–61.

Laclau, Ernesto, and Chantal Mouffe. 1985. *Hegemony and Socialist Strategy: Towards a Radical Democratic Politics.* London: Verso.

Lamont, Michele, and Marcel Fournier (eds.). 1992. *Cultivating Differences: Symbolic Boundaries and the Making of Inequality.* Chicago: University of Chicago Press.

Lincoln, James R., and Arne L. Kalleberg. 1985. "Work Organization and Workforce Commitment: A Study of Plants and Employees in the U.S. and Japan." *American Sociological Review* 50:738–60.

Mason, William M., George Y. Wong, and Barbara Entwisle. 1983. "Contextual Analysis Through the Multilevel Linear Model." Pp. 72–103 in Karl F. Schuessler (ed.), *Sociological Methodology, 1983–84*. San Francisco: Jossey-Bass.

Mishel, Lawrence R., and Jared Bernstein. 1994. *The State of Working America, 1994–95*. Armonk, NY: M. E. Sharpe.

Peterson, Richard A., and Albert Simkus. 1992. "How Musical Tastes Mark Occupational Status Groups." Pp. 152–86 in Michele Lamont and Marcel Fournier (eds.), *Cultivating Differences: Symbolic Boundaries and the Making of Inequality*. Chicago: University of Chicago Press.

Peterson, Richard R. 1989. "Firm Size, Occupational Segregation, and the Effects of Family Status on Women's Wages." *Social Forces* 68:397–414.

Pfeffer, Jeffrey, and James N. Baron. 1988. "Taking the Workers Back Out: Recent Trends in the Structuring of Employment." Pp. 257–303 in Barry M. Staw and L. L. Cummings (eds.), *Research in Organizational Behavior*, Volume 10. Greenwich, CT: JAI Press.

Podolny, Joel M., and James N. Baron. 1995. "Resources and Relationships: Social Networks, Mobility, and Satisfaction in the Workplace." Manuscript, Graduate School of Business, Stanford University.

Preston, Samuel H., and Cameron Campbell. 1993. "Differential Fertility and the Distribution of Traits: The Case of IQ." *American Journal of Sociology* 98:997–1019.

Reskin, Barbara. 1993. "Sex Segregation in the Workplace." *Annual Review of Sociology* 19:241–70.

Roos, Patricia A. 1983. "Marriage and Women's Occupational Attainment in Cross-Cultural Perspective." *American Sociological Review* 48:852–64.

Rosenbaum, James E., and Takehiko Kariya. 1989a. "From High School to Work: Market and Institutional Mechanisms in Japan." *American Journal of Sociology* 94:1334–65.

———. 1989b. "Japan Offers Way to Link School, Jobs." *Forum for Applied Research and Public Policy* 4:63–70.

———. 1991. "Do School Achievements Affect the Early Jobs of High School Graduates in the United States and Japan?" *Sociology of Education* 4:78–95.

Saunders, Peter. 1989. "Left Write in Sociology." *Network* 44:3–4.

Sewell, William H., and Robert M. Hauser. 1975. *Education, Occupation, and Earnings: Achievements in the Early Career*. New York: Academic Press.

Shavit, Yossi, and Hans-Peter Blossfeld (eds.). 1993. *Persistent Inequality: Changing Educational Stratification in Thirteen Countries*. Boulder: Westview Press.

Sobel, Michael E. 1985. "Social Mobility and Fertility Revisited: Some New Models for the Analysis of Mobility Effects." *American Sociological Review* 46:893–906.

Sobel, Michael E., Michael Hout, and Otis Dudley Duncan. 1985. "Exchange, Structure, and Symmetry in Occupational Mobility." *American Journal of Sociology* 91:359–72.

Sowell, Thomas. 1975. *Affirmative Action Reconsidered: Was It Necessary in Academia?* Washington, DC: American Enterprise Institute for Public Policy Research.

Stark, David. 1987. "Rethinking Internal Labor Markets: New Insights from a Comparative Perspective." *American Sociological Review* 51:492–504.

Treiman, Donald J. 1970. "Industrialization and Social Stratification." Pp. 207–34 in Edward O. Laumann (ed.), *Social Stratification: Research and Theory for the 1970s*. Indianapolis: Bobbs-Merrill.

———. 1977. *Occupational Prestige in Comparative Perspective*. New York: Academic.

Uri, Noel D., and J. Wilson Mixon Jr. 1992. "Effects of U.S. Equal Employment Opportunity and Affirmative Action Programs on Women's Employment Stability." *Quality and Quantity* 26:113–26.

Vining, D. R. 1986. "Social Versus Reproductive Success: The Central Theoretical Problems of Human Sociobiology." *Behavioral and Brain Sciences* 9:167–216.

Walker, Michael A., and Walter Block (eds.). 1982. *Discrimination, Affirmative Action, and Equal Opportunity: An Economic and Social Perspective*. Vancouver: Fraser Institute.

Warner, W. Lloyd. 1949. *Social Class in America*. Chicago: Science Research Associates.

Weakliem, David. 1993. "Class Consciousness and Political Change: Voting and Political Attitudes in the British Working Class, 1964 to 1970." *American Sociological Review* 58:382–97.

Wethington, Elaine, and Ronald C. Kessler. 1989. "Employment, Parental Responsibility, and Psychological Distress: A Longitudinal Study of Married Women." *Journal of Family Issues* 10:527–46.

Wharton, Amy S., and James N. Baron. 1987. "So Happy Together? The Impact of Gender Segregation on Men at Work." *American Sociological Review* 52:574–87.

Williams, Robin M., Jr., and Gerald D. Jaynes (eds.). 1989. *A Common Destiny: Blacks and American Society*. Washington, DC: National Academy Press.

Wise, Arthur E. 1967. *Rich Schools, Poor Schools*. Chicago: University of Chicago Press.

Zielinski, Henryk. 1954. *Population Changes in Poland, 1939–1950*. New York: Mid-European Studies Center, National Committee for a Free Europe.

PART SIX

Appendixes

A

Biographical Sketches of Contributors

James N. Baron (coeditor; coauthor, "Social Differentiation and Inequality") is the Walter Kenneth Kilpatrick Professor of Organizational Behavior and Human Resources and associate dean for academic affairs at the Graduate School of Business, Stanford University. After graduating from Reed College in 1976, he received an M.S. in 1977 from the University of Wisconsin and his Ph.D. in 1982 from the University of California-Santa Barbara, both in sociology. His experiences and perceptions as a sociology major at Reed were quite similar to those chronicled in Paul Siegel's essay in this volume. (Unlike Siegel, Baron correctly answered the final exam question about the one-eyed man being king in the country of the blind. However, Pock's first handwritten comment on that same exam, scrawled in red ink in the margin, was "cut off the words and get to the point," advice that some might say still rings true nearly twenty five years later.) Baron's current research interests include economic sociology, gender and ethnic inequality in organizations, social networks in the workplace, and the creation and evolution of employment systems in high-technology companies.

Haldor Byrkjeflot (coauthor, "The Logic of Employment Systems") is a graduate student in the Department of Sociology at the University of California-Berkeley. He has written on the development of Norway's service sector. His dissertation examines the emergence of the German and American managerial structures between 1920 and 1960, charting how German and American managers pursued different kinds of careers that included different technical training and different specializations. His argument is that because German managers remained closer to production processes, there was no separation between engineers and managers. In contrast, American managers began to move away from manufacturing backgrounds to become more professionalized and concerned with marketing and financial affairs. As a result, German firms remained relatively small, not vertically integrated, and less diversified than their American counterparts.

Angelique Chan (coauthor, "The Decline of Infant Mortality in China") received her B.A. from Reed in 1989 and her Ph.D. in sociology from UCLA in 1995. She is presently on a postdoctoral fellowship at the Population Studies Center of the University of Michigan.

M.D.R. Evans (coauthor, "Currents and Anchors") graduated from Reed College in 1976, and went on to receive an M.A. from the University of Illinois and a Ph.D. in sociology from the University of Chicago. She has worked for the past ten years at the Institute of Advanced Studies at the Australian National University, where she is currently senior research fellow. She works in a wide range of fields, mainly on the question of how markets and norms shape human conduct. Her book *Prejudice or Productivity: Ethnicity, Language, and Discrimination* is forthcoming from Westview Press. She characterizes her Reed experience as follows: "I came to Reed College as a bewildered 17-year-old intending vaguely to be a French literature major. Luckily, satisfying Reed's breadth requirements led me to take introductory sociology with John Pock. That outstanding course forever changed the way I think and drew me into sociology as a vocation. John asked the most interesting questions at seminars, and I yearned to learn the secrets of such insightful thinking. To this end, I sat behind him at a seminar by a visiting scholar to observe what notes he might scrawl. He put pen to paper and I peeked over his shoulder. He wrote: 'Get cottage cheese.' Nonetheless, I hope I have learned something of his art of asking questions."

Neil Fligstein (coauthor, "The Logic of Employment Systems"), a professor of sociology at the University of California-Berkeley, graduated from Reed College in 1973. He received his master's degree in 1976 and his Ph.D. in 1979 from the sociology department at the University of Wisconsin-Madison. He was on the faculty of the University of Arizona from 1979 to 1990. The author of two books, *Going North* (Academic Press, 1981) and *The Transformation of Corporate Control* (Harvard University Press, 1990), and over 20 papers, he is currently working on two projects. The first is a theoretical project that attempts to consider a theory that unifies elements of political sociology, social movements theory, and organizational theory. The second is an empirical project that tries to make sense of the large-scale institution-building projects of the European Community during the 1980s.

David B. Grusky (coeditor; coauthor, "The Structure of Career Mobility in Microscopic Perspective" and "Social Differentiation and Inequality") is associate professor of sociology at Stanford University and coeditor of the Westview Press Social Inequality Series. After graduating from Reed College in 1980, he attended graduate school at the University of Wisconsin-Madison, where he received his Ph.D. in sociology in 1985. He was then an assistant professor at the University of Chicago before moving to his current resting place at Stanford University. He is carrying out research on the underlying contours of social mobility and sex segregation; the structure of racial, ethnic, and cross-national variability in social mobility; the rise and fall of social classes under advanced industrialism; the sources of modern attitudes toward gender inequality; and long-term trends in patterns of occupational and geographic mobility. He is editor of the recently published *Social Stratification: Class, Race, and Gender in Sociological Perspective* (Westview Press) and reports that his next book, tentatively titled "All I Really Know I Learned in Sociology 210," examines the pedagogical returns to gruffness and high standards.

Carol A. Heimer (author, "Gender Inequalities in the Distribution of Responsibility") is a research fellow at the American Bar Foundation and associate professor of sociology at Northwestern University. She received her B.A. from Reed in 1973 and her Ph.D. in sociology from the University of Chicago in 1981. She is currently writing an empirical book on how responsibility for critically ill infants is distributed among parents and hospital staff members and a more theoretical book on the social organization of responsibility. Her previous work includes *Reactive Risk and Rational Action* (University of California Press, 1985), which is not as dry as it sounds. Her recent paper "Doing Your Job and Helping Your Friends" won the 1995 Theory Prize from the Theory Section of the American Sociological Association.

William Lavely (coauthor, "The Decline of Infant Mortality in China") received his B.A. from the University of Michigan in 1971 and his Ph.D. in sociology in 1982 from the University of Michigan. Currently he is associate professor of sociology and international studies and research associate in the Center for Studies in Demography and Ecology, both at the University of Washington in Seattle.

Hye-kyung Lee (coauthor, "Income Differences Among 31 Ethnic Groups in Los Angeles") is associate professor of sociology at Pai Chai University in Taejon, Korea. She has a bachelor's degree in English from Ehwa Women's University in Seoul and in 1987 received her doctorate in sociology from UCLA, where she was a student of her coauthor in this volume, Don Treiman. Her current research is on international labor migration in several Asian countries.

Robert D. Mare (author, "Demography and the Evolution of Educational Inequality") is professor of sociology at the University of Wisconsin-Madison. He received his B.A. from Reed in 1973 and his Ph.D. in sociology from the University of Michigan in 1977. His research interests include demographic aspects of social stratification, educational inequality and mobility, the sociology of marriage markets, and quantitative methods of social research. He is currently the editor of *Demography*.

Karen Oppenheim Mason (coauthor, "Currents and Anchors") graduated from Reed in 1964 and received her Ph.D. from the University of Chicago in 1970. She subsequently held positions at the University of Wisconsin-Madison, Research Triangle Institute, and the University of Michigan, before joining the East-West Center in Honolulu, where she is currently senior fellow. In addition to having a long-standing interest in gender attitudes, she is concerned with the intersections among family, gender, and demographic change, particularly in Asia and the Pacific. Her coedited book *Women's Position and Demographic Change* (Clarendon Press) appeared in late 1993, and another such volume, *Gender and Family Change in Industrialized Societies* (Clarendon Press), appeared in 1995. She reports that "like my coauthor, Mariah Evans, I, too, came to Reed as a bewildered 17-year-old (approximately 15 years before Mariah did) with vague intentions to major in English literature and with 12 years of training as a moralistic thinker under my belt. John Pock's introductory sociology lectures—and even more so, his often tense but incredibly challenging conferences—taught me for the first time to think analytically about social issues, an eye-opening experience that released me from the bondage of English literature and turned me into a social scientist. It is a testament to the strong sense of connection that John Pock produced in his students that Mariah and I, from different generations, came eventually to know each other as friends and collaborators."

William M. Mason (coauthor, "The Decline of Infant Mortality in China") graduated from Reed in 1963 and received his Ph.D. in 1970 from the University of Chicago. He taught at the University of Chicago, Duke, and the University of Michigan before moving in 1990 to UCLA, where he is currently professor of sociology and statistics. His research interests include the methodology of cohort analysis, the study of political alienation, multilevel analysis, and the comparative analysis of human fertility and contraception. His chapter in this volume is part of a larger project on infant mortality and son preference in China since the revolution. Mason remembers John Pock as the most influential instructor he ever had and as "certainly the most compelling thinker I experienced at Reed." He writes that "John dynamically and insightfully expressed his conceptualizations of the contributions of anthropologists and other sociologists. He taught the sociology of everyday life without saying so. He synthesized as no textbook I know of has ever done. Uniquely, John explained (and often disagreed with) intellectual orientations and key ideas in my courses in *other* fields, and that included biology, history, mathematics, philosophy, and economics, as well as those cross-disciplinary amalgams known then as 'humanities' courses. Although the connections are probably less than obvious, even to those who know us both, John's teaching and thought processes have been a 'mother lode' that I have mined ever since I first attempted to absorb them. To John and the late Howard Jolly I owe a once inordinately detailed knowledge of the works of Talcott Parsons, which turned out to be dysfunctional in graduate school. About this I have no regrets. What better point in one's life is there to spend time pondering oracles?"

Martina Morris (author, "Vive la Différence") graduated from Reed in 1980 and received her Ph.D. in sociology from the University of Chicago in 1989. She holds a joint appointment in the departments of sociology and statistics at Penn State and has degrees in both fields. Her work has focused on the development of generalized linear models for dynamic network analysis and new methods for interdistributional comparison and decomposition. Her main substantive area of research is in the population dynamics of AIDS transmission, where she has developed methods for empirically modeling the impact of network biases (such as assortative mixing by age or race) on the spread of infection. She has gathered survey data on this topic in several countries to date, including the United States, Thailand, and Uganda. Her papers in this area have appeared in such journals as *Nature*, the *American Journal of Epidemiology*, *Social Networks*, and *Mathematical Biosciences*. Morris also has an active research agenda in the area of earnings inequality, as reflected by the paper in this volume. With colleagues A.D. Bernhardt and M.S. Handcock, she has developed new methods for visualizing and analyzing changes in the United States earnings distribution, which retain full distributional information and are therefore more informative than other measures regarding issues of distributive justice. Papers on this topic have appeared in the *American Sociological Review* and the *American Journal of Sociology*. Morris and Handcock are also writing a monograph on relative distribution techniques for the new Springer Verlag series on Statistics in the Social Sciences.

Morris recalls that "I took my first sociology class because my friend Larry Jones said 'if you spend 4 years at Reed and don't take a course with Pock, you've just wasted $20,000' (at $5K/year, what it used to cost) ... Pock's grasp of what matters in social processes, and his unwavering commitment to critical thought, provided a set of intellectual tools that made it impossible not to be a sociologist. Not that he made it easy. All of us 'Sunday Supplement Marxists' from the Pepsi Generation found ourselves in very deep water with this man. At the time, it seemed like an excruciatingly painful way to learn, more sinking than swimming for sometimes years at a stretch. But ... somewhere along the line, you began to realize that you understood things, and that understanding, with all its flinty unyielding discipline, was the reward of academic life ... I miss his growling mug these days, but the internal dialogue continues on pretty much a daily basis."

Hiromi Ono (coauthor, "The Decline of Infant Mortality in China") graduated from Reed in 1988, then spent a year in the demography department at Berkeley, and ultimately moved to the sociology department at UCLA, where she received her Ph.D. in 1995. Her dissertation, written under the supervision of fellow Reed graduate Bill Mason, examines trends in divorce in the United States. She is currently a lecturer in the Department of Sociology and a research associate at the Center for Child and Family Policy Studies, both at UCLA. Her current research examines racial and ethnic differences in health service utilization among older Americans. Ono expresses gratitude for John Pock's role in determining her life course. She writes: "I came to the United States from Japan when I was 17 and could barely speak English when I arrived. A year later I found myself at Reed. When I first entered Reed, I did not know that there was a profession called 'sociologist.' Now, I have started to make my living as a sociologist. This beats being an unhappy Japanese housewife, which John used to joke could be in store for me. John not only helped me understand classical theories in sociology; he also helped me with a wide variety of other problems such as learning English grammar and adapting to life in the United States. One of the most important things he did was to believe in my abilities, and his belief fueled my belief in myself, which today carries me through difficult times. John provided me with a great education in sociology and the tools to survive."

Paul M. Siegel (author, "How Pock Shaped Me") has a diploma from Reed College dated June 1962 but is listed as a member of the class of 1961. This demonstration of the unreliability of administrative records should have cautioned him about his current (1995–1996) undertaking, in which administrative records are employed in making postcensal estimates of income and poverty for small areas (all counties) of the United States. Since leaving the sociology faculty of the University of Michigan in fall 1980, Siegel has been employed by the Census Bureau—as chief of the Education and Social Stratification Branch, then as chief of the Education Analysis Staff, and presently as special assistant to the chief of the Housing and Household Economic Statistics Division. At Michigan he had the luxury of being the human ecologist that Dudley Duncan and Amos Hawley convinced the Population Studies Center and the sociology department they should have. Between his stints at Reed and Michigan, he was at the National Opinion Research Center and the sociology department at the University of Chicago, where he received his doctorate in 1970 working under the strong influence of Bill Hodge and Pete Rossi. He thinks of his current (largely technical) work on poverty estimation as loosely tied to his earlier research in stratification and inequality.

Jesper B. Sørensen (coauthor, "The Structure of Career Mobility in Microscopic Perspective") is an assistant professor of sociology at the University of Notre Dame. He received his Ph.D. in sociology from Stanford University in 1996. His current research focuses on the consequences of career mobility for organizational outcomes and on the determinants of interorganizational mobility patterns. His areas of interest include organizational theory, labor markets and careers, stratification theory, economic sociology, and research design and methods.

Donald J. Treiman (coeditor; coauthor, "Income Differences Among 31 Ethnic Groups in Los Angeles" and "Social Differentiation and Inequality") graduated from Reed in 1962. He is currently professor of sociology at UCLA. He did his graduate work at Chicago, finishing in 1967, and taught at the University of Wisconsin-Madison and Columbia University before moving to UCLA in 1975. His research interests center on the comparative study of social stratification and, most recently, on social mobility in transitional societies. He currently has research under way on South Africa, Eastern Europe, and China. He also maintains an interest in the social structure of that peculiar place, Los Angeles, where he lives and works, which is reflected in the piece on income differences he prepared for this volume. Treiman entered Reed expecting to become a "college history teacher," because that was as close to what he was interested in as anything he could imagine at the time. For him, the introductory soc/anthro course, as taught by John Pock, was a revelation—namely, that "sociology is a field in which you could empirically investigate your ideas about how the social world works and decide whether they were right or wrong, instead of just talking about them." He was hooked for life and has never regretted it, although he has been dismayed in recent years by what he regards as the retrograde foray of so much of sociology into post-modern hermeneutics. He remains an unreconstructed positivist—an intellectual stance he thinks he acquired from John Pock, although Pock may deny it. (He is also an unreconstructed "tax-and-spend" Democrat, so perhaps all that is revealed is that he is unable to swing with the times.)

William Tudor (author, "The Social Construction of Modern Intelligence") received his B.A. in history from Reed College in 1965 and his Ph.D. in sociology from Vanderbilt University. Since 1973 he has been a member of the faculty at Reed, where he is presently chair of the Division of History and Social Sciences and chair of the Department of Sociology. His professional life focuses on courses he teaches in historical sociology; the sociology of religion; personality and social systems; deviant behavior; research methods; and introductory sociology. His research has been published in the *American Sociological Review,* the *Journal of Health and Social Behavior,* and *Social Forces.*

B

Reed College Students Who Became
Professional Sociologists,
1957–1991

Class	Name	Graduate School	Current Position
1957	Keith L. Miller	Illinois	Dept. of Human Development, University of Kansas
1958	Francesca Cancian	Harvard	Dept. of Sociology, University of California-Irvine
1958	Ruth L. Love	Columbia	Retired from Office of Conservation, Bonneville Power Administration
1958	Harry Mackler	Columbia	Retired from Dept. of Sociology, University of Toronto
1959	Robert W. Hodge	Chicago	Deceased. Last position: Dept. of Sociology, University of Southern California
1959	Patricia L. Krisch	Chicago	Retired from Population Research Center, University of Chicago
1959	Gerald D. Suttles	Illinois	Dept. of Sociology, University of Chicago
1960	Richard P. Gale	Michigan State	Dept. of Sociology, University of Oregon
1960	Jerome R. Kirk	Hopkins	Dept. of Sociology, University of California-Irvine
1960	Janice Stroud	Berkeley	Durham Mental Health Center
1961	Joseph Harry	Oregon	Dept. of Sociology, Northern Illinois University
1962	David Elesh	Columbia	Dept. of Sociology, Temple University
1962	Elinor Lerner	Berkeley	Dept. of Sociology, Richard Stockton State College, New Jersey
1962[a]	Barbara Reskin	University of Washington	Dept. of Sociology, Ohio State University
1962	Paul M. Siegel	Chicago	U.S. Bureau of the Census
1962	Donald J. Treiman	Chicago	Dept. of Sociology, University of California-Los Angeles

1962[a]	Joseph S. Uris	Portland State University	Dept. of Sociology, Portland State University
1963	William M. Mason	Chicago	Dept. of Sociology, University of California-Los Angeles
1963	Bruce Saunders	Berkeley	No longer in sociology
1964	Johanna S. Brenner	UCLA	Women's Studies Program, Portland State University
1964	Marlene Lockheed	Stanford	World Bank
1964	Karen Oppenheim Mason	Chicago	Program on Population, East-West Center, Honolulu
1964	David R. Roth	UCSB	Bureau of Labor and Industries, State of Oregon
1965	Richard Conviser	Hopkins	Office of the Health Plan Administrator, State of Oregon
1965	Donald L. Greene	USC	Social Science Division, Taft College
1965	T. Robert Harris	Hopkins	Dept. of Mathematics, University of North Dakota
1965	Angela V. Lane	Chicago	U.S. Bureau of the Census
1965	Gwendolyn L. Lewis	Princeton	Higher Education Programs, U.S. Dept. of Agriculture
1965	William Tudor	Vanderbilt	Dept. of Sociology, Reed College
1966	Philip W. Blumstein	Vanderbilt	Deceased. Last position: Dept. of Sociology, University of Washington
1966	Galen Cranz	Chicago	Dept. of Architecture, University of California-Berkeley
1966	Jon Lauglo	Chicago	Dept. of Sociology, University of Trondheim, Norway
1966	Michael S. Teitelbaum	Oxford	Alfred P. Sloan Foundation
1967	Mark S. Gould	Harvard	Dept. of Sociology and Anthropology, Haverford College
1967	Sheila L. Klatzky	Chicago	No longer in sociology

Class	Name	Graduate School	Current Position
1968	Larry Nutt	Chicago	Dept. of Criminal Justice, Richard Stockton State College, New Jersey
1968	Jonathan M. Unger	Sussex	Contemporary China Center, Australian National University
1969	Harry Travis	Wisconsin	DEMOSTIX Corp., Washington, D.C.
1970	Jonathan B. Fields	University of Washington	Oregon Health Sciences University School of Nursing
1970	Sally E. Findley	Brown	School of Public Health, Columbia University
1970	Susan A. Stephens	Michigan	Center for Assessment and Policy Development, Pennsylvania
1970	Dean R. Gerstein	Harvard	National Opinion Research Center (Washington, D.C.)
1971	Carol Conell	Michigan	Kaiser-Permanente Foundation
1971	Susan Kinne	University of Washington	Center for Disability Policy and Research, University of Washington
1971[a]	Gail Kligman	Berkeley	Dept. of Sociology, University of California-Los Angeles
1971	Anne L. Potter	Stanford	Oregon Research Consulting Group
1973	Peter Cattan	Vanderbilt	U.S. Bureau of Labor Statistics
1973	Neil Fligstein	Wisconsin	Dept. of Sociology, University of California-Berkeley
1973	Carol A. Heimer	Chicago	Dept. of Sociology, Northwestern University
1973	John D. Loft	Chicago	Abt Associates
1973	Robert D. Mare	Michigan	Dept. of Sociology, University of Wisconsin
1975	Linda A. Jacobsen	Wisconsin	Equifax National Decision Systems, San Diego

1975	Toni Richards	Michigan	State of California
1976	James N. Baron	UCSB	Graduate School of Business, Stanford University
1976	Mariah D. R. Evans	Chicago	Institute of Advanced Studies, Australian National University
1978	Lisa Greenwell	Indiana	Leonard Davis School of Gerontology, University of Southern California
1978	David E. Moore	University of Washington	Battelle, Seattle
1979[a]	George Steinmetz	Wisconsin	Dept. of Sociology, University of Chicago
1980	Julia Adams	Wisconsin	Dept. of Sociology, University of Michigan
1980	David B. Grusky	Wisconsin	Dept. of Sociology, Stanford University
1980	Martina Morris	Chicago	Depts. of Sociology and Statistics, Pennsylvania State University
1982	Kathryn L. Kost	Princeton	Alan Guttmacher Institute
1986	John Manzo	Wisconsin	Dept. of Sociology and Anthropology, University of South Alabama
1988	Hiromi Ono	UCLA	Dept. of Sociology, University of California-Los Angeles
1989	Angelique Chan	UCLA	Postdoctoral program, Population Studies Center, University of Michigan
1989	Marin E. Clarkberg	Chicago	Graduate school, Dept. of Sociology, University of Chicago
1990[a]	Timothy J. Berard	Boston University	Graduate school, Dept. of Sociology, Boston University
1991	Elizabeth A. Dundon	Stanford	Graduate school, Dept. of Sociology, Stanford
1991[a]	Elizabeth D. Kessler	Wisconsin	Graduate school, Dept. of Sociology, Wisconsin
1991	Ellen R. Reese	UCLA	Graduate school, Dept. of Sociology, University of California-Los Angeles

[a] Transferred from Reed to another undergraduate institution.

About the Book and Editors

The field of social stratification is being transformed and reshaped by advances in theory and method as well as by new approaches to the analysis of macroeconomic, institutional, demographic, and ascriptive sources of inequality. In this tribute to John C. Pock, the editors have brought together established and emerging stars in the field. The result is an important new statement on contemporary developments and controversies in stratification scholarship. The chapters address such matters as recent trends in gender attitudes and the gender gap in earnings, race and class differentials in life chances and income, cross-national and institutional variability in employment systems and inequality, the division of domestic labor within households, and the implications of demographic change for social inequality.

James N. Baron is Associate Dean for Academic Affairs and Walter Kenneth Kilpatrick Professor of Organizational Behavior and Human Resources in the Graduate School of Business at Stanford University. **David B. Grusky** is associate professor of sociology at Stanford University. **Donald J. Treiman** is professor of sociology at The University of California at Los Angeles.